CAMBRIDGE

Brighter Thinking

GW01454347

A Level Further Mathematics for AQA

Mechanics Student Book (AS/A Level)

Jess Barker, Nathan Barker, Michele Conway and Janet Such
Course consultant: Stephen Ward

CAMBRIDGE
UNIVERSITY PRESS

University Printing House, Cambridge CB2 8BS, United Kingdom

One Liberty Plaza, 20th Floor, New York, NY 10006, USA

477 Williamstown Road, Port Melbourne, VIC 3207, Australia

314–321, 3rd Floor, Plot 3, Splendor Forum, Jasola District Centre, New Delhi – 110025, India

103 Penang Road, #05-06/07, Visioncrest Commercial, Singapore 238467

Cambridge University Press is part of the University of Cambridge.

It furthers the University's mission by disseminating knowledge in the pursuit of
education, learning and research at the highest international levels of excellence.

www.cambridge.org
Information on this title:
www.cambridge.org/ 9781316644539 (Paperback)
www.cambridge.org/ 9781316644348 (Paperback with Cambridge Elevate edition)

First published 2017

20 19 18 17 16 15 14 13 12 11 10 9 8 7

Printed in Great Britain by CPI Group (UK) Ltd, Croydon CR0 4YY

A catalogue record for this publication is available from the British Library

ISBN 978-1-316-64453-9 Paperback
ISBN 978-1-316-64434-8 Paperback with Cambridge Elevate edition

Additional resources for this publication at www.cambridge.org/education

Message from AQA

This textbook has been approved by AQA for use with our qualification. This means that we have checked that it broadly covers
the specification and we are satisfied with the overall quality. Full details of our approval process can be found on our website.

We approve textbooks because we know how important it is for teachers and students to have the right resources to support
their teaching and learning. However, the publisher is ultimately responsible for the editorial control and quality of this book.

Please note that when teaching the A/AS Level Further Mathematics (7366, 7367) course, you must refer to AQA's
specification as your definitive source of information. While this book has been written to match the specification, it cannot
provide complete coverage of every aspect of the course.

A wide range of other useful resources can be found on the relevant subject pages of our website: www.aqa.org.uk

IMPORTANT NOTE
AQA has not approved any Cambridge Elevate content

Contents

Introduction

You have probably been told that mathematics is very useful, yet it can often seem like a lot of techniques that just have to be learnt to answer examination questions. You are now getting to the point where you will start to see where some of these techniques can be applied in solving real problems. However as well as seeing how maths can be useful we hope that anyone working through this book will realise that it can also be incredibly frustrating, surprising and ultimately beautiful.

The book is woven around three key themes from the new curriculum:

Proof

Maths is valued because it trains you to think logically and communicate precisely. At a high level maths is far less concerned about answers and more about the clear communication of ideas. It is not about being neat – although that might help! It is about creating a coherent argument which other people can easily follow but find difficult to refute. Have you ever tried looking at your own work? If you cannot follow it yourself it is unlikely anybody else will be able to understand it. In maths we communicate using a variety of means – feel free to use combinations of diagrams, words and algebra to aid your argument. And once you have attempted a proof, try presenting it to your peers. Look critically (but positively) at some other people's attempts. It is only through having your own attempts evaluated and trying to find flaws in other proofs that you will develop sophisticated mathematical thinking. This is why we have included lots of common errors in our Work it out boxes – just in case your friends don't make any mistakes!

Problem solving

Maths is valued because it trains you to look at situations in unusual, creative ways, to persevere and to evaluate solutions along the way. We have been heavily influenced by a great mathematician and maths educator George Polya who believed that students were not just born with problem-solving skills – they were developed by seeing problems being solved and reflecting on their solutions before trying similar problems. You may not realise it but good mathematicians spend most of their time being stuck. You need to spend some time on problems you can't do, trying out different possibilities. If after a while you have not cracked it then look at the solution and try a similar problem. Don't be disheartened if you cannot get it immediately – in fact, the longer you spend puzzling over a problem the more you will learn from the solution. You may never need to integrate a rational function in the future, but we firmly believe that the problem solving skills you will develop by trying it can be applied to many other situations.

Modelling

Maths is valued because it helps us solve real-world problems. However, maths describes ideal situations and the real world is messy! Modelling is about deciding on the important features needed to describe the essence of a situation and turning that into a mathematical form, then using it to make predictions, compare to reality and possibly improve the model. In many situations the technical maths is actually the easy part – especially with modern technology. Deciding which features of reality to include or ignore and anticipating the consequences of these decisions is the hard part. Yet it is amazing how some fairly drastic assumptions – such as pretending a car is a single point or that people's votes are independent – can result in models which are surprisingly accurate.

More than anything else this book is about making links – links between the different chapters, the topics covered and the themes above, links to other subjects and links to the real world. We hope that you will grow to see maths as one great complex but beautiful web of interlinking ideas.

Maths is about so much more than examinations, but we hope that if you take on board these ideas (and do plenty of practice!) you will find maths examinations a much more approachable and possibly even enjoyable experience. However always remember that the results of what you write down in a few hours by yourself in silence under exam conditions is not the only measure you should consider when judging your mathematical ability – it is only one variable in a much more complicated mathematical model!

How to use this book

Throughout this book you will notice particular features that are designed to aid your learning. This section provides a brief overview of these features.

In this chapter you will learn how to:
- calculate the work done by a force
- calculate kinetic energy
- use the work–energy principle
- equate gravitational potential energy to work done against gravity
- understand and use the power of a driving force.

Before you start…

GCSE	You should be able to solve simultaneous equations both for two linear equations and for one linear and one quadratic equation.	1	Solve these equations. $4x + 5y = 8$ $6x + 4y = 5$
A Level Mathematics Student Book 1, Chapter 17	You should know the equations of linear motion with constant acceleration.	2	A particle of mass 2 kg is dropped from a height of 6 metres above a pond. What is the speed of the particle at the instant when it hits the water?

Learning objectives
A short summary of the content that you will learn in each chapter.

Before you start
Points you should know from your previous learning and questions to check that you're ready to start the chapter.

WORKED EXAMPLE
The left-hand side shows you how to set out your working. The right-hand side explains the more difficult steps and helps you understand why a particular method was chosen.

Key point
A summary of the most important methods, facts and formulae.

PROOF
Step-by-step walkthroughs of standard proofs and methods of proof.

Common error
Specific mistakes that are often made. These typically appear next to the point in the Worked example where the error could occur.

WORK IT OUT
Can you identify the correct solution and find the mistakes in the two incorrect solutions?

Tip
Useful guidance, including ways of calculating or checking answers and using technology.

Each chapter ends with a **Checklist of learning and understanding** and a **Mixed practice exercise**, which includes **past paper questions** marked with the icon.

In between chapters, you will find extra sections that bring together topics in a more synoptic way.

FOCUS ON …
Unique sections relating to the preceding chapters that develop your skills in proof, problem-solving and modelling.

CROSS-TOPIC REVIEW EXERCISE
Questions covering topics from across the preceding chapters, testing your ability to apply what you have learned.

You will find **practice papers** towards the end of the book, as well as a **glossary** of key terms (picked out in colour within the chapters), and **answers** to all questions. Full **worked solutions** can be found on the Cambridge Elevate digital platform, along with a **digital version** of this Student Book.

Maths is all about making links, which is why throughout this book you will find signposts emphasising connections between different topics, applications and suggestions for further research.

⏮ Rewind

Reminders of where to find useful information from earlier in your study.

📷 Focus on ...

Links to problem-solving, modelling or proof exercises that relate to the topic currently being studied.

⏭ Fast forward

Links to topics that you may cover in greater detail later in your study.

ℹ Did you know?

Interesting or historical information and links with other subjects to improve your awareness about how mathematics contributes to society.

Colour coding of exercises

The questions in the exercises are designed to provide careful progression, ranging from basic fluency to practice questions. They are uniquely colour-coded, as shown here.

1 A sequence is defined by $u_n = 2 \times 3^{n-1}$. Use the principle of mathematical induction to prove that $u_1 + u_2 + \ldots + u_n = 3^n - 1$.

2 Show that $1^2 + 2^2 + \ldots + n^2 = \frac{n(n+1)(2n+1)}{6}$

3 Show that $1^3 + 2^3 + \ldots + n^3 = \frac{n^2(n+1)^2}{4}$

4 Prove by induction that $\frac{1}{1 \times 2} + \frac{1}{2 \times 3} + \frac{1}{3 \times 4} + \ldots + \frac{1}{n(n+1)} = \frac{n}{n+1}$

5 Prove by induction that $\frac{1}{1 \times 3} + \frac{1}{3 \times 5} + \frac{1}{5 \times 7} + \ldots + \frac{1}{(2n-1) \times (2n+1)} = \frac{n}{2n+1}$

6 Prove that $1 \times 1! + 2 \times + 3 \times 3! \ldots + n \times n! = (n+1)! - 1$

7 Use the principle of mathematical induction to show that $1^2 - 2^2 + 3^2 - 4^2 + \ldots + (-1)^{n-1} n^2 = (-1)^{n-1} \frac{n(n+1)}{2}$.

8 Prove that $(n+1) + (n+2) + (n+3) + \ldots + (2n) = \frac{1}{2} n(3n+1)$

9 Prove using induction that $\sin\theta + \sin 3\theta + \ldots + \sin(2n-1)\theta = \frac{\sin^2 n\theta}{\sin\theta}$, $n \in \mathbb{Z}^+$

10 Prove that $\sum_{k=1}^{n} k \, 2^k = (n-1) 2^{n+1} + 2$

Black – practice questions which come in several parts, each with subparts i and ii. You only need attempt subpart i at first; subpart ii is essentially the same question, which you can use for further practice if you got part i wrong, for homework, or when you revisit the exercise during revision.

Green – practice questions at a basic level.

Blue – practice questions at an intermediate level.

Red – practice questions at an advanced level.

Purple – challenging questions that apply the concept of the current chapter across other areas of maths.

Yellow – designed to encourage reflection and discussion.

A – indicates content that is for A Level students only.

1 Work, energy and power 1

In this chapter you will learn how to:

- calculate the work done by a force
- calculate kinetic energy
- use the work–energy principle
- equate gravitational potential energy to work done against gravity
- understand and use the power of a driving force.

Before you start…

GCSE	You should know how to convert units of distance, speed and time.	1	Convert 15 000 metres to kilometres.
A Level Mathematics Student Book 1, Chapter 18	You should know how to calculate the weight of an object from its mass, and know the unit of weight.	2	Calculate the weight of a car of mass 1150 kg, stating the unit with your answer.
A Level Mathematics Student Book 1, Chapter 18	You should be able to use Newton's second law of motion: $F = ma$.	3	A resultant force of 50 N acts on an object of mass 2.5 kg. Calculate the acceleration of the object.

The relationship between work and energy

In this chapter, you will learn the definition of the **work done** by a force, which is a quantity that is measured in joules, the same units that are used for **energy**. You will learn about propulsive and resistive forces. You will learn that work done by a propulsive force is equivalent to **kinetic energy** gained. Work done against a resistive force is equivalent to kinetic energy lost. The driving force of a car engine can cause a car to accelerate; work done by the car engine increases the kinetic energy of the car. Resistances to motion can cause a car to decelerate; work done against these forces decreases the kinetic energy of the car. You will also learn about power, which is the rate of doing work.

Principles of work, energy and power are crucial in engineering, enabling engineers to design machines to do useful work. Hydroelectric power stations work by converting the work done by falling water first into kinetic energy, as the hydroelectric turbines rotate, and then into electricity.

⏮ **Rewind**

You have already studied the effect of a force or system of forces in A Level Mathematics Student Book 1, Chapter 18.

⏭ **Fast forward**

In Chapter 5, you will learn about elastic potential energy and its conversion to kinetic energy.

Section 1: The work done by a force

Work is done by a force when the object it is applied to moves.

Some forces promote movement while others resist it. For example, when you cycle into a breeze, your pedalling promotes movement but the breeze acts against your movement. Forces that promote movement are **propulsive forces** and those that resist movement are **resistive forces**.

Other propulsive forces include the **tension** in a rope being used to drag an object across the ground and the driving force of a vehicle engine. The driving force of an engine is often described as its **tractive force**. Other resistive forces include vehicle braking and resistance from still air.

Weight is a special case because it can either resist or promote movement. When you cycle uphill your weight acts as a resistive force – you do work **against your own weight**. But when you cycle downhill your weight acts as a propulsive force – **your weight does work on you**. Work done by weight is usually described as 'work done by gravity'. Work done against weight is usually described as 'work done against gravity'.

> ### 🔑 Key point 1.1
>
> For a force acting in the direction of motion:
>
> $$\text{work done} = \text{force} \times \text{distance}$$
>
> Work done is measured in joules (J):
>
> $$1 \text{ joule} = 1 \text{ newton} \times 1 \text{ metre}$$
> $$1\,\text{J} = 1\,\text{N\,m}$$

For example, a force of 5 newtons acting on an object that moves 15 metres in the direction of the force does $5 \times 15 = 75$ joules of work. Doubling the force to 10 newtons over the same distance would double the amount of work done to 150 joules. Likewise, doubling the distance moved to 30 metres with an unchanged force of 5 newtons would double the amount of work done to 150 joules.

WORKED EXAMPLE 1.1

A box is pushed 5 m across a horizontal floor by a horizontal force of 25 N. Calculate the work done by the force.

Work done = force × distance	Use the definition of work done.
$\quad = 25 \times 5\,\text{J}$	State the units of work done (J) with your answer.
$\quad = 125\,\text{J}$	

WORKED EXAMPLE 1.2

A lorry driver driving along a horizontal road applies a braking force of 75 kN for 25 m. Calculate the work done by the brakes, giving your answer in kilojoules (kJ).

75 kN = 75 000 N — Convert 75 kN to 75 000 N as you need to work in standard units.

Work done by brakes = braking force × distance — Use the definition of work done.

$= 75\,000 \times 25$ J

$= 187\,5000$ J

$= 1880$ kJ (3 s.f) — Change J to kJ.

Tip

Work done by the brakes against movement is equivalent to work done by the lorry against the brakes.

WORKED EXAMPLE 1.3

A 50 kg crate is lifted 12 m by means of a rope and pulley system. Calculate the work done against gravity.

Work done = force × distance — Apply the definition of work done to the gravitational force. Force becomes weight and distance becomes height gained.

∴ Work done against gravity = weight × height gained

Weight of crate = 50 × 9.8 — Calculate the weight of the crate, using the approximation for the acceleration due to gravity of 9.8 m s^{-2}.

$= 490$ N

Work done against gravity = weight × height gained

$= 490 \times 12$ J — You have used a value of g to 2 s.f. so this is an appropriate degree of accuracy for your final answer.

$= 5880$ J

$= 5900$ J (2 s.f.)

Key point 1.2

When a mass, m, is raised or lowered through a height h:

work done by or against gravity = weight × height

work done = $mg \times h$

Fast forward

In Section 3 you will learn the equivalence of work done by or against gravity and gravitational potential energy.

WORKED EXAMPLE 1.4

A competitor of mass 75 kg dives from a diving board that is 10 metres high into a pool. Air resistance averages 12 newtons as he descends 10 metres through the air. Resistance from the water then averages 3000 newtons as he descends 2.0 metres further. Calculate:

a the total work done by gravity as he descends 12 metres
b the total work done against air and water resistance during this descent.

a Work done by gravity $= mgh$

$$= 75g \times 12$$

$$\approx 8800 \text{ joules (2 s.f.)}$$

> You have used a value of g (9.8 m s^{-2}) to 2 s.f. so this is an appropriate degree of accuracy for your final answer.

b Work done against air resistance $= 12 \times 10 = 120$ joules

Work done against water resistance $= 3000 \times 2 = 6000$ joules

Total work done against resistances $= 6120$ joules

> Use force × distance to calculate the work done by each of the resistances.

WORKED EXAMPLE 1.5

A van of mass 1250 kg travels along a straight road. The driving force of the vehicle engine is 500 newtons and resistance to motion is 220 newtons, on average. The van travels 1.5 km from one delivery to the next, descending 8 metres in height. Find:

a the work done by the vehicle engine
b the work done by gravity
c the work done against resistance.

a 1.5 km = 1500 metres

> Convert distance to SI units.

Work done by vehicle engine $= 500 \times 1500$

$$= 750\,000 \text{ joules}$$

> Use force × distance to calculate the work done by the vehicle engine.

b Work done by gravity $= mgh$

$$= 1250g \times 8$$

$$= 98\,000 \text{ joules}$$

c Work done against resistance $= 220 \times 1500$

$$= 330\,000 \text{ joules}$$

> Use force × distance to calculate the work done against resistance.

EXERCISE 1A

In this exercise, unless otherwise instructed, use $g = 9.8 \text{ m s}^{-2}$, giving your final answers to an appropriate degree of accuracy.

1 A parcel is dragged 5 metres across a horizontal floor by means of a horizontal rope. The tension in the rope is 12 N. Calculate the work done by the tension in the rope.

2 Susan climbs a vertical rock 32 m high. Susan's mass is 65 kg. Calculate the work done by Susan against gravity.

3 Sunil descends a vertical ladder. His mass is 82 kg and the work done by gravity is 2150 J. Find the height Sunil descends.

4 In this question use $g = 10 \text{ m s}^{-2}$, giving your final answer to an appropriate degree of accuracy.

A ball of mass 100 g is dropped from a window. Calculate the work done by gravity as it falls vertically to the ground 6.0 m below.

5 A puck slides 50 metres across an ice rink, against a resistive force of 2.5 N. Calculate the work done against resistance.

6 A cyclist travelling on horizontal ground applies a driving force of 25 N against a headwind of 10 N and a resistance from friction of 5.0 N. The cyclist travels 1.2 km. Find:

a the work done by the cyclist

b the total work done against wind and friction.

7 A fish basket is raised from the sea floor to a fishing boat at sea level, 18 metres above. The mass of the basket is 15 kg. The resistance to motion from the seawater is 50 N. Calculate the total work done, against gravity and water resistance, in raising the fish basket.

8 A driving force of 400 N does 50 kJ of work moving a van along a horizontal road from A to B. Resistance to motion averages 185 N. Calculate the work done against resistance as the van moves from A to B.

Section 2: Kinetic energy and the work–energy principle

Kinetic energy is the energy an object has because it is moving.

Key point 1.3

An object of mass m moving with speed v has kinetic energy $\frac{1}{2}mv^2$.

If mass is measured in kilograms (kg) and speed is measured in metres per second (m s^{-1}), kinetic energy is measured in joules (J).

Tip

If speed is not given in m s^{-1}, you should convert to m s^{-1} before you start the rest of your calculations.

WORKED EXAMPLE 1.6

A particle of mass 1.5 kg is moving with kinetic energy 48 joules. Calculate the speed of the particle.

Kinetic energy $= \frac{1}{2}mv^2$ Use the formula for kinetic energy.

Substituting and rearranging to find speed:

$$48 = \frac{1}{2} \times 1.5 \times v^2$$

As mass was given in kg and kinetic energy in joules, speed is in m s^{-1}.

$$\therefore v^2 = 64$$
$$\Rightarrow v = \pm 8 \text{ m s}^{-1}$$

Since speed is a positive quantity, $v = 8 \text{ m s}^{-1}$

WORKED EXAMPLE 1.7

A cyclist slows down from 25 km h^{-1} to 10 km h^{-1}. The combined mass of the cyclist and her bicycle is 95 kg. Calculate the loss of kinetic energy.

Let u be the starting speed and v be the final speed.

$u = \dfrac{25}{3.6} = 6.944\,\text{m s}^{-1}$ and $v = \dfrac{10}{3.6} = 2.778\,\text{m s}^{-1}$

> To convert km h^{-1} to m s^{-1} you must multiply by the conversion factor $\dfrac{1000}{3600}$, which simplifies to division by 3.6.

Loss of kinetic energy = initial kinetic energy − final kinetic energy

Loss of kinetic energy $= \dfrac{1}{2}mu^2 - \dfrac{1}{2}mv^2$

Loss of kinetic energy $= \dfrac{1}{2} \times 95 \times 6.944^2 - \dfrac{1}{2} \times 95 \times 2.778^2$

$\qquad\qquad = 1920\,\text{J (3 s.f.)}$

WORKED EXAMPLE 1.8

A

Calculate the increase in kinetic energy when a boat of mass 2.0 tonnes changes velocity from $(3.0\mathbf{i} + 4.0\mathbf{j})$ m s^{-1} to $(4.5\mathbf{i} + 4.5\mathbf{j})$ m s^{-1}. Give your answer in kJ.

$(\text{Starting speed})^2 = 3^2 + 4^2 = 25$

$\quad(\text{Final speed})^2 = 4.5^2 + 4.5^2 = 40.5$

> Use Pythagoras' theorem to convert the velocity vectors to speeds. You need the square of the speed, not the velocity vector, for the kinetic energy formula.

Gain in kinetic energy = final kinetic energy − initial kinetic energy

Gain in kinetic energy $= \dfrac{1}{2}m(v^2 - u^2)$

> You can write $\dfrac{1}{2}mv^2 - \dfrac{1}{2}mu^2$ in factorised form.

2 tonnes = 2000 kg

> Convert 2 tonnes to 2000 kg.

Gain in kinetic energy $= \dfrac{1}{2} \times 2000 \times (40.5 - 25)$

$\qquad\qquad\quad \approx 15.5\,\text{kJ}$

> Divide by 1000 to convert joules to kJ.

The **work–energy principle** is an essential idea in mechanics that enables you to calculate and compare the work necessary to cause a change in kinetic energy.

🔑 Key point 1.4

The work done by a force on an object causes an equal increase in its kinetic energy.

$$\text{Work done} = \dfrac{1}{2}mv^2 - \dfrac{1}{2}mu^2$$

💡 Tip

Remember that gravity acts as:

- a propulsive force when the object is moving downwards
- a resistive force when the object is moving upwards.

Work done by propulsive forces causes an increase in kinetic energy. Work done against resistive forces causes a loss of kinetic energy. To use the work–energy principle you must calculate the total work done on the moving object.

Total work done = work done by propulsive forces

− work done against resistive forces

WORKED EXAMPLE 1.9

A particle of mass 1.6 kg is at rest on a smooth horizontal plane. It is acted on by a constant horizontal force of 8.0 N. Find the speed of the particle after it has travelled 5.0 metres.

Work done = force × distance

$$= 8 \times 5$$

$$= 40 \text{ joules}$$

Applying the work–energy principle:

$$40 = \frac{1}{2} \times 1.6 \times v^2$$

$$v^2 = 50$$

$$\Rightarrow v = 7.1 \,\mathrm{m\,s^{-1}} \ (2 \text{ s.f.})$$

Work done = force × distance

Work–energy principle: work done = $\frac{1}{2}mv^2$

WORKED EXAMPLE 1.10

Stephen is driving his car along a horizontal road at 55 km h⁻¹ when he notices a broken-down vehicle, just off the road, 150 m ahead. Stephen and his car together have a mass of 1025 kg and the total resistance to motion is assumed constant at 500 N. Stephen believes he should slow down and that he can slow down sufficiently without applying the brakes. Calculate Stephen's speed, in km h⁻¹, as he reaches the broken-down vehicle, taking account of the resistance to motion.

Assume that Stephen allows the resistance to motion to slow his car down over 150 m. There is no driving or braking force.

Work done against resistance = resistive force × distance

$$= 500 \times 150$$

$$= 75\,000 \text{ J}$$

Calculate the work done against resistance.

$$55\,\mathrm{km\,h^{-1}} = \frac{55}{3.6}$$

$$\approx 15.28 \,\mathrm{m\,s^{-1}}$$

Convert 55 km h⁻¹ to m s⁻¹.

Loss of kinetic energy = initial kinetic energy − final kinetic energy

Loss of kinetic energy $= \frac{1}{2} \times m \times (u^2 - v^2)$

Using the work–energy principle:

Write down the expression for loss of kinetic energy.

$$75\,000 = \frac{1}{2} \times 1025(u^2 - v^2)$$

Rearranging and solving for v:

Work–energy principle:

work done against resistance = loss of KE

$$u^2 - v^2 = \frac{2 \times 75\,000}{1025}$$

$$\approx 146.3$$

$$v^2 \approx 15.28^2 - 146.3$$

$$v = 9.337 \,\mathrm{m\,s^{-1}}$$

Substitute in the value for u.

$$v \approx 9.337 \times 3.6 \,\mathrm{km\,h^{-1}}$$

Convert back to km h⁻¹

$$v = 33.6 \,\mathrm{km\,h^{-1}} \ (3 \text{ s.f.})$$

In this exercise, unless otherwise instructed, use $g = 9.8 \text{ m s}^{-2}$, giving your final answers to an appropriate degree of accuracy.

1 Calculate the kinetic energy of a cyclist and her bicycle, having a combined mass of 70 kg, travelling at 12 m s^{-1}. Give your answer in kJ.

2 Calculate the mass of an athlete who is running at 8.5 m s^{-1}, with kinetic energy 3500 J.

3 Calculate the speed of a bus of mass 20 tonnes with kinetic energy 1100 kJ. Give your answer in km h^{-1}.

4 A box of mass 5.0 kg is pulled from A to B across a smooth horizontal floor by a horizontal force of magnitude 10 N. At point A, the box has speed 1.5 m s^{-1} and at point B the box has speed 2.8 m s^{-1}. Ignoring all other resistive forces, find:

   a the increase in kinetic energy of the box

   b the work done by the force

   c the distance AB.

5 A car driver brakes on a horizontal road and slows down from 20 m s^{-1} to 12 m s^{-1}. The mass of the car and its occupants is 1150 kg.

   a Find the loss in kinetic energy.

   b Given that the work done against resistance to motion is 50 kJ, find the work done by the brakes.

6 A child of mass 35 kg descends a smooth slide, after propelling herself onto the top at 1.6 m s^{-1}. Ignoring air resistance, calculate her speed at the bottom of the slide, which is 2.1 metres lower than the top.

7 A bullet of mass 10 grams passes horizontally through a target of thickness 5.0 cm. The speed of the bullet is reduced from 240 m s^{-1} to 90 m s^{-1}. Calculate the magnitude of the average resistive force exerted on the bullet.

8 A train of mass 100 tonnes is travelling at 108 km h^{-1} on horizontal tracks, when the driver sees a speed reduction sign. The train's speed must be reduced to 75 km h^{-1} over 500 m. Resistance to motion is approximately 8 kN. Calculate the braking force required, in kN.

9 A package of mass 500 grams slides down a parcel chute of length 3.5 metres, starting from rest. The bottom of the chute is 2.2 metres below the top. The speed of the package at the bottom of the chute is 4.5 m s^{-1}. Find the resistance to motion on the chute.

10 Eddy cycles up a hill. His mass, together with that of his bicycle, is 92 kg. His driving force is 125 N and resistance from friction is 45 N. Eddy travels 350 metres along the road, which rises through a vertical height of 32 metres. His starting speed is 8.2 m s^{-1}. Find his final speed.

Section 3: Potential energy, mechanical energy and conservation of mechanical energy

Consider an object of mass m falling freely under gravity from height h_1 to height h_2, with starting speed u and final speed v.

Since the only external force acting on the object is gravity, the work–energy principle becomes:

work done by gravity = increase in kinetic energy

$$\Rightarrow mg(h_1 - h_2) = \frac{mv^2}{2} - \frac{mu^2}{2}$$

Rearranging this gives:

$$mgh_1 - mgh_2 = \frac{mv^2}{2} - \frac{mu^2}{2}$$

$$\Rightarrow mgh_1 + \frac{mu^2}{2} = mgh_2 + \frac{mv^2}{2}$$

Each side of this equation is made up of the sum of two terms, one of which is kinetic energy. The other term is **gravitational potential energy**. Gravitational potential energy is equal to the work done by gravity causing an object of weight mg to fall through height h if no external forces act on the object.

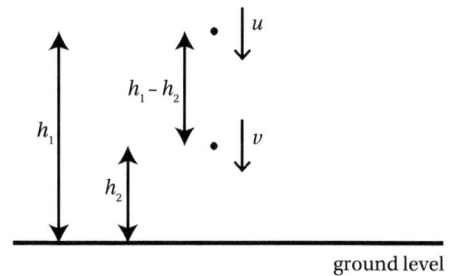

Key point 1.5

Gravitational potential energy (GPE) = mgh, where h is the height above ground (zero) level.

Tip

Whilst you can choose any height as your ground (zero) level it is usually best to choose the lowest height reached by the moving object.

If no external force acts on the object, the sum of kinetic energy and gravitational potential energy is conserved. The sum is usually called **mechanical energy**.

Key point 1.6

If the only force acting on an object is its weight then mechanical energy is conserved.

$$\text{GPE} + \text{KE} = mgh + \frac{1}{2}mv^2 = \text{constant}$$

where h is the vertical height above the zero level.

This diagram may help you to understand the formula for conservation of mechanical energy more easily. As an object descends vertically in height it speeds up, so gravitational potential energy is converted into kinetic energy. As an object ascends vertically in height it slows down, so kinetic energy is converted into gravitational potential energy.
An object will stop its vertical ascent when all of its kinetic energy has been converted to gravitational potential energy.

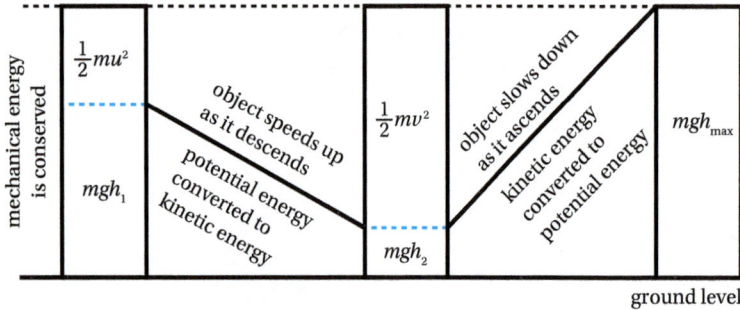

WORKED EXAMPLE 1.11

Faisal throws a ball of mass 125 grams upwards from ground level, with a speed of 12.5 m s^{-1}. Assuming no external forces apply, calculate:

a   the speed of the ball after it has risen 5.0 metres
b   the maximum height gained by the ball.

a   Starting KE $= \dfrac{1}{2} \times 0.125 \times 12.5^2$ .... Convert 125 g to 0.125 kg.

$= 9.766 \text{ J}$

Starting KE $= mgh +$ final KE .... Use conservation of mechanical energy over
$9.766 = 0.125g \times 5 +$ final KE   the first 5 metres of the ascent.
Final KE $= 3.635 \text{ J}$

Take the gravitational potential energy at ground level to be zero.

Calculate the final kinetic energy of the ball.

$\dfrac{1}{2}mv^2 = 3.635$ .... Calculate the final speed of the ball.

Final speed $= \sqrt{\dfrac{3.635}{0.5 \times 0.125}}$

$= 7.6 \text{ m s}^{-1} \text{ (2 s.f.)}$

b   Starting KE $= mgh_{max}$ .... Use conservation of mechanical energy over
the whole ascent (final kinetic energy is zero). All the kinetic energy will have been converted into gravitational potential energy.

$= 0.125 \, g \times h_{max}$ .... Calculate the maximum height gained.

$\Rightarrow h_{max} = 8.0 \text{ metres (2 s.f.)}$

Using energy to solve problems

The principle of conservation of mechanical energy applies to the situation where the only force acting on an object is its weight.

You have already used the work–energy principle to solve problems involving other propulsive and resistive forces. You are now ready to combine the work–energy principle and the principle of conservation of energy:

$$(GPE_1 + KE_1) + \text{work done by driving forces}$$
$$- \text{work done against resistive forces} = (GPE_2 + KE_2)$$

When using this formula you must remember that you do not need to include work done by gravity or work done against gravity as these are already accounted for.

When an object moves vertically upwards or downwards you can work out the change of gravitational potential energy. When an object moves diagonally upwards or downwards it is only the vertical component of the movement that causes a change in gravitational potential energy – you need not consider the horizontal component of movement. This simplification often makes the energy approach to problems very useful.

WORKED EXAMPLE 1.12

A 1.5 kg package is attached to one end of an inextensible string. The string and package are being raised by the action of a pulley. The tension in the string is 18 N. Find the height gained by the package as it increases in speed from 1.2 m s^{-1} to 3.2 m s^{-1}.

Increase in KE $= \dfrac{1}{2} \times 1.5 \times (3.2^2 - 1.2^2)$ · · · · · · · · · · · Calculate the increase in kinetic energy

$\qquad = 6.6 \text{ joules}$

Propulsive work done − resistive work done $= 6.6$ joules · · · work–energy principle:

$\qquad$ total work done = increase in KE

$18 \times h - 1.5g \times h = 6.6$ · · · · · · · · · · · · · · · · · · work done $= \text{tension} \times h - mg \times h$

$\qquad h = \dfrac{6.6}{18 - 1.5g} = 2.0 \text{ metres}$

WORKED EXAMPLE 1.13

Helen cycles from rest at the top of a sloping track, 35 m above the valley floor. She pedals downhill, then continues along a horizontal track, before ascending 10 m on an uphill track and stopping. The total distance she travels is 500 m. The average resistance to motion is 55 N. The combined mass of Helen and her bicycle is 62 kg. Calculate the total work done by Helen and the average driving force she applies.

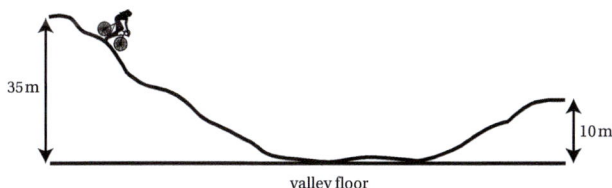

35 m

10 m

valley floor

Continues on next page

$mgh_1 + KE_1 +$ work done by Helen $-$ work done against resistance $= mgh_2 + KE_2$

> Use the work–energy principle and the principle of conservation of energy.

$KE_1 = KE_2 = 0$

> Helen has no kinetic energy at the start of her ride and none at the end.
>
> You do not need to consider her motion throughout her ride – just at the start and at the end.

Work done against resistance = resistive force $\times$ distance
$$= 55 \times 500$$
$$= 27\,500 \text{ J}$$

> Calculate the work Helen does against resistance.
>
> The distance used is the total distance along the road.

$62g \times (35 - 10) +$ work done by Helen $= 27\,500$

> Let both kinetic initial and final energy be zero and rearrange:
>
> $mgh_1 - mgh_2 +$ work done by Helen $-$ work done against resistance $= 0$
>
> $mgh_1 - mgh_2$ is the loss of potential energy of Helen and her bicycle.

Work done by Helen $\approx 27\,500 - 15\,200$
$$\approx 12\,000 \text{ J}$$

Helen's average driving force

> Use Helen's work done, together with her distance travelled, 500 m, to calculate her average driving force.

$$= \frac{\text{work done by Helen}}{\text{distance}}$$
$$= \frac{12\,000}{500}$$
$$= 25 \text{ N (2 s.f.)}$$

ⓘ Did you know?

Conservation of energy is an important principle throughout Physics. Work done by a moving object against resistance, which is lost mechanical energy, is converted to other forms of energy such as heat and noise. This means that total energy is still conserved. The mechanical equivalent of heat was first proposed by James Joule and explains the relationship between mechanical energy and heat energy.

EXERCISE 1C

In this exercise, unless otherwise instructed, use $g = 9.8 \text{ m s}^{-2}$, giving your final answers to an appropriate degree of accuracy.

1 Calculate the increase in potential energy when a mass of 5.0 kg is raised by 25 m.

2 In this question, use $g = 10 \text{ m s}^{-2}$, giving your final answers to an appropriate degree of accuracy.

Calculate the loss of potential energy when a mass of 2 tonnes is lowered through 10 m.

3 A boy of mass 68 kg gains 3600 J of potential energy by climbing a vertical rope. Calculate the height he gains.

4 A toy train loses 1.5 J of potential energy when it descends a spiral track, losing 50 cm in height. Find the mass of the toy train.

5 Felipe strikes a golf ball off an elevated tee. The golf ball has mass 45 grams and Felipe imparts an initial speed of 35 m s^{-1} to the ball.

  a Find the initial kinetic energy of the golf ball.

The ball lands on the green 25 metres below the tee.

  b Calculate the loss of potential energy of the ball.

  c Calculate the kinetic energy of the ball as it lands on the green.

  d Calculate the speed of the golf ball as it lands on the green.

6 Anita dives off a highboard into a diving pool. When Anita leaves the highboard she has a speed of 7.5 m s^{-1} and she is 8.0 metres above the water surface. Anita's mass is 60 kg.

  a Find Anita's kinetic energy as she leaves the highboard.

  b Calculate Anita's kinetic energy as she enters the water.

  c Calculate Anita's speed as she enters the water.

  d What modelling assumptions have you made to simplify your calculations?

7 Wing serves a 58 gram tennis ball with a speed of 9.5 m s^{-1} from a height 3.0 metres above the level of the tennis court. Assuming there are no resistive forces acting on the ball, calculate:

  a the kinetic energy of the ball as Wing serves it

  b the potential energy lost by the ball as it descends to the level of the court

  c the kinetic energy of the ball as it strikes the court

  d the speed of the tennis ball as it strikes the court.

8 Preeti descends a smooth slide starting from rest. Her mass is 58 kg. Overall, her change in vertical height above the ground is 5.8 m and her speed at the bottom of the slide is 6.5 m s^{-1}. Calculate the work done against resistance during her descent.

9 A package of mass 0.80 kg is projected down a smooth sloping parcel chute with a speed of 2.2 m s^{-1}. The height of the bottom of the chute is 7.5 m vertically below the top. Assuming there are no external resistive forces, calculate:

  a the loss of potential energy of the package

  b the speed of the package at the bottom of the chute.

10 Karol slides on his sledge down a straight track of length 210 m, descending 32 m. The combined mass of Karol and his sledge is 72 kg. Karol's starting speed is 2.8 m s^{-1} and his speed at the end of his descent is 10.5 m s^{-1}. Calculate the average resistance to motion, R N, during Karol's descent.

11 Loretta and her bicycle have a combined mass of 75 kg. Loretta cycles up a straight hill AB, accelerating from rest at A to 4.0 m s^{-1} at B. The level of point A is 5.5 m below the level of B. Find:

   a   the increase in kinetic energy of Loretta and her bicycle as she cycles from A to B

   b   the increase in potential energy of Loretta and her bicycle.

   During her ride, the resistance to motion is constant at 60 N parallel to the road surface and Loretta does 8500 J of work.

   c   Calculate the distance from A to B.

Section 4: Power

Power is the rate of doing work. Average power is defined as the total work done by a force divided by the time taken.

> ### 🔑 Key point 1.7
>
> When the force applied is constant:
>
> $$\text{average power} = \frac{\text{work done}}{\text{time taken}}$$

Often, you consider power in relation to a driving force but it applies equally to any constant force acting on an object. Power is measured in watts (W). 1 joule per second is equal to 1 watt.

> ### ℹ️ Did you know?
>
> James Watt (1736–1819) was a Scottish engineer and scientist.
>
> The unit of power is named after him.

WORKED EXAMPLE 1.14

A crane lifts a 2.5 tonne concrete block 35 m in 25 seconds. Calculate the average power rating of the crane during the lift, giving your answer in kW.

Work done against gravity = weight × height gained   Calculate the work done by the crane lifting the block against gravity.

$$= 2500g \times 35$$

$$= 87\,500g \text{ J}$$

Power $= \dfrac{87\,500g}{25}$ Use the definition of power $= \dfrac{\text{work done}}{\text{time taken}}$

$= 34\,000 \text{ W or } 34 \text{ kW (2 s.f.)}$

WORKED EXAMPLE 1.15

The engine brakes on a truck have a power rating of 25 kW. Calculate the total work done in 5.0 seconds by the braking force at this average power rating, giving your answer in kJ.

Work done by brakes = $250\,000 \times 5$

> Rearrange the definition of power to make work done the subject.
>
> work done = power × time

= $1250\,000$ J or 1250 kJ

> Convert your answer to kJ.

WORKED EXAMPLE 1.16

A pump is used to raise water from a well. In one minute, 1500 litres of water are raised 8 metres before being ejected into a tank at a speed of 7.5 m s^{-1}. The density of water is 1000 kg m^{-3}.

a   Calculate the gain of potential energy of the water per second.
b   Calculate the gain of kinetic energy of the water ejected per second.
c   Calculate the power of the pump, in watts.

There are 1000 litres in 1 m^3, with a mass of 1000 kg.

> Work out the mass of 1500 litres of water.

The mass of 1500 litres of water is 1500 kg.

a   Gain of PE of water per second = $\dfrac{1500g \times 8}{60}$

= 1960 J

> Use mgh to calculate the gain in potential energy of the water per second.

b   Gain of KE of water per second = $\dfrac{\frac{1}{2} \times 1500 \times 7.5^2}{60}$

= 703.125 J

> Use $\frac{1}{2}mv^2$ to calculate the gain of kinetic energy of the water per second.

c   Total gain of mechanical energy per second = 2700 W

> Use conservation of mechanical energy:
> work done by the pump
> = gain in GPE + gain in KE
>
> The gain of total mechanical energy per second is the power of the pump.

You can use an alternative formula for power when solving problems.

From the definitions of power and work done:

$$\text{Power} = \frac{\text{work done}}{\text{time taken}} = \frac{\text{force} \times \text{distance}}{\text{time taken}} = \text{force} \times \frac{\text{distance}}{\text{time}} = \text{force} \times \text{speed}$$

This definition allows you to work out power at a specific point in time if you know the force and the speed. This is often referred to as 'instantaneous power' and can be used to work out power when either the force or the velocity varies over time.

Key point 1.8

Power = tractive force × speed

WORKED EXAMPLE 1.17

Chris is cycling on a horizontal road. He is moving at a constant speed of 8.0 m s⁻¹ with a power output of 200 W. Calculate the total resistance to Chris and his bicycle, in newtons.

$200 =$ tractive force $\times 8$ Power $=$ tractive force $\times$ speed
$\Rightarrow$ tractive force $= 25$ N

tractive force $-$ total resistive force $= 0$ As Chris is travelling at constant speed
$\therefore$ tractive force $=$ total resistive force   the resultant force is zero.
$\therefore$ total resistive force $= 25$ N

WORKED EXAMPLE 1.18

Julia is riding her motorbike along a horizontal road. She is travelling with constant speed 90 km h⁻¹, at an engine power of 15 kW. Julia decides to overtake and increases to full power, 20 kW. Assuming the resistance to motion is unchanged, calculate Julia's acceleration. Julia and her motorbike have a combined mass of 465 kg.

90 km h⁻¹ $= 25$ m s⁻¹   Convert Julia's speed to m s⁻¹.

Power $=$ tractive force $\times$ speed   Use the definition of power, but
$\Rightarrow$ tractive force $= \dfrac{\text{power}}{\text{speed}}$ rearrange to make tractive force the subject.

For the motorbike: Calculate the tractive force of Julia and
Tractive force $= \dfrac{15\,000}{25} = 600$ N   her motorbike when she is travelling at constant speed.

tractive force $-$ resistance to motion $= 0$ As Julia is cruising at constant speed the
$\therefore$ tractive force $=$ resistance to motion   resultant force is zero. Hence calculate
$\therefore$ resistance to motion $= 600$ N   the resistive force.

When Julia increases to full power: When Julia increases the power, the
tractive force increases so that it is
Tractive force $= \dfrac{\text{power}}{\text{speed}}$ greater than the resistive force, and
she accelerates. Calculate the resultant
$= \dfrac{20\,000}{25}$ force.
$= 800$ N

Resultant force $=$ tractive force $-$ resistance to motion
$= 800$ N $- 600$ N
$= 200$ N

Using $F = ma$:   Use $F = ma$ to calculate Julia's initial
acceleration.
$200 = 465 \times$ acceleration

$= 0.430$ m s⁻² (3 s.f.)

WORKED EXAMPLE 1.19

A car of mass 1250 kg is travelling along a straight horizontal road against a resistance to motion of $kv^{\frac{1}{2}}$ N, where v is the speed of the car and k is a constant. When the engine is producing a power of 13.5 kW, the car has speed 12.5 m s^{-1} and is accelerating at 0.45 m s^{-2}.

a Find the value of k.

The maximum constant speed of the car on this road is 28 m s^{-1}.

b Find the engine's maximum power, giving your answer in kW.

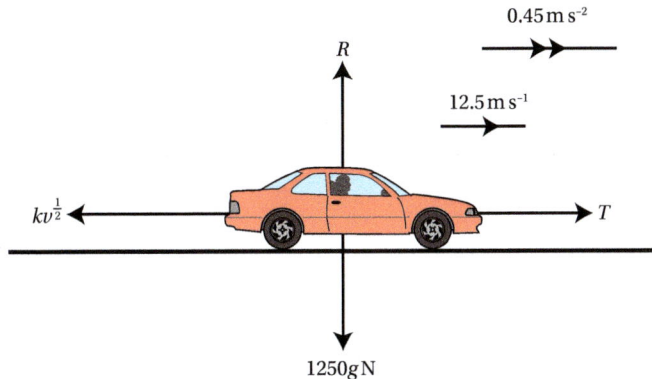

a Resultant force = $T - kv^{\frac{1}{2}}$ . . . .

Let T be the tractive force of the car engine.

Resistance varies with $v^{\frac{1}{2}}$.

Resultant force = T − resistance.

$$T = \frac{power}{speed}$$ . . . .

Rearrange the formula:
power = force × speed.

$$\Rightarrow T = \frac{13\,500}{12.5}$$ . . . .

Calculate T.

$$= 1080 \text{ N}$$

Resultant force = mass × acceleration . . . .

Use $F = ma$.

$$1080 - k \times 12.5^{\frac{1}{2}} = 1250 \times 0.45$$

$$k = \frac{1080 - 1250 \times 0.45}{\sqrt{12}}$$ . . . .

Rearrange to find the value of k.

$$= 146 \text{ units (3 s.f.)}$$

b $T' - kv^{\frac{1}{2}} = 0$ . . . .

Let the new driving force be T'.

As the car is now moving with constant speed the resultant force is now zero.

$$T' = \frac{maximum\ power}{speed}$$

$$\Rightarrow \frac{maximum\ power}{28} - 146.4 \times 28^{\frac{1}{2}} = 0$$

Maximum power = $146.4 \times 28^{\frac{1}{2}} \times 28$ . . . .

Rearrange to find the maximum power rating of the car engine.

$$= 22 \text{ kW (2 s.f.)}$$

EXERCISE 1D

In this exercise, unless otherwise instructed, use $g = 9.8 \text{ m s}^{-2}$, giving your final answers to an appropriate degree of accuracy.

1   A 38 tonne truck is able to brake from 65 km h^{-1} to rest in 20 seconds. Find the average power rating of the brakes.

2   A crane lifts a 2 tonne concrete block 25 m in 12 seconds. Find the average power of the crane.

3   A lift of mass 800 kg can accommodate up to 12 people, who are assumed to have combined mass no more than 1500 kg. Calculate the average power required by the lift motor to raise the maximum load through 60 m in 45 s.

4   A car engine has a maximum driving force of 750 N when travelling at 80 km h^{-1}. Calculate the average power of the engine.

5   A train engine has a power rating of 2.5 MW. Calculate the tractive force when the train is travelling at 216 km h^{-1}.

6   Find the average power exerted by a climber of mass 78 kg when climbing a vertical distance of 35 m in 3 minutes.

A 7   A boat is travelling at a constant speed of 16 km h^{-1}. The boat has mass 10.5 tonnes and the engine is working at its maximum power output of 8 kW. Calculate the work done when the boat is displaced $(5.0\mathbf{i} + 6.0\mathbf{j})$ km.

8   Find the average power of an engine that lifts 500 bags of flour 5 m in 1 hour. Each bag of flour has mass 50 kg.

9   A pump is used to raise water from a well that is 12 metres deep. Water is raised at a rate of 50 kg per second. It is ejected into a pipe at a speed of 5.5 m s^{-1}.

   a   Calculate the gain of potential energy of the water per second.

   b   Calculate the gain of kinetic energy of the water ejected per second.

   c   Calculate the average power of the pump, in watts.

10   Victoria is cycling on level ground. Victoria and her bicycle have a combined mass of 61.5 kg and she is working at a rate of 380 W. Given that Victoria is accelerating at 0.65 m s^{-2}, find the sum of the resistive forces acting on Victoria and her bicycle at the instant when her speed is 7.5 m s^{-1}.

11   Stan is driving his 35 tonne truck on a horizontal road. Stan accelerates from 50 km h^{-1} to 65 km h^{-1}, which is his maximum speed at 500 kW power output. Find the maximum acceleration of the truck, assuming that total resistance is constant.

12   Vince is driving his van against a constant resistance to motion of 5500 N. The van has mass 2.8 tonnes and engine power 125 kW. Vince's acceleration at the instant when his speed is u m s^{-1} is 0.90 m s^{-2}. Calculate u.

13   The resistance to motion of a car is $kv^{\frac{3}{2}}$ newtons, where v m s^{-1} is the speed of the car and k is a constant. The power of the car's engine is 12 kW and the car has a constant speed of 27.5 m s^{-1} along a horizontal road. Show that $k \approx 3.0$.

14 A rocket, *Athena*, of mass 500 kg is moving in a straight line in space, without any resistance to motion. *Athena's* rocket motor is working at a constant rate of 500 kW and its mass is assumed to be constant. *Athena's* speed increases from 90 m s⁻¹ to 140 m s⁻¹ in time t seconds.

   a Calculate the value of t.

   b Calculate *Athena's* acceleration when its speed is 120 m s⁻¹.

✎ Checklist of learning and understanding

In this chapter you have learned the relationship between mechanical work and mechanical energy. You have learned the work–energy principle and the principle of conservation of energy. You have used the definition of power to solve problems.

- Work done = force × distance
- Work done against gravity = weight × height gained
- Gravitational potential energy: GPE = mgh
- Kinetic energy = $\frac{1}{2}mv^2$
- Work–energy principle: work done = change in energy
- Average power = $\dfrac{\text{work done}}{\text{time taken}}$
- Power = tractive force × speed

Mixed practice 1

In this exercise, unless otherwise instructed, use $g = 9.8 \text{ m s}^{-2}$, giving your final answers to an appropriate degree of accuracy.

1. An osprey, flying at 5 m s^{-1}, is carrying a 2.5 kg salmon towards the chicks in its nest, when it drops the fish 15 metres into the loch. Assume there is no air resistance and calculate:

   a the kinetic energy of the salmon when it is dropped by the osprey

   b the potential energy lost by the salmon as it falls to the water surface

   c the kinetic energy, and hence the speed, of the salmon as it enters the water.

2. Inge, who has mass 62 kg, takes part in a ski-jumping contest. She achieves a speed of 20 m s^{-1} at the point of take-off and lands at a point in the landing zone 18 metres vertically below. Assuming there is no air resistance, calculate:

   a Inge's kinetic energy at take-off

   b Inge's loss of gravitational potential energy as she descends through 18 metres

   c Inge's kinetic energy and hence her speed, as she lands.

3. Leo throws a stone of mass 500 grams into the sea from the top of a cliff 50 metres above sea level. He throws the stone with speed 8 m s^{-1}.

   a Calculate the kinetic energy of the stone as it leaves Leo's hand.

   b Calculate the potential energy lost by the stone as it enters the sea.

   c Calculate the kinetic energy of the stone as it enters the sea and, hence, its speed at this time.

4. Carol, a circus performer, is on a swing. She jumps off the swing and lands in a safety net. When Carol leaves the swing, she has a speed of 7 m s^{-1} and she is at a height of 8 metres above the safety net.

   Carol is to be modelled as a particle of mass 52 kg being acted upon only by gravity.

   a Find the kinetic energy of Carol when she leaves the swing.

   b Show that the kinetic energy of Carol when she hits the net is 5350 J, correct to 3 significant figures.

   c Find the speed of Carol as she hits the net.

   [© AQA 2013]

5. A car travels along a straight horizontal road. The resistance to motion is kv N, where v is the speed of the car, measured in m s^{-1}. The car travels at a constant speed of 25 m s^{-1} and the engine of the car works at a constant rate of 21 kW. Show that $k = 33.6$.

6. Find the average power produced by a climber of mass 82 kg in climbing a vertical distance of 65 metres in 3 minutes.

7 A pump is being used to empty a flooded basement.

In one minute, 400 litres of water are pumped out of the basement.

The water is raised 8 metres and is ejected through a pipe at a speed of $2\ \text{m s}^{-1}$.

The mass of 400 litres of water is 400 kg.

a Calculate the gain in potential energy of the 400 litres of water.

b Calculate the gain in kinetic energy of the 400 litres of water.

c Hence calculate the power of the pump, giving your answer in watts.

[© AQA 2011]

8 A cyclist rides from rest up an inclined rough track with an average pedalling force of 38 N. She travels a distance of 850 metres along the track, whilst gaining 25 metres in height. Resistance to motion from the track averages 18 N. The cyclist and her bicycle have a mass of 68 kg . Calculate her speed at the end of her ride.

9 A child of mass 28 kg descends a slide of length 25 metres, losing 4.5 metres in height. She starts from rest and reaches the bottom of the slide at $6.5\ \text{m s}^{-1}$. Find the average resistive force from the slide during her descent.

10 A car travels along a straight horizontal road. When its speed is $v\ \text{m s}^{-1}$, the car experiences a resistance force of magnitude $25v$ newtons.

a The car has a maximum constant speed of $42\ \text{m s}^{-1}$ on this road.

Show that the power being used to propel the car at this speed is 44 100 watts.

b The car has mass 1500 kg.

Find the acceleration of the car when it is travelling at $15\ \text{m s}^{-1}$ on this road under a power of 44 100 watts.

[© AQA 2012]

11 A train consists of an engine and five carriages. A constant resistance force of 3000 N acts on the engine and a constant resistance force of 400 N acts on each of the five carriages.

The maximum constant speed of the train on a horizontal track is $90\ \text{km h}^{-1}$.

a Show that this speed is $25\ \text{m s}^{-1}$.

b Hence find the maximum power output of the engine. Give your answer in kilowatts.

[© AQA 2011]

12 A train, of mass 22 tonnes, moves along a straight horizontal track. A constant resistance force of 5000 N acts on the train. The power output of the engine of the train is 240 kW.

Find the acceleration of the train when its speed is $20\ \text{m s}^{-1}$.

[© AQA 2013]

13 Alan is driving a train of mass 65 tonnes at its maximum speed of 42.5 m s⁻¹ on a straight horizontal track. Its engine is working at 850 kW.

a   Find the magnitude of the resistance acting on the train.

When the train is travelling at 42.5 m s⁻¹, Alan disengages the engine and the train slows down. Assume that the total resistance is unchanged.

b   Use a work–energy calculation to find how far the train travels as it reduces its speed from 42.5 m s⁻¹ to 32.5 m s⁻¹.

A 14 Calculate the loss of kinetic energy when a boat of mass 3.5 tonnes reduces in velocity from $(3.0\mathbf{i} + 4.0\mathbf{j})$ m s⁻¹ to $(2.5\mathbf{i} + 3.0\mathbf{j})$ m s⁻¹.

15 Use the equation of motion, $F = ma$, together with the formula $v^2 = u^2 + 2as$, to derive the relation $Fs = \frac{1}{2}m(v^2 - u^2)$.

16 A particle of mass 500 grams moves along the x-axis under the action of a propulsive force F. The particle's displacement, s metres, depends on time, t seconds, as shown: $s = 3t^2 + 2t$

Find the power of force F when $t = 5$ seconds.

17 A van of mass 1500 kg travels along a horizontal road against a constant resistive force of 225 N. The van travels with constant acceleration from rest, at time $t = 0$ seconds, to 15 m s⁻¹ at time $t = 30$ seconds. It then travels at constant speed for 120 seconds before decelerating to rest over 25 seconds. The speed–time graph illustrates the motion.

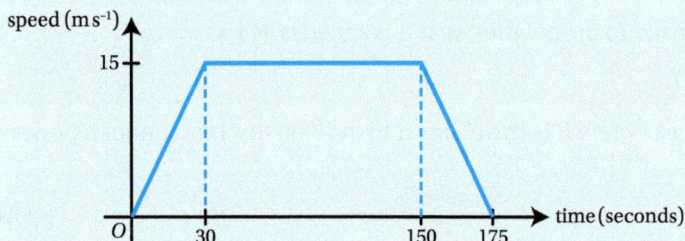

Calculate the power of the vehicle engine when:

a $t = 20$ seconds

b $t = 120$ seconds.

Calculate the power of the van's brakes when:

c $t = 160$ seconds.

2 Dimensional analysis

In this chapter you will learn how to:

- understand the concept of dimensions
- use the language and symbols of dimensional analysis
- understand the connections between units and dimensions
- check the validity of a formula by using dimensional considerations
- predict formulae by using dimensional analysis.

Before you start…

A Level Mathematics Student Book 1, Chapter 2	You should be able to work with indices and surds.	1 Simplify each expression. a $\dfrac{r^5 r^8}{r^9}$ b $(r^4)^3$ c $8^{-\frac{4}{3}}$ d $\dfrac{3\sqrt{6}}{\sqrt{27}}$
GCSE	You should be able to rearrange formulae.	2 Make x the subject of the formula. $y = \dfrac{x^2 z t^3}{t+1}$
GCSE	You should be able to solve simultaneous equations.	3 Solve these simultaneous equations. $2x + 3y = 2$ $3x - 2y = 16$
GCSE	You should be able to express direct and indirect proportion in mathematical terms.	4 P is inversely proportional to r^2. If $P = 2$ when $r = 2$, what is the value of P when $r = 6$?
GCSE	You should know common area and volume formulae.	5 What, in terms of π, is: a the volume b the surface area of a sphere of radius 3 cm?
A Level Mathematics Student Book 1, Chapter 16	You should be familiar with the SI units of mass (kg), length (m) and time (s).	6 What are the SI units of velocity?

Continues on next page

A Level Mathematics Student Book 2, Chapter 7	You should know the definition of a radian.	7 What is the angle, in radians, of a sector of a circle of radius 4 cm and arc length 5 cm?
A Level Mathematics Student Book 1, Chapter 16	You should know the definitions and units of velocity and acceleration.	8 A particle moving in a straight line with constant velocity travels 10 m in 2 seconds. What is its velocity? State the units. 9 A particle moving in a straight line with constant acceleration increases its velocity from 8 m s^{-1} to 15 m s^{-1} in 10 seconds. What is the acceleration? State the units.
A Level Mathematics Student Book 1, Chapter 18	You should know the definition and units of force.	10 A mass of 3 kg is acted on by a constant force of 12 N. What is its acceleration? State the units.
Chapter 1	You should know the definitions of kinetic energy $\left(\frac{1}{2}mv^2\right)$ and potential energy (mgh).	11 A mass of 3 kg is held at a height of 2 metres vertically above the ground. The particle is released from rest. By equating its loss in potential energy to its gain in kinetic energy, find its speed at the instant when it hits the ground. Use $g = 9.8 \text{ m s}^{-2}$, giving your final answer to an appropriate degree of accuracy.

What is dimensional analysis?

In dimensional analysis you look at the type of quantity you are dealing with rather than the specific units. You use it as a mathematical way of checking that equations and formulae are consistent, and that you are combining like quantities, and also to predict and establish formulae.

Section 1: Defining and calculating dimensions

The **dimension** of a given quantity describes what sort of quantity you are measuring; for example, any distance or length, whatever its units, has the dimension of length and has the symbol **L**.

You can use square brackets to represent 'the dimension of' so, for example, [metres] = **L**.

The dimension of distance is **L**. The diameter of a pin, the radius of a circle, the length of a running track and the distance from London to Hong Kong would all be measured in different units but they are all measurements of length or distance and have the dimension **L**.

The other common dimensions that you use in Mechanics are **M** for mass and **T** for time.

The mass of a spider, the mass of an elephant, the mass of a sphere might all be measured in different units but they are all measurements of mass with the dimension **M**.

Similarly time, whether measured in seconds, days or centuries, has the dimension **T**. If t is a time in seconds, then it has dimension **T**. $2t$ and $60t$ will also be times with dimension **T**. The 2 and the 60 do not affect the units as they are numbers and numbers are dimensionless.

Some branches of science use other dimensions, for example, the dimensions of temperature, electric current, amount of light and amount of matter.

> **i) Did you know?**
>
> In the USA, there is a unit of mass called a slug!

> **i) Did you know?**
>
> There is a connection between dimensional analysis and the greenhouse effect.
>
> The concept of dimensional analysis is often attributed to Joseph Fourier, a famous French mathematician and physicist. He is best known for the Fourier series, which is widely used in Mathematics and Physics, and for his work on heat flow.
>
> Fourier is widely recognised as being the first scientist to suggest that the Earth's atmosphere would act as an insulation layer – the idea now known as the greenhouse effect.

> **🔑 Key point 2.1**
>
> The dimensions of quantities in Mechanics can be expressed in terms of **M** for mass, **L** for length and **T** for time.
>
> Square brackets are used to abbreviate the phrase 'the dimension of', so for example, [time] = **T**.

> **⏩ Fast forward**
>
> Dimensionless constants are explored in greater detail later in this chapter.

Finding dimensions

To find the dimensions of quantities that are multiplied or divided, you combine their dimensions in the same way as the quantities are combined.

WORKED EXAMPLE 2.1

Find the dimensions of:

a velocity   **b** acceleration   **c** force = mass × acceleration.

a If an object is moving with constant velocity v in a straight line and it moves a distance s in time t, then you have the relationship:

$v = \dfrac{s}{t}$ State an equation for velocity.

Continues on next page

$$[v] = \frac{[s]}{[t]}$$

$$= \frac{\mathbf{L}}{\mathbf{T}}$$

$$= \mathbf{LT^{-1}}$$

Write down the dimensions of the right-hand side of the equation and simplify. The dimension of distance is **L** and of time is **T**. Use negative indices when you divide by dimensions.

In more general terms:

$$v = \frac{ds}{dt}$$

State the general case.

$$[v] = \frac{[ds]}{[dt]}$$

$$= \frac{[s]}{[t]}$$

$$= \frac{\mathbf{L}}{\mathbf{T}}$$

$$= \mathbf{LT^{-1}}$$

Find the dimensions – ds has the same dimensions as s and dt has the same dimensions as t.

$\frac{ds}{dt}$ has the same dimensions as $\frac{s}{t}$.

b If a particle starts from rest and moves with constant acceleration a in a straight line gaining speed v in time t, then:

$$a = \frac{dv}{dt}$$

State a definition of acceleration.

$$[a] = \frac{[dv]}{[dt]}$$

$$= \frac{[v]}{[t]}$$

$$= \frac{\mathbf{LT^{-1}}}{\mathbf{T}}$$

$$= \mathbf{LT^{-2}}$$

Find the dimensions. $\frac{dv}{dt}$ has the same dimensions as $\frac{v}{t}$.

c $\quad F = ma$

State an equation for force...

$$[\text{force}] = [m][a]$$

$$= \mathbf{MLT^{-2}}$$

...and take dimensions of both sides of the equation.

WORKED EXAMPLE 2.2

Work out the dimensions of:

a area **b** kinetic energy.

a $[\text{area}] = [\text{length}][\text{length}]$

$\quad = \mathbf{L^2}$

Area formulae always involve multiplying two lengths together or squaring a length.

Continues on next page

Tip

Vector quantities such as velocity and **displacement** have the same dimensions as their **scalar** equivalents (speed and distance). Remember that vectors have magnitude and direction, but scalar quantites have only magnitude, not direction.

b   Kinetic energy $= \frac{1}{2}mv^2$ ····· State the formula for kinetic energy.

$$[\text{kinetic energy}] = \left(\frac{1}{2}\right)[m][v^2]$$

$$= [m][v]^2$$

To find the dimensions, you need to multiply the dimension of m by the square of the dimensions of v.

$\frac{1}{2}$ is a constant so has no dimensions and does not affect the calculation of dimensions.

$$[m][v]^2 = \mathbf{M(LT^{-1})^2}$$

$$= \mathbf{ML^2T^{-2}}$$

Remove the brackets and simplify the result.

Dimensionless quantities

If all the dimensions cancel out, then the quantity is dimensionless. This is true of many quantities in Mechanics that are described as coefficients. Examples are the coefficient of restitution (which you will meet in Chapter 3) and the coefficient of friction.

The coefficient of friction, μ, between two surfaces is defined as the ratio of the limiting frictional force, F, to the normal reaction force, R. Both F_{LIM} and R have the dimensions of force that you worked out in Worked example 2.1.

$$\mu = \frac{F_{\text{LIM}}}{R}$$

$$[\mu] = \frac{[F_{\text{LIM}}]}{[R]}$$

$$= \frac{\mathbf{MLT^{-2}}}{\mathbf{MLT^{-2}}}$$

$$= \mathbf{M^0L^0T^0}$$

$$= 1$$

So μ is dimensionless.

You can leave out dimensionless quantities when you are working out the dimensions of a formula or expression, or you can put in the number 1 to represent the dimensionless quantity.

> **Rewind**
>
> You met the coefficient of friction in A Level Mathematics Student Book 2, Chapter 18. In this chapter, you will be given the definition when it is required, as a reminder.

Key point 2.2

Numerical constants, such as the real numbers, π and e, are dimensionless. For example, in the formula $C = 2\pi r$, 2 and π are dimensionless.

EXERCISE 2A

1 Find the dimensions of each quantity, or state if it is dimensionless.

   a linear acceleration (a) **b** acceleration due to gravity (g)

   c force (ma) **d** weight

   e momentum (mv) **f** π in the formula $C = 2\pi r$

   g volume   **h** density (mass per unit volume)

   i moment of a force F (force × distance)

   j pressure (force per unit area)

2 State the dimensions of $\sin \theta$.

3 State the dimensions of $\tan^2 \theta$.

4 **a** Find the dimensions of potential energy (mgh).

   b Are these the same as the dimensions of kinetic energy?

5 **a** Work out the dimensions of work done
     (work done = force × distance).

   b How does this compare to the dimensions of kinetic or potential energy?

6 The coefficient of restitution e is defined as

$e = \dfrac{\text{relative velocity of separation}}{\text{relative velocity of approach}}$. Find $[e]$.

7 The refractive index n of a material is defined as $n = \dfrac{c}{v}$ where c is the speed of light in a vacuum and v is the speed of light through the material. Find $[n]$.

8 State the dimensions of $\dfrac{\mathrm{d}F}{\mathrm{d}t}$ where F is a force and t is time.

9 **a** Given that all forms of mechanical energy have the same dimensions, find the dimensions of mechanical energy.

   b The mechanical energy stored in an elastic string of initial length l extended by a distance x is $\dfrac{\lambda x^2}{2l}$, where λ is the modulus of elasticity of the string. Find $[\lambda]$.

10 Newton's law of gravitational attraction states that the force of attraction between two masses m_1 and m_2 that are a distance r apart is $\dfrac{Gm_1 m_2}{r^2}$, where G is the gravitational constant. Find $[G]$.

11 The energy-frequency relationship for slow moving particles is given by the formula $\lambda = \dfrac{h}{mv}$, where λ is the wavelength, m is the mass of the particle, v is the velocity of the particle and h is Planck's constant. Find the dimensions of h.

Tip

Once you have established the dimensions of a quantity, then the dimensions will be the same however you calculate it.

Kinetic energy and potential energy have different formulae but they are both expressions of mechanical energy and so have identical dimensions.

Forces such as friction, tension, thrust and reaction force all have the same dimensions however they are described.

Section 2: Units and dimensions of sums, differences and angles

> ## 🔑 Key point 2.3
>
> You can only add and subtract terms that have the same dimensions.
>
> When you add or subtract two or more quantities with the same dimensions, then the resulting sum or difference will also have the same dimensions.

If you add two or more lengths, then the answer is also a length with dimension $\mathbf{L}$. If you add and subtract several forces the answer is also a force.

You can add 10 minutes to 3 hours or you can add 6 kilometres to 5 miles but you cannot add 10 seconds to 6 metres to give any form of meaningful result.

> **❗ Common error**
>
> Remember that you can only add or subtract quantities if they have the same dimensions. They do not however have to have the same units.

You can only add or subtract terms with the same dimensions to give a consistent formula. You can use this principle to check whether or not a formula is dimensionally consistent; this is called an error check.

The sum $u+v$ where u and v are speeds is also a speed and has the dimension of speed.

In dimensional terms:

$$\begin{aligned}[u+v] &= [u]+[v]\\ &= \mathbf{LT^{-1}}+\mathbf{LT^{-1}}\\ &= \mathbf{LT^{-1}}\end{aligned}$$

The sum $\displaystyle\sum_{i=1}^{n} m_i v_i$ has the same dimensions as mv which is:

$$\begin{aligned}[m][v] &= (\mathbf{M})(\mathbf{LT^{-1}})\\ &= \mathbf{MLT^{-1}}\end{aligned}$$

The integral $\displaystyle\int_0^t v\,\mathrm{d}t$ is a sum and has the same dimension as $v\,\mathrm{d}t$ which is:

$$\begin{aligned}[v][\mathrm{d}t] &= (\mathbf{LT^{-1}})\mathbf{T}\\ &= \mathbf{L}\end{aligned}$$

For sums and differences, you should check that the dimensions of the terms that you are adding or subtracting are the same. Then the dimensions of the answers will also be the same.

For products and quotients you must multiply or divide the dimensions.

> **💡 Tip**
>
> Many dimensional analysis questions look very complicated as they involve formulae, often with indices. Do not let the look of the question put you off, it's just about applying rules!

WORKED EXAMPLE 2.3

Given that a, r, r_1, r_2 and h are lengths and m_1 and m_2 are masses, check that the terms being added or subtracted have the same dimensions and find the dimensions of the result.

a $ar^2 + arh$ **b** $\left[\dfrac{m_1 r_1 + m_2 r_2}{m_1 + m_2} \right]$ **c** $\sqrt{\dfrac{r_1^{\,3} + r_2^{\,3}}{r_1 + r_2}}$

a $[ar^2 + arh] = [ar^2] + [arh]$

$\qquad\qquad = \mathbf{L}^3 + \mathbf{L}^3$

$\qquad\qquad = \mathbf{L}^3$

> The dimensions of both terms are $\mathbf{L}^3$, so the dimension of their sum is also $\mathbf{L}^3$.

b $\left[\dfrac{m_1 r_1 + m_2 r_2}{m_1 + m_2} \right] = \dfrac{[m_1 r_1] + [m_2 r_2]}{[m_1 + m_2]}$

$\qquad\qquad\qquad = \dfrac{\mathbf{ML}}{\mathbf{M}}$

$\qquad\qquad\qquad = \mathbf{L}$

> The dimensions of both terms in the numerator are $\mathbf{ML}$ so the dimension of their sum is also $\mathbf{ML}$. The dimensions of both terms in the denominator are $\mathbf{M}$, so the dimension of their sum is also $\mathbf{M}$. The dimension of the quotient is $\mathbf{L}$.

c $\left[\sqrt{\dfrac{r_1^{\,3} + r_2^{\,3}}{r_1 + r_2}} \right] = \sqrt{\dfrac{r_1^{\,3} + r_2^{\,3}}{r_1 + r_2}}$

$\qquad\qquad = \sqrt{\dfrac{[r_1^{\,3}] + [r_2^{\,3}]}{[r_1] + [r_2]}}$

$\qquad\qquad = \sqrt{\dfrac{\mathbf{L}^3}{\mathbf{L}}}$

$\qquad\qquad = \mathbf{L}$

> The dimensions of both terms of the numerator are $\mathbf{L}^3$, so the dimension of their sum is also $\mathbf{L}^3$.
>
> The dimensions of both terms of the denominator are $\mathbf{L}$, so the dimension of their sum is also $\mathbf{L}$.
>
> Divide $\mathbf{L}^3$ by $\mathbf{L}$ giving $\mathbf{L}^2$ and take the square root.

WORKED EXAMPLE 2.4

Is the equation $v^2 = u^2 + 2gt$, where u and v are velocities, g is the acceleration due to gravity and t is time, dimensionally consistent?

Checking the dimensions of each term:

> To check an equation for consistency you need to find the dimensions of each term and show that they all have the same dimensions.

Velocity involves dividing distance by time so has dimensions $\mathbf{LT^{-1}}$.

> Find the dimensions of v^2 by squaring the dimensions of v.

$[v^2] = [v]^2$

$\qquad = (\mathbf{LT^{-1}})^2$

$\qquad = \mathbf{L^2 T^{-2}}$

Continues on next page

Similarly $[u^2] = \mathbf{L}^2\mathbf{T}^{-2}$

The dimensions of u^2 will be the same as those of v^2 as they are both velocities.

$$[2gt] = [2][g][t]$$
$$= [g][t]$$
$$[g][t] = (\mathbf{L}\mathbf{T}^{-2})\mathbf{T}$$
$$= \mathbf{L}\mathbf{T}^{-1}$$

Find the dimension of $2gt$ by multiplying the dimensions of 2 and g (acceleration) and t.

As the dimensions of the three terms are not the same the equation is not dimensionally consistent so cannot be correct.

Dimensions of angles and trigonometric functions

The definition of an angle in radians is the ratio:

$$\text{angle in radians} = \frac{\text{arc length}}{\text{radius}}$$

As both arc length and radius are lengths then the dimensions of angle are $\frac{\mathbf{L}}{\mathbf{L}} = \mathbf{L}^0(=1)$ which is dimensionless.

All trigonometric functions are dimensionless for the same reason – each is the ratio of two quantities with the same dimensions.

⏪ **Rewind**

You learned about radians in A Level Mathematics Student Book 2, Chapter 7.

🔑 **Key point 2.4**

An angle has units but is dimensionless.

WORKED EXAMPLE 2.5

What are the dimensions of angular velocity, $\omega = \dfrac{\mathrm{d}\theta}{\mathrm{d}t}$ where θ is an angle in radians?

Angular velocity $\omega = \dfrac{\mathrm{d}\theta}{\mathrm{d}t}$ radians per second

where θ is the angle in radians

Define the quantity involved – angular velocity is rate of change of angle and has the symbol ω.

$$[\omega] = \frac{[\mathrm{d}\theta]}{[\mathrm{d}t]}$$
$$= \frac{1}{\mathbf{T}}$$
$$= \mathbf{T}^{-1}$$

Equate the dimensions of all terms in the equation.

ⓘ Did you know?

The metric system originated during the French Revolution of the 1790s. It was intended to provide a unified system of measures that used the metre and kilogram as standard units of length and mass, respectively. The name of the system, **SI**, stands for *système international d'unités*. The units are now commonly used by the scientific communities of most developed nations. The main units are metres for length, kilograms for mass and seconds for time. The wider adoption of this system, sometimes known as MKS after the units, was the result of an initiative, started in the late 1940s, to standardise units. At that time, the UK was using feet, pounds and seconds as standard and most of Europe was using centimetres, grams and seconds (cgs).

Definitions of some SI units

Some common SI units have particular names.

The **newton** is the unit of force. 1 newton (N) is the force required to give a mass of 1 kilogram an acceleration of 1 metre per second per second.

The **joule** is the unit of work and energy. 1 joule (J) is the work done (or energy transferred) to an object when a force of 1 newton acts on that object in the direction of motion for a distance of 1 metre.

The **newton metre** is the unit of moment (or torque). It is the effect of a force of 1 newton applied perpendicularly to a moment arm of 1 metre.

The **moment** of a force about a point is force × perpendicular distance to the line of action of that force.

The **watt** is the unit of power. 1 watt (W) is a rate of energy transfer or a rate of working of 1 joule per second.

The **pascal** is the unit of pressure. 1 pascal is the pressure exerted by a force of 1 newton acting on an area of 1 square metre. Pressure is force per unit area.

⏮ Rewind

Recall the formula for force from A Level Mathematics Student Book 1, Chapter 18:

force = mass × acceleration.

⏮ Rewind

Recall the formula for work done from Chapter 1,

work done = force × distance.

EXERCISE 2B

In this exercise, these letters refer to specific quantities:

- u and v represent velocities
- r, s, h, x and y represent distance or displacement
- F represents force
- a represents acceleration
- θ represents an angle
- t represents time.

1 Given that r, l and h are measurements of length, state the dimensions of:

  a $r+l+h$ **b** h^2+rl **c** r^2l-h^3.

2 Given that m_i are masses, x_i are distances and v_i are speeds, state the dimensions of:

  a $m_1v_1+m_2v_2$ **b** $\frac{1}{2}mv_2^2-\frac{1}{2}mv_1^2$

  c $\displaystyle\sum_1^n m_ix_i^2$ **d** $\displaystyle\int v\,\mathrm{d}t$.

3 Given that m_i are masses and x_i are distances, state the dimensions of $\dfrac{\displaystyle\sum_1^n m_ix_i}{\displaystyle\sum_1^n m_i}$.

4 Given that m represents mass, u and v represent speeds, a represents acceleration, t and T represent times and l and h represent distances, find the dimensions of each term in these equations and hence determine which equations are dimensionally consistent.

  a $v^2=u^2+2as$ **b** $s=ut+\frac{1}{2}at$

  c $\frac{1}{2}mv^2-\frac{1}{2}mu^2=mgh$ **d** impulse (force × time) = change in momentum

  e $T=2\pi\sqrt{\dfrac{l^2}{g}}$

5 **a** Write down the dimensions of angular acceleration, commonly written as θ.

  b Is the formula $\theta=-\frac{g}{l}\theta$ dimensionally consistent? Give a dimensional argument for your answer.

6 In simple harmonic motion (SHM) the restoring force measured towards the centre of the motion is proportional to the displacement, x, measured away from the centre of the motion.

  a Write this as an equation, in terms of m, x and t, using k as the constant of proportionality.

  b Find the dimensions of k.

7 Angular momentum is defined as $I\omega$ where I is the moment of inertia $\left(\sum mr^2\right)$ and ω is angular velocity.

  a Work out the dimensions of angular momentum.

  b Are these the same as the dimensions of linear momentum, where linear momentum is defined

  as $\sum mv$?

  c Explain why angular momentum is sometimes call 'moment of momentum'.

8 The rotational kinetic energy of a rigid body about an axis is defined as $\frac{1}{2}I\omega^2$ where I is the moment of inertia $\left(\sum mr^2\right)$ of the body about that axis and ω is the angular velocity.

  a Work out the dimensions of rotational kinetic energy.

  b Is this the same as the dimensions of translational kinetic energy?

9 Young's modulus, E, for a solid is defined as $E = \dfrac{\text{stress}}{\text{strain}}$. Stress is the pressure in the solid and strain is defined as the ratio of extension to the original length.

  a Write a formula for E in terms of $F, A, l,$ and x, where F is the force exerted on the solid, A is its cross-sectional area, l is the original length and x is the extension.

  b What are the dimensions of E?

10 A student writes the equation for the path of a projectile as:

$$y = x \tan \theta - \frac{gx}{2v^2} \sec^2 \theta$$

  a Find the term in this equation that is dimensionally inconsistent.

  b Suggest an alteration to one variable in this term that would make it dimensionally consistent.

WORK IT OUT 2.1

A particle of mass m is fixed at the midpoint of an elastic string of natural length $2l$. The string is then fixed to two points A and B on a smooth horizontal surface, $AB = 2a$ and $a > l$. When the particle is displaced through a small distance x along the perpendicular bisector of AB it is thought to perform small oscillations. The modulus of elasticity of the string is λ and it has the dimensions of force. Use dimensional analysis to determine which option gives the correct formula for the periodic time of these oscillations.

  A $T = 2\pi\sqrt{\dfrac{ma^2l}{2\lambda(a-l)}}$

  B $T = 2\pi\sqrt{\dfrac{mal}{2\lambda(a-l)}}$

  C $T = 2\pi\sqrt{\dfrac{mal}{2\lambda(a-l)^2}}$

Which is the correct solution? Identify the errors made in the incorrect solutions.

Solution 1	Solution 2	Solution 3
Formula A:	Formula B:	Formula C:
$T = 2\pi\sqrt{\dfrac{ma^2l}{2\lambda(a-l)}}$ is correct	$T = 2\pi\sqrt{\dfrac{mal}{2\lambda(a-l)}}$ is correct	$T = 2\pi\sqrt{\dfrac{mal}{2\lambda(a-l)^2}}$ is correct
because the right-hand side has the dimensions of time.	because the right-hand side has the dimensions of time.	because the right-hand side has the dimensions of time.

Tip

You can derive dimensions of a quantity either from its formula or from its units. Any formula for that quantity will have the same dimensions. The volume of an icosahedron will have the same dimensions as the dimensions of a cube: $\mathbf{L}^3$. You only need to know that it is a volume to state its dimensions; you do not need to know the specific formula.

Section 3: Finding dimensions from units and derivatives, conversion of units and predicting formulae

This process is similar to finding the dimensions of a quantity from its formula.

WORKED EXAMPLE 2.6

A pascal is a unit of pressure. Pressure is force per unit area $\left(\dfrac{\text{force}}{\text{area}}\right)$. The poiseuille (PI) is the (very rarely used!) SI unit of dynamic viscosity. It is equivalent to pascal seconds (Pa s). Find the dimensions of a poiseuille.

	To find the dimensions of dynamic viscosity you do not need to know its formula, or even what it is, as long as you know its units. You are told that it is measured in pascal seconds.
$\text{pressure} = \dfrac{\text{force}}{\text{area}}$	A pascal is a unit of pressure so you can find its dimensions from the definition of pressure as force per unit area.
$[\text{Pa}] = \left[\dfrac{\text{force}}{\text{area}}\right]$	Simplify the dimensions of a pascal...
$\quad = \dfrac{[\text{mass}][\text{acceleration}]}{[\text{area}]}$	
$[\text{Pa}] = \dfrac{\text{MLT}^{-2}}{\text{L}^2}$	
$\quad = \text{ML}^{-1}\text{T}^{-2}$	
$[\text{poiseuille}] = [\text{Pa}][\text{s}]$	...then multiply by the dimension of seconds to give the required dimensions.
$\quad = \text{ML}^{-1}\text{T}^{-2}\text{T}$	
$\quad = \text{ML}^{-1}\text{T}^{-1}$	

You have seen that angles have units but not dimensions. This makes it difficult to predict units from dimensions. For example, angular velocity, ω, has dimension T^{-1} but units of radians per second. Frequency also has dimension T^{-1} but has units of hertz (Hz, sometimes called cycles per second).

🔑 Key point 2.5

You can predict dimensions from units or formulae but it is **not** always possible to predict units from dimensions.

There are quantities that you might think of as constants that have dimensions even if they are not always written with units.

The tension T in an elastic string of initial length l which has been stretched to $(l+x)$ is given by the formula $T = \lambda \frac{x}{l}$, where λ is the modulus of elasticity for the string.

λ is a physical constant, so if the string were made of a different material, then it would have a different value. λ has the same units and dimensions as the tension. Other examples of physical constants are surface tension and the gravitational constant.

> **Common error**
>
> Do not assume that a quantity represented by a letter is dimensionless unless you are told specifically that it is.

> **▶▶I Fast forward**
>
> You will study the tension in an elastic string in Chapter 5.

WORKED EXAMPLE 2.7

a Derive the dimensions of λ, the modulus of elasticity.
b State the units of λ.

a The tension (force) T in an elastic string or spring of initial length l, which has been stretched to $(l+x)$, is given by:

$T = \lambda \dfrac{x}{l}$

First state a formula involving λ.

$\lambda = \dfrac{Tl}{x}$

Then rearrange it to give a formula for λ.

$[\lambda] = \dfrac{[T][l]}{[x]}$

$= \dfrac{MLT^{-2}L}{L}$

$= MLT^{-2}$

Find the dimensions of each term and combine them.

b The units are newtons as $\dfrac{x}{l}$ is dimensionless.

As x and l have the same dimensions, their quotient will be dimensionless so it is reasonable to assume that T and λ will have the same units – newtons – which is in keeping with the dimensions.

Finding dimensions of second derivatives

You saw in Worked example 2.1 that the dimensions of acceleration are **LT^{-2}**. You know that acceleration can be written as $a = \dfrac{d^2x}{dt^2}$, but how do you find the dimensions of acceleration from this?

> **I◀◀ Rewind**
>
> You learned about non-uniform acceleration in A Level Mathematics Student Book 1, Chapter 16.

You know that:

$$[v] = \frac{[dx]}{[dt]}$$

$$= \frac{[x]}{[t]}$$

$$= \mathbf{LT^{-1}}$$

It follows that:

$$\frac{d^2x}{dt^2} = \frac{d}{dt}\left(\frac{dx}{dt}\right)$$

So $\left[\dfrac{d^2x}{dt^2}\right] = \left[\dfrac{d}{dt}\left(\dfrac{dx}{dt}\right)\right]$

$$= \left[\frac{x}{t^2}\right]$$

$$= \frac{\mathbf{L}}{\mathbf{T^2}}$$

$$= \mathbf{LT^{-2}}$$

> **❗ Common error**
>
> You should recognise that
>
> $$\frac{d^2x}{dt^2} \neq \left(\frac{dx}{dt}\right)^2$$
>
> so you cannot say that:
>
> $$[a] = \left[\frac{d^2x}{dt^2}\right]$$
>
> $$= \left[\frac{dx}{dt}\right]^2$$
>
> $$= \frac{[x]^2}{[t]^2}$$
>
> $$= \mathbf{L^2T^{-2}}$$

Using dimensions to convert units

If two quantities are equal, then their dimensions must be the same, whatever their units. So to find a conversion factor you first need to find the dimensions of the quantities involved and then put these into the expressions for each quantity in the formula. For example, if you are converting hours to seconds, the conversion factor for the **T** dimension is $60 \times 60 = 3600$. So if the dimension of the quantity required involves $\mathbf{T^2}$, then the conversion factor involves 3600^2.

WORKED EXAMPLE 2.8

In the centimetres, grams and seconds (cgs) system, a force measures 30 000 dynes. What is this in newtons?

[force] = $\mathbf{MLT^{-2}}$

For **M**, 1 gram = 0.001 kg

For **L**, 1 centimetre = 0.01 metres

For **T**, 1 second = 1 second

You do not need to know the definition of a dyne to solve this problem, since you are told that it is a force. You just need to know the dimensions of force.

State the dimensions of force (mass × acceleration).

For each dimension, put in its conversion factor from cgs to SI units.

The conversion factor is

$0.001 \times 0.01 \times 1^{-2} = 0.00001$

Put these conversions into the dimensions $\mathbf{MLT^{-2}}$ to find the conversion factor.

30 000 dynes = 30 000 × 0.00001 newtons

$$= 0.3\,N$$

Apply this to the question.

37

Using dimensions to predict formulae

> ### 🔑 Key point 2.6
>
> You can use dimensional analysis to predict formulae by equating the dimensions of the terms of the proposed formula.

> ### ⏮ Rewind
>
> Recall from Section 1 that numerical constants, and other dimensionless quantities such as trigonometric functions, ratios and angles, can be left out of the calculation or given the dimension 1.

If you take dimensions of both sides of a proposed formula and then equate the indices of each dimension, you will get a set of simultaneous equations. You will need to know, or be able to derive, the dimensions of common quantities such as density, force, pressure and acceleration.

WORKED EXAMPLE 2.9

Pressure, P, is measured in newtons per square metre. Surface tension, S, is defined as force per unit length $\left(\dfrac{\text{force}}{\text{length}}\right)$.

a Derive the dimensions of pressure.

b Find the dimensions of surface tension.

c The pressure P inside an ideal soap bubble is given by the formula $P = 2R^\alpha S^\beta$, where 2 is a dimensionless constant, R is the radius of the sphere and S is the surface tension. Find the values of α and β and hence find the formula for P.

a $[\text{pressure } (P)] = \left[\dfrac{\text{newtons}}{\text{metres}^2}\right]$

$= \dfrac{[\text{force}]}{[\text{metres}]^2}$

$[P] = \dfrac{[\text{mass} \times \text{acceleration}]}{[\text{metres}]^2}$

$= \dfrac{\mathbf{M} \times \mathbf{LT^{-2}}}{\mathbf{L}^2}$

$= \mathbf{ML^{-1}T^{-2}}$

Use the units of pressure given to write an expression for the dimensions. Newtons are units of force so have the units of force or mass × acceleration. Metres are units of length.

Simplify the indices to give a single expression for the dimensions.

b $[\text{surface tension } (S)] = \left[\dfrac{\text{force}}{\text{length}}\right]$

$= \dfrac{[\text{mass} \times \text{acceleration}]}{[\text{length}]}$

$[S] = \dfrac{\mathbf{MLT^{-2}}}{\mathbf{L}}$

$= \mathbf{MT^{-2}}$

Use the definitions of force and length to find the dimensions of surface tension in the same way.

c $P = 2R^\alpha S^\beta$

Write down the formula given in the question.

$[P] = [R]^\alpha [S]^\beta$

Write the dimensional equation, remembering that 2 is dimensionless so can be left out.

$\mathbf{ML^{-1}T^{-2}} = \mathbf{L}^\alpha (\mathbf{MT^{-2}})^\beta$

Substitute in the dimensions of each quantity…

Continues on next page

For $M : 1 = \beta$

For $L : -1 = \alpha$

For $T : -2 = -2\beta$

...and equate the indices of the dimensions on each side of the equation to find the values of α and β.

This gives $\alpha = -1$ and $\beta = 1$.

Put these values of α and β back into the given formula and simplify.

$\therefore P = 2R^{-1}S^{1}$

$\quad = \dfrac{2S}{R}$

WORKED EXAMPLE 2.10

A simple pendulum consists of a particle of mass m suspended at the end of an inextensible string of length l. The pendulum is initially hanging at rest and then it is displaced through a small angle θ and released to make small oscillations.

a It is thought that the formula for the periodic time T of the small oscillations is of the form $T = Am^{\alpha}l^{\beta}g^{\gamma}$, where A is a dimensionless constant and g is the acceleration due to gravity. Use dimensional analysis to find the values of α, β and γ and hence find an equation for T.

b What deductions can you make from this formula?

c In an experiment it is found that $T = \dfrac{2\pi}{\sqrt{5}}$ when $l = 2$. Using $g = 10 \text{ m s}^{-2}$, find the value of A.

a $T = Am^{\alpha}l^{\beta}g^{\gamma}$ (1)

$[T] = \mathbf{T}$

The periodic time T has dimension $\mathbf{T}$.

$\mathbf{T} = [Am^{\alpha}l^{\beta}g^{\gamma}]$

$\quad = [A][m^{\alpha}][l^{\beta}][g^{\gamma}]$

The dimensions of both sides of the equation must be the same and are equal to $\mathbf{T}$.

A is dimensionless.

$[m] = \mathbf{M}$

$[l] = \mathbf{L}$

$[g] = \mathbf{LT}^{-2}$

State the dimensions of each of the terms...

$\mathbf{T} = \mathbf{M}^{\alpha}(\mathbf{LT}^{-2})^{\gamma}\mathbf{L}^{\beta}$

$\quad = \mathbf{M}^{\alpha}\mathbf{L}^{\beta+\gamma}\mathbf{T}^{-2\gamma}$

...then combine them as the formula states and simplify.

Equating indices of $\mathbf{T}$:

$\mathbf{T}^{1} = \mathbf{T}^{-2\gamma}$ so $1 = -2\gamma$ giving $\gamma = -\dfrac{1}{2}$

Equating indices of $\mathbf{M}$:

$\mathbf{M}^{O} = \mathbf{M}^{\alpha}$ so $0 = \alpha$

Equating indices of $\mathbf{L}$:

$\mathbf{L}^{O} = \mathbf{L}^{\beta+\gamma}$ so $0 = \beta + \gamma$ giving $\beta = \dfrac{1}{2}$

Continues on next page

This gives:

$\alpha = 0$

$\beta = \dfrac{1}{2}$

$\gamma = -\dfrac{1}{2}$

So $T = Am^0 l^{\frac{1}{2}} g^{-\frac{1}{2}}$

$\quad = A\sqrt{\dfrac{l}{g}}$

> Solve the equations to find the values of α, β and γ…
>
> …and then substitute these values into equation (1) and state a formula for A.

b You can deduce that for displacements through a small angle θ the periodic time is independent of θ and is also independent of m. T will be the same whatever the mass m of the particle.

> You now need to consider your answer as the question asks for a deduction. You see that the formula does not include m or θ, so the periodic time T will be the same whatever the mass of the particle as long as the length of the string is unchanged, for small angle displacements θ.

c $A^2 = \dfrac{T^2 g}{l}$

$A^2 = \dfrac{4\pi^2 \times 10}{\dfrac{5}{2}} = 4\pi^2$

$A \;= 2\pi$

So $T = 2\pi\sqrt{\dfrac{l}{g}}$

> Rearrange the expression for T to make A the subject and substitute the values given to find A.

EXERCISE 2C

1 A watt is a unit of 1 joule per second. Derive the dimensions of watts.

2 The sievert is a unit of 1 joule per kilogram. Derive the dimensions of sieverts.

3 Work out the dimensions of $\dfrac{\mathrm{d}^2\omega}{\mathrm{d}t^2}$, where ω is an expression for angular velocity.

4 A yank is defined to be the rate of change of force with time. What are the dimensions of yank?

5 Using the standard notation, the area of a triangle can be written as area $= \dfrac{1}{2}ab \sin C$. By stating the dimensions of each of the components (area, $\dfrac{1}{2}$, a, b and $\sin C$) and combining them, show that this formula is dimensionally correct.

6 In a simple harmonic motion the displacement x can be written as $x = a\sin \omega t$, where x is the displacement and a is the amplitude (greatest distance from the centre of oscillation).

    a Use a dimensional argument to explain why this formula is dimensionally consistent.

    b Find the dimensions of ω.

7 **a** State the dimensions of force.

  b In the centimetres, grams and seconds (cgs) system, a force has magnitude 45 000 dynes. Calculate this in newtons.

8 The sine formula states that $\dfrac{a}{\sin A} = \dfrac{b}{\sin B} = \dfrac{c}{\sin C} = 2R^{\alpha}$, where R is the radius of the circumcircle of the triangle and α is a constant. Use dimensional analysis to find the value of α, showing the steps in your argument clearly.

9 Decibels are used to describe how loud a noise is. A formula for sound level in decibels is sound intensity $(\text{dB}) = 10 \log_{10} \left(\dfrac{I}{I_0} \right)$, where I is the sound output, in watts, and I_0 is the threshold level sound output, in watts.

  a Write down the dimensions of decibels.

  b A speaker has a sound output of 100 000 times the threshold level. Express this in decibels.

10 **a** State the dimensions of acceleration.

  b An equation for oscillations of a damped simple harmonic motion when a system is displaced through a small distance x is given by $\dfrac{d^2 x}{dt^2} + A \dfrac{dx}{dt} = -Bx$ where A and B are constants. Given that this equation is dimensionally consistent find:

   i the dimensions of A **ii** the dimensions of B.

11 **a** What are the dimensions of force?

  b The thrust, F, of a propeller blade is a force which is thought to have a formula of the form:
  $$F = 0.5 \rho^{\alpha} A^{\beta} (v_1^2 - v_0^2)^{\gamma}$$
  where ρ is the density of the air, A is the surface area and v_0 and v_1 are velocities.
  Use dimensional analysis to find the values of α, β and γ and hence find a formula for F in terms of ρ, A, v_1^2 and v_0^2.

12 **a** Tension is a force. What are the dimensions of tension?

  b The periodic time, t, of the vibration of a piano wire, of mass m, length l and tension F is thought to be of the form
  $$t = 2\pi F^{\alpha} m^{\beta} l^{\gamma}$$
  where 2 and π are dimensionless constants.
  Use dimensional analysis to find the values of α, β and γ and hence find a formula for t in terms of F, m and l.

13 The Froude number, Fr, is a dimensionless constant which can be used in analysing channel and river flows. The formula for Fr is of the form:
  $$Fr = v^{\alpha} g^{\beta} h^{\gamma}$$
  where v is the velocity of the water in the channel, g is the acceleration due to gravity and h is a relative depth.

  a Use dimensional analysis to find β and γ in terms of α.

  b Take $\alpha = 1$ to find a formula for Fr in terms of v, g and h.

14 A light inextensible string of length l is fixed at one end and has a particle of mass m fixed at the other end. The mass m is moving at constant speed v in a horizontal circle of radius r and the string is fully extended. The string makes an angle θ with the downward vertical. Given that $\tan \theta = v^{\alpha} r^{\beta} g^{-1}$, use a dimensional argument to find a formula for $\tan \theta$ in terms of v, r and g, where g is the acceleration due to gravity.

Section 4: Summary of dimensions and units

Exercise 2D is a summary of common units and dimensions.

EXERCISE 2D

Copy and complete this table.

Quantity	Dimension	SI unit
Time		
Mass		
Weight (mg)		newton (N)
Length/displacement		
Area		
Volume		
Velocity		
Acceleration	LT^{-2}	
Acceleration due to gravity		m/s² or m s⁻²
Force (ma)		newton (N)
Kinetic energy $\left(\frac{1}{2}mv^2\right)$		joule (J)
Gravitational potential energy (mgh)		
Work done (force × distance moved)		joule (J)
Moment of a force (force × distance)		newton metres (N m)
Power $\left(\text{rate of doing work:} \dfrac{dW}{dt}\right)$		watt (W)
Momentum (mv)		kg m s⁻¹
Impulse (force × time)		newton seconds (N s)
Moment of inertia $\left(\sum mr^2\right)$		
Angular velocity $\left(\omega = \dfrac{d\theta}{dt}\right)$		
Density $\left(\dfrac{\text{mass}}{\text{volume}}\right)$		
Pressure $\left(\dfrac{\text{force}}{\text{area}}\right)$		pascal (Pa)
Periodic time (time for one complete cycle)		
Frequency (1 ÷ periodic time)		hertz (Hz)
Surface tension $\left(\dfrac{\text{force}}{\text{length}}\right)$		

Checklist of learning and understanding

- In Mechanics, dimensions describe a quantity in terms of three basic dimensions **M**ass, **L**ength and **T**ime. Other dimensions are used in other branches of Mathematics and Science.
- Square brackets are used to denote 'the dimensions of', for example, [time] = **T**.
- You can only add and subtract terms that have the same dimensions; the resulting sum or difference will also have the same dimensions.
- A formula must be dimensionally consistent to be valid.
- Angles and numerical constants are dimensionless.
- If two quantities are equal, then they have the same dimensions.
- You can find the dimensions of a quantity from its definition, from an equation describing it or from its units.
- Quantities can have units but be dimensionless, for example, radians are dimensionless.
- You cannot predict units from dimensions as some dimensionless quantities have units.
- In dimensional calculations, you can give dimensionless quantities the dimensional value 1.
- You can use dimensional analysis to predict formulae by equating dimensions on both sides of a proposed formula.

Mixed practice 2

1 Given that a, b, h, l and r are lengths and that numerical constants are dimensionless, what could be a formula for volume? Choose from these options.

A $V = 2\pi r l$ **B** $V = \dfrac{h}{2}(a+b)$ **C** $V = \dfrac{hl}{2}(a+b)$

2 If $[\text{density}] = M^\alpha L^\beta T^\gamma$, what is the value of β? Choose from these options.

A 3   **B** −3   **C** −2

3 State the dimensions of:

a $2\pi\sqrt{\dfrac{l}{g}}$ **b** $\dfrac{d^2v}{dt^2}$, where v is an expression for speed.

4 Heron's (or Hero's) formula for the area of a triangle with sides of length a, b, and c is $A = \sqrt{s(s-a)(s-b)(s-c)}$, where s is half the perimeter. Show, with full explanation, why this formula is dimensionally consistent.

5 **a** Tension in a string is a force. What are the dimensions of tension?

b In each formula, T is the tension in a string, m is a mass, v is a velocity, r is a length and θ is an angle. Which of the formulae is/are dimensionally consistent? If the formula is inconsistent state which term is incorrect.

     i $T - mg\cos\theta = \dfrac{mv}{r}$ **ii** $T - mg\cos\theta = \dfrac{mv^2}{r}$ **iii** $T - g\cos\theta = \dfrac{mv^2}{r}$

6 **a** State the dimensions of potential energy.

b In the centimetres, grams and seconds (cgs) system a particle has potential energy of 5.2×10^8 ergs. Calculate this in joules.

7 In a simple harmonic motion of a mass m the restoring force is proportional to the displacement. It can be shown that, at time t, the displacement x and the acceleration a are:

$$x = A\cos\left(\sqrt{\dfrac{k}{m}}t\right)$$

$$a = -\dfrac{k}{m}A\cos\left(\sqrt{\dfrac{k}{m}}t\right)$$

Find the dimensions of:

a A **b** k.

8 The radial force on a particle moving in a circle is thought to be of the form $F = m^\alpha v^\beta r^\gamma$. By writing each of the components in term of its dimensions, and equating indices, form three equations to find the values of α, β and γ and hence find the formula for F.

9 **a** State the dimensions of force.

b Newton's law of gravitational attraction states that the force of attraction, F, between two bodies of masses m_1 and m_2 is dependent on the masses, the distance r between them and the constant G and it can be written as $F = G^\alpha m_1^\beta m_2^\gamma r^\delta$.

Write down, with reasons, the relationship between β and γ.

c Given that the dimensions of G are $M^{-1}L^3T^{-2}$, use a dimensional proof to find a formula for F.

10 a Give the dimensions of angular acceleration.

b An equation for oscillations of a damped pendulum of length l displaced by a small angle θ is given by $\dfrac{d^2\theta}{dt^2} + A\dfrac{d\theta}{dt} = -B\theta$, where A and B are constants. Given that this equation is dimensionally consistent, find the dimensions of A.

c By expressing B as a product of powers of l and g, find an expression for B in terms of l and g.

11 Surface tension is defined as force per unit length.

a State the dimensions of surface tension.

b When liquid forms a puddle on a clean horizontal surface, the depth d of the puddle has a maximum value which can be written as $d = AS^\alpha \rho^\beta g^\gamma$, where A is a dimensionless constant, S is surface tension, g is the acceleration due to gravity and ρ is the density of water. Use dimensional analysis to find a formula for d.

c Given that $d = 5.4$ mm when $S = 0.073$ N m^{-1}, and 1 m^3 of water has a mass of approximately 1000 kg, find the value of A.

12 Tension is a force.

a State the dimensions of tension.

b Frequency, f, has dimension $\mathbf{T}^{-1}$. Mersenne's law states that the fundamental frequency of a string is of the form $f = \dfrac{1}{2} l^\alpha F^\beta \mu^\gamma$, where $\dfrac{1}{2}$ is a dimensionless constant, l is the length of the string, F is the tension in the string and μ is the mass per unit length of the string. Use dimensional analysis to find the values of α, β and γ and hence find the formula for f.

13 A ball of mass m is travelling vertically downwards with speed u when it hits a horizontal floor. The ball bounces vertically upwards to a height h.

It is thought that h depends on m, u, the acceleration due to gravity g, and a dimensionless constant k, such that $h = km^\alpha u^\beta g^\gamma$, where α, β and γ are constants.

By using dimensional analysis, find the values of α, β and γ.

[©AQA 2009]

14 a Pressure is force per unit area. Derive the dimensions of pascals – the units of pressure.

b Dynamic viscosity μ is measured in pascal seconds. Derive the dimensions of μ.

c The terminal velocity v_T of a small spherical particle, of radius r and density ρ, falling vertically down though a medium of density ρ_1 and dynamic viscosity μ, is given by $v_T = A\dfrac{r^\alpha g^\beta (\rho - \rho_1)}{\mu}$, where A is a dimensionless constant and g is the acceleration due to gravity. Use dimensional analysis to find the values of α and β.

15 The formula for the lifting force F generated on a wing of an aeroplane is of the form $F = k\rho^\alpha v^\beta A^\gamma$, where k is a dimensionless constant, ρ is the air density, v is the air speed and A is the surface area of the wing. Use dimensional analysis to find the values of α, β and γ and hence find the formula for F.

16 The speed, v m s^{-1}, of a wave travelling along the surface of the sea is believed to depend on:

the depth of the sea, d m

the density of the water, ρ kg m^{-3}

the acceleration due to gravity, g m s^{-2} and

a dimensionless constant, k

so that $v = kd^\alpha \rho^\beta g^\gamma$, where α, β and γ are constants.

By using dimensional analysis, show that $\beta = 0$ and find the values of α and γ.

[©AQA 2008]

17 Surface tension, S, is defined as force per unit length.

   a State the dimensions of S.

   b State the dimensions of density.

   c The average height, h, of a liquid in a capillary tube can be written as $h = AS\rho^\alpha r^\beta g^\gamma$, where A is a dimensionless constant for the liquid, S is the surface tension, ρ is the density of the liquid, r is the internal radius of the tube and g is the acceleration due to gravity. Use a dimensional argument to find the values of α, β and γ and hence find a formula for h.

   d In this question part use $g = 9.8$ m s^{-2}, giving your final answer to an appropriate degree of accuracy. 1 m^3 of water has a mass of approximately 1000 kg. Water rises up a vertical capillary tube which has a diameter of 0.3 mm. Given that $A = 2$ and $S = 0.072$ N m^{-1}, what is the height of water in the tube, in millimetres?

18 The equation:
$$\frac{F}{d^\alpha u^\beta \rho^\gamma} = c$$
where c is a constant, F is a force, d is a diameter, u is a velocity and ρ is a density is dimensionally consistent. Find the values of α, β and γ and hence find a formula for F.

3 Momentum and collisions 1

In this chapter you will learn how to:

- understand momentum and impulse in mathematical terms with units
- understand that linear momentum is conserved in a collision between objects that are free to move
- understand that impulse on a body is equal to the change in momentum
- calculate impulse of variable forces
- understand Newton's experimental law for collisions
- analyse and solve problems involving simple collisions in a straight line
- use vectors to analyse and solve problems involving simple collisions in two dimensions.

Before you start…

GCSE	You should be able to solve simultaneous equations both for two linear equations and for one linear and one quadratic equation.	1	Solve these equations. $4x + 5y = 8$ $6x + 4y = 5$
A Level Mathematics Student Book 1, Chapter 17	You should know the equations of linear motion with constant acceleration.	2	A particle of mass 2 kg is dropped from a height of 6 metres above a pond. What is the speed of the particle at the instant when it hits the water?
A Level Mathematics Student Book 1	You should understand the definitions and units of velocity, acceleration and force.	3	Write down the units of: a velocity b acceleration c force.
A Level Mathematics Student Book 1, Chapter 18	You should know Newton's second law: force = mass × acceleration.	4	A constant force of 15 N acts on a particle of mass 2 kg. Find the acceleration of the particle.
Chapter 1	You should know the definitions of kinetic and potential energy.	5	The speed of a particle of mass 0.1 kg is $4\,\mathrm{m\,s^{-1}}$. Find its kinetic energy.

What are momentum and impulse?

You use and understand the principles of impulse and momentum instinctively in everyday life. If you hit a ball with a tennis racquet, you know that the ball will move in the direction in which you hit it – and the harder you hit it the faster and further it will go because it receives a greater impulse. A ball rolling down a slope gathers momentum. A hammer hitting a nail sends the nail forward in the direction of the blow and the hammer bounces back slightly in your hands. Events such as playing snooker or air hockey, applying the brakes in a vehicle, pile-driving the foundations of a building, hitting or kicking a ball and the wind blowing the sails of a boat and carrying it forward can all be modelled in terms of these concepts.

Section 1: Momentum and impulse

If you apply a single force to a stationary object, then any movement of the object will be in the direction of the force.

WORKED EXAMPLE 3.1

A toboggan of mass 40 kilograms moving at $3\,\mathrm{m\,s^{-1}}$ starts to slide down a smooth slope. The component of its weight acting down the slope is 80 N. Find its speed after:

a 5 seconds   **b** 10 seconds.

Using Newton's second law:	To calculate the speed, you need to know the acceleration, a.
$F = ma$	
$80 = 40a$ so $a = 2\,\mathrm{m\,s^{-2}}$	
Using the equations of motion with constant acceleration:	The motion is in a straight line with constant acceleration and with an initial speed of $3\,\mathrm{m\,s^{-1}}$.
$\quad\quad\quad v = u + at$	
$\quad\quad\quad v = 3 + 2t$	
a Substituting $t = 5$:	You are asked to find the speed so you do not need to state the direction. Speed is the magnitude of the velocity.
$\quad\quad\quad v = 3 + 2t$	
$\quad\quad\quad\quad = 13\,\mathrm{m\,s^{-1}}$	
b Substituting $t = 10$:	
$\quad\quad\quad v = 3 + 2t$	
$\quad\quad\quad\quad = 23\,\mathrm{m\,s^{-1}}$	

If the force continues to act in the same direction, and there is no resistance, the object will move more and more quickly; it gains **momentum**, which is calculated as the product of the mass and the velocity of a moving object.

WORKED EXAMPLE 3.2

An object of mass m is moving at $u\,\mathrm{m\,s^{-1}}$ on a smooth surface in a straight line. A constant force of F N is applied to it in the direction of the motion for t seconds. If the final velocity of the object is $v\,\mathrm{m\,s^{-1}}$, show that $Ft = mv - mu$.

$F = ma$	State Newton's second law, $F = ma$. The force and mass are constant so the acceleration is constant.
$v = u + at$	Use the equations of motion in a straight line with constant acceleration to find the final velocity, v, from the initial velocity, u.
Multiplying through by m:	
$mv = mu + mat$	
Substituting F for the term ma:	
$mv = mu + Ft$	
$Ft = mv - mu$	Rearrange the equation as shown.

🔑 Key point 3.1

For an object of mass m and velocity v:

$$\text{momentum} = mv$$

The units of momentum are $kg\,m\,s^{-1}$.

When a force acting on an object changes its momentum it exerts an **impulse** on the object.

🔑 Key point 3.2

The impulse (I) of a constant force is:

$$I = Ft = mv - mu$$

where $mv - mu$ is a change of momentum.

The units of impulse are newton seconds, N s.

💡 **Tip**

The units $kg\,m\,s^{-1}$ and N s are equivalent, and you can use either for momentum.

Momentum, force, impulse and velocity are all vectors and can be expressed in vector format.

WORKED EXAMPLE 3.3

A football of mass 450 grams is travelling along the ground at $20\,m\,s^{-1}$. Calculate its momentum.

Positive direction →

 $20\,m\,s^{-1}$

$450\,g = 0.45\,kg$ .... Convert the mass from grams to kilograms.

$\text{Momentum} = mv$ .... State the formula for momentum.

Substituting the values into the formula:

$\text{Momentum} = 0.45 \times 20$

$= 9\,kg\,m\,s^{-1}$

💡 **Tip**

1 As force, impulse and momentum are all vector quantities, their direction matters. So it is often helpful to draw a diagram and to identify and label a direction on the diagram as positive.
2 Always check the units and convert to kilograms, metres and seconds, if necessary.

WORKED EXAMPLE 3.4

A particle of mass m kg is at rest on a smooth, horizontal surface. It is hit with an impulse of I N s. What is its velocity immediately after the impulse?

Impulse = change in momentum .... State the impulse-momentum principle.

$I = mv - mu$

Continues on next page

Initial momentum $= m \times 0$
$= 0$
Final momentum $= m \times v$
$= mv$
Change in momentum $= mv - 0$
$= mv$
$I = mv$

So $I = mv$ giving $v = \dfrac{I}{m}$ m s^{-1}.

> Work out the change in momentum by subtracting the initial momentum from the final momentum.

> Equate the impulse to the change in momentum.

Modelling

When you make a mathematical model you look at a simplified situation. Initially, you model all objects as point masses without taking into account their size and what they are made of. As you learn more about the situation you can make better models and can put in more accurate data.

Focus on ...

You will learn more about mathematical modelling in Focus on ... Modelling 1.

WORKED EXAMPLE 3.5

A toy sailing boat of mass 800 grams is blown along by a constant wind acting horizontally with a force of 0.2 N. Given that the boat is initially at rest, find its velocity after 10 seconds.

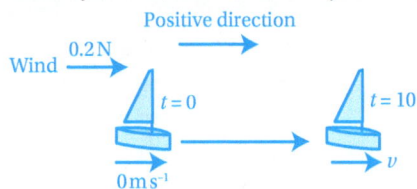

$u = 0$
$m = 800\,\text{g} = 0.8\,\text{kg}$
$F = 0.2$
$t = 10$

> State the values you are given and convert grams to kilograms.

Let the final velocity be v.

> Define any unknowns.

Impulse = change in momentum

> State the formula for impulse.

$Ft = mv - mu$

Substituting the values:

$2 = 0.8v - 0.8 \times 0$
$= 0.8v$

> As you are asked for velocity, you must also state the direction.

So $v = 2.5\,\text{m s}^{-1}$ in the direction of the wind.

Tip

You don't have to draw a complicated diagram, as long as it is clear and contains all the relevant information. For example, you can represent boats by dots and the wind by an arrow. Remember to include the direction you are taking as positive.

WORKED EXAMPLE 3.6

A football of mass 450 grams is travelling along the ground at 20 m s^{-1} when it is kicked and starts to move with a speed of 25 m s^{-1}. Find the impulse given to the football by the footballer's kick if:

a the ball is now moving in the opposite direction   **b** the ball continues to move in the same direction.

$m = 450 \text{ g} = 0.45 \text{ kg}$ Check the units and change grams to kilograms.

a

Before 20 m s^{-1}

25 m s^{-1} ←
After

+ve →

$u = 20 \text{ m s}^{-1}$ State the values you know. v has a negative sign
$v = -25 \text{ m s}^{-1}$ as the football is moving in the negative direction
after it has been kicked.

Change in momentum $= mv - mu$ To find the impulse you need to find the change in momentum.

$$mv - mu = (0.45 \times -25) - (0.45 \times 20)$$ Substitute the values and calculate.
$$= -11.25 - 9$$
$$= -20.25$$

Impulse $= -20.25 \text{ N s}$ or 20.25 N s in the opposite direction to the approaching ball.   The impulse is negative, telling you that it is in the opposite direction to the original direction of the ball so the ball was moving towards the footballer, who then kicked it away. You need to give the direction as well as the magnitude of the impulse.

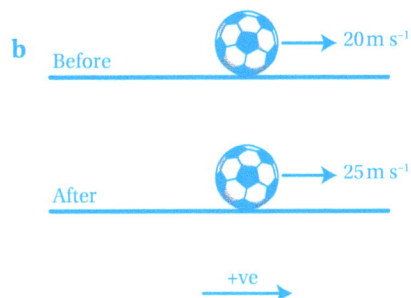

b
Before 20 m s^{-1}

After 25 m s^{-1}

+ve →

$u = 20 \text{ m s}^{-1}$ State the values you know. v has a positive sign as
$v = 25 \text{ m s}^{-1}$ it is moving in the positive direction.

Change in momentum $= mv - mu$ To find the impulse you need to find the change in momentum.

Continues on next page

$$mv - mu = (0.45 \times 25) - (0.45 \times 20)$$
$$= 11.25 - 9$$
$$= 2.25 \, \text{kg m s}^{-1}$$

Impulse = 2.25 N s or 2.25 N s in the same direction as the initial movement of the ball.

Substitute the values and calculate.

The impulse is positive, telling you that it is in the same direction as the original direction of the ball so the ball was moving away from the footballer, who then kicked it in the same direction.

Vector notation

Force, impulse, momentum and velocity are all vector quantities. They have a direction as well as a magnitude. You can apply the same principles and equations if these quantities are given in vector form.

> **! Common error**
>
> Velocity and impulse are vector quantities so you must show the direction, with motion in one direction. You do this by using plus and minus signs.

WORKED EXAMPLE 3.7

A toy sailing boat of mass 800 grams is blown along by a constant wind of force $(0.25\mathbf{i} + 0.5\mathbf{j})$ N. Given that the boat is initially at rest, find its velocity after 10 seconds.

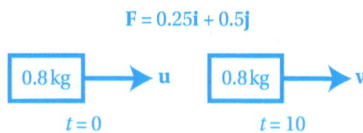

$\mathbf{F} = 0.25\mathbf{i} + 0.5\mathbf{j}$

Draw a clear diagram.

$\underline{u} = 0$

$m = 800 \, g = 0.8 \, \text{kg}$

$\underline{F} = 0.25 \underline{i} + 0.5 \underline{j}$

$t = 10$

State the values you are given and convert grams to kilograms.

Let the final velocity be $\underline{v} = a\underline{i} + b\underline{j}$

Define any unknowns.

Impulse $= \underline{F}t = m\underline{v} - m\underline{u}$

State the formula.

Substituting the values:

$10(0.25 \underline{i} + 0.5 \underline{j}) = 0.8(a\underline{i} + b\underline{j}) - 0.8(0\underline{i} + 0\underline{j})$

Equating the $\underline{i}$ values of both sides of the equation

$2.5 = 0.8a - 0$ so $a = 3.125$

Equating the $\underline{j}$ values of both sides of the equation

$5 = 0.8b - 0$ so $b = 6.25$

$\underline{v} = (3.125 \underline{i} + 6.25 \underline{j}) \, \text{m s}^{-1}$

State the value of velocity vector **v**.

Continues on next page

Alternative solution

$\underline{u} = O$

$m = 800\,g = 0.8\,kg$

$\underline{F} = \begin{pmatrix} 0.25 \\ 0.5 \end{pmatrix}$

State the values you are given and convert grams to kilograms.

$t = 10$

Let the final velocity be $\underline{v} = \begin{pmatrix} a \\ b \end{pmatrix}$

Define any unknowns.

Impulse $= \underline{F}t$

State the formula.

$\qquad = m\underline{v} - m\underline{u}$

Substituting the values:

$10\begin{pmatrix} 0.25 \\ 0.5 \end{pmatrix} = 0.8\begin{pmatrix} a \\ b \end{pmatrix} - 0.8\begin{pmatrix} O \\ O \end{pmatrix}$

Equating the $\underline{i}$ values (top line) of both sides of the equation:

$2.5 = 0.8a - O$ so $a = 3.125$

Equating the $\underline{j}$ values (bottom line) of both sides of the equation:

$5 = 0.8b - O$ so $b = 6.25$

$\underline{v} = (3.125\,\underline{i} + 6.25\,\underline{j})\,m\,s^{-1}$

State the value of the velocity vector **v**.

Impulse of a variable force

Not all forces are constant. The more you stretch an elastic band, the greater the force trying to pull it back. The force increases with the extension of the band.

A graph of force against time for a constant force is a horizontal line. The impulse is calculated as the area between the force line and the time axis.

If the graph is not made up of straight lines, you need to use integration to find the area.

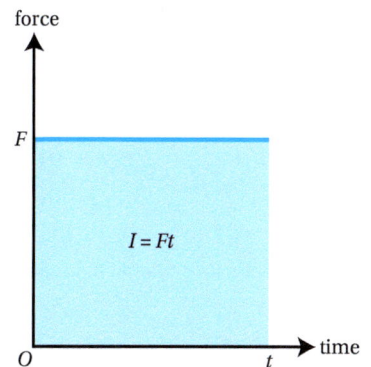

🔑 Key point 3.3

The impulse, I N s, of a variable force F N acting for a time t seconds, where $t_1 \leqslant t \leqslant t_2$, is:

$$I = \int_{t_1}^{t_2} F \, dt$$

⏪ Rewind

You looked at non-uniform acceleration in A Level Mathematics Student Book 1, Chapter 16.

WORKED EXAMPLE 3.8

The force–time graph for the force F acting on a mass of 2 kg is shown.

The mass, A, is initially moving in a straight line with velocity 5 m s^{-1} and the force is acting along the same straight line in the direction of motion.

Calculate the speed of A after:

a 4 seconds   **b** 10 seconds.

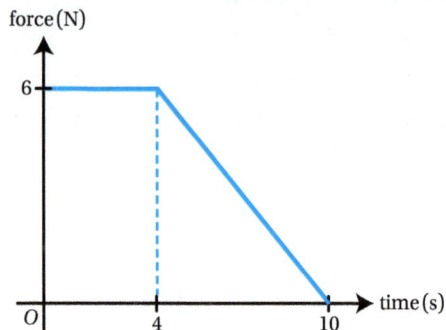

a Let v be the velocity of A after 4 seconds.   First define the unknown quantity.

$I = Ft$

$\quad = mv - mu$ Use impulse = change in momentum.

Total impulse in the first 4 seconds $= 6 \times 4$ The impulse in the first 4 seconds is the area under the graph between $t = 0$ and $t = 4$.

$\qquad\qquad\qquad\qquad = 24\,\text{N s}$

Change in momentum $= mv - mu$ Use change in momentum = final momentum – initial momentum

$\qquad\qquad\qquad = 2v - 2 \times 5$

$\qquad\qquad\qquad = 2v - 10$

$2v - 10 = 24$

Therefore $v = 17\,\text{m s}^{-1}$

b Let w be the velocity of A after 10 seconds.   Define the unknown.

Total impulse in the first 10 seconds is: The impulse in the first 10 seconds is the area under the graph between $t = 0$ and $t = 10$, which is a trapezium of height 6 and opposite parallel sides of 4 and 10.

$\frac{1}{2}h(a+b) = \frac{1}{2}6(4+10)$

$\qquad\qquad = 42\,\text{N s}$

Change in momentum $= mw - mu$

$\qquad\qquad\qquad = 2w - 2 \times 5$

Using $I = mw - mu$ and solving for w: You could have used the result from part **a** to help you calculate the answer for part **b** but it is safer to start again, in case you had made an error.

So $2w - 10 = 42$

Therefore $w = 26\,\text{m s}^{-1}$

WORKED EXAMPLE 3.9

A smooth sphere of mass 2 kg is acted on by a variable force $F = (3t^2 - 6t + 8)$ newtons acting in the direction of motion of the sphere.

a Find the magnitude of the impulse between $t = 0$ and $t = 4$.

b When $t = 0$ the speed of the sphere is $2\ \text{m s}^{-1}$. Calculate the speed of the particle after 4 seconds.

a Let the speed of the particle after 4s be v.   Define the unknown quantity.

$$\text{Impulse} = \int F\, dt$$ To find the change in momentum you need to integrate F from $t = 0$ to $t = 4$.

Integrating between $t = 0$ to $t = 4$ and substituting in the limits:

$$I = \int_0^4 (3t^2 - 6t + 8)\, dt$$

$$= \left[\frac{3t^3}{3} - \frac{6t^2}{2} + 8t \right]_0^4$$

$$= \left[\frac{3 \times 64}{3} - \frac{6 \times 16}{2} + 32 \right] - [0]$$

$$= 64 - 48 + 32$$

$$= 48\ \text{N s}$$

b Change in momentum $= mv - mu$ Write an expression for the change in momentum.

$2v - 2 \times 2 = 2v - 4$

Using $I = mv - mu$ and solving for v:

$2v - 4 = 48$

Therefore $v = 26\ \text{m s}^{-1}$

ⓘ Did you know?

Rockets are an example of a momentum–impulse problem in which the situation is constantly changing. Fuel is expelled from the back of the rocket, so the mass of the rocket decreases. Look up the Tsiolkovsky rocket equation.

$$\int_{v_0}^{v_1} dv = \int_{m_0}^{m_1} \frac{dm}{m}$$

EXERCISE 3A

1 Calculate the momentum, in kg m s^{-1}, for each situation. Change to SI units (kg, m, s) before you start, if necessary.

a A rocket of mass 15 kg and velocity 150 m s^{-1}.

b A cat of mass 4.5 kg and velocity 5 m s^{-1}.

    c   A marble of mass 10 grams and velocity 20 m s^{-1}.

    d   A car of mass 1200 kg and velocity 60 km h^{-1}.

    e   A rhino of mass 1.4 tonnes running at 20 m s^{-1}.

2   A bullet of mass 5 grams is fired from a gun. Its momentum is 4.5 kg m s^{-1} as it leaves the gun. Work out its velocity.

3   A car is moving at a velocity of 15 m s^{-1}. Its momentum is $18\,000 \text{ kg m s}^{-1}$. Find its mass, in metric tonnes.

4   What impulse is generated by an engine that exerts a force of 6 N for 20 seconds?

5   Work out the impulse generated by an engine that exerts a force of 6 N for 2 minutes.

6   The table shows the velocity, in metres per second (m s^{-1}), of a particle of mass m kg before and after an impulse is applied to it. Calculate the impulse, in newton seconds (N s), in each case.

   The first one is done for you.

Positive direction $\longrightarrow$		
Initial velocity (m s^{-1})	**Final velocity** (m s^{-1})	**Impulse** (N s)
$\rightarrow 4$	$\rightarrow 6$	$(+6m)-(+4m)=+2m$
$\rightarrow 4$	$\rightarrow 2$	
$\rightarrow 4$	$6 \leftarrow$	
$8 \leftarrow$	$3 \leftarrow$	
$3 \leftarrow$	$\rightarrow 8$	

7   A sailing boat of mass 600 kg is stationary on the sea when it is blown by a wind that exerts a constant horizontal force of 10 N. Calculate the speed of the boat, in metres per second, after 5 minutes.

8   A motor boat of mass 600 kg is moving in a straight line at a speed of 8 m s^{-1}. The drag of the water produces a constant force of 10 N in the direction opposite to the direction of motion of the boat. How long does it take for the speed of the boat to halve?

9   A gyrfalcon of mass 1.2 kg is flying at 15 m s^{-1} with a following wind that exerts a constant force of 0.6 N in the direction in which the gyrfalcon is flying. Find its speed, in metres per second, 10 seconds later.

10   A gyrfalcon of mass 1.2 kg is flying at 15 m s^{-1} into a wind that exerts a constant force of 0.6 N in the direction opposite to the flight of the gyrfalcon. Calculate its speed, in metres per second, 10 seconds later.

11   A football of mass 500 grams is kicked along the ground and hits a vertical wall at right angles. As it hits the wall, its speed is 20 m s^{-1} and it bounces straight back with a speed of 15 m s^{-1}. Find the impulse of the wall on the ball.

12   A bowling ball of mass 2 kg is rolled along the ground and hits a vertical wall at right angles. As it hits the wall, its speed is 15 m s^{-1} and it bounces straight back with a speed of 10 m s^{-1}. Calculate the impulse of the wall on the ball.

13   A motorbike of mass 250 kg slows down from 25 m s^{-1} to 15 m s^{-1} in 20 seconds. Find the magnitude, in newtons, of the constant braking force.

14 A motorbike of mass 200 kg accelerates from 18 km h^{-1} to 72 km h^{-1} in 20 seconds. Work out the magnitude, in newtons, of the constant accelerating force produced by the engine.

15 A motorbike, of mass 250 kg, is moving with velocity $(40\mathbf{i} + 30\mathbf{j})$ m s^{-1} when it is acted on by an accelerating force $(50\mathbf{i} + 60\mathbf{j})$ N for 10 seconds. Calculate its velocity after 10 seconds.

16 A motorbike, of mass 200 kg, slows from a velocity of $(40\mathbf{i} + 50\mathbf{j})$ m s^{-1} to a velocity of $(20\mathbf{i} + 15\mathbf{j})$ m s^{-1} in 10 seconds. Calculate the braking force.

17 A ball of mass 500 grams is acted on by a force of $(2 + t^2)$ for 3 seconds. When $t = 0$, the velocity of the ball is 3 m s^{-1}. Find the velocity of the ball when $t = 3$ seconds.

18 A ball of mass 500 grams is acted on by a force of $(2 + kt)$ where k is a constant. When $t = 0$, the velocity of the ball is 3 m s^{-1}. When $t = 5$ seconds, the velocity of the ball is 85.5 m s^{-1}. Find the value of k.

(i) Did you know?

Cannon on Spanish galleons were originally mounted on the highest part of the ship to give the best possible advantage over the enemy. It was soon realised that the impulse of the cannon's recoil on the ship at such a height was making the ship unstable and likely to overturn, so the cannon were moved down to the lower decks.

Section 2: Collisions and the principle of conservation of momentum

In a game of snooker, if the cue ball hits a stationary red ball it exerts a force on it, causing it to move along the line of the collision. From Newton's third law, there is an equal and opposite reaction on the cue ball. As the time for which the collision force acts is the same for both balls – the time for which the two balls are in contact – then the impulse, I, (force × time) on the two balls is also the same but in opposite directions.

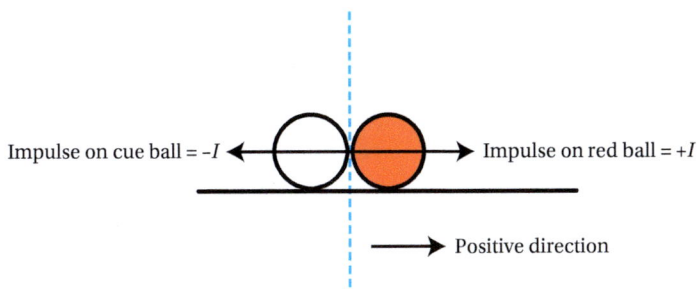

Impulse on cue ball = $-I$ Impulse on red ball = $+I$

Positive direction

The total impulse on the two balls along the line of the collision is $-I + I = 0$.

As the total impulse is zero then there is no change in the total momentum of the two balls. This means that linear momentum is conserved in a collision between two objects that are free to move. This is called **the principle of conservation of linear momentum.**

Consider two objects, A and B, of mass m_1 and m_2, moving with velocities u_1 and u_2 in a straight line. After they collide, their velocities are v_1 and v_2. If you ignore any external forces:

the impulse on A (the change in its momentum) $= m_1v_1 - m_1u_1$

the impulse on B (the change in its momentum) $= m_2v_2 - m_2u_2$

the impulse on $A = -$(the impulse on B)
$m_1v_1 - m_1u_1 = -(m_2v_2 - m_2u_2)$
$m_1v_1 - m_1u_1 = -m_2v_2 + m_2u_2$

Rearranging gives:

$m_1u_1 + m_2u_2 = m_1v_1 + m_2v_2$

$m_1u_1 + m_2u_2$ is the total momentum before the collision and $m_1v_1 + m_2v_2$ is the total momentum after the collision.

Key point 3.4

Total momentum before collision = total momentum after collision

$$m_1u_1 + m_2u_2 = m_1v_1 + m_2v_2$$

WORKED EXAMPLE 3.10

A ball of mass $3m$ kg is moving at 10 m s^{-1} when it collides with a second ball of mass $2m$ kg moving towards it on the same straight line with a velocity of 6 m s^{-1}. If the second ball now moves in the opposite direction at 6 m s^{-1} find:

a the final speed of the ball of mass $3m$ kg
b the magnitude, in terms of m, of the impulse on the ball of mass $3m$ kg.

Positive direction $\longrightarrow$

$3m$ → 10 m s^{-1} 6 m s^{-1} ← $2m$

Initial

Draw a clear diagram with the positive direction marked and labelled with the SI units.

$3m$ → v $2m$ → 6 m s^{-1}

Final

a Let the final velocity of the mass $3m$ be v.

Define the unknown.

Using the principle of conservation of linear momentum:
Total momentum before collision =
    total momentum after collision
$m_1u_1 + m_2u_2 = m_1v_1 + m_2v_2$

Continues on next page

Substituting the values and solving for v:

$3m \times 10 + 2m \times (-6) = 3m \times v + 2m \times 6$

$30m - 6(2m) = 3mv + 2m(6)$

$18m = 3mv + 12m$

$v = 2\,\text{m s}^{-1}$

So the final speed is $2\,\text{m s}^{-1}$.

Use -6 to show that this velocity is in the opposite direction.

Note that you were asked for speed so you should not include the minus sign with your answer or state the direction.

The ball of mass $3m$ moves at $2\,\text{m s}^{-1}$ in the direction of its initial motion.

b For the impulse on the $2m$ mass:

impulse = change in momentum

$\quad = $ final momentum $-$ initial momentum

$\quad = 2m(6) - 2m(-6)$

$\quad = 24m\,\text{N s}$

The impulse on the ball of mass $3m$ is equal and opposite so is $-24m$ or $24m$ in the negative direction. Its magnitude is $24m$ N s.

The impulse on the two balls is equal and opposite so it is sensible to find the impulse on the $2m$ mass as you are given its velocities. This will give the correct answer even if you have made a mistake calculating the velocity of the mass $3m$. However, you can use the impulse on the ball of mass $3m$ kg to check your answer.

WORKED EXAMPLE 3.11

A snooker cue ball of mass 160 grams is travelling at $10\,\text{m s}^{-1}$. It hits a blue ball of mass 170 grams, travelling in the same direction at $6\,\text{m s}^{-1}$. If the blue ball continues to move in the same direction but at $9\,\text{m s}^{-1}$ find:

a the magnitude of the impulse on the blue ball
b the magnitude of the impulse on the cue ball
c the speed of the cue ball after the collision.

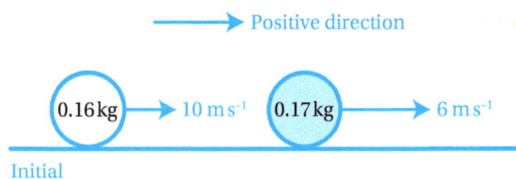

Draw diagrams to show the situation clearly. Make sure that you identify and label a direction as positive.

Convert 160 g and 170 g to 0.16 kg and 0.17 kg.

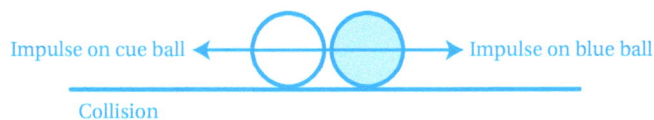

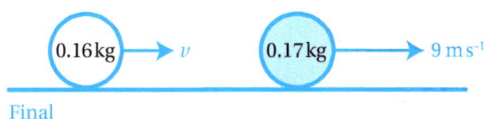

Continues on next page

a Impulse = change in momentum

$$I = mv - mu$$

For the blue ball:

$$I = 0.17 \times 9 - 0.17 \times 6$$
$$= 1.53 - 1.02$$
$$= 0.51 \, \text{N s}$$

The impulse on the blue ball is 0.51 N s in the direction of the motion.

.... For the blue ball only, find the impulse by finding the change in momentum.

b The impulse on the cue ball is equal and opposite and so it is -0.51 N s.
The magnitude of this impulse is 0.51 N s.

.... The impulse on the cue ball is equal and opposite to the impulse on the blue ball. The magnitude is the modulus of this so you omit the minus sign in the answer. Only omit the minus sign if you are asked for the magnitude, otherwise leave it in as it indicates direction.

c The impulse on the cue ball = -0.51 N s
Let the final speed of the cue ball be v.

.... State the values you know and define the unknown quantity.

Impulse = final momentum − initial momentum
Initial momentum = 0.16×10
Final momentum = $0.16v$

.... State the formula and the values.

$$I = mv - mu$$
$$-0.51 = 0.16v - 0.16 \times 10$$

.... Put impulse equal to the change in momentum. Here you **do** need to write the minus sign.

Rearranging to find v:

$$0.16v = -0.51 + 0.16 \times 10$$
$$0.16v = -0.51 + 1.6$$
$$\text{So } v = 6.81 \, \text{m s}^{-1} \, (3 \text{ s.f.})$$

.... The final speed is positive showing that the cue ball continues to move in the same direction but is slower than before.

WORK IT OUT 3.1

Two particles of masses m_1 and m_2 collide. Their speeds before the collision are $4\,\mathrm{m\,s^{-1}}$ and $3\,\mathrm{m\,s^{-1}}$, respectively, and they are moving in the same direction, which is taken as the positive direction. After the collision, their speeds are v_1 and v_2 respectively.

Three possible sets of values for v_1 and v_2 are provided. Which set is possible? Explain why the other two sets are not possible.

	Solution 1	Solution 2	Solution 3
$v_1\,(\mathrm{m\,s^{-1}})$	+5	+4.5	+5
$v_2\,(\mathrm{m\,s^{-1}})$	+2	+5	+4

Masses that combine

In some situations, two objects **coalesce**, or move as one object, after a collision. This means that you add their masses together after the collision.

WORKED EXAMPLE 3.12

A toy truck of mass 2 kg is travelling at $10\,\mathrm{m\,s^{-1}}$ when it hits a stationary toy truck of mass 3 kg. The two trucks move off together. Find their speed immediately after the collision.

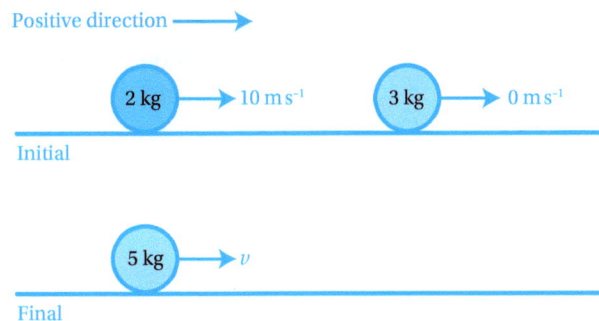

Draw a diagram, labelling the masses, speeds and the positive direction.

Using the principle of conservation of linear momentum:

State the formula.

Total momentum before collision =

   total momentum after collision

$m_1u_1 + m_2u_2 = m_1v_1 + m_2v_2$

Let the speed of the combined trucks be v.

Define the unknown quantity.

Substituting the values and solving for v:

$(2 \times 10) + (3 \times 0) = 5 \times v$

$5v = 20$

$v = 4\,\mathrm{m\,s^{-1}}$

Also, there are situations in which an object can be resolved into two or more parts.

WORKED EXAMPLE 3.13

A kitten, of mass 700 g, is sitting on the back of a toy train of mass 2.5 kg which is free to move on a straight horizontal track. The train is at rest when the kitten jumps off the train. The initial direction of the kitten is horizontal and in the direction of the track. The initial velocity of the kitten is 2 m s^{-1}. What is the initial velocity of the train?

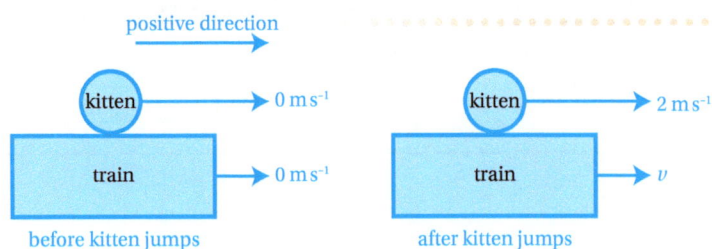

positive direction

kitten — 0 m s^{-1} kitten — 2 m s^{-1}

train — 0 m s^{-1} train — v

before kitten jumps   after kitten jumps

Draw a diagram.

Applying the principle of conservation of linear momentum:

$(0.7 \times 0) + (2.5 \times 0) = (0.7 \times 2) + 2.5v$

$v = -0.56$ m s^{-1} in the opposite direction to the kitten's jump.

Solve for v.

Further examples: multiple collisions and using change in kinetic energy

Harder examples often involve multiple collisions. You will need to split such problems into parts and treat each collision as a separate event. As usual, you need to draw clear diagrams and set out your working clearly.

When you are dealing with a loss of kinetic energy in collisions, you need to subtract the final kinetic energy from the initial kinetic energy.

⏪ Rewind

You studied change in kinetic energy in Chapter 1.

WORKED EXAMPLE 3.14

Three particles P, Q and R, of masses m kg, $2m$ kg and $3m$ kg are moving with velocities 2.5 m s^{-1}, 2 m s^{-1} and 1 m s^{-1} respectively, as shown in the diagram.

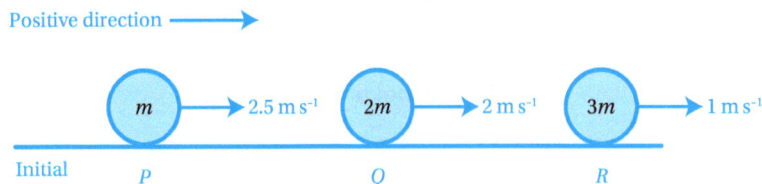

Positive direction ⟶

m — 2.5 m s^{-1} $2m$ — 2 m s^{-1} $3m$ — 1 m s^{-1}

Initial P Q R

Particle P collides with particle Q, which then goes on to collide and coalesce with particle R. The combined particle moves with speed 1.5 m s^{-1}.

a Find the speed of Q after the first collision.
b Calculate the kinetic energy lost by P in the collision with Q.

Continues on next page

a Collision 1

Positive direction ⟶

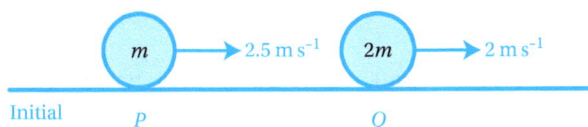

Initial P   Q

m ⟶ 2.5 m s⁻¹   2m ⟶ 2 m s⁻¹

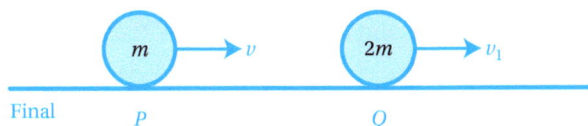

Final P   Q

m ⟶ v 2m ⟶ v_1

> Two collisions need two sets of diagrams. Label the speeds clearly with their directions and mark the positive direction. The signs of the final answers will give the directions of the motion.
>
> Draw the diagram for the first collision.
>
> Let v_1 m s⁻¹ be the speed of Q after the collision.

Using the principle of conservation of momentum for the collision between P and Q:

total momentum before collision =
    total momentum after collision

$m_1 u_1 + m_2 u_2 = m_1 v + m_2 v_1$

$2.5m + 2(2m) = mv + 2mv_1$

> State the formula.

Dividing through by m:

$2.5 + 4 = v + 2v_1$ (1)

> You now have one equation in two unknowns so you need more information to solve for the two velocities.

For the collision between Q and R:

Positive direction ⟶

> Draw the diagram for the second collision.

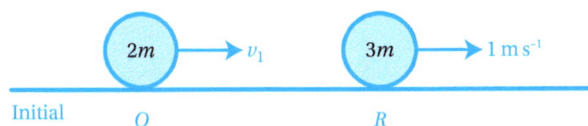

Initial Q   R

2m ⟶ v_1 3m ⟶ 1 m s⁻¹

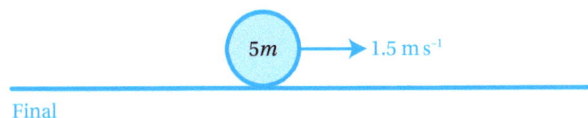

Final

5m ⟶ 1.5 m s⁻¹

Using the principle of conservation of momentum:

total momentum before collision =
    total momentum after collision

$m_1 u_1 + m_2 u_2 = m_1 v_1 + m_2 v_2$

$2mv_1 + 3m \times 1 = 5m \times 1.5$

Dividing through by m and solving for v_1:

$2v_1 = 7.5 - 3$

$2v_1 = 4.5$

So $v_1 = 2.25$ m s⁻¹

Continues on next page

b Substituting into equation (1):

$6.5 = v + 2 \times 2.25$

$6.5 = v + 4.5$

So $v = 2$

Kinetic energy (KE) $= \frac{1}{2}mv^2$

Initial KE of P is $\frac{1}{2}m(2.5)^2 = 3.175m$

Final KE of P is $\frac{1}{2}m(2)^2 = 2m$

Loss in KE is $3.175m - 2m = 1.175m$ J.

To find the loss in kinetic energy of P you need to find its velocity after the collision with Q.

State the formula for kinetic energy.

Find the initial KE...

...and the final KE...

...and subtract.

WORKED EXAMPLE 3.15

A particle A, of mass 2 kg, is moving with velocity $(2\mathbf{i} + 3\mathbf{j})$ m s^{-1} when it collides with particle B, of mass 1.5 kg, which is moving with velocity $(\mathbf{i} + 2\mathbf{j})$ m s^{-1}. The particles coalesce during the collision. Find:

a the velocity of the combined particle after the collision
b the total loss in kinetic energy, as a result of the collision.

a Using the principle of conservation of linear momentum in vector form:

$m_1\underline{u}_1 + m_2\underline{u}_2 = m_1\underline{v}_1 + m_2\underline{v}_2$

$2\begin{pmatrix} 2 \\ 3 \end{pmatrix} + 1.5\begin{pmatrix} 1 \\ 2 \end{pmatrix} = 3.5\begin{pmatrix} a \\ b \end{pmatrix}$

Substitute in the values. It is easier to work with column vectors.

$\begin{pmatrix} 4 \\ 6 \end{pmatrix} + \begin{pmatrix} 1.5 \\ 3 \end{pmatrix} = \begin{pmatrix} 3.5a \\ 3.5b \end{pmatrix}$

Equating the $\underline{\mathbf{i}}$ components:

$4 + 1.5 = 3.5a$

$a = \frac{5.5}{3.5}$

$= \frac{11}{7}$ m s^{-1}

Equating the $\underline{\mathbf{j}}$ components:

$6 + 3 = 3.5b$

$b = \frac{9}{3.5}$

$= \frac{18}{7}$ m s^{-1}

$\underline{v} = \frac{11}{7}\underline{\mathbf{i}} + \frac{18}{7}\underline{\mathbf{j}}$

Give the answer in the original format.

Continues on next page

b $KE = \frac{1}{2}mv^2$

> You need to be able to find v^2, which is a scalar quantity.

Let the velocity of the combined particles be $a\underline{i} + b\underline{j}$.

> Write an expression for the velocity vector.

$$(\text{Initial velocity of } A)^2 = |2\underline{i} + 3\underline{j}|^2$$
$$= 2^2 + 3^2$$
$$= 13$$

> Find the square of the magnitude of the velocity of A (the square of the speed of A).

$$(\text{Initial velocity of } B)^2 = |\underline{i} + 2\underline{j}|^2 = 1^2 + 2^2 = 5$$

> Find the square of the magnitude of the velocity of B (the square of the speed of B).

$$\text{Initial KE} = \left(\frac{1}{2} \times 2 \times 13\right) + \left(\frac{1}{2} \times 1.5 \times 5\right)$$
$$= 16.75 \text{ J}$$

> The initial KE is the sum of $KE_A + KE_B$.

$$|\text{Velocity of combined particle}|^2 = \left(\frac{11}{7}\right)^2 + \left(\frac{18}{7}\right)^2$$
$$= \frac{445}{49}$$

> Find the square of the magnitude of the velocity of the combined particle.

$$\text{So, final KE} = \left(\frac{1}{2} \times 3.5 \times \frac{445}{49}\right) = \frac{445}{28}$$

$$\text{Loss in KE} = 16.75 - \frac{445}{28}$$
$$= 0.857 \text{ J}$$

> Loss in KE = initial KE – final KE.

Modelling in collision questions

If you are dealing with collisions between spheres, unless you are told otherwise, you can assume that:

- they are smooth
- the spheres are not spinning
- the impulse during the collision acts along the line of centres.

EXERCISE 3B

1   Use the conservation of linear momentum to fill in this table. m_1 and m_2 are the masses (in kilograms) of two particles moving in the same straight line, with initial velocities u_1 and u_2 respectively. The particles collide and their velocities after their collision are v_1 and v_2 respectively. The velocities are given in metres per second ($m\,s^{-1}$) and the signs indicate direction.

m_1	m_2	u_1	u_2	v_1	v_2
3	4	+10	+2		+6
2	4	+6	−2	−2	
2	5		+2	+0.5	+5
2		+8	−2	−1	+1.6

2 A ball, A, of mass 1.5 kg is travelling at 3 m s^{-1}. It collides with a stationary ball, B, of mass 2 kg. Ball A is brought to rest in the collision. Find the speed of ball B immediately after the collision.

3 A ball, A, of mass 2 kg, moving at 8 m s^{-1}, collides with a ball, B, of mass 2.5 kg, moving towards it at 10 m s^{-1} in the same straight line. If ball A then moves in a direction opposite to its original path, at a velocity of 6 m s^{-1}, find the final speed of ball B.

4 A cat of mass 3.5 kg jumps onto a stationary toy train of mass 1.5 kg that is free to move on a straight horizontal track. The velocity of the cat in the direction of the track immediately before it lands on the truck is 2 m s^{-1}. Find the speed of the cat and the train, in the direction of the track, immediately after it lands.

5 A croquet ball of mass 450 grams is at rest when a croquet mallet hits it with a force, instantly producing an impulse of 2.1 N s.

    a Find the exact speed of the ball at the instant it leaves the croquet mallet.

    b The ball immediately hits another croquet ball of mass 400 grams which is at rest. Given that the second ball moves off at 3 m s^{-1}, find the speed of the first ball immediately after the collision.

6 Particle, A, of mass 0.7 kg, is moving with velocity 8 m s^{-1} towards particle B, of mass 0.9 kg. Particle B is moving towards A, in the same straight line, at a velocity of 6 m s^{-1}. The particles coalesce. Calculate the magnitude and direction of the velocity of the combined particles.

7 Particle A, of mass 0.8 kg, is moving, with velocity 8 m s^{-1} towards particle B. Particle B is moving towards particle A, in the same straight line, with velocity 6 m s^{-1}. The two particles collide. After the collision the two particles move in opposite directions, both with speed 4 m s^{-1}. Find the mass of particle B.

8 A truck of mass 600 kg is travelling along a straight track at a velocity of 60 km h^{-1} when it collides with a second, stationary, truck of mass 800 kg, which then starts to move with velocity 30 km h^{-1}. Calculate the velocity of the first truck immediately after the impact.

9 A skateboard of mass 2 kg is moving at 14 m s^{-1} when it hits a ball of mass 200 grams, which is at rest. Immediately after the collision the skateboard moves at 12 m s^{-1} in the same straight line and in the same direction. Find the speed of the ball immediately after the collision.

10 A football of mass 380 grams, moving at v m s^{-1}, hits a second football of mass 420 grams moving directly towards it, in the same straight line, at 8 m s^{-1}. After the collision the two footballs both have a speed of $0.75v$ but in opposite directions. Find the value of v. What assumption have you made about the two footballs?

11 A particle A, of mass m kg, is moving along a straight line with speed 5 m s^{-1}. It collides with another particle, B, of mass 3 kg, moving towards it on the same straight line at a speed of 3 m s^{-1}. After the collision the particles coalesce and move at a speed of v m s^{-1}.

    a Find expressions for the two possible values of v, in terms of m.

    b In each case the magnitude of v is 2 m s^{-1}. Find the two possible values of m.

12 A ball, A, of mass 2 kg, is moving at 5 m s^{-1} when it hits another ball, B, of mass 3 kg, moving in the same direction and in the same straight line at 3 m s^{-1}. The magnitude of the speed of A after the collision is 3.5 m s^{-1}, and the speed of B after the collision is v m s^{-1}.

By calculating the total kinetic energy before and after the collision, show that A cannot change direction as a result of the collision.

Section 3: Restitution and kinetic energy

Newton discovered that there is a constant ratio between the relative velocities of the spheres before and after the collision which is independent of the masses of the two spheres but depends on the materials from which the spheres are made. This constant is called the coefficient of restitution.

> ### 🔑 Key point 3.5
>
> Newton's experimental law of collisions states that:
>
> $$\frac{\text{relative velocity of separation}}{\text{relative velocity of approach}} = e \text{ or } \frac{v_2 - v_1}{u_1 - u_2} = e, 0 \leq e \leq 1$$
>
> where e is a constant called the **coefficient of restitution**.
>
> The value of e varies, depending on the material properties of the objects involved in the collision.

For a **perfectly elastic collision**, $e = 1$ and there is no loss of total kinetic energy.

The kinetic energy of the individual spheres may change but the total of their kinetic energies will remain the same. For example:

Initial momentum is $2 \times 10 + 3 \times 6 = 38 \text{ kg m s}^{-1}$.

Final momentum is $2 \times 5.2 + 3 \times 9.2 = 38 \text{ kg m s}^{-1}$, so momentum is conserved.

Initial kinetic energy is $\frac{1}{2} \times 2 \times 10^2 + \frac{1}{2} \times 3 \times 6^2 = 154 \text{ J}$.

Final kinetic energy is $\frac{1}{2} \times 2 \times (5.2)^2 + \frac{1}{2} \times 3 \times (9.2)^2 = 154 \text{ J}$ so there is no loss in kinetic energy.

If the spheres coalesce then $e = 0$, and there is loss of kinetic energy. This is sometimes called a **perfectly inelastic collision**. For example:

Initial momentum is $2 \times 10 + 3 \times 6 = 38 \text{ kg m s}^{-1}$.

Final momentum $= 5 \times 7.6 = 38 \text{ kg m s}^{-1}$, so momentum is conserved.

Initial kinetic energy is $\frac{1}{2} \times 2 \times 10^2 + \frac{1}{2} \times 3 \times 6^2 = 154 \text{ J}$.

Final kinetic energy is $\frac{1}{2} \times 5 \times (7.6)^2 = 144.4 \text{ J}$ so kinetic energy is lost.

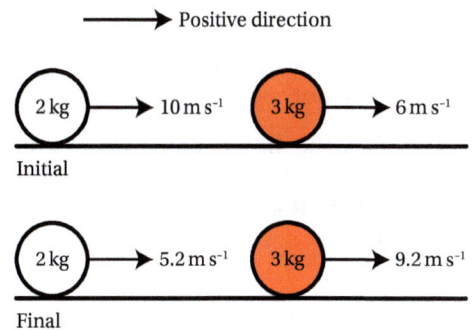

Positive direction

2 kg → 10 m s⁻¹   3 kg → 6 m s⁻¹

Initial

2 kg → 5.2 m s⁻¹   3 kg → 9.2 m s⁻¹

Final

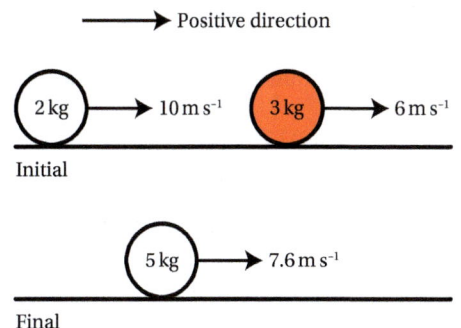

Positive direction

2 kg → 10 m s⁻¹   3 kg → 6 m s⁻¹

Initial

5 kg → 7.6 m s⁻¹

Final

In all other collisions, the total kinetic energy of the system decreases and $0 < e < 1$.

The outcome of the collision depends on the material that the objects are made of. For example:

Initial momentum is $2 \times 10 + 3 \times 6 = 38$ kg m s^{-1}.

Final momentum is $2 \times 7 + 3 \times 8 = 38$ kg m s^{-1}, so momentum is conserved.

Initial kinetic energy is $\frac{1}{2} \times 2 \times 10^2 + \frac{1}{2} \times 3 \times 6^2 = 154$ J.

Final kinetic energy is $\frac{1}{2} \times 2 \times 7^2 + \frac{1}{2} \times 3 \times 8^2 = 145$ J so kinetic energy is lost.

Again momentum is conserved but kinetic energy is lost. The loss in kinetic energy is slightly lower than if the particles had coalesced.

Applying Newton's experimental law

Consider a collision between two particles of masses m_1 and m_2 with initial velocities u_1 and u_2 and final velocities v_1 and v_2.

Newton's experimental law gives:

$$\frac{v_2 - v_1}{u_1 - u_2} = e$$

Unless $v_2 > v_1$ the spheres will not separate. Similarly, unless $u_1 > u_2$ the spheres will not collide.

You can rewrite the equation in three other ways.

- $e(u_1 - u_2) = (v_2 - v_1)$
- $\frac{v_1 - v_2}{u_1 - u_2} = -e$
- $(v_1 - v_2) = -e(u_1 - u_2)$

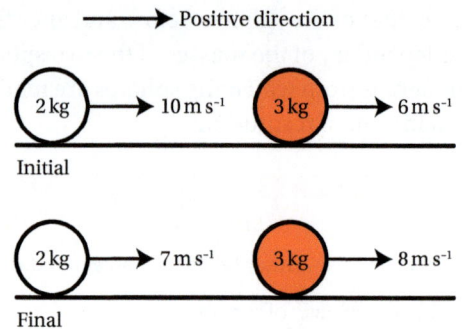

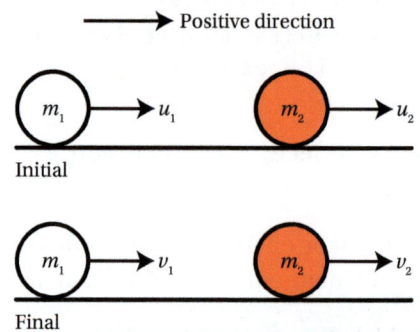

Tip

Take care to put the velocities in the correct order, with the correct signs. A clearly labelled diagram showing directions and a statement of Newton's experimental law will help to prevent errors but you **must** learn the formula.

WORKED EXAMPLE 3.16

Two spheres of masses $3m$ and $2m$ are moving towards each other with velocities 4 m s^{-1} and 5 m s^{-1} respectively. After the collision, they move away from each other with velocities 2.5 m s^{-1} and 3.5 m s^{-1} respectively.

a Find the value of the coefficient of restitution between the two spheres.

b Calculate, in terms of m, the kinetic energy loss for the particle of mass $3m$.

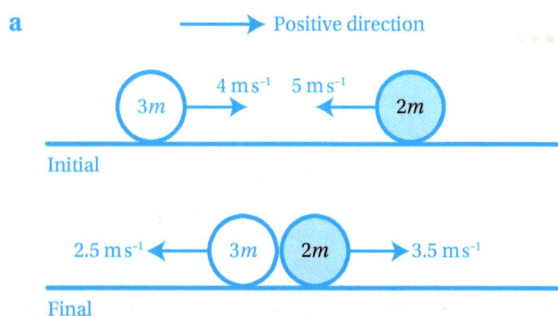

a

Draw a clear diagram.

Continues on next page

Newton's experimental law gives:

$\dfrac{v_2 - v_1}{u_1 - u_2} = e$

$u_1 = +4, u_2 = -5$

$v_1 = -2.5\,\text{m s}^{-1}, v_2 = +3.5\,\text{m s}^{-1}$

> State the values, remembering that signs indicate direction. Do not leave this step out as it helps to prevent errors with signs.

$e = \dfrac{3.5 - (-2.5)}{4 - (-5)}$

$= \dfrac{6}{9}$

$= \dfrac{2}{3}$

> Always check that e is positive and between 0 and 1. If it isn't, check that you have substituted correctly and have the fraction the correct way up. Remember that the final velocities go on the top line.

b Initial KE of the $3m$ mass is $\dfrac{1}{2} \times 3m \times 4^2 = 24m$ J

> Find the initial KE...

Final KE of the $3m$ mass is

$\dfrac{1}{2} \times 3m \times 2.5^2 = 9.375m$ J

> ...and the final KE.

Loss in KE $= (24 - 9.375)m$

$= 14.625m$ J

> Then subtract.

WORKED EXAMPLE 3.17

Two spheres A and B, of masses 0.4 kg and 0.5 kg respectively, are moving towards each other with velocities 6 m s⁻¹ and 3 m s⁻¹ respectively. The kinetic energy lost in the collision is 9 J.

a Find the speeds and directions of A and B immediately after the collision.
b What does this tell you about the coefficient of restitution between A and B?

a Positive direction ⟶

Initial

Final

> Draw a clear diagram and choose a direction to be positive.

Using the principle of conservation of momentum:

total momentum before collision =

total momentum after collision

$m_1 u_1 + m_2 u_2 = m_1 v_1 + m_2 v_2$

$(0.4 \times 6) - (0.5 \times 3) = 0.4v_1 + 0.5v_2$

$24 - 15 = 9 = 4v_1 + 5v_2 \qquad (1)$

> Multiply through by 10 to simplify the numbers.

Continues on next page

Initial KE $= \frac{1}{2} \times 0.4 \times 6^2 + \frac{1}{2} \times 0.5 \times 3^2$

$\qquad = 9.45\,\text{J}$

Find the KE before the collision.

Initial KE $-$ final KE $= 9$

So final KE $= 0.45\,\text{J}$

Find the KE after the collision by subtracting the amount of KE lost from the initial KE.

Final KE $= \frac{1}{2} \times 0.4 \times v_1^2 + \frac{1}{2} \times 0.5 \times v_2^2$

$\qquad = 0.2v_1^2 + 0.25v_2^2$

Write an expression for the KE after the collision and equate this to 0.45.

So $0.2v_1^2 + 0.25v_2^2 = 0.45$ $\qquad$ (2)

Solving (1) and (2) simultaneously:

$v_1 = 1\,\text{m s}^{-1}$ and $v_2 = 1\,\text{m s}^{-1}$.

You now have two equations, one linear and one quadratic, for the two unknowns. Solve them simultaneously.

b As the velocities have the same magnitude and act in the same direction, the particles coalesce (become one) so $e = 0$.

State the value of e, the coefficient of restitution and comment on your answer.

WORKED EXAMPLE 3.18

Two spheres of masses 300 grams and 500 grams are moving in the same direction, in the same straight line, with velocities $5\,\text{m s}^{-1}$ and $4\,\text{m s}^{-1}$ respectively. The coefficient of restitution between the spheres is 0.6. Find the velocities of the spheres immediately after the impact.

Draw a clear diagram. Show the positive direction. Convert units as necessary.

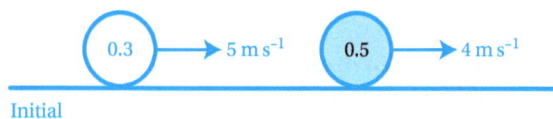

Initial

Final

$u_1 = 5,\, u_2 = 4$

State what you know.

Using the principle of conservation of momentum:

total momentum before collision =

$\quad$ total momentum after collision

$m_1u_1 + m_2u_2 = m_1v_1 + m_2v_2$

$0.3 \times 5 + 0.5 \times 4 = 0.3v_1 + 0.5v_2$ $\qquad$ (1)

$0.3v_1 + 0.5v_2 = 3.5$ $\qquad$ (2)

Substitute into the equation and simplify.

Continues on next page

Newton's experimental law gives:

$$\frac{v_2 - v_1}{u_1 - u_2} = e$$

$u_1 = +5, u_2 = +4$

$$\frac{v_2 - v_1}{5 - 4} = 0.6$$

State the known values with their signs.

$v_2 - v_1 = 0.6$

$v_2 = v_1 + 0.6$ \qquad (3)

Substituting (3) into (2):

$0.3v_1 + 0.5(v_1 + 0.6) = 3.5$

$3v_1 + 5(v_1 + 0.6) = 35$

$8v_1 = 32$

Multiply through by 10 to make the numbers easier and solve.

$v_1 = 4 \text{ m s}^{-1}$ and $v_2 = 4.6 \text{ m s}^{-1}$

Checking back in (1):

LHS $\quad 0.3 \times 5 + 0.5 \times 4 = 3.5$

RHS $\quad 0.3 \times 4 + 0.5 \times 4.6 = 3.5$

Check your answers by substituting back into the unsimplified conservation of momentum equation (1).

Collisions between a moving object and a fixed object

If a body hits a fixed wall, momentum is not conserved, because the wall is usually not free to move. However, Newton's experimental law still holds, so you can use the coefficient of restitution to calculate velocities for impacts involving a fixed object.

Consider a particle of mass m kg moving with velocity u m s^{-1} on a smooth horizontal plane as it collides with a fixed wall at right angles to its path and rebounds with velocity $-v$ m s^{-1} away from the wall. The coefficient of restitution between the wall and the particle is e.

Newton's experimental law states that:

$$\frac{v_2 - v_1}{u_1 - u_2} = e$$

$u_2 = v_2 = 0$ (as the wall does not move), $u_1 = u$ and $v_1 = -v$, so the equation reduces to $\frac{v}{u} = e$ or $v = eu$ where u and $-v$ are the velocities of the particle before and after the collision with the wall. Therefore the final velocity of the particle is $-eu$ or eu away from the wall.

Impulse of the wall on the particle = change in momentum of the particle

$$I = \text{final momentum} - \text{initial momentum}$$
$$= -mv - mu$$
$$= -meu - mu$$
$$= -mu(e + 1)$$

which is negative because the positive direction has been defined as being towards the wall and this impulse acts away from the wall.

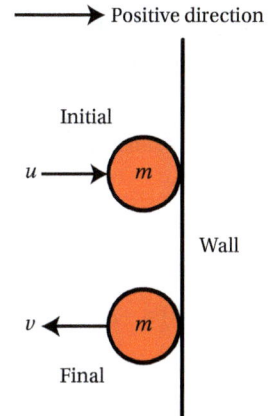

🔑 Key point 3.6

If an object, P, moving with velocity u, collides at right angles with a fixed object, then the object rebounds with velocity v where:

$$v = -eu$$

WORKED EXAMPLE 3.19

A football of mass 450 grams, moving with velocity 25 m s^{-1}, hits a fixed wall at right angles. The coefficient of restitution between the football and the wall is 0.8.

a At what speed does the ball rebound from the wall?
b Find the magnitude and direction of the impulse of the ball on the wall.
c Calculate the loss in kinetic energy of the football.

a

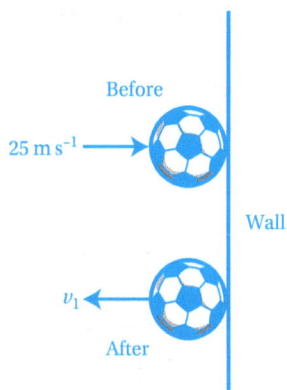

Always draw a diagram so you don't get confused with signs. Show the positive direction with an arrow.

Newton's experimental law gives:

$v = -eu$

Substituting in the values:

$v_1 = -e(25)$

$v_1 = -0.8(25) = -20 \text{ m s}^{-1}$

So the ball rebounds from the wall with speed 20 m s^{-1}.

You cannot use conservation of momentum as the wall is not free to move but you can use Newton's experimental law.

b Impulse = change in momentum

To find impulse you need force × time or change in momentum. As the wall does not move, you can only find the change in momentum of the football.

The impulse of the wall on the ball is:

$0.45(-20) - 0.45(25) = -9 - 11.25$

$\qquad\qquad\qquad = -20.25 \text{ N s}$

Find the impulse of the wall on the ball.

Therefore the impulse of the ball on the wall is 20.25 N s towards the wall.

The impulse of the ball on the wall is equal and opposite to the impulse of the wall on the ball.

Continues on next page

c   Initial KE $= \frac{1}{2}mv^2$

$$= \frac{1}{2} \times 0.45 \times 25^2$$

$$= 140.625$$

> To find the loss in kinetic energy you subtract the final KE from the initial KE of the ball.

Final KE $= \frac{1}{2} \times 0.45 \times 20^2$

$$= 90$$

Loss in KE $= 140.625 - 90$

$$= 50.625 \text{ J}$$

WORKED EXAMPLE 3.20

A ball of mass 400 grams is dropped from rest at a height of 2 m onto a smooth horizontal surface. It instantly bounces back vertically and reaches a height of 1.5 m.

a   Find the impulse of the ball on the ground at the instant of the collision , in terms of g.

b   Calculate the value of the coefficient of restitution between the ball and the ground.
Give your answer in surd form.

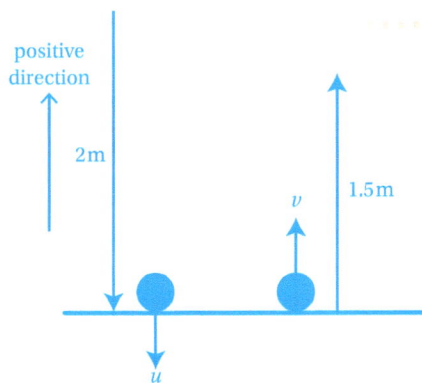

> To find impulse, you need to know either force and time or change in momentum. Momentum depends on velocity so find the velocity at which the ball hits the ground and then the velocity at which the ball leaves the ground. You can use either the conservation of energy equation or the equations of uniform acceleration.

a   As the ball falls:

loss in PE is $mgh = 0.4 \times g \times 2 = 0.8g$ J

gain in kinetic energy is $\frac{1}{2}mu^2 = 0.2u^2$

so $0.2u^2 = 0.8g$

> This example uses energy. Equating potential energy (PE) loss to kinetic energy (KE) gain you can find the velocity at which the ball hits the ground.

$u = \sqrt{4g}$ in the downwards or negative direction.

As the ball bounces up:

gain in PE is $mgh = 0.4 \times g \times 1.5 = 0.6g$ J

> You can use energy equations again to find the velocity v at which the ball leaves the ground.

loss in KE is $\frac{1}{2}mv^2 = 0.2v^2$

so $0.2v^2 = 0.6g$

$v = \sqrt{3g}$

Continues on next page

Taking the upwards direction as positive, impulse on the ball is:

$$mv - mu = 0.4(\sqrt{3g} - (-\sqrt{4g}))$$
$$= 0.4(\sqrt{3g} + \sqrt{4g})\,\text{N s}$$
vertically upwards

You then use the relationship between impulse and momentum to find the impulse of the ground on the ball.

State which direction you are taking as positive.

In the question the values are given to 1 s.f. so this is an appropriate degree of accuracy for your final answer.

The impulse of the ball on the ground is therefore $0.4(\sqrt{3g} + \sqrt{4g})\,\text{N s}$ vertically down.

This is equal and opposite to the impulse of the ball on the ground.

b Newton's experimental law gives:

$$v = -eu$$

Substituting the values and simplifying:

$$-e = \frac{v}{u}$$

$$= -\frac{\sqrt{3g}}{\sqrt{4g}}$$

$$\therefore e = \frac{\sqrt{3}}{2}$$

Range of values of e

The value of e affects what happens after a collision as it determines the final velocities of the colliding bodies and enables you to calculate whether further collisions will occur.

Rewind

You learned about gravitational potential energy, kinetic energy and the principle of conservation of mechanical energy in Chapter 1.

Tip

If two objects moving in the same straight line are going to collide, then there are two possibilities: either they are moving towards each other from opposite directions, or one is following the other and the follower is travelling faster than the object it is following.

WORKED EXAMPLE 3.21

Small spheres P of mass $3m$ and Q of mass $2m$ are lying in a smooth horizontal groove, which is a straight line ending in a vertical wall which is at right angles to the groove. P is projected with velocity u m s^{-1} towards Q, which is initially at rest. The coefficient of restitution between P and Q is 0.4. Q then hits the wall and rebounds. The coefficient of restitution between Q and the wall is 0.5.

a Find the velocity of Q as it rebounds from the wall.
b State, with reasons, whether or not there will be any further collisions between P and Q.

Continues on next page

a

Positive direction

$3m$ →u_1 $2m$ →u_2

Initial

$3m$ →v_1 $2m$ →v_2

Final

> Draw a clear diagram of the first collision only. Do not try to cram both collisions onto one diagram.
>
> Label u_1, u_2, v_1 and v_2 on the diagram to ensure you get Newton's law the correct way round.

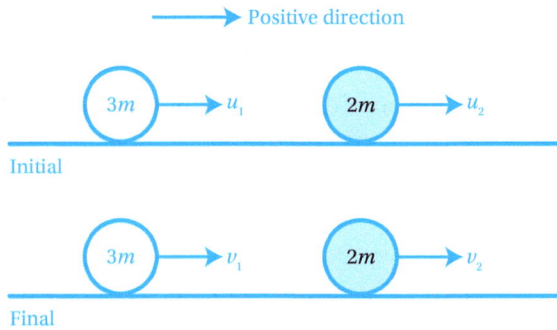

Using the principle of conservation of momentum:

total momentum before collision =
    total momentum after collision

$m_1u_1 + m_2u_2 = m_1v_1 + m_2v_2$

Substituting in the values and dividing through by m:

$3mu + 2m(0) = 3mv_1 + 2mv_2$

$3u + 0 = 3v_1 + 2v_2$ (1)

> Divide through by m as every term contains m. There is no need to define the unknowns if they are clearly shown on the diagram.

Newton's experimental law gives:

$\dfrac{v_2 - v_1}{u_1 - u_2} = e$

> State the formula.

Substituting in the values and simplifying:

$\dfrac{v_2 - v_1}{u - 0} = 0.4$

$v_2 - v_1 = 0.4u$

$v_1 = v_2 - 0.4u$ (2)

Substituting (2) into (1):

$3u = 3(v_2 - 0.4u) + 2v_2$

$5v_2 = 4.2u$

> The question asks you to find v_2.

$v_2 = 0.84u \text{ m s}^{-1}$

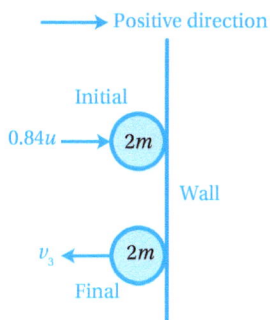

Positive direction

> Now deal with the collision with the wall.
>
> Draw a new diagram.

Initial

$0.84u$ → $2m$

Wall

v_3 ← $2m$

Final

Newton's experimental law gives:

$v = -eu$

> Momentum is not conserved as the wall is fixed so you use Newton's experimental law.

Substituting in the values and solving for v_3:

$v_3 = -0.5(0.84u)$

    $= -0.42u$

> Don't forget to include u with your answer.

Continues on next page

The final velocity of Q is $0.42\,\text{m s}^{-1}$ away from the wall.

> Explain that the minus sign indicates direction and state that direction.

b From (2):

$v_1 = v_2 - 0.4u$

$\quad = 0.84u - 0.4u$

$\quad = +0.44u$

The final velocity of P is $0.44u\,\text{m s}^{-1}$ towards the wall.

> To find out if there are any further collisions you need to know the velocity of P after the first collision and then compare the final velocities of P and Q.

As P is moving towards the wall and Q is moving away from the wall they will be moving towards each other so there will be at least one further collision.

> The directions of P and Q are important, as well as their speeds. Here the two particles are moving towards each other so they will collide again whatever their velocities.

WORKED EXAMPLE 3.22

A sphere, P, of mass $2m$ kg, moving at a velocity of $6\,\text{m s}^{-1}$, hits a sphere, Q, of mass $4m$ kg, which is at rest on a smooth horizontal surface. The coefficient of restitution between P and Q is 0.8. Q then hits a smooth vertical wall at right angles and rebounds. The coefficient of restitution between Q and the wall is e. Find the range of values of e for which there is a further collision between Q and P.

Positive direction $\longrightarrow$

> Draw a diagram for the first collision, with the positive direction labelled.

$2m$ $\rightarrow 6\,\text{m s}^{-1}$ $\qquad$ $4m$ $\rightarrow 0\,\text{m s}^{-1}$

Initial

$2m$ $\rightarrow v_1$ $\qquad$ $4m$ $\rightarrow v_2$

Final

Using the principle of conservation of linear momentum:

> Use the principle of conservation of linear momentum.

$m_1u_1 + m_2u_2 = m_1v_1 + m_2v_2$

$(2 \times 6) + (4 \times 0) = 2v_1 + 4v_2$

$2v_1 + 4v_2 = 12 \qquad (1)$

> Simplify the equation.

Using Newton's experimental law:

$\dfrac{v_2 - v_1}{u_1 - u_2} = e$

$0.8(6 - 0) = v_2 - v_1$

$v_2 - v_1 = 4.8 \qquad (2)$

> Simplify the equation.

$v_1 = -1.2\,\text{m s}^{-1}$ and $v_2 = 3.6\,\text{m s}^{-1}$

> Solve (1) and (2) simultaneously and check your answers in equation (1).

Continues on next page

Using Newton's experimental law for the collision between Q and the wall:

$v = -eu$

The speed of Q after the collision with the wall is $3.6e$ away from the wall.

Q is following P. The speed of P is $1.2\,\text{m s}^{-1}$ away from the wall and the speed of Q is $3.6e\,\text{m s}^{-1}$ away from the wall. If Q collides with P then:

$3.6e > 1.2$

$e > \dfrac{1}{3}$

After the collision with the wall, Q has velocity $-3.6e$, so it is moving away from the wall.

Now consider what is actually happening. If there is to be another collision then Q must be moving in the same direction as P and be moving faster than P.

EXERCISE 3C

1. A small sphere, of mass m, moving with speed u on a smooth horizontal plane, hits a vertical wall at right angles and rebounds. The coefficient of restitution between the sphere and the wall is e. Find:

   a the speed of the sphere after the collision

   b the magnitude of the impulse of the wall on the sphere

   c the loss in kinetic energy of the sphere

   when:

   i $u = 4\,\text{m s}^{-1}$ and $e = 0.3$ ii $u = 10\,\text{m s}^{-1}$ and $e = 1.0$

   iii $u = 60\,\text{m s}^{-1}$ and $e = 0$ iv $u = 40\,\text{m s}^{-1}$ and $e = 0.8$

   v $u = 10\,\text{m s}^{-1}$ and $e = 0.6$.

2. A 3 kg mass, P, moving at $4\,\text{m s}^{-1}$, collides with a second mass of 2 kg, Q, moving towards it on the same straight line with speed $5\,\text{m s}^{-1}$. The coefficient of restitution between the two masses is 0.5. Find the speeds and directions of P and Q after the collision.

3. Particle A, of mass 0.5 kg, moving at $5\,\text{m s}^{-1}$, collides with particle B, of mass 1 kg, moving towards it at a speed of $3\,\text{m s}^{-1}$ on the same straight line. After the collision, A moves in the opposite direction with a speed of $0.6\,\text{m s}^{-1}$. Find:

   a the speed and direction of B after the collision

   b the coefficient of restitution between A and B.

4. A small, smooth sphere of mass 1.5 kg, at rest on a smooth horizontal floor, is hit with a blow of impulse 24 N s and immediately hits a vertical wall at right angles. If it rebounds with velocity $12\,\text{m s}^{-1}$, find:

   a the coefficient of restitution between the wall and the sphere

   b the magnitude of the impulse of the wall on the sphere

   c the loss in kinetic energy of the sphere.

5   A small, smooth sphere of mass m kg, at rest on a smooth horizontal floor, is hit with a blow of impulse J N s and immediately hits a vertical wall at right angles. If it rebounds with velocity v m s^{-1}, find expressions, in terms of J, m and v, for:

   a   the coefficient of restitution between the wall and the sphere

   b   the magnitude of the impulse of the wall on the sphere

   c   the loss in kinetic energy of the sphere.

6   A small smooth ball-bearing, A, of mass 4 kg and with velocity v m s^{-1}, collides with another small, smooth ball-bearing, B, of mass 2.5 kg, moving in the same direction with velocity 10 m s^{-1}. After the collision, A and B are moving in the same direction, A with velocity 13.75 m s^{-1} and B with velocity v m s^{-1}.

   a   Find the value of v.

   b   Find the value of e, the coefficient of restitution between A and B.

   c   What is the total loss of kinetic energy in the collision?

7   A particle, A, of mass 200 grams, is moving at 10 m s^{-1} when it hits a vertical wall, at right angles to the wall, and rebounds. The coefficient of restitution between the wall and the particle is 0.6. The particle then hits another smooth particle, B, of mass 400 grams, which is initially at rest. After the collision, A is at rest and B is moving at v_B m s^{-1}. Find the value of v_B and hence the coefficient of restitution between A and B.

8   A small sphere, A, of mass 400 grams, moving in a straight line with velocity 8 m s^{-1}, collides with another small sphere, B, of mass 600 grams, which is moving directly towards A, along the same straight line, with velocity 6 m s^{-1}. The coefficient of restitution between the spheres is 0.8.

   a   Find the magnitude and direction of the velocities of the two spheres immediately after the collision.

   b   Calculate the magnitude of the impulse on B.

9   A particle of mass 400 grams is dropped from a height of 2 m on to a smooth horizontal surface and bounces back vertically up to a height h. The coefficient of restitution between the ball and the surface is 0.6. Find the value of h.

10   Two small spheres, A of mass $4m$ and B of mass m, are moving directly towards each other along a smooth horizontal surface, with velocities $2u$ and $3u$ respectively. The coefficient of restitution between the two spheres is 0.75.

   a   Find the magnitude and direction of the velocities of the two spheres immediately after the collision.

   b   Calculate the total loss of kinetic energy in the collision.

11   Two particles, A and B, each of mass m, are moving in the same direction, in the same straight line, with speeds 6 m s^{-1} and 3 m s^{-1} respectively, on a smooth horizontal surface when they collide. If the coefficient of restitution between the two particles is 0.8, find the speed and direction of the two particles immediately after the collision.

12   A ball of mass m kg is dropped from a height h_1 metres onto a smooth horizontal surface and bounces back vertically up to a height h_2. The coefficient of restitution between the ball and the surface is e. Find the ratio of h_1 to h_2.

13   Two particles, A and B, each of mass 400 grams, are moving in the same direction, in the same straight line, with speeds 6 m s^{-1} and 3 m s^{-1} respectively, on a smooth horizontal surface when they collide. At the instant of collision, each particle receives an impulse of 0.96 N s.

   a   Find the magnitude and direction of the velocities of the particles immediately after the collision.

   b   Calculate the coefficient of restitution between the two particles.

14 Two smooth spheres, A and B, each of mass 40 grams move towards each other along the same straight horizontal line and collide when they are moving with speeds $5 \, \text{m s}^{-1}$ and $3 \, \text{m s}^{-1}$, respectively. Immediately after the collision A moves with velocity $2.2 \, \text{m s}^{-1}$ away from B.

    a Calculate the velocity of B immediately after the collision.

    b Work out the coefficient of restitution between the two spheres.

    c Find the magnitude of the impulse exerted on A in the collision.

15 Two particles, A, of mass 2 kg, and B, of mass 3 kg, collide and coalesce to form a single particle, C. Immediately before the collision, the velocity of A is $(3\mathbf{i}+5\mathbf{j}) \, \text{m s}^{-1}$ and the velocity of B is $(6\mathbf{i}-3\mathbf{j}) \, \text{m s}^{-1}$.

    a Find the velocity of C immediately after the collision.

    b Calculate the total loss of kinetic energy in the collision.

16 A small ball of mass 500 grams is dropped from rest at a height of 2.5 m onto a smooth horizontal surface. It instantly bounces vertically up and reaches a height of 2 m. Calculate the impulse of the ground on the ball at the instant of the collision. Use $g = 10 \, \text{m s}^{-2}$, giving your final answer to an appropriate degree of accuracy.

17 A ball-bearing, A, of mass 450 grams, is thrown vertically down with a speed of $4 \, \text{m s}^{-1}$ from a height of 2 m. It bounces back and just reaches its original height. Find the coefficient of restitution between A and the ground. Use $g = 10 \, \text{m s}^{-2}$, giving your final answer to an appropriate degree of accuracy.

Checklist of learning and understanding

- Momentum is mass $\times$ velocity or momentum $= mv$.
- Impulse of a constant force is force $\times$ time $=$ change in momentum.
- $I = Ft = mv - mu$
- The units of impulse and momentum are equivalent and are newton seconds (N s) or kg m s^{-1}.
- Momentum, force, impulse and velocity are all vectors and can be expressed in vector form.

- The impulse generated by a variable force acting from time t_1 to time t_2 is $\displaystyle\int_{t_1}^{t_2} F \, \mathrm{d}t$.

- In general terms, if two objects of mass m_1 and m_2 are moving with velocities u_1 and u_2 in a straight line and they collide, then, if their velocities after the collision are v_1 and v_2:
  - total momentum before collision $=$ total momentum after collision
  - $m_1u_1 + m_2u_2 = m_1v_1 + m_2v_2$
  - this is the principle of conservation of linear momentum.
- Newton's experimental law of collisions states that:

  $\dfrac{\text{relative velocity of separation}}{\text{relative velocity of approach}} = e$ or $\dfrac{v_2 - v_1}{u_1 - u_2} = e, \, 0 \leqslant e \leqslant 1$

  where e is a constant called the coefficient of restitution. The value of e varies depending on the material properties of the objects involved in the collision.
- For a perfectly elastic collision, $e = 1$ and there is no loss of total kinetic energy.
- If the spheres coalesce, then $e = 0$, and there is loss of kinetic energy. This may be called a perfectly inelastic collision.
- In all other collisions the total kinetic energy of the system decreases and $0 < e < 1$.
- If an object P, which is free to move with velocity u, collides with a fixed object, which is at right angles to the plane of movement of P, then the object rebounds with velocity $v = -eu$ where e is the coefficient of restitution between P and the fixed object.

Mixed practice 3

1 A mass of 2 kg, which is initially at rest, is hit by a blow of impulse J N s. State the speed of the mass immediately after the impulse. Choose from these options.

A $2J\,\text{m}\,\text{s}^{-1}$ **B** $J\,\text{m}\,\text{s}^{-1}$ **C** $\dfrac{J}{2}\,\text{m}\,\text{s}^{-1}$ **D** $\sqrt{J}\,\text{m}\,\text{s}^{-1}$

2 A mass A, of 5 kg, initially at rest and free to move on a smooth horizontal surface, is acted on by a force F for 12 seconds. The graph of F is shown. State the speed of A after the 12 seconds. Choose from these options.

A $72\,\text{m}\,\text{s}^{-1}$ **B** $54\,\text{m}\,\text{s}^{-1}$ **C** $19.2\,\text{m}\,\text{s}^{-1}$ **D** $18\,\text{m}\,\text{s}^{-1}$

E $14.4\,\text{m}\,\text{s}^{-1}$

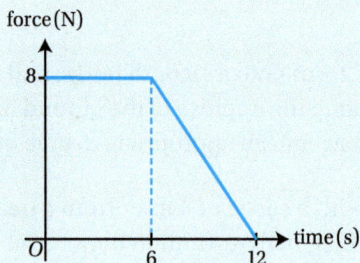

3 A toy train of mass 300 grams is moving along a straight horizontal track at a speed of $2.8\,\text{m}\,\text{s}^{-1}$. This toy train collides with another toy train, of mass 200 grams, which is at rest on the same track. During the collision, the two trains lock together and then move together.

Find the speed of the trains immediately after the collision.

[© AQA 2013]

4 A trolley, of mass 5 kg, is moving in a straight line on a smooth horizontal surface. It has a velocity of $6\,\text{m}\,\text{s}^{-1}$ when it collides with a stationary trolley, of mass m kg. Immediately after the collision, the trolleys move together with velocity $2.4\,\text{m}\,\text{s}^{-1}$.

Find m.

[© AQA 2011]

5 Two particles, A of mass 7 kg and B of mass 3 kg, are moving on a smooth horizontal plane when they collide. Just before the collision, the velocity of A is $(3\mathbf{i} + 8\mathbf{j})\,\text{m}\,\text{s}^{-1}$ and the velocity of B is $(6\mathbf{i} - 5\mathbf{j})\,\text{m}\,\text{s}^{-1}$. During the collision, the particles coalesce to form a single combined particle.

Find the velocity of the single combined particle after the collision.

[© AQA 2012]

6 Two particles, A and B, are moving on a smooth horizontal plane when they collide. The mass of

A is 6 kg and the mass of B is m kg. Before the collision, the velocity of A is $\begin{pmatrix} 2 \\ 4 \end{pmatrix}\,\text{m}\,\text{s}^{-1}$ and the

velocity of B is $\begin{pmatrix} 3 \\ -2 \end{pmatrix}\,\text{m}\,\text{s}^{-1}$. After the collision, the velocity of A is $\begin{pmatrix} 1 \\ 3 \end{pmatrix}\,\text{m}\,\text{s}^{-1}$ and the velocity of

B is $\begin{pmatrix} 7 \\ b \end{pmatrix}\,\text{m}\,\text{s}^{-1}$.

a Find m.

b Find b.

[© AQA 2010]

7 Two particles, A and B, have masses of m and km respectively, where k is a constant. The particles are moving on a smooth horizontal plane when they collide and coalesce to form a single particle. Just before the collision the velocities of A and B are $(4\mathbf{i} + 2\mathbf{j})$ m s^{-1} and $(6\mathbf{i} - 2\mathbf{j})$ m s^{-1} respectively. Immediately after the collision the combined particle has velocity $(5.2\mathbf{i} - 0.4\mathbf{j})$ m s^{-1}.

Find k.

[© AQA 2014]

8 Two particles, A and B, are moving towards each other along the same straight horizontal line when they collide. Particle A has mass 5 kg and particle B has mass 4 kg. Just before the collision, the speed of A is 4 m s^{-1} and the speed of B is 3 m s^{-1}. After the collision, the speed of A is 0.6 m s^{-1} and both particles move on the same straight horizontal line.

Find the two possible speeds of B after the collision.

[© AQA 2013]

9 Three uniform smooth spheres, A, B and C, have equal radii and masses m, $2m$ and $6m$ respectively. The spheres lie at rest in a straight line on a smooth horizontal surface with B between A and C. The sphere A is projected with speed u directly towards B and collides with it.

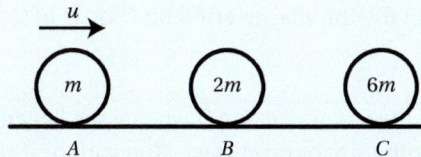

The coefficient of restitution between A and B is $\frac{2}{3}$.

a i Show that the speed of B immediately after the collision is $\frac{5}{9}u$.

ii Find, in terms of u, the speed of A immediately after the collision.

b Subsequently, B collides with C. The coefficient of restitution between B and C is e. Show that B will collide with A again if $e > k$, where k is a constant to be determined.

c Explain why it is not necessary to model the spheres as particles in this question.

[© AQA 2015]

10 A smooth sphere A, of mass m, is moving with speed $4u$ in a straight line on a smooth horizontal table. A smooth sphere B, of mass $3m$, has the same radius as A and is moving on the table with speed $2u$ in the same direction as A.

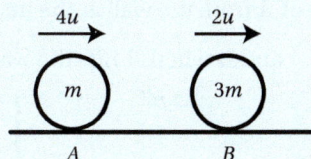

The sphere A collides directly with sphere B. The coefficient of restitution between A and B is e.

a Find, in terms of u and e, the speeds of A and B immediately after the collision.

b Show that the speed of B after the collision cannot be greater than $3u$.

c Given that $e = \frac{2}{3}$, find, in terms of m and u, the magnitude of the impulse exerted on B in the collision.

[© AQA 2013]

11 Three smooth spheres, A, B and C, of equal radii have masses 1 kg, 3 kg and x kg respectively. The spheres lie at rest in a straight line on a smooth horizontal surface with B between A and C. The sphere A is projected with speed $3u$ directly towards B and collides with it.

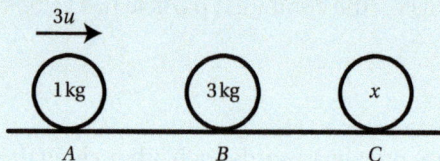

The coefficient of restitution between each pair of spheres is $\frac{1}{3}$.

a Show that A is brought to rest by the impact, and find the speed of B immediately after the collision in terms of u.

b Subsequently, B collides with C.

Show that the speed of C immediately after the collision is $\frac{4u}{3+x}$.

Find the speed of B immediately after the collision in terms of u and x.

c Show that B will collide with A again if $x > 9$.

d Given that $x = 5$, find the magnitude of the impulse exerted on C by B in terms of u.

[© AQA 2010]

12 Two small smooth spheres, A and B, are the same size and have masses $2m$ and m respectively. Initially, the spheres are at rest on a smooth horizontal surface. The sphere A receives an impulse of magnitude J and moves with speed $2u$ directly towards B.

a Find J in terms of m and u.

b The sphere A collides directly with B. The coefficient of restitution between A and B is $\frac{2}{3}$. Find, in terms of u, the speeds of A and B immediately after the collision.

c At the instant of collision, the centre of B is at a distance s from a fixed smooth vertical wall which is at right angles to the direction of motion of A and B, as shown in the diagram.

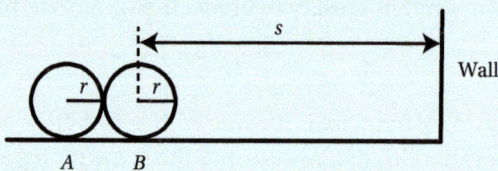

Subsequently, B collides with the wall. The radius of each sphere is r.

Show that the distance of the centre of A from the wall at the instant that B hits the wall is $\frac{3s + 12r}{5}$.

d The diagram shows the positions of A and B when B hits the wall.

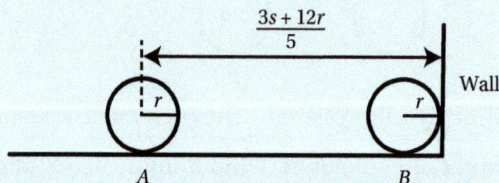

The sphere B collides with A again after rebounding from the wall. The coefficient of restitution between B and the wall is $\frac{2}{5}$.

Find the distance of the **centre of B** from the wall at the instant when A and B collide again.

[© AQA 2014]

13 Two particles, A, of mass $2m$, and B, of mass $3m$, are at rest on a smooth horizontal plane. A is hit with a blow of impulse $8m$ N s in the direction AB. A collides with B, which then hits a smooth vertical wall at right angles. The coefficient of restitution between A and B is 0.8 and the coefficient of restitution between B and the wall is e. Find the range of values of e for which there is at least one more collision between A and B. Give your answer as a fraction.

14 Three particles, P of mass m, Q of mass $2m$ and R of mass $7m$, are at rest in the same horizontal line on a smooth horizontal surface. P is projected along the plane towards Q at a velocity of 6 m s^{-1} and the coefficient of restitution between P and Q is 0.7. Q then collides with R. The coefficient of restitution between Q and R is e. Find the range of values of e for which there is a further collision between Q and P. Give your answer as a fraction.

4 Circular motion 1

In this chapter you will learn how to:

- model motion of a particle moving in a horizontal circular path under a constant speed
- link linear speed and angular speed of a particle moving in a horizontal circular path
- find the acceleration and forces acting on a particle moving in a horizontal circular path.

A If you are following the A Level course, you will also learn how to:

- use velocity and angular velocity as vector quantities
- solve problems relating to motion in a horizontal circular path in 3D.

Before you start…

GCSE	You should know how to calculate the arc length for a given proportion of a circle.	1	A particle moves around a circular track with speed 3 m s^{-1}. Given that it takes 3 seconds to run $\frac{1}{12}$ of the circumference, find the length of the circular track.
A Level Mathematics Student Book 1, Chapter 15	You should know how to write column vectors and what they mean.	2	Write down the vector that translates a point from coordinates (2, 3) to (−3, 10).
GCSE	You should be able to work with trigonometric ratios.	3	A point (3, 4) lies on a circle of radius 5 centred at the origin. Find the angle made with the positive x-axis of the straight line that goes through the origin and the point (3, 4).
A Level Mathematics Student Book 1, Chapter 16	You should be able to use calculus to work with simple rates of change related to distance, speed, acceleration and time.	4	An object is accelerating with a constant acceleration of 3 m s^{-2}. Find an expression for its velocity and displacement, given that the initial velocity is 2 m s^{-1} and the initial displacement is 3 m.
A Level Mathematics Student Book 2, Chapter 7	You should be able to work in radians as an angular measure.	5	Find the angle, in radians, that is equivalent to an angle of 150°.

What is different about motion in a circle?

In your work on kinematics so far you have considered the velocity of a particle as a vector quantity with magnitude (speed) and direction. When a particle moves in a circular path the direction of the velocity is constantly changing. You need to consider a new way of measuring how the particle is moving over time. To do this you look at how the angle changes with respect to time.

WORKED EXAMPLE 4.1

A particle P is moving at a constant rate anticlockwise along a circle, centre O, of radius 5 cm. The particle takes 20 seconds to make one revolution of the circle.

a Calculate the angle (in radians) through which the particle moves in 1 second.
b Find the arc length traced out by the particle every second.

a

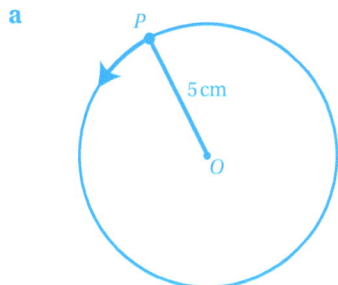

It is a good idea to draw a diagram first.

The particle moves through 2π in 20 seconds.

It moves through $\dfrac{\pi}{10}$ in 1 second.

Hence it moves through an angle of $\dfrac{\pi}{10} = 0.314$ rad (3 s.f.).

Take the angle in a full turn and divide by the time taken to make one revolution to find the angle turned through in 1 second.

b $l = \theta r$

$l = \dfrac{\pi}{10} \times 5$

$= \dfrac{\pi}{2}$ cm

$= 1.57$ cm (3 s.f.)

Start with the formula for arc length and then substitute the value found in part **a**. This will give the distance travelled along the arc every second.

Section 1: Linear speed versus angular speed

Let O be the centre of a circle of radius r and let A be a fixed point on the circumference. At time t the particle P is at an angle of θ measured in radians anticlockwise from the radius OA. If the particle is travelling at a constant **angular speed** around the circle then the rate of change of the angle θ with respect to time t is a constant and is denoted by ω, which means that $\dfrac{d\theta}{dt} = \omega$, where ω is measured in radians per second.

As it is equal to the arc length, the distance the particle P has travelled along the circumference is given by $s = r\theta$. Given that linear speed v (the **tangential speed**) is a change in distance s with respect to change in time t, you can relate this to the angular speed by:

$$v = \frac{ds}{dt} = \frac{d(r\theta)}{dt}$$

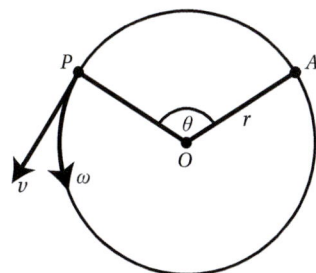

⏮ **Rewind**

Arc length is covered in A Level Mathematics Student Book 2, Chapter 7.

You can remove r from the differentiation since it is a constant:

$$\frac{d(r\theta)}{dt} = r\frac{d\theta}{dt}$$
$$= r\omega$$

since you know that $\frac{d\theta}{dt} = \omega$.

> **Tip**
>
> Sometimes ω is denoted by $\dot{\theta}$, which is just $\frac{d\theta}{dt}$. This gives the formula for linear speed as $v = r\dot{\theta}$.

🔑 Key point 4.1

For a particle P, moving in a circular path of radius r, centre O, and with constant angular speed ω, linear (tangential) speed is given by $v = r\omega$.

WORKED EXAMPLE 4.2

Two marbles are moving in two clockwise circles, both centred at the origin O. One circle has radius 2 cm and the other has radius 5 cm. Both marbles have a constant angular speed of 3.5 rad s^{-1}. Calculate:

a the linear speed for each marble
b the time taken for each marble to complete one full circle.

a

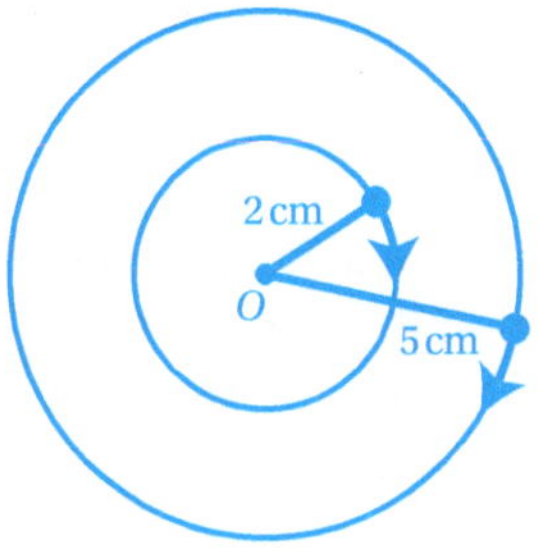

Draw a diagram.

$v = r\omega$

You know that $v = r\omega$.

For the circle radius 2 cm:
$v = 2 \times 3.5$
$\quad = 7\ cm\,s^{-1}$

For the circle radius 5 cm:
$v = 5 \times 3.5$
$\quad = 17.5\ cm\,s^{-1}$

b $\omega = 3.5\ rad\,s^{-1}$

Each marble moves through 3.5 rad in 1 second.

Each moves through 1 rad in $\frac{2}{7}$ s

You know that angular speed is the amount of turn with respect to time. Both particles have the same angular speed and, consequently, will take the same time to complete one full circle.

Each moves through 2π rad in $\frac{4\pi}{7}$ s

One full turn takes 1.80 seconds (3 s.f.)

You know how long it takes to complete 1 radian. Multiply this by 2π to find the time taken to complete a full turn.

WORKED EXAMPLE 4.3

A particle moves in a circular orbit of radius 2 m at a constant frequency of 0.6 revolutions per minute.

a How many revolutions does the particle complete in 1 second?
b Find the angular speed of the particle, in radians per second.
c Find the linear speed of the particle.

a $0.6 \div 60 = 0.01$ revolutions per second

You know that 1 minute = 60 seconds. The particle will travel far less in 1 second than in 1 minute.

b $2\pi \times 0.01 = \dfrac{\pi}{50}$ radians turned in a second

$\omega = 0.0628$ rad s^{-1} (3 s.f.)

Angular speed is the angle turned through in 1 second so use the result for part **a** to consider what proportion of a full turn has taken place in 1 second.

c $v = r\omega$

$= 2 \times \dfrac{\pi}{50}$

$= \dfrac{\pi}{25}$

$= 0.126$ m s^{-1} (3 s.f.)

You know that $v = r\omega$.

Tip

It is important to ensure that you are using the correct units for your angular speed, linear speed, distance and time.

WORK IT OUT 4.1

Two particles, A and B, are moving in clockwise circles, of radius 5 cm and 7 cm respectively, both centred at O. Particle A moves at a linear speed of 2.5 m s^{-1} and particle B moves at an angular speed of 6 rad s^{-1}. Which particle has the greater angular speed?

Which is the correct solution? Identify the errors made in the incorrect solutions.

Solution 1	Solution 2	Solution 3
Angular speed: $\omega = \dfrac{v}{r}$	Angular speed $\omega = rv$	Angular speed: $\omega = \dfrac{v}{r}$
For particle A:	$r = 5$ cm $= 0.05$ m	$r = 5$ cm $= 0.05$ m
angular speed $\omega = 2.5 \div 5$ $= 0.5$ rad s^{-1}	For particle A:	For particle A:
Therefore, particle B has the greater angular speed.	angular speed $\omega = 0.05 \times 2.5$ $= 0.125$ rad s^{-1}	angular speed $\omega = 2.5 \div 0.05$ $= 50$ rad s^{-1}
	Therefore, particle B has the greater angular speed.	Therefore, particle A has the greater angular speed.

EXERCISE 4A

1 A particle is travelling around a circular path, with angular speed ω and linear speed v. The radius of the circular orbit is r.

  a **i** Given that $\omega = 3.4$ rad s^{-1} and $r = 3$ m, find the value of v.

       ii Given that $\omega = 2.11$ rad s^{-1} and $r = 0.2$ m, find the value of v.

  b **i** Given that $v = 7$ m s^{-1} and $\omega = 4$ rad s^{-1}, find the value of r.

       ii Given that $v = 3.2$ m s^{-1} and $\omega = 0.2$ rad s^{-1}, find the value of r.

  c **i** Given that the radius of the circular path is 30 cm and the linear speed is 3 metres per minute, find the value of ω.

       ii Given that the radius of the circular path is 124 mm and the linear speed is 10 km h^{-1}, find the value of ω.

  d **i** Given that the particle makes two revolutions of a circular path of radius 2 cm every second, find the value of v.

       ii Given that the particle makes 10 revolutions of a circular path of radius 3 m every minute, find the value of v.

2 **a** A particle takes 15 seconds to move round a circle, at a constant linear speed of 30 m s^{-1}. Find:

      i the angular speed, in radians per second (rad s^{-1})

      ii the radius of the circle, in metres.

  b A marble completes 20 revolutions every 30 seconds, with a linear speed of 10 m s^{-1}. Find:

      i the angular speed, in radians per second (rad s^{-1})

      ii the radius of the circle, in metres.

  c A ball takes 1 minute to move round a circle, at a constant linear speed of 5 m s^{-1}. Find:

      i the angular speed, in radians per second (rad s^{-1})

      ii the radius of the circle, in metres.

3 A cyclist rides clockwise round a circular track of radius 75 m at a linear speed of 8 m s^{-1}.

  a Find the angular speed, in radians per second (rad s^{-1}).

  b Calculate the time it takes for the cyclist to complete one circuit.

4 A spinning disc of radius 10 cm completes one revolution every 45 seconds.

  a Calculate the angular speed of the spinning disc, in radians per second (rad s^{-1}).

  b Find the linear speed of a point at the edge of the spinning disc.

  c Find the radius of the spinning disc if a point at its edge has a linear speed of 1 m s^{-1}.

5 Two gear wheels, A and B, one of radius 5 cm and one of radius 10 cm, are connected. Given that the angular speed of wheel A is 0.5 rad s^{-1}, find the angular speed of B.

6 An athlete runs at 7 m s^{-1} along the inside path of the track, as shown in the diagram.

    a How long does it take for the athlete to complete one circuit?

    b Find the angular speed of the athlete as he runs around the circular parts of the track.

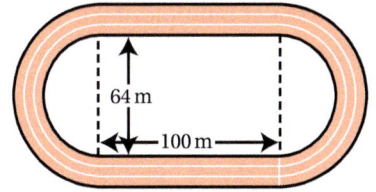

7 Metis is a moon of Jupiter. It completes one orbit approximately every 7 hours. The orbit has an average distance from Jupiter of approximately 128 000 km.

    a What assumptions do you need to make to be able to calculate its angular speed?

    b Making these modelling assumptions:

       i find the angular speed, in revolutions per minute (rev min^{-1}) and radians per second (rad s^{-1})

      ii work out the linear speed of this moon, in kilometres per second (km s^{-1}).

Section 2: Acceleration in horizontal circular motion

When a particle moves in a circular path there must be a resultant force that keeps the particle moving in a circle, otherwise the particle would stop turning and continue to move in a straight line.

If there is a force acting on the particle to keep it in a circular orbit, by Newton's second law, there must be an acceleration. The diagram shows a particle moving in a horizontal circle in the xy-plane.

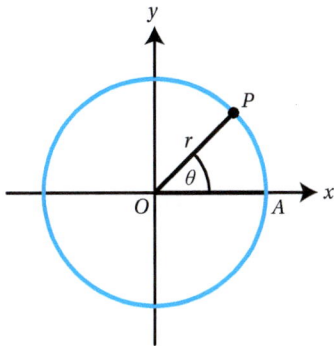

A If you consider the position of the particle P in this diagram, it has coordinates $(r \cos \theta, r \sin \theta)$, where $\theta = 0$ when $t = 0$. Let ω be the constant angular speed. Then the angle θ measured anticlockwise from the line OA at time t is ωt. You can replace θ by ωt to get the position vector.

$$\mathbf{r} = \begin{pmatrix} r \cos \theta \\ r \sin \theta \end{pmatrix} = \begin{pmatrix} r \cos \omega t \\ r \sin \omega t \end{pmatrix}$$

Differentiating with respect to time gives the **velocity vector** and differentiating again gives the **acceleration vector**. However, this requires differentiation of sine and cosine functions and using the chain rule, which is covered in your A level Mathematics studies. For now, you can just state the result needed: $\mathbf{a} = -\omega^2 \mathbf{r}$. So the acceleration is a

Rewind

Recall Newton's laws of motion, which you studied in A Level Mathematics Student Book 1, Chapter 18.

Tip

The use of vectors will only be examined at A level.

Rewind

You learned about vectors in A Level Mathematics Student Book 1, Chapter 15.

Rewind

Refer to A Level Mathematics Student Book 2, Chapter 10, for differentiation using the chain rule. You could try question 10 in Exercise 4B, to derive $\mathbf{a} = -\omega^2 \mathbf{r}$.

negative scalar multiple of the direction vector **r**. This means that the acceleration is directed towards the centre of the circular motion.

The direction of the velocity vector is along the tangent at the point P.

The formula for acceleration is given by $a = v\omega$, where v is the linear speed and ω is the angular speed.

Since $v = r\omega$ you can write $a = r\omega^2$ and since $w = \dfrac{v}{r}$ you can write $a = \dfrac{v^2}{r}$.

This means that you have a relationship between a and any two of the three variables v, ω and r.

As the linear speed is given by $v = r\omega$ and hence $v = \dfrac{\omega}{r}$, you can also write the magnitude of the acceleration as $|\mathbf{a}| = \dfrac{v^2}{r}$.

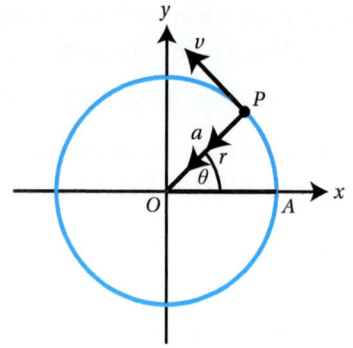

Tip

The proof of this result is beyond the scope of this section.

WORKED EXAMPLE 4.4

A particle P of mass 5 kg is travelling in the xy-plane. The particle's position vector is given by

$$\begin{pmatrix} 2\cos \pi t - 2 \\ 2\sin \pi t + 1 \end{pmatrix} \text{ metres, where } 0 < t < 2 \text{ is the time in seconds.}$$

a Show that the particle is moving in a circular orbit.
b Find the linear speed of the particle.
c Find the force keeping the particle P in a circular orbit.

a $x = 2\cos \pi t - 2$

  $y = 2\sin \pi t + 1$

The position vector gives the x- and y-coordinates.

For a particle to move in a circular orbit the Cartesian equation for the particle's path must be of the form $(x-a)^2 + (y+b)^2 = r^2$.

This is the general equation for a circle.

Using the identity $\sin^2 t + \cos^2 t = 1$:

You want to eliminate t.

$$\sin^2 \pi t + \cos^2 \pi t = \left(\frac{y-1}{2}\right)^2 + \left(\frac{x+2}{2}\right)^2 = 1$$

$$(x+2)^2 + (y-1)^2 = 4$$

This is a Cartesian equation of a circle, centre $(-2, 1)$ of radius 2. So, the particle P is moving in a circular orbit.

Continues on next page

b Differentiating the position vector with respect to t:

$$\begin{pmatrix} -2\pi \sin \pi t \\ 2\pi \cos \pi t \end{pmatrix}$$

The velocity vector is the derivative of the position vector.

Calculating the magnitude gives the speed:

$$\sqrt{(-2\pi \sin \pi t)^2 + (2\pi \cos \pi t)^2} = 6.3 \, \text{m s}^{-1} \, (2 \text{ s.f.})$$

c Differentiating the velocity vector with respect to t:

$$\begin{pmatrix} -2\pi \cos \pi t \\ -2\pi \sin \pi t \end{pmatrix}$$

The acceleration vector is the derivative of the velocity vector.

$$F = 5 \times 2 \times \pi = 31 \, \text{N} \, (2 \text{ s.f.})$$

Since $F = m|\mathbf{a}|$ and $|\mathbf{a}|$ is constant.

Since you can find the acceleration of a particle of mass m kg moving in a horizontal circular path you can apply Newton's second law, $F = ma$, to find the horizontal resultant force that acts on the particle. As acceleration is directed towards the centre, the resultant force must also be directed towards the centre. This force is often referred to as the **centripetal force**.

💡 **Tip**

Sometimes the acceleration is written as $r\ddot{\theta}$, where $r\ddot{\theta}$ is $\frac{d^2\theta}{dt^2}$. This gives the formula for acceleration as $a = r\ddot{\theta}$.

🔑 **Key point 4.2**

For a particle P, moving in a circular path of radius r, centre O and with constant angular speed ω, the acceleration is given by $v\omega$, $r\omega^2$ or $\frac{v^2}{r}$, towards the centre of the circle.

You need to know Key point 4.2 for the AS Level course. For the A Level course you will also need to know the vector notation.

📷 **Focus on ...**

In Focus on ... Proof 1, you will investigate the connection between the equations for linear motion with constant acceleration in a straight line and motion in a circle involving angular equivalents of s, u, v and a.

WORKED EXAMPLE 4.5

A ball of mass 200 grams is attached to a light inextensible string of length 150 cm. One end of the string is fixed on a smooth horizontal table and the ball moves in a circular path with linear speed 4 m s^{-1}. Calculate:

a the acceleration of the ball   **b** the tension in the string.

a

Draw a diagram, labelling the direction of the acceleration.

⏮ **Rewind**

When modelling with a rope, you can make the assumptions that it is light and inextensible in order to produce a simple mathematical model of the situation, as you did in A Level Mathematics Student Book 1, Chapter 19.

Continues on next page

$v = 4\,\text{m s}^{-1}, r = 1.5\,\text{m}$ .... Convert centimetres to metres.

$a = \dfrac{v^2}{r}$

You know that $a = \dfrac{v^2}{r}$.

$= \dfrac{4^2}{1.5}$

$= \dfrac{16}{1.5}$

$= 10.7\,\text{m s}^{-2}$ (3 s.f.) towards the centre of the circle

b   Using Newton's second law: .... The resultant force directed towards the centre of the circular motion comes from the tension in the string.

$T = ma$

$m = 0.2\,\text{kg}$

$T = 0.2 \times \dfrac{16}{1.5}$

$= \dfrac{32}{15}$

$= 2.13\,\text{N}$ (3 s.f.)

WORKED EXAMPLE 4.6

A toy car of mass 1 kg moves at an angular speed of $\dfrac{\pi}{30}$ rad s^{-1} around a circular path of radius 20 m. Calculate the centripetal force required to keep the toy car travelling in this circular path.

.... Draw a diagram.

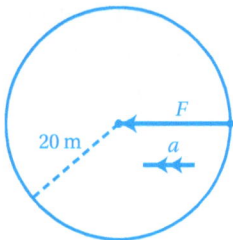

Using Newton's second law: .... The centripetal force is towards the centre of the circle.

$F = ma$

$= 1 \times a$

$a = r\omega^2$

$= 20 \times \left(\dfrac{\pi}{30}\right)^2$

$= 0.219\,\text{m s}^{-2}$ (3 s.f.)

Hence $F = 1 \times 0.219$

$= 0.219\,\text{N}$ (3 s.f.)

EXERCISE 4B

1 A particle of mass m kg is travelling around a circular path of radius r m. It has angular speed ω rad^{-1}, linear speed v m s^{-1} and the magnitude of the acceleration is a a m s^{-2}.

  a   **i**   Given that $\omega = 4$ and $a = 5$, find the value of r.

      ii   Given that $\omega = 2.33$ and $a = 7$, find the value of r.

  b   **i**   Given that $v = 5$ and $a = 7$, find the value of r.

      ii   Given that $v = 3.56$ and $a = 9$, find the value of r.

  c   **i**   Given that $m = 20$, $r = 0.3$ and the force keeping the particle in a circular motion is 340 N, find the value of v.

      ii   Given that $m = 35$, $r = 0.5$ and the force keeping the particle in a circular motion is 150 N, find the value of v.

  d   **i**   Given that $m = 5$, $r = 2$ and the force keeping the particle in a circular motion is 90 N, find the value of ω.

      ii   Given that $m = 0.5$, $r = 0.4$ and the force keeping the particle in a circular motion is 30 N, find the value of ω.

2   **a**   A ball of mass 2 kg is travelling, with constant linear speed 2 m s^{-1}, in a circular path of radius 1 m on a smooth table.

      i   Find the acceleration due to the circular motion.

      ii   Find the magnitude of the resultant force acting on the ball.

      iii   Draw a diagram of the situation.

  b   A car of mass 2900 kg is travelling in a circular path of diameter 50 m with a constant linear speed of 35 km h^{-1}.

      i   Find the acceleration due to the circular motion.

      ii   Find the magnitude of the resultant force acting on the car.

      iii   Draw a diagram of the situation.

  c   A particle of mass 200 grams is attached to a light inextensible string of length 15 cm that is fixed at the other end so that the particle is spinning in a circular path on a smooth table. The particle is moving at a constant rate of 1 revolution every 20 seconds.

      i   Find the acceleration due to the circular motion.

      ii   Find the magnitude of the resultant force acting on the particle.

      iii   Draw a diagram of the situation.

3 A car of mass 3500 kg travels along a horizontal road around a bend that is an arc of a circle of radius 35 m. The maximum speed at which the car can travel on this circular bend without moving outwards tangentially from the centre is 25 km h^{-1}. Calculate the acceleration and the maximal centripetal force on the car towards the centre of the circle.

4 Find the tension required in a light inextensible string of length 30 cm to keep a particle of mass 2 kg spinning in a horizontal circular path when:

  a   the linear speed of the particle is 3 m s^{-1}

  b   the angular speed is 6 rad s^{-1}.

5 Emily is on a roundabout that is rotating at a constant angular speed ω. She is sitting halfway between the centre and the edge. Emily moves to a position that is $\frac{1}{3}$ away from the edge. Describe the effect on the force that Emily experiences, acting towards the centre of the roundabout. Provide calculations to support your argument.

A **6** A car travels at a constant speed along a bend in the road that is formed by an arc of a circle of radius 55 m.

    a Find the greatest linear speed, in kilometres per hour (km h^{-1}), at which the car can travel around the bend without moving outwards at a tangent, given that the coefficient of friction between the tyres of the car and the surface of the road is estimated as 0.1.

    b Comment on whether this is a sensible estimate for the value of the coefficient of friction for the model.

> ⏮ **Rewind**
>
> **A** You will have used the coefficient of friction if you have worked through A Level Mathematics Student Book 2, Chapter 18.

7 A particle is on a rough horizontal disc at a distance of 13 cm from its centre. When the disc is rotating at a constant speed of 12 rev min^{-1} the particle is on the point of moving outwards at a tangent. Calculate the coefficient of friction between the marble and the disc.

8 Two particles, A and B, of mass 40 grams and 30 grams respectively, are attached to opposite ends of a light inextensible string of length 30 cm. Particle A rests on a rough horizontal spinning table. The coefficient of friction between the table and the particle is 0.4 and the string passes through a smooth hole in the centre of the table. The hole is too small to allow either particle to pass through it. Particle B hangs freely below the table. Particle A is moving on the spinning table in a circular path with constant angular speed about the centre of the table.

Find the linear speed of particle A when the system is in equilibrium, with particle A on the point of moving off at a tangent, and particle B is hanging 15 cm below the table.

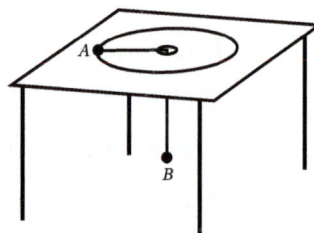

> 💡 **Tip**
>
> Remember that it is the resultant force acting horizontally towards the centre of the circular motion that you use for the force in $F = ma$.

9 Road surface conditions are being assessed for a horizontal bend in a road that is formed by an arc of a circle of radius 25 m. The road surface could be made of asphalt or concrete. The coefficient of friction between car tyres and asphalt is 0.72, and between car tyres and concrete it is 0.85.

    a List the assumptions that need to be made.

    b Calculate the maximum safe linear speed, in kilometres per hour (km h^{-1}), at which a car could travel around the bend without veering off at a tangent for:

        i a surface made from asphalt   **ii** a surface made from concrete.

    c When the surface is wet, the coefficient of friction between the car tyres and asphalt is 0.25 and between the car tyres and concrete is 0.45. What are the maximum safe limits in wet weather?

    d Given that concrete is more expensive that asphalt, which road surface would you recommend for the bend in the road?

10 Let the position of particle P in the diagram have coordinates $(r \cos \theta, r \sin \theta)$. Let ω be the constant angular speed so that the angle θ measured from the line OA anticlockwise at time t is ωt.

a Show that:

   i the position vector of P is given by $\mathbf{r} = \begin{pmatrix} r \cos \omega t \\ r \sin \omega t \end{pmatrix}$

   ii the linear (tangential) velocity of P is $\mathbf{v} = \begin{pmatrix} -r\omega \sin \omega t \\ r\omega \cos \omega t \end{pmatrix}$

   iii the acceleration of P is given by $\mathbf{a} = \begin{pmatrix} -r\omega^2 \cos \omega t \\ -r\omega^2 \sin \omega t \end{pmatrix}$.

b The direction of the acceleration is along a radius, directed towards the centre O, and of magnitude $r\omega^2$.

   Use the scalar product to show that the velocity vector is perpendicular to the radius.

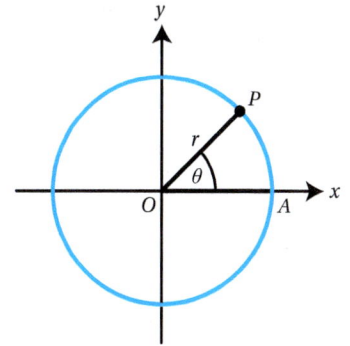

> ⏮ **Rewind**
>
> The scalar product is covered in A Level Further Mathematics Student Book 1, Chapter 9.

Section 3: Horizontal circular motion in 3D

The examples you have seen so far in this chapter have all had a single horizontal force keeping a particle in a circular path. You are now going to consider situations where the forces are not necessarily acting horizontally but the particle is still moving in a horizontal circular path with a constant angular speed. This will require you to consider the components of a force.

🔑 Key point 4.3

When solving problems in three dimensions for particles moving in a horizontal circular path you need to resolve the forces parallel and perpendicular to the plane containing the circular path. For the object to continue to move in a horizontal circle, the sum of the perpendicular forces must be zero. The resultant force towards the centre of the circle must equal $mr\omega^2$, where m is the mass of the particle, r is the radius of the circle and w is the angular speed.

One example of this is the **conical pendulum**.

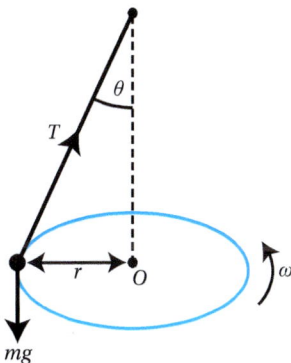

The particle is moving in a horizontal circle at a constant angular speed ω attached to a light inextensible string that makes an angle of θ with the downward vertical.

WORKED EXAMPLE 4.7

A particle A of mass 200 grams is attached to the lower end of a light inextensible string with the upper end fixed at B. When the particle moves in a horizontal circular path, the string traces out the curved surface of a cone and makes an angle of $60°$ with the downward vertical. The centre of the circular path lies directly below the point B at a distance of 2 m.

Use $g = 9.8 \text{ m s}^{-2}$, giving your final answers to an appropriate degree of accuracy.

a Find the tension in the string.

b Find the angular speed of the particle.

a

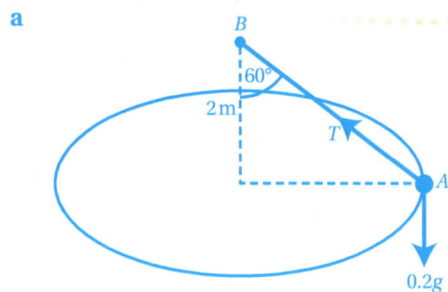

Draw a diagram.

The particle is not moving vertically.

Make sure that all units are consistent. In this case the mass should be in kilograms.

Resolving vertically:

$T \cos 60° - mg = 0$

Therefore $T = \dfrac{mg}{\cos 60°}$

$T = 0.2 \times 9.8 \div 0.5$

$= 3.9 \text{ N (2 s.f.)}$

Resolve the forces vertically and use Key point 4.3. Remember that g is the acceleration due to gravity.

b Resolving horizontally:

$T \sin 60° = ma$

So $3.92 \sin 60° = 0.2a$

Hence $a = 3.92 \times \sin 60° \div 0.2$

$= 17.0 \text{ m s}^{-2} \text{ (3 s.f.)}$

Resolve the forces horizontally in the direction of the acceleration and use Key point 4.3.

$r = 2 \tan 60°$

You can find the radius of the circular motion using trigonometry.

Use $a = r\omega^2$

So $\omega = \sqrt{\dfrac{a}{r}}$

Substituting the values for r and a:

$= \sqrt{\dfrac{17.0}{2 \tan 60°}}$

$= \sqrt{4.9} = 2.2 \text{ rad s}^{-1} \text{ (2 s.f.)}$

📷 **Focus on …**

You will learn more about a simple pendulum in Focus on … Modelling 2.

WORKED EXAMPLE 4.8

In this question use $g = 9.81 \text{ m s}^{-2}$, giving your final answers to an appropriate degree of accuracy.

A particle P of mass 0.8 kg is attached to two light rods AP and BP, as shown in the diagram, where A, B, P and C all lie in the same vertical plane. The lengths of AB, BC and CP are 0.25, 0.07 and 0.24 metres respectively.

The particle is moving in a horizontal circle with linear speed 3 m s⁻¹.

a Calculate the tension in the rod BP.

b Calculate the magnitude of the force in the rod AP and determine if the rod is in tension or compression.

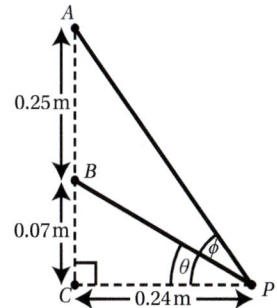

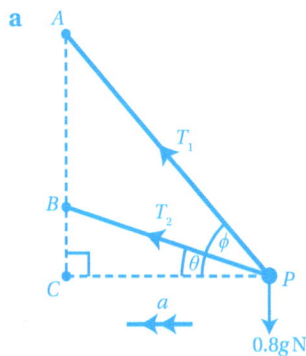

a

Draw a diagram, showing the forces acting on P.

Resolving the forces at P vertically:

$T_1 \sin \phi + T_2 \sin \theta = 0.8g$

$\qquad = 7.848$

Resolving the forces horizontally in the direction of the acceleration:

$T_1 \cos \phi + T_2 \cos_2 \theta = m \dfrac{v^2}{r}$

$\qquad = 30$

Find the trigonometric ratios for the angles in the question.

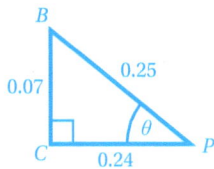

$\sin \theta = \dfrac{0.07}{0.25} = \dfrac{7}{25}$

$\cos \theta = \dfrac{0.24}{0.25} = \dfrac{24}{25}$

$\tan \theta = \dfrac{0.07}{0.24} = \dfrac{7}{24}$

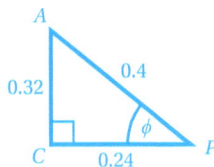

$\sin \phi = \dfrac{0.32}{0.4} = \dfrac{4}{5}$

$\cos \phi = \dfrac{0.24}{0.4} = \dfrac{3}{5}$

$\tan \phi = \dfrac{0.32}{0.24} = \dfrac{4}{3}$

Substituting the values and solving the simultaneous equations:

$\dfrac{4}{5} T_1 + \dfrac{7}{25} T_2 = 7.848$

$\dfrac{3}{5} T_1 + \dfrac{24}{25} T_2 = 30$

Continues on next page

$$60T_1 + 21T_2 = 588.6$$
$$60T_1 + 96T_2 = 3000$$

$$T_2 = 32.152 = 32.2 \, \text{N} \, (3 \, \text{s.f.})$$

Find the tension T_2 by eliminating T_1.

b Substituting the value for T_2 to find T_1:

$$60T_1 + 21T_2 = 588.6$$
$$60T_1 = 588.6 - 21 \times 32.152$$
$$T_1 = -1.4432$$
$$= -1.44 \, (3 \, \text{s.f.})$$

You can use the other equation to check your answers.

Magnitude of the force is 1.44 N.

The force is directed towards P. The rod is in compression.

The initial assumption was that T_1 was acting towards A. As the value of T_1 is negative, the direction must have been incorrect and the rod is in compression.

⏮ **Rewind**

Recall from A Level Mathematics Student Book 1, Chapter 19, that a rod can be under tension or compression.

WORKED EXAMPLE 4.9

In this question use $g = 9.81 \, \text{m s}^{-2}$, giving your final answers to an appropriate degree of accuracy.

The fixed points A, B and C are in a vertical line with A above B and B above C. A particle Q of mass 3 kg is joined to A, to B and to a particle P of mass 2 kg by three light rods where the length of rod AQ is 2 m and the length of rod QP is 1 m. Particle Q moves in a horizontal circle with centre B. Particle P moves in a horizontal circle with centre C at the same constant angular speed ω as Q, in such a way that A, B, P and Q are coplanar. The rod AQ makes an angle of $30°$ with the downward vertical, rod QP makes an angle of $45°$ with the downward vertical and rod BQ is horizontal.

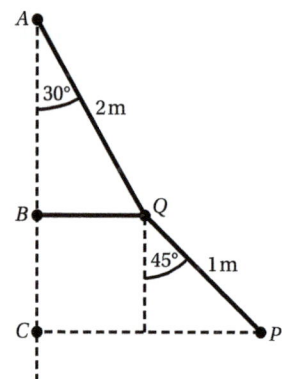

a Calculate the angular speed ω.
b Find the tension in the rod AQ.
c Find the force in the rod BQ and determine if the rod is in tension or compression.

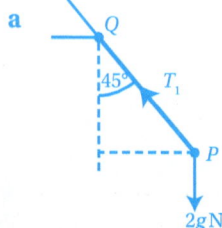

a

Draw a diagram showing the forces acting on P.

Continues on next page

$$F = ma$$

Resolving the forces horizontally in the direction of the acceleration:

$$T_1 \sin 45 = 2r\omega^2$$

You want an equation that involves the tension in the rod QP.

Resolving the forces vertically at P:

$$T_1 \cos 45 = 2g$$
$$T_1 = 27.7 \, \text{N} \, (3 \, \text{s.f.})$$

You want to find the tension in the rod QP.

$$r = |AQ|\sin 30° + |QP|\sin 45°$$
$$r = 2\sin 30° + 1\sin 45°$$
$$r = 2\sin 30° + \sin 45°$$

You need to find the radius of the circle motion for P. This will involve finding the horizontal distance CP, which is made up of two parts.

$$\omega = \sqrt{\frac{T_1 \sin 45°}{2r}}$$

$$= \sqrt{\frac{2g \sin 45°}{2(2\sin 30° + \sin 45°)\cos 45}}$$

$$\omega = 2.40 \, \text{rad s}^{-1} \, (3 \, \text{s.f.})$$

You can then substitute the expression for T_1 and the radius r of the circular motion into a rearranged equation to find ω.

b

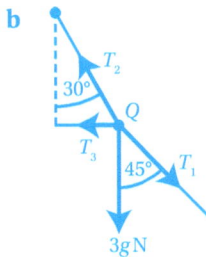

Draw a diagram first, showing the forces acting on Q.

Resolving the forces vertically at Q:

$$T_2 \cos 30° = 3g + T_1 \cos 45°$$
$$T_2 \cos 30° = 5g$$
$$T_2 = 56.6 \, \text{N} \, (3 \, \text{s.f.})$$

You want to find the tension in the rod AQ.

c Resolving the forces horizontally in the direction of the acceleration:

$$F = ma$$
$$T_3 + T_2 \sin 30° - T_1 \sin 45° = 3r\omega^2$$
$$T_3 = 3r\omega^2 + T_1 \sin 45° - T_2 \sin 30°$$

Use the values already found for ω, T_1 and T_2 to find the tension in BQ.

$$T_3 = 3(2\sin 30°)\omega^2 + T_1 \sin 45° - T_2 \sin 30°$$
$$T_3 = 8.54 \, \text{N} \, (3 \, \text{s.f.})$$

Find the radius of the circular motion for Q by finding the horizontal distance BQ.

The rod is in tension.

Since the value of the tension is positive, the rod is in tension.

EXERCISE 4C

In this exercise, unless otherwise instructed, use $g = 9.8$ m s^{-2}, giving your final answers to an appropriate degree of accuracy.

1 A particle of mass m kg is moving in a horizontal circle at a constant angular speed ω rad s^{-1} attached to a light inextensible string of length l metres that makes an angle of θ with the downward vertical.

  a **i** Given that $m = 2$ and $\theta = 20°$, find the tension in the string.

      ii Given that $m = 3.5$ and $\theta = 35°$, find the tension in the string.

  b **i** Given that $m = 2$, $\omega = 3$ and $l = 2$, find the tension in the string.

      ii Given that $m = 3.5$, $\omega = 3$ and $l = 1.5$, find the tension in the string.

  c **i** Given that $\theta = 30°$ and $l = 2.2$, find the value of ω.

      ii Given that $\theta = 60°$ and $l = 3.75$, find the value of ω.

  d **i** Given that $\omega = 3.25$ and $l = 1.2$, find the size of angle θ.

      ii Given that $\omega = 5.2$ and $l = 3.2$, find the size of angle θ.

2 These incomplete force diagrams show simple conical pendulums. Each consists of a light, inextensible string of length l m suspended from a point A and a bob of mass m kg at point B. The bob moves in a horizontal circle centred vertically below A and the string forms an angle θ with the downward vertical. B moves with a constant angular speed ω rad s^{-1} and the tension in the string AB is T N.

  a Find the value of θ.
            b Find the angular speed ω.

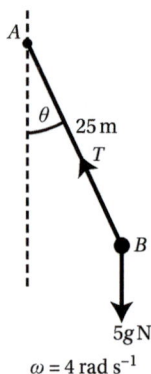

$\omega = 4$ rad s^{-1}

ω unknown

  c Find the tension in the string.
            d Find the mass of the bob.

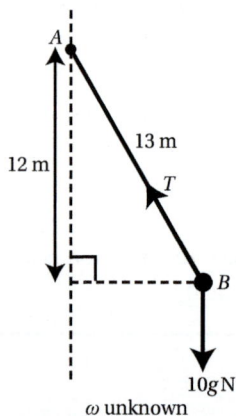

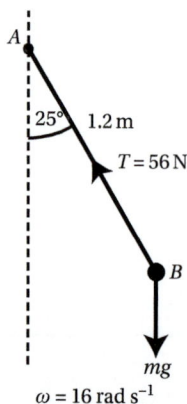

ω unknown

$\omega = 16$ rad s^{-1}

3 A smooth bead B of mass 500 grams is threaded onto a light inextensible string. The two ends of the string are attached to fixed points X and Y, where X is vertically below Y.

The string is taut and the bead rotates about the axis YX. The bead moves with a constant angular speed in a horizontal circular path of radius 0.8 m. Given that angle YXB is 60° and angle XYB is 30°, calculate:

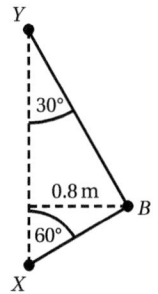

  a the tension in the string

  b the angular speed.

4 The fixed points A and B are in a vertical line, with A above B at a distance of 1.80 m. A particle P of mass m kg is attached to two light inextensible strings, so that AP is 1.44 m and BP is 1.08 m. The particle P rotates at a constant angular speed of ω rad s^{-1} with both strings BP and AP taut.

  a Find the tension in AP in terms of m, g and ω.

  b Find the tension in BP in terms of m, g and ω.

  c Calculate a lower bound for the angular speed ω, given that BP remains taut.

5 The fixed points A, B and C are in a vertical line with A above B and B above C. A particle Q of mass 3 kg is joined to A, to B and to a particle P of mass 2 kg, by three light rods where the length of rod AQ is 2 m and the length of rod QP is 1 m. Particle Q moves in a horizontal circle with centre B. Particle P moves in a horizontal circle with centre C at the same constant angular speed ω rad s^{-1} as Q, in such a way that A, B, P and Q are coplanar. The rod AQ makes an angle of 30° with the downward vertical, rod QP makes an angle of 30° with the downward vertical and rod BQ is horizontal (see diagram).

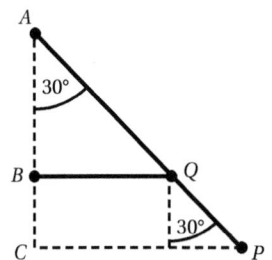

  a Calculate the angular speed ω.

  b Find the tension in the rod AQ.

  c Find the magnitude of the force in the rod BQ and state whether the rod is in tension or compression.

6 A hemispherical bowl of radius r is fixed with its rim horizontal. A bead B of mass m is moving in a horizontal circle around the smooth inside surface of the bowl. The centre of the circle is $\frac{3}{5}r$ below the centre of the bowl.

  a Find the magnitude of the reaction force between the bowl and the bead in terms of m and g.

  b Find the linear speed of the bead in terms of g and r.

7 The fixed points A and B, B under A, lie in the same vertical plane. A particle P of mass 3 kg is joined to the point A by a light rod of length 1.3 m and to the point B by a light rod that is horizontal. The particle P moves in a horizontal circle with centre B at a constant angular speed ω rad s^{-1}.

  a If the angle the rod AP makes with the downward vertical is 45 degrees, calculate the tension in the rod AP.

  b Given that the particle P moves in a horizontal circle at a constant angular speed ω rad s^{-1}, calculate a lower bound for ω which would mean that the rod BP is in tension.

  c If the angular speed of P is 2 rad s^{-1}, calculate the magnitude and direction of the force in the rod BP.

8   A conical pendulum consists of a light inextensible string AB of length 2 m. The string is fixed at the end A and a small ball of mass 3 kg is attached at the end B. The ball moves in a horizontal circle, with centre vertically below the point A, with constant linear speed 3 m s^{-1}. Find the tension in the string and the radius of the circle.

Checklist of learning and understanding

For a particle moving in a horizontal circular path of radius r m and at a constant angular speed ω rad s^{-1}:

- linear speed is given by $v = r\omega$
- acceleration is given by $v\omega$, $r\omega^2$ or $\dfrac{v^2}{r}$ and is directed towards the centre of the circular motion.

When solving problems in three dimensions for particles moving in a horizontal circular path you need to resolve the forces parallel and perpendicular to the plane containing the circular path. For the object to continue to move in a horizontal circle, the sum of the perpendicular forces must be zero. The resultant force towards the centre of the circle must equal $mr\omega^2$, where m is the mass of the particle, r is the radius of the circle and ω is the angular speed.

Mixed practice 4

In this exercise, unless otherwise instructed, use $g = 9.8 \text{ m s}^{-2}$, giving your final answers to an appropriate degree of accuracy.

1 A particle is travelling around a circular path of radius 30 cm at a constant linear speed of 3 m s^{-1}. Find its angular speed. Choose from these options.

    A 0.1 rad s^{-1} **B** 90 rad s^{-1} **C** 10 rad s^{-1} **D** 0.9 rad s^{-1}

2 A particle of mass 300 grams is travelling around a circular path of radius 340 mm and makes 20 full circles every minute. Calculate the force keeping the particle in circular motion, giving the answer correct to 3 significant figures. Choose from these options.

    A 0.447 N **B** 447 N **C** 0.0113 N **D** 0.214 N

A 3 A particle is moving in a horizontal circle at a constant angular speed 3.4 rad s^{-1} attached to a light inextensible string of length 2 metres. Find the angle that the string makes with the downward vertical to 3 significant figures. Choose from these options.

    A $77.8°$ **B** $23.0°$ **C** $25.1°$ **D** $64.9°$

4 A particle of mass 200 grams moves in a circle of radius 5 m with constant linear speed 8 m s^{-1}.

  a Find the angular speed of the particle.

  b Find the time it takes for one revolution.

  c Find the force acting on the particle to keep it in a circular orbit.

A 5 In this question use $g = 9.81 \text{ m s}^{-2}$, giving your final answers to an appropriate degree of accuracy. A particle of mass m kg moves with a constant linear speed of $v \text{ m s}^{-1}$ in a horizontal circle of radius r m on a rough table with coefficient of friction 0.6. The particle is on the point of moving away tangentially.

  a Draw a diagram to display the forces acting on the particle and the acceleration.

  b If the radius of the horizontal circle is 30 cm, find the linear speed.

6 A particle of mass 0.5 kg is attached to a light inextensible string of length 350 cm. The string is fixed on a smooth horizontal table and the ball moves in a circular path with constant angular speed 1.96 rad s^{-1}.

  a What is the acceleration of the ball?

  b What is the tension in the string?

7 A car of mass 1.2 tonnes moves at linear speed of 5.2 m s^{-1} around a circular path of radius 25 m. What is the frictional force required to keep the car travelling in this circular path?

8 A light rod AB, of length l, has one particle of mass m attached at A and a second particle of mass $3m$ attached at B. The rod is attached at the point C and is free to rotate in a horizontal circle with a constant angular speed about the point C. Given that the tensions in parts AC and CB of the rod are equal, show that the length AC is $\frac{3}{4}l$.

9 Two particles, P and Q, are connected by a light inextensible string which passes through a smooth hole in a smooth horizontal table. Particle P, of mass m kg, moves on the table, with constant angular speed in a circle of radius 0.25 m around the hole. Particle Q, of mass $4m$ kg, hangs vertically in equilibrium under the table, as shown in the diagram. Find the angular speed of P.

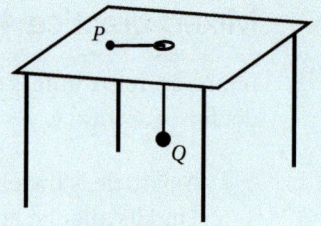

A 10 A small smooth ring R of mass m is threaded onto a light inextensible string of length $49L$. The two ends of the string are fixed at the points A and B, where B is vertically below A at a distance of $7L$. The ring is moving with constant linear speed in a horizontal circle with centre B and radius $24L$.

    a Find the tension in the string in terms of m and g.

    b Find the linear speed in terms of g and L.

    c How did you use the assumption that the ring was smooth?

A 11 A particle P of mass 200 g is travelling in the xy-plane. The particle's position vector is given by $\begin{pmatrix} 2\cos \pi t \\ 2\sin \pi t \end{pmatrix}$ m, where $0 < t < 2$ is the time in hours.

    a Show that the particle is moving in a circular orbit.

    b Find the linear speed of the particle.

    c Find the magnitude of the acceleration towards the centre of the circular motion.

    d Find the force directed towards the centre of the circular motion required to keep the particle P in a circular orbit.

A 12 A particle Q is travelling in the xy-plane. The particle's position vector is given by $\begin{pmatrix} 1+3\cos 2t \\ 2+3\sin 2t \end{pmatrix}$ m, where $0 < t < \pi$.

    a Show that the particle is moving in a circular orbit and hence find the centre and radius of the circular motion.

    b Find the linear speed of the particle.   **c** Find the acceleration vector for the particle.

A 13 In this question use $g = 10$ m s^{-2}, giving your final answers to an appropriate degree of accuracy. A car of mass m kg moves around a bend which is banked at a constant angle of 22 degrees to the horizontal. The car is modelled as a particle moving in a horizontal circle of radius 10 m at a constant angular speed. Calculate the linear speed of the car in km h^{-1} given that:

    a there is no sideways frictional force on the car

    b the coefficient of friction between the tyres and the surface is 0.25 and it is on the point of:

        i slipping down the slope   **ii** slipping up the slope.

A 14 A circular cone is fixed so that the apex A of the cone is sitting on a horizontal surface and the perpendicular height for the cone is perpendicular to the horizontal surface. The angle the cone makes with the horizontal surface is θ. A particle P of mass m kg moves on the inner surface of the cone. The particle is joined to A by a light inextensible string AP, of length l. The particle moves in a horizontal circle with constant linear speed v and the sting is taut. If the inside of the cone is smooth:

    a show that the reaction force can be written in the form $mg\cos\theta + mv^2 l^{-1}\tan\theta$

    b find the tension in the string, in terms of m, l, v, g and $\sin\theta$

    c show that the motion of the particle is only possible when $v^2 > gl\sin\theta$.

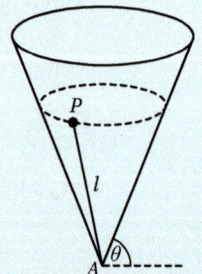

A 15 A particle of mass m is suspended from a fixed point A by a light inextensible string. The point A is at a height $4L$ above a smooth horizontal table and the particle moves on the table in a horizontal circle of radius $3L$ with constant linear speed $\sqrt{2gL}$.

  a Find the reaction force between the particle and the table.

  The modelling assumption that the table was smooth was not correct. The coefficient of friction for the table top is 0.4.

  b If the particle is on the point of slipping towards the centre of motion, does this affect the reaction force calculated in part **a**? Use calculations to support your answer.

  c Calculate the new tension in the string.

A 16 A particle P of mass 2.2 kg is travelling in the xy-plane. The particle's position vector is given by

$$\begin{pmatrix} 6\cos \pi t - 1 \\ 3 + 6\sin \pi t \end{pmatrix} \text{ m, where } 0 < t < 2.$$

  a Show that the particle is moving in a circular orbit and hence find the centre and radius of the circular motion.

  b Find the velocity and acceleration vectors for the particle P.

  c Show that the velocity and acceleration vectors are perpendicular.

A 17 A particle X is travelling in the xy-plane in a circular orbit centre $(-2, 1)$. The velocity vector for X is given by $\begin{pmatrix} -2\pi \cos \pi t \\ 2\pi \sin \pi t \end{pmatrix}$ m s^{-1}, where t is the time in seconds. Find the position vector for the particle X and describe the direction of movement of the particle X.

18 A parcel is placed on a flat rough horizontal surface in a van. The van is travelling along a horizontal road. It travels around a bend of radius 34 m at a constant speed. The coefficient of friction between the parcel and the horizontal surface in the van is 0.85.

Model the parcel as a particle travelling around part of a circle of radius 34 m and centre O, as shown in the diagram.

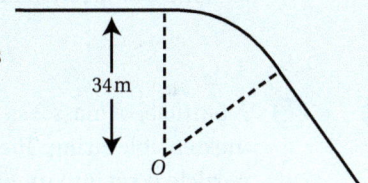

Find the greatest speed at which the van can travel around the bend without causing the parcel to slide.

[© AQA 2012]

19 In this question use $g = 9.81$ m s^{-2}, giving your final answers to an appropriate degree of accuracy.
Two particles, A and B, are connected by a light inextensible string which passes through a hole in a smooth horizontal table. The edges of the hole are also smooth.
Particle A, of mass 1.4 kg, moves on the table, with constant speed in a circle of radius 0.3 m around the hole. Particle B, of mass 2.1 kg, hangs in equilibrium under the table, as shown in the diagram.

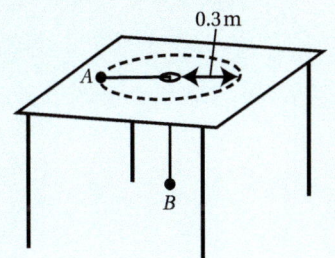

  a Find the angular speed of particle A.

  b Find the speed of particle A.

  c Find the time taken for particle A to complete one full circle around the hole.

[© AQA 2012]

20 A particle, of mass 8 kg, is attached to one end of a length of elastic string. The particle is placed on a smooth horizontal surface. The other end of the elastic string is attached to a point O fixed on a horizontal surface.

The elastic string has natural length 1.2 m and modulus of elasticity 192 N.

The particle is set in motion on the horizontal surface so that it moves in a circle, centre O, with constant speed 3 m s^{-1}.

Find the radius of the circle.

▶▶ **Fast forward**

Question 20 requires topics covered in Chapter 5.

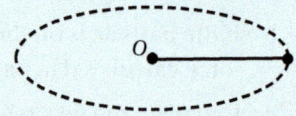

[© AQA 2010]

21 Two light inextensible strings each have one end attached to a particle, P, of mass 6 kg. The other ends of the strings are attached to the fixed points B and C. The point C is vertically above the point B. The particle moves, at constant speed, in a horizontal circle, with centre 0.6 m below point B, with the strings inclined at 40° and 60° to the vertical, as shown in the diagram. Both strings are taut.

a As the particle moves in the horizontal circle, the tensions in the two strings are equal.

Show that the tension in the strings is 46.4 N, correct to three significant figures.

b Find the speed of the particle.

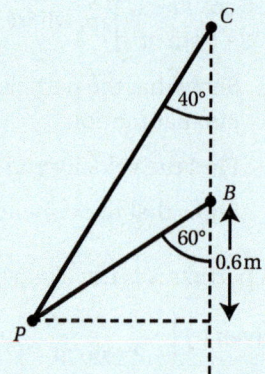

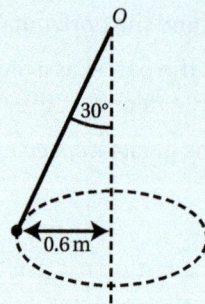

[© AQA 2009]

22 A particle, of mass 2 kg, is attached to one end of a light inextensible string. The other end is fixed to the point O. The particle is set into motion, so that it describes a horizontal circle of radius 0.6 metres, with the string at an angle of 30° to the vertical. The centre of the circle is vertically below O.

a Show that the tension in the string is 22.6 N, correct to three significant figures.

b Find the speed of the particle.

[© AQA 2006]

5 Work, energy and power 2

In this chapter you will learn how to:

- calculate the work done by a variable force f(x) when displacement is along the x-axis
- understand and use Hooke's law for elastic strings and springs
- calculate the work done extending an elastic string and the work done extending or compressing an elastic spring
- include elastic potential energy in problems involving conservation of energy.

A If you are following the A Level course, you will also learn how to:

- calculate the work done by a force acting at an angle to the movement.

Before you start…

Chapter 1	You should know that work done is the product of force and displacement and that it is measured in joules.	1	Calculate the work done by gravity when a stone of mass 2 kg falls vertically 10 m.
Chapter 1	You should know that kinetic energy is defined as $\frac{1}{2}mv^2$ and that it is measured in joules.	2	Calculate the change in kinetic energy when a boy of mass 72 kg increases his running speed from 4.2 m s^{-1} to 6.0 m s^{-1}.
Chapter 1	You should know that a force acting on an object causes a change in its kinetic energy. This is the work–energy principle.	3	Find the horizontal resistive force that causes an ice hockey puck of mass 150 g to reduce speed from 2.1 m s^{-1} to 0.65 m s^{-1} over 25 m.
A Level Mathematics Student Book 1, Chapter 14 and Student Book 2, Chapter 11	You should be able to integrate a function between limits x_1 and x_2 to find a quantity, $\int_{x_1}^{x_2} f(x)\,dx$.	4	Find $\int_0^{\pi} \sin x\,dx$.

Extending your knowledge of work and energy

You are now going to learn new ways to apply concepts of work, energy and power.

First, forces can vary. The weight of a body is approximately constant close to the Earth's surface and the change in gravitational potential energy caused by a change in height above a fixed point can be accurately modelled as the work done by or against constant weight. In this chapter, you will learn how to work with forces that vary with distance. A particularly important example is the force in an elastic spring or string, which increases with extension (Hooke's law). As a spring is extended, you do work against an increasing tension. The work is stored as elastic potential energy.

Second, forces can act obliquely to the direction of movement. If a force is applied in the direction of movement (or directly against it) then work done

⏮ **Rewind**

You learned about the work done by a constant force in the direction of movement and the work–energy principle in Chapter 1. You also learned about conservation of mechanical energy. These ideas are crucial to understanding how energy is converted to useful work.

is the product of force and distance moved. If a force acts at an angle to the direction of movement you need to adapt this definition. Effectively, you get less than the full value of the force because of its oblique direction. You will learn how to deal with this situation as you work through this chapter.

Section 1: Work done by a variable force f(x)

You know that for a constant driving force acting in the direction of motion:

$$\text{work done} = \text{force} \times \text{distance moved}$$

If the force is always parallel to the motion but the magnitude of the force is changing you need to use integration to find the work done.

> **ℹ Did you know?**
>
> Springs have many practical uses. In mountain bikes springs called shock absorbers are used to absorb any unevenness in the road surface. When your bike hits a bump, the spring compresses. The compression absorbs some of the energy that would otherwise pass straight through to the rider. There is elastic potential energy in the spring. If you hit a bump too hard you can break your shock absorber – you have gone beyond its elastic limit.

> **🔑 Key point 5.1**
>
> If an object is moved in a straight line from a position x_1 to a position x_2 by the action of a variable force $f(x)$ that depends on displacement, x, work done is defined as:
>
> $$\text{work done} = \int_{x_1}^{x_2} f(x)\,dx$$

WORKED EXAMPLE 5.1

Find the work done by a force of $(8.0x + 15)$ newtons that displaces an object from $x = 2.0$ metres to $x = 5.0$ metres.

$$\text{Work done} = \int_{2}^{5} (8x + 15)\,dx$$

$$\text{Work done} = \int_{x_1}^{x_2} f(x)\,dx$$

Let $x_1 = 2$ and $x_2 = 5$.

$$= \left[4x^2 + 15x \right]_{2}^{5}$$

Integrate and substitute the limits of integration.

$$= (4 \times 5^2 + 15 \times 5) - (4 \times 2^2 + 15 \times 2)$$

$$= 175 - 46$$

$$= 129 \text{ joules}$$

WORKED EXAMPLE 5.2

A car of mass 1020 kg moves from rest at a point A on a horizontal surface. The driving force is constant at 1800 N and resistance to motion is modelled as $\dfrac{x^2}{8}$ N. The car moves 120 m to point B.

a   Find the work done by the driving force and the work done against resistance as the car travels from A to B.

b   Find the speed of the car at B.

Continues on next page

a The work done by the driving force $= 1800 \times 120$

$= 216\,000$ J

As the driving force is constant, you can use the definition of the work done by a constant force.

The work done against resistance $= \int_0^{120} \dfrac{x^2}{8}\,\mathrm{d}x$

Use integration to find the work done against the variable resistive force.

$= \left[\dfrac{x^3}{24}\right]_0^{120}$

Let $x_1 = 0$ and $x_2 = 120$.

$= \dfrac{120^3}{24}$

Integrate and substitute the limits of integration.

$= 72\,000$ J

b Work done by driving force – work done against resistance = increase in kinetic energy

Use the work–energy principle.

$216\,000 - 72\,000 = \dfrac{1}{2} \times 1020 \times v^2$

Car moves from rest $\Rightarrow u = 0$.

$\therefore v^2 = \dfrac{144\,000 \times 2}{1020}$

Rearrange to find the car's final speed.

$v = 16.8\,\mathrm{m\,s^{-1}}$

WORKED EXAMPLE 5.3

An object is moving in a horizontal straight line against a resistive force that is directly proportional to its distance from its starting point, $f(x) = kx$. The work done against resistance as the object travels from the origin, $x = 0$ m, to a point 15 m away, $x = 15$ m, is 337.5 kJ. Find:

a the magnitude of k **b** the units of k.

a Work done $= \displaystyle\int_{x_1}^{x_2} f(x)\,\mathrm{d}x$

Use the definition of work done by a force that depends on displacement.

Work done $= \displaystyle\int_0^{15} kx\,\mathrm{d}x$

Integrate between the given limits to find an expression for work done in terms of k.

$= \left[\dfrac{kx^2}{2}\right]_0^{15}$

Use the given value for work done to calculate k.

$= \dfrac{225k}{2}$

But work done $= 337\,500$ J

Resistive force is given as kx. Consider dimensions, given that all measurements are in standard units.

$\therefore \dfrac{225k}{2} = 337\,500$

So $k = 3000$

b Since f is a force (units N), k must have units $\mathrm{N\,m^{-1}}$.

1 Calculate the work done by a force $f(x)$ newtons moving an object along the x-axis from x_1 metres to x_2 metres. Use the formula

$$\text{work done} = \int_{x_1}^{x_2} f(x)\,dx.$$

	$f(x)$	x_1	x_2
a	$2\sqrt{x}$	5	7.5
b	$5\cos x$	0	$\dfrac{\pi}{2}$
c	$10\sin^2 x$	π	2π
d	$200 - 10x$	5	10

2 The work done by a force kx^2 N moving an object from $x = 1.0$ m to $x = 2.0$ m is 210 J. Find the value of k.

3 The work done by a force $\dfrac{1}{2x}$ N moving an object from $x = 4$ m to $x = a$ m is ln 4 J. Find an exact value for a.

4 A vehicle of mass 850 kg moves along a horizontal road with driving force 500 N. It starts from rest at $x = 0$ m and experiences a resistance to motion of $2x$ N. Find the speed of the vehicle when it reaches $x = 100$ m.

5 A particle of mass 3.5 kg moves along a horizontal axis with driving force 50 N. The particle starts from rest at $x = 0$ m and experiences a resistance to motion of $\sqrt{x}$ N. Find the speed of the particle when it reaches $x = 256$ m.

6 A truck of mass 30 tonnes, travelling along a horizontal road, experiences a resistance to motion of $2500x$ N. The truck is travelling at 45 km h^{-1} when the driver applies the brakes with a constant braking force of 10 000 N. Find how far the truck travels, after the brakes are applied, before coming to rest.

7 A vehicle of mass 960 kg starts from rest at $x = 0$ m and moves in a straight line parallel to the x-axis. There is a driving force of $5 + 2x^2$ N and a resistive force of $8x$ N. Derive an expression to represent work done after the vehicle has travelled X m. Use a numerical method to find the value of X when the vehicle is travelling at 25 m s^{-1}.

Section 2: Hooke's law, work done against elasticity and elastic potential energy

Robert Hooke was an English experimental scientist, born in 1635. He found that the extension caused when stretching an **elastic string** obeyed a simple rule. The same rule applied to compression of an **elastic spring**. The rule is known as Hooke's Law. Hooke measured the force required and found that, providing the object was not deformed past its **elastic limit**:

- when stretching: force $\propto$ extension
- when compressing: force $\propto$ compression

Elastic **strings** may be extended but not compressed. Elastic **springs** may be extended and compressed. Extension or compression must occur within the elastic limit of the string or spring.

As you stretch or compress an elastic object, you do work against elasticity and this work is stored as **elastic potential energy**.

Rewind

In Chapter 1 you learned that when gravity is the only force acting on a object:

total mechanical energy = kinetic energy + gravitational potential energy

Fast forward

You will learn more about elastic potential energy later in this chapter.

Total mechanical energy = kinetic energy (KE) + gravitational potential energy (GPE) + elastic potential energy (EPE)

You can use this extended definition of mechanical energy to solve problems about the motion of objects attached to elastic strings or springs.

Hooke's law for elastic strings and springs

When an elastic string or spring is extended from its natural length, there is a force in the string or spring that acts in the opposite direction to the extending force.

When an elastic spring is compressed from its natural length, there is a **thrust** in the spring that acts in the opposite direction to the compressing force.

In each case, the tension or thrust acts in the direction that would restore the string or spring to its natural length.

You can relate the extension or compression of an elastic spring to the tension or thrust in the spring by the proportionality equation:

$$T = kx$$

In this equation T represents tension or thrust, x is the extension or compression of the spring and k is its **stiffness**. The same proportionality equation applies to extension of an elastic string.

An alternative approach is to use a **modulus of elasticity**, λ. In the proportionality equation k is replaced by $\frac{\lambda}{l}$, where l is the natural length of the spring or string. The modulus of elasticity, λ, is the force required to double the length of an elastic string or spring.

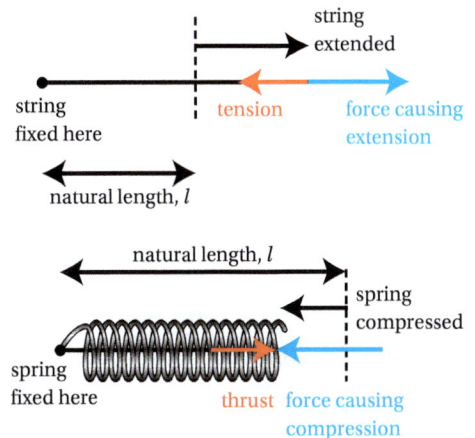

string extended

string fixed here   tension   force causing extension

natural length, l

natural length, l

spring compressed

spring fixed here   thrust   force causing compression

> ### ⏪ Rewind
>
> You have already encountered the modulus of elasticity in Chapter 2.

🔑 Key point 5.2

Hooke's law for an elastic string or spring is:

$$T = kx \text{ or } T = \frac{\lambda x}{l}$$

Stiffness, k, has units newtons per metre (N m^{-1}) and the modulus of elasticity, λ, is measured in newtons (N).

- A low value for k or λ means that the string or spring is quite flexible and easy to extend or compress.
- A high value for k or λ means the string or spring is quite stiff and difficult to extend or compress.

An important assumption is that the elastic string or spring is **light**, that is, its mass can be ignored. If the string were not light then the tension or thrust in the string or spring could vary along its length.

WORKED EXAMPLE 5.4

A light elastic spring, which has modulus of elasticity 85 N and natural length 1.8 m, has one end attached at a fixed point, A. A horizontal force, of magnitude 40 N, is applied to the spring, causing a compression. The spring rests in equilibrium. Find the distance by which the spring is compressed from its natural length.

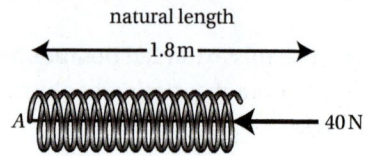

natural length
$\xleftarrow{\hspace{1cm}}$ 1.8 m $\xrightarrow{\hspace{1cm}}$

A ⟵ 40 N

$T - 40 = 0$	Since the spring is in equilibrium there is zero resultant force.
$\Rightarrow T = 40$	
$x = \dfrac{Tl}{\lambda}$	Rearrange the formula for Hooke's law to make extension the subject.
$x = \dfrac{40 \times 1.8}{85}\,\text{m} \Rightarrow x = 0.847\,\text{m}$	The compression of the spring is less than its natural length. This is a simple check of validity.
The compression of the spring is 0.847 m.	

WORKED EXAMPLE 5.5

A light elastic string is attached to a fixed point and hangs vertically, in equilibrium, with an object of mass 400 grams attached to its lower end. The string has natural length 0.8 m and the object is resting 1.3 m below the point of suspension. Find the stiffness of the string as a multiple of g, the acceleration due to gravity. Hence find the modulus of elasticity of the string.

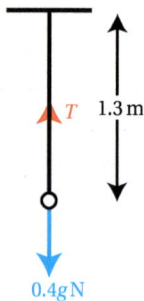

(diagram: T upward, 1.3 m, $0.4g$ N downward)	Draw a diagram showing the forces acting on the particle.
400 grams = 0.4 kg	Convert grams to kilograms.
$T - 0.4g = 0 \Rightarrow T = 0.4g$	Since the string is in equilibrium there is zero resultant force.
$T = kx \Rightarrow k = \dfrac{T}{x}$	Rearrange the formula for Hooke's law to make k the subject. x is the difference between the stretched and unstreched lengths of the string.
$k = \dfrac{0.4\,g}{0.5} \Rightarrow k = 0.8\,g\,\text{N m}^{-1}$	Leave your answer for k as a multiple of g, the acceleration due to gravity, as required.
$k = \dfrac{\lambda}{l} \Rightarrow \lambda = kl$	Convert from 'stiffness' to modulus of elasticity.
$\lambda = 0.8g \times 0.8\,\text{N}$	
$\Rightarrow \lambda = 0.64g\,\text{N}$	

WORKED EXAMPLE 5.6

An object of mass 1.5 kg is attached to the end of a light elastic string of length 1.5 m. The other end of the string is fixed to point A. The object is then held at A and released. The modulus of elasticity of the string is 50 N. Find the extension of the string when the object reaches its maximum speed, and hence its distance below A at this time.

Using $F = ma$ $1.5g = 1.5a$	To start with the object falls under gravity for 1.5 m. $T = 0$ when the object is falling freely under gravity.
$1.5g - T = 1.5a$	As the string extends beyond its natural length the increasing tension in the string reduces the acceleration.
When $a = 0$: $1.5g = T$	Speed reaches its maximum value when $a = 0$.
$1.5g = \frac{\lambda x}{l} \Rightarrow 1.5g = \frac{50x}{1.5}$	Use Hooke's law to find T.
$x = \frac{2.25g}{50}$ $\quad = 0.44\,\text{m}$	Rearrange to find the extension.
So the object is 1.94 m below A when it reaches maximum velocity.	Find the total distance fallen.

WORKED EXAMPLE 5.7

An object P of mass 10 kg is attached to the lower ends of two parallel light elastic strings. One string is of natural length 0.50 metres with modulus of elasticity 25 N. The other string is of natural length 0.4 metres with modulus of elasticity 30 N. The free ends of the strings are attached to a point A and P hangs in equilibrium vertically below A. Find the distance AP.

Let the tensions in the strings be T_1 and T_2. $T_1 + T_2 - 10g = 0$	The mass hangs in equilibrium so there is zero resultant force on P.
Let distance AP be D metres. $T_1 = \frac{25(D - 0.5)}{0.5}$ and $T_2 = \frac{30(D - 0.4)}{0.4}$	Use $\frac{\lambda x}{l}$ for the tensions in the strings. Extension $= D - l$ in each case.
$50(D - 0.5) + 75(D - 0.4) = 10g$	Substitute your expressions for tension.
$125D = 55 + 10g \Rightarrow D = 1.2\,\text{metres}$	Rearrange to find the value of D.

Work done extending an elastic string

The force required to extend an elastic string or spring varies with the extension of the string. This means that you cannot find the work done simply by multiplying force and distance. You need to integrate to find the work done against a variable force.

🔑 Key point 5.3

Work done extending an elastic string is given by:

$$\frac{k}{2}(x_2^2 - x_1^2) \text{ or } \frac{\lambda}{2l}(x_2^2 - x_1^2)$$

You can use the same method to calculate the work done in compressing an elastic spring from compression x_1 to compression x_2.

PROOF 1

An elastic string has modulus of elasticity λ and natural length l. Prove that the work done extending from extension x_1 to extension x_2 is $\frac{\lambda}{2l}(x_2^2 - x_1^2)$.

$\text{Work done} = \displaystyle\int_{x_1}^{x_2} T \, \mathrm{d}x$	The string is extended from x_1 to x_2. Integrate your expression for T from x_1 to x_2.
$\phantom{\text{Work done}} = \displaystyle\int_{x_1}^{x_2} \frac{\lambda x}{l} \, \mathrm{d}x$	
$\text{Work done} = \dfrac{\lambda}{l} \left[\dfrac{x^2}{2} \right]_{x_1}^{x_2}$	Take the constants out of the integration.
$\text{Work done} = \dfrac{\lambda}{2l}(x_2^2 - x_1^2)$	Substitute the limits.

You can also write the formula in terms of stiffness, k, as shown in Key point 5.3.

WORKED EXAMPLE 5.8

Find the work done when a light elastic string of natural length 1.2 m and modulus of elasticity 80 N is stretched from a length of 1.5 m to 1.8 m.

$x_1 = 0.3 \text{ m and } x_2 = 0.6 \text{ m}$	Work out the starting and ending extensions.
$\text{Work done} = \dfrac{\lambda}{2l}(x_2^2 - x_1^2)$	Use the formula for work done against elasticity.
$\text{Work done} = \dfrac{80}{2 \times 1.2}(0.6^2 - 0.3^2)$	Substitute in the values.
$\phantom{\text{Work done}} = 9.0 \text{ J}$	

⚠ Common error

When calculating the work done against elasticity, make sure you take the difference of the squares of the extensions, not the square of the difference!

$$x_2^2 - x_1^2 \neq (x_2 - x_1)^2$$

Elastic potential energy

The work done extending a light elastic string or spring is stored as **elastic potential energy**. When the string or spring is released, it contracts towards its natural length and elastic potential energy is converted to kinetic energy.

Similarly, the work done compressing a spring is stored as elastic potential energy. When the spring is released it expands towards its natural length, converting elastic potential energy to kinetic energy.

Rewind

In Chapter 1 you learned that work done against gravity is stored as gravitational potential energy and that when the only force acting on an object is its weight, the sum of kinetic and gravitational potential energy is conserved.

Key point 5.4

Elastic potential energy (EPE) is the energy stored in a string or spring extended by x, or a spring compressed by x:

$$\text{EPE is } \frac{kx^2}{2} \text{ or, alternatively, } \frac{\lambda x^2}{2l}$$

Key point 5.5

Using the principle of conservation of energy, when an object is acted on only by its weight and the force in an elastic string or spring:

$$\text{GPE} + \text{EPE} + \text{KE} = \text{constant}$$

where GPE is gravitational potential energy, EPE is elastic potential energy and KE is kinetic energy.

WORKED EXAMPLE 5.9

A light elastic spring with natural length 15 cm rests on a smooth horizontal table. One end is attached to a fixed point, A, and a 250 gram mass is attached at the other end, B, held 10 cm from A. The modulus of elasticity of the spring is 600 N.

a Find the elastic potential energy in the spring.

The spring is released and B moves horizontally away from A.

b Find how fast the mass is travelling when the spring reaches its natural length.

a $\text{EPE} = \dfrac{\lambda x^2}{2l}$

$\lambda = 600\,\text{N}$

$x = 0.15 - 0.10$ .... Convert centimetres to metres.

$\quad = 0.05\,\text{m}$

$l = 0.15\,\text{m}$

$\text{EPE} = \dfrac{600 \times 0.05^2}{2 \times 0.15}$

$\quad = 5\,\text{J}$

b $\text{EPE}_1 + \text{KE}_1 = \text{EPE}_2 + \text{KE}_2$ .... When the spring reaches its natural length, all its EPE has been converted to KE.

$\text{KE}_1 = 0$ and $\text{EPE}_2 = 0$.

$5 = \dfrac{1}{2} \times 0.25 \times v^2$

$v^2 = 40$

$v = 6.3\,\text{m}\,\text{s}^{-1}$

WORKED EXAMPLE 5.10

One end of a light elastic string, of natural length 0.80 m and modulus of elasticity 50 N, is attached to a fixed point O. A particle P, of mass 1.5 kg, is attached to the other end of the string. P is released from rest at O and falls vertically. Assuming there is no air resistance, find:

a the extension of the string when P is at its lowest position

b the acceleration of P at its lowest position.

a $mgh = \text{final EPE}$

Use the principle of conservation of energy:

$$GPE_1 + EPE_1 + KE_1 = GPE_2 + EPE_2 + KE_2$$

Let the lowest point be the zero level for GPE.

$$GPE_2 = 0$$

$GPE_1 = mgh$, where h is the height fallen.

P is stationary at O and at its lowest position.

$$KE_1 = KE_2 = 0$$

At O the string is not extended.

$$EPE_1 = 0$$

$mg(l+x) = \dfrac{\lambda x^2}{2l}$

Take x to represent extension, as usual.

Substituting in the given values and rearranging:

$1.5g(0.8+x) = \dfrac{50x^2}{2 \times 0.8}$

$\Rightarrow 11.76 + 14.7x = 31.25x^2$

$\Rightarrow 31.25x^2 - 14.7x - 11.76 = 0$

Solving for x:

$x = 0.89$ metres

Take the positive solution for x. This is the maximum extension of the string.

b $T - mg = ma$

At the maximum extension of the string, take upwards as positive, and use $F = ma$.

The acceleration will be greatest when the mass is at the lowest point.

$\dfrac{\lambda x}{l} - mg = ma$

Use Hooke's law, $T = \dfrac{\lambda x}{l}$ for the tension.

When $x = 0.8922$:

Use the value for the maximum extension found in part **a**.

$\dfrac{50 \times 0.8922}{0.8} - 1.5g = 1.5a$

$a = \dfrac{50 \times 0.8922}{0.8 \times 1.5} - g$

$a = 27\,\text{m s}^{-2}$

WORKED EXAMPLE 5.11

A light elastic spring, of natural length 20 cm, has one end fixed to a horizontal surface with the other end vertically above it. A sphere of mass 0.80 kg rests on the top of the spring, which is in equilibrium, 12 cm above the surface.

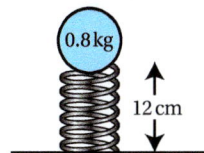

a Show that modulus of elasticity of the spring is $2g$ N.

The spring is compressed a further 3.0 cm.

b Find the maximum speed of the sphere in the subsequent vertical motion.

a $T - mg = 0$

> The sphere rests in equilibrium so the resultant force is zero.

$\dfrac{\lambda x}{l} - mg = 0$

> Use Hooke's law, $T = \dfrac{\lambda x}{l}$.

$\dfrac{\lambda \times 0.08}{0.2} = 0.8g$

> Compression = 8 cm = 0.08 metres.

$\lambda = 2g$ N, as required

b $KE + GPE + EPE = constant$

> Use the principle of conservation of mechanical energy for the upward movement.

Let x be the final compression of the spring:
$mgh = 0.8g(0.11 - x)$

> Let the GPE at the start of the upward movement be zero $\Rightarrow GPE_1 = 0$.
>
> $GPE_2 = mgh$, where h is the distance moved.
>
> $h =$ starting compression $-$ final compression

$\dfrac{2g \times 0.11^2}{2 \times 0.2} = \dfrac{1}{2} \times 0.8v^2 + 8.8g(0.11 - x) + \dfrac{2g \times x^2}{2 \times 0.2}$

> $EPE_1 = KE_2 + GPE_2 + EPE_2$

$0.4v^2 + 0.8624 - 7.84x + 49x^2 = 0.5929$

> Simplify, substituting $g = 9.8$.

$v^2 = -122.5(x^2 - 0.16x) - 0.67375$

> Rearrange to express v^2 in terms of a quadratic in x.

$v^2 = 0.110 - (x - 0.08)^2$

> Complete the square to find the stationary point for v^2.

Maximum speed ≈ 0.33 m s^{-1} when $x = 8$ cm.

> The maximum speed arises at the equilibrium compression of the spring.

📷 **Focus on …**

You will use alternative methods of finding the maximum speed in Focus on … Problem solving 2.

WORK IT OUT 5.1

A light elastic string has one end attached to a fixed point O and the free end is attached to a particle P of mass m kg. Particle P is released from rest at O and falls a distance $(l + x)$ metres, where l metres is the natural length of the string and x is its extension. David wants to work out an expression for P's kinetic energy. Which of these energy equations should he use?

Solution 1	Solution 2	Solution 3
$\frac{1}{2}mv^2 = mg(l+x) + \frac{\lambda x^2}{2l}$	$mg(l+x) = \frac{1}{2}mv^2 + \frac{\lambda x^2}{2l}$	$\frac{1}{2}mv^2 = mg(l+x) = \frac{\lambda x^2}{2l}$

EXERCISE 5B

In this exercise, unless otherwise instructed, use $g = 9.8\ \text{m s}^{-2}$, giving your final answers to an appropriate degree of accuracy.

1. Calculate the tension in a light elastic string when it is extended from a natural length of 0.8 m by 0.25 m. The modulus of elasticity is 85 N.

2. Calculate the thrust in a light elastic spring that is compressed from its natural length of 0.35 m to 0.25 m. The modulus of elasticity is 150 N.

3. A light elastic string of natural length 60 cm is extended by 15 cm. The tension in the string is 55 N. Find the stiffness and hence the modulus of elasticity.

4. A light elastic spring is compressed from its natural length of 40 cm. The thrust in the spring is 45 N and the modulus of elasticity is 145 N. Find the compression of the spring.

5. A light elastic string is attached to a fixed point and hangs vertically, in equilibrium, with an object of mass 1.5 kg attached to its lower end. The string has natural length 0.85 m and the modulus of elasticity is 120 N. Find the extension of the string.

6. A light elastic string is attached to a fixed point and hangs vertically, in equilibrium, with an object of mass 1250 grams attached to its lower end. The string has natural length 1.1 m and the object is resting 1.5 m below the point of suspension. Find the stiffness and hence the modulus of elasticity of the string.

7. A light elastic spring of natural length 0.75 m has one end attached to a fixed point on a smooth horizontal surface. A horizontal force is applied to the other end of the spring, causing a compression of 20 cm. The modulus of elasticity of the spring is 125 N. Find the magnitude of the force causing the compression.

8. A light elastic spring of natural length 85 cm has one end attached to a fixed point on a smooth horizontal surface. The spring is extended by a horizontal force of magnitude 105 N. The modulus of elasticity is 200 N. Find the extension of the spring.

9. Find the elastic potential energy stored in a light elastic spring of natural length 1.2 m and modulus of elasticity 250 N when it is compressed to a length of 1.02 m.

10. Find the increase of elastic potential energy when a light elastic string of natural length 1.8 m and modulus of elasticity 125 N is extended from 2.05 m to 2.8 m.

11 A light elastic string of natural length 1.4 m is extended from 1.5 m to 1.75 m. The work done against elasticity extending the string is 21 J. Find the modulus of elasticity of the string.

12 A light elastic spring with modulus of elasticity 360 N and natural length 1.2 m is compressed from its natural length. The elastic potential energy stored within the spring is 65 J. Find the length of the compressed spring.

13 An object P of mass 1.2 kg is attached to one end of a light elastic string of natural length 1.25 m with its other end attached to a fixed point, O. The modulus of elasticity of the string is 65 N. P is dropped from O. Find the extension of the string when the object reaches its maximum velocity.

14 One end of a light elastic string of natural length 95 cm and modulus of elasticity 75 N is attached to a fixed point O. A particle P, of mass 1.75 kg, is attached to the other end of the string. P is released from rest at O and falls vertically. Assuming there is no air resistance, find:

   a   the extension of the string when P is at its lowest position

   b   the acceleration of P at its lowest position, stating its direction.

15 A particle of mass 1.6 kg is attached to the free end of an elastic string of natural length 1.5 m. The other end is attached to a fixed point, O. The particle is held 1.8 m below O and released. Given the modulus of elasticity of the string is 158 N, find how far the particle is from O when it comes to instantaneous rest.

16 An object Q, of mass 8.0 kg, is attached to the lower ends of two parallel light elastic strings. One string is of natural length 0.40 metres with modulus of elasticity 35 N. The other string is of natural length 0.60 metres with modulus of elasticity 42 N. The free ends of the strings are attached to a point O and Q hangs in equilibrium vertically below O. Find the distance OQ.

17 A light elastic spring with natural length 18 cm rests on a smooth horizontal table. One end is attached to a fixed point A and a 280 gram mass is attached at the other end B, held 12 cm from A. The modulus of elasticity of the spring is 550 N.

   a   Find the elastic potential energy in the spring.

   The spring is released and B moves horizontally away from A.

   b   Find how fast the mass is travelling when it is 16 cm from A.

18 A light elastic string has natural length l, modulus of elasticity λ and extension x. Show that the work done extending from $(l + x_1)$ to $(l + x_2)$ can be expressed as the change in string tension multiplied by the mean extension of the string.

Section 3: Work done by a force at an angle to the direction of motion

In the problems you met in Chapter 1, all the forces always acted in the direction of movement, either promoting motion or resisting it directly. However, in many cases, the forces causing motion are not in the direction of motion. Examples are:

- a man dragging a sledge along horizontal ground by pulling on a rope that is angled upwards
- a child descending a slide under gravity; the child's weight acts vertically downwards but she travels down the slide at an angle to the vertical.

🔑 Key point 5.6

If a force is acting at an angle θ to the direction of movement:

$$\text{work done} = \text{force} \times \cos\theta \times \text{distance}$$

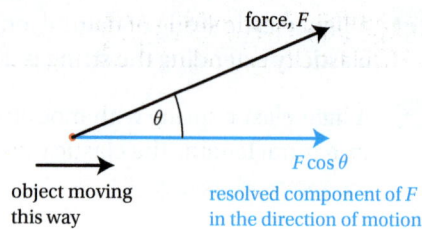

The resolved component that is perpendicular to the direction of motion, $F\sin\theta$, does no work.

WORKED EXAMPLE 5.12

Jamal is dragging his son on a sledge along horizontal ground. He is pulling a rope, attached to the sledge, at an angle of 30° to the horizontal. The tension in the rope is 50 N. Find the work Jamal does dragging the sledge 85 m.

Work done = force $\times \cos\theta \times$ distance	Use the definition of work done by a force acting at an angle to the direction of motion.
$\Rightarrow$ Work done $= 50 \times \cos 30° \times 85$ $= 3700$ J	

WORKED EXAMPLE 5.13

Irina walks up a steady slope inclined at 15° to the horizontal. Irina's mass is 55 kg and she walks 185 metres along the slope. Find the work Irina does against gravity as she walks up the slope, giving your answer in kilojoules (kJ).

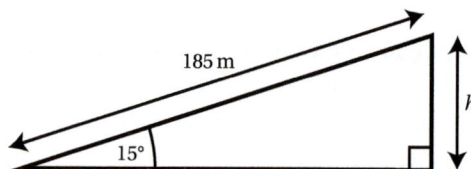

Work done = force $\times \cos\theta \times$ distance	Use the definition of work done by a force acting at an angle to the direction of motion.
$\theta = 75°$	The slope makes an angle of 15° with the horizontal but 75° with the vertical.
$\Rightarrow$ work done $= 55g \times \cos 75° \times 185$ $= 25.8$ kJ (3 s.f.)	Irina does work against gravity. Her weight is $55g$ newtons acting vertically downwards. The component of her weight parallel to the slope is $55g \times \cos 75°$.

WORKED EXAMPLE 5.14

A girl of mass 20 kg descends a straight smooth slide, starting from rest. The slide is 5 m in length and inclined at 10° to the horizontal. Use work and energy to calculate the speed of the girl at the bottom of the slide.

Let θ be the angle between the vertical and the slope.
$\theta = 80°$

> The slope makes an angle of 10° with the horizontal but 80° with the vertical.

Work done by girl's weight $= \text{weight} \times \cos\theta \times \text{distance}$
$$= 20g \times \cos 80° \times 5$$
$$\approx 174 \text{ J}$$

> Calculate the work done by gravity, using $g = 10 \text{ m s}^{-2}$, as the data in the question is given to 1 significant figure.

$174 = \dfrac{1}{2} \times 20 \times v^2$

> Use the work–energy principle.
> work done by gravity
> = increase of kinetic energy

$v = 4 \text{ m s}^{-1}$

The girl is travelling at approximately 4 m s^{-1} at the bottom of the slide.

WORKED EXAMPLE 5.15

A box of mass 500 g is projected with speed 2.5 m s^{-1} up a smooth inclined plane. The plane slopes at 20° to the horizontal. By considering conservation of energy, calculate how far the box travels up the plane.

Let θ be the angle between the vertical and the slope.
$\theta = 70°$

> The slope makes an angle of 20° with the horizontal but 70° with the vertical.

$GPE_1 = 0$
Let the distance travelled up the slope be x.

> Let gravitational potential energy at start of movement be zero ($GPE_1 = 0$).

At the end of the movement:
$GPE_2 = 0.5g \times \cos 70° \times x$
$$\approx 1.676x \text{ J}$$

> As the box travels a distance x up the plane, its gravitational potential energy increases.
>
> This is equivalent to the work done against the weight of the box: $\text{weight} \times \cos\theta \times \text{distance}$.

$KE_1 = GPE_2$
$\dfrac{1}{2} \times 0.5 \times 2.5^2 = 1.676x$
$x = 0.93 \text{ m}$
The box travels 0.93 m up the plane.

> Compare mechanical energy when the box is projected with mechanical energy when it comes to rest: $GPE_1 + KE_1 = GPE_2 + KE_2$.
>
> $KE_2 = 0$ (when the box comes to rest).

EXERCISE 5C

In this exercise, unless otherwise instructed, use $g = 9.8\,\text{m s}^{-2}$, giving your final answers to an appropriate degree of accuracy.

1 A force of 25 newtons is acting at a constant 20° to the line of movement of a particle that moves 5.0 metres. Calculate the work done by the force.

2 A force of 1.8 kN is acting at a constant 25° to the line of movement of a particle that moves 1.2 metres. Calculate the work done by the force. Give your answer in kilojoules (kJ).

3 A particle is acted on by a force of 12 newtons acting at a constant angle of 15° to its direction of movement. The force does 850 joules of work. Find the distance moved by the particle.

4 A particle is acted on by a force of F newtons acting at a constant angle of 8° to its direction of movement. The force does 1250 joules of work in moving the particle 55 metres. Find the value of F.

5 A particle is acted on by a force of 10.5 newtons acting at a constant angle to its direction of movement. The force does 750 joules of work moving the particle through 125 metres. Find the constant angle.

6 Calculate the increase in potential energy when a mass of 500 grams is moved 10 m up a plane inclined at 25° to the horizontal.

7 Calculate the loss of potential energy when a mass of 1.5 kg descends 20 m along a plane inclined at 35° to the horizontal.

8 A car is towed at constant speed along a horizontal straight road. The tow rope is at 30° to the horizontal and the tension in the tow rope is 180 N. The work done by the force is 4800 J. Calculate the distance moved by the car.

9 A block of mass 3.0 kg is released from rest on a smooth plane inclined at 18° to the horizontal, and descends 50 m down the plane. Calculate:

a the loss of potential energy of the block

b the gain in kinetic energy of the block.

10 A block of mass 20 kg is dragged up a smooth slope from rest at point X to point Y. The distance XY is 28 m and the slope is inclined at 6° to the horizontal. The rope used to drag the block is parallel to the slope and has a tension of 30 N. Find:

a the work done by the tension in the rope

b the change in potential energy of the block

c the speed of the block at point Y.

Section 4: Problem solving involving work, energy and power

More complex problems may combine the work–energy principle and the principle of conservation of energy. You may be working with any of the propulsive or resistive forces you have met in Chapter 1 and this chapter.

WORKED EXAMPLE 5.16

An object, P, of mass 2.0 kg, is attached to the ends of two light elastic strings with the same natural length, 0.75 m, but different moduli of elasticity. One of the strings is attached to a point A and the other is attached to point B on the same horizontal level as A, such that the distance AB is 2.0 m. P hangs in equilibrium. The distance AP is 1.5 m and BP is 0.90 m. Calculate the modulus of elasticity of each of the strings.

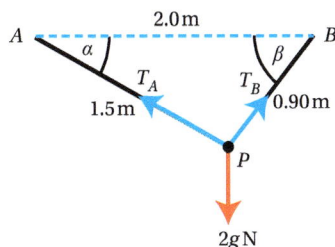

Draw a clearly labelled diagram.

$$\alpha = \cos^{-1}\frac{1.5^2 + 2^2 - 0.9^2}{2 \times 2 \times 1.5}$$

$$\approx 24.95°$$

$$\beta = \cos^{-1}\frac{0.9^2 + 2^2 - 1.5^2}{2 \times 0.9 \times 2}$$

$$= 44.67°$$

Use the cosine rule to find angles PAB (α) and PBA (β). Work to four significant figures at this stage.

Resolving horizontally, taking left as positive:
$$T_A \cos \alpha - T_B \cos \beta = 0$$

$$\therefore T_A \cos \alpha = T_B \cos \beta$$

$$\text{and } T_A = \frac{\cos \beta}{\cos \alpha} \times T_B$$

Resolve horizontally and get an expression for T_A in terms of T_B.

Resolving vertically, taking upwards as positive:
$$T_A \sin \alpha + T_B \sin \beta - 2g = 0$$

$$\frac{\cos \beta}{\cos \alpha} \times T_B \sin \alpha + T_B \sin \beta - 2g = 0$$

$$T_B = \frac{2g}{\cos \beta \tan \alpha + \sin \beta} \Rightarrow T_B \approx 18.96 \text{ N}$$

Resolve vertically and then substitute for T_A.

Rearrange, to make T_B the subject, and calculate T_B.

$$\text{But } T_A = \frac{\cos \beta}{\cos \alpha} \times T_B \Rightarrow T_A \approx 14.87 \text{ N}$$

Now calculate T_A.

$$\lambda = \frac{Tl}{x}$$

Use Hooke's law.

$$\lambda_A = \frac{14.87 \times 0.75}{(1.5 - 0.75)}$$

$$= 14.9 \text{ N (3 s.f.)}$$

$$\lambda_B = \frac{18.96 \times 0.75}{(0.9 - 0.75)}$$

$$= 95 \text{ N (2 s.f.)}$$

Use Hooke's law for each string to find each modulus of elasticity.

WORKED EXAMPLE 5.17

A light elastic string, of natural length 0.80 m, has one end fixed to point A on a rough plane inclined at 30° to the horizontal. The string has modulus of elasticity 150 N. A particle P, of mass 2.1 kg, is attached to the free end of the string. P is released from rest at A and descends the plane to B, where it comes to rest. Given that the coefficient of friction between P and the plane is 0.35:

a find the distance AB

b determine whether the particle remains stationary at B or starts to travel back up the plane.

Draw a clearly labelled diagram.

a Work done by gravity − work done against tension − work done against friction = increase in kinetic energy

Use the work–energy principle. work done by propulsive forces − work done against resistive forces = increase in kinetic energy

Work done by gravity − work done against tension − work done against friction = 0

The particle is at rest at A and at B so the increase in kinetic energy is zero.

Work done by gravity $= mgh$

$$= 2.1g \sin 30°(0.8 + x)$$

Work done against friction $= F(0.8 + x)$

where x is the extension in the string.

The distance travelled down the slope by P is the natural length, 0.8 metres, plus the extension (x) in the string.

Let F be the frictional force.

Work done against tension $= \dfrac{\lambda x^2}{2l}$

$$2.1g \sin 30°(0.8 + x) - F(0.8 + x) - \dfrac{\lambda x^2}{2l} = 0$$

$$F = 2.1g \cos 30° \times \mu$$

Whilst P is moving, $F = \mu R$, where $R = 2.1g \cos 30°$.

$$\left(2.1g \times \dfrac{1}{2} - 2.1g \times \dfrac{\sqrt{3}}{2} \times 0.35\right)(0.8 + x) - \dfrac{150x^2}{1.6} = 0$$

Substitute for F in the work–energy equation.

$$4.052(0.8 + x) - 93.75x^2 = 0$$

$$93.75x^2 - 4.052x - 3.242 = 0$$

Simplify to get a quadratic equation and take the positive value for the extension.

$$x \approx 0.2088 \text{ metres}$$

$$x = 0.21 \text{ metres (2 s.f.)}$$

Continues on next page

b At $x \approx 0.2088$ metres:

$$T = \frac{\lambda x}{l}$$

$$= 39.2\,\text{N} \,(3\,\text{s.f.})$$

Find the tension in the string when it is at its maximum extension.

$T - 2.1g \sin 30° = 29\,\text{N}$ towards A.

Calculate the total force parallel to the plane without friction.

$$F = 2.1g \times \frac{\sqrt{3}}{2} \times 0.35$$

$$= 6.2\,\text{N away from } A.$$

Using the expression for F from part **a**.

resultant force $= T - 2.1g \sin 30°$

resultant force $= 29 - 6.2 > 0$

∴ the particle will start to travel back up the plane.

Consider the resultant force up the plane.

WORKED EXAMPLE 5.18

One end of a light elastic string, of natural length 0.80 metres and modulus of elasticity $0.75mg$ newtons, is attached to a fixed point O on a smooth plane inclined at an angle α to the horizontal, where $\sin \alpha = \frac{3}{8}$.

A particle P, of mass m kg, is attached to the other end of the string. P is released from rest at O and travels down the plane without reaching the bottom. Find the maximum speed of P as it travels down the plane.

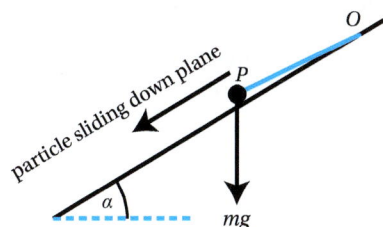

Draw a clearly labelled diagram.

Let the extension of the elastic string be x.

Component of the weight of P ∥ to the plane is $mg \sin \alpha$.

At maximum speed: $Mg \sin \alpha - T = 0$

P has maximum speed when the acceleration is zero because there is no resultant force parallel to the plane.

and $T = \frac{\lambda x}{l}$

Use Hooke's law.

$$= \frac{0.75mgx}{0.8}$$

$$mg \times \frac{3}{8} = \frac{15}{16}mgx$$

x is the 'equilibrium extension'.

$x \approx 0.4$

P has travelled 1.2 m from O when it reaches its maximum speed.

The distance from O is the natural length plus the extension.

Continues on next page

GPE + EPE + KE is constant.

$GPE_1 = KE_2 + EPE_2$

Let $GPE_2 = 0$ (when P is travelling at its maximum speed).

$KE_1 = 0$ (P moves from rest.)

$EPE_1 = 0$

Substituting and rearranging to find v:

$$mg \times \frac{3}{8} \times 1.2 = \frac{1}{2}mv^2 + \frac{0.75\,mg \times 0.4^2}{2 \times 0.8}$$

$4.41 = 0.5v^2 + 0.735$ so $v = 2.7\,\text{m s}^{-1}$ (2 s.f.)

WORKED EXAMPLE 5.19

a A car of mass 1150 kg moves along a straight horizontal road. The resistance to motion is 580 N; the engine is working at 14.5 kW and the car is moving with constant speed. Find the constant speed of the car in kilometres per hour (km h^{-1}).

b The same car now moves up a hill inclined at 4° to the horizontal. The car's engine continues working at 14.5 kW and the resistance to motion is unchanged. Find the new, constant, speed of the car up the hill, in kilometres per hour (km h^{-1}).

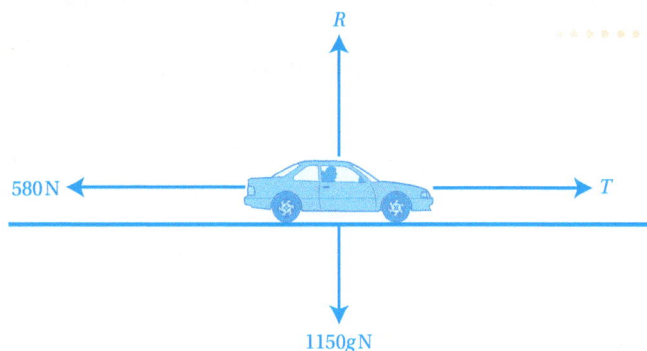

Draw a clearly labelled diagram.

T is the constant tractive force.

a Resolving horizontally, taking right as positive:

Tractive force − resistive force = 0

Constant speed $\Rightarrow$ resultant force = 0

$T - 580 = 0$

$\therefore T = 580\,\text{N}$

$14.5\,\text{kW} = 14\,500$ watts

Convert kilowatts to watts.

$14\,500 = 580 \times \text{speed}$

Use power = tractive force × speed.

$\Rightarrow \text{speed} = \dfrac{14\,500}{580}$

Rearrange the formula to find the speed.

$= 25\,\text{m s}^{-1}$

$25\,\text{m s}^{-1} = 90\,\text{km h}^{-1}$

Convert metres per second to kilometres per hour.

Continues on next page

b When travelling uphill:

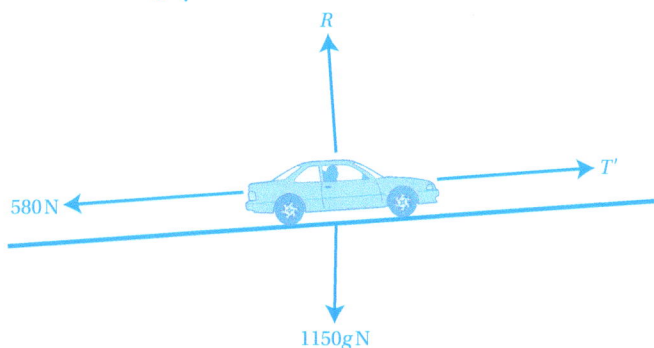

Draw a clearly labelled diagram. Use T' to represent the new tractive force.

tractive force – resistive force – component of weight acting parallel to road surface = 0

$T' - 580 - 1150g \sin 4° = 0$

$\therefore T' = 580 + 1150g \sin 4°$

Rearrange to find the tractive force.

$T' = 1366\,\text{N}$

Power = tractive force × speed

Use power = tractive force × speed.

$14\,500 \approx 1366 \times \text{speed}$

$\Rightarrow \text{speed} = \dfrac{14\,500}{1366}$

Rearrange to find speed.

$= 10.6\,\text{m s}^{-1}$ (3 s.f.)

$10.6\,\text{m s}^{-1} = 38.2\,\text{km h}^{-1}$

Convert m s^{-1} to km h^{-1}.

The new speed is $38\,\text{km h}^{-1}$ (2 s.f.).

WORKED EXAMPLE 5.20

A car and driver of combined mass 1150 kg accelerate from rest up a road inclined at 5° to the horizontal, with average resistance to motion of 850 newtons. The car engine is working at a constant rate of 32 kW. The car reaches a speed of $15\,\text{m s}^{-1}$ after it has travelled 80 m. Calculate the time taken.

To find the time taken when the vehicle engine is operating at constant power, find the total work done and use the definition:

$$\text{power} = \frac{\text{work done}}{\text{time}} \Rightarrow \text{time} = \frac{\text{work done}}{\text{power}}$$

Work done by engine – work done against resistance

$+\,\text{KE}_1 + \text{GPE}_1 = \text{KE}_2 + \text{GPE}_2$

Mechanical energy is increased because the car is accelerating up a hill. This increase in mechanical energy comes from the car engine. But some of the work done by the engine is expended on resistance to motion.

Continues on next page

Work done by engine = work done against resistance + KE_2 + GPE_2

$KE_1 = 0$ (Car moves from rest.)

Let $GPE_1 = 0$ (At the start of the travel).

Work done against resistance = 850×80 J

Calculate the total work done by the car's engine.

$KE_2 = \dfrac{1}{2} \times 1150 \times 15^2$ J

$PE_2 = 1150g \times \sin 5° \times 80$ J

$\Rightarrow$ work done by engine

$= 850 \times 80 + \dfrac{1}{2} \times 1150 \times 15^2 + 1150g \times 80 \sin 5°$

$= 276\,000$ J (3 s.f.)

32 kW = 32 000 watts

Convert kilowatts to watts.

Time $= \dfrac{276\,000}{32\,000}$ s

Divide the work done by the engine's constant power output.

Time = 8.6 s (2 s.f.)

EXERCISE 5D

In this exercise, unless otherwise instructed, use $g = 9.8$ m s^{-2}, giving your final answers to an appropriate degree of accuracy.

1. A block of mass 2.0 kg is being pushed in a straight line along horizontal ground by a force of 16 N inclined at 12° above the horizontal. The block moves a distance of 6.5 m in 7.0 seconds. Find:

   a the work done by the force

   b the power with which the force is working.

2. Darius is pulling a wheeled suitcase of mass 2.5 kg up a plane inclined at 10° to the horizontal. The strap he is holding is taut, with tension 7.5 N, and angled at 30° to the horizontal. The resistance to motion is 2.5 N.

   a Calculate the increase in the suitcase's kinetic energy as it moves 10 m up the slope.

   Darius trips slightly and releases the strap. The suitcase comes to rest before rolling back down the hill against the same resistance to motion.

   b Find the speed of the suitcase after it has travelled 5 m down the slope from rest.

3. A block of mass 1.25 kg is projected up an inclined plane at 1.5 m s^{-1} and comes to rest after travelling 75 cm up the plane. Given that the resistance to motion up the plane is constant at 0.50 N, find the inclination of the plane, to the nearest degree.

4. A parcel of mass 250 g is projected up a smooth plane inclined at 15° to the horizontal with a speed 2.5 m s^{-1}. Find:

   a the speed of the parcel after it has travelled 50 cm up the plane

   b how far the parcel travels up the plane before it stops moving.

5 A car and driver of combined mass 1025 kg accelerate from rest down a road inclined at $3°$ to the horizontal, with average resistance to motion of 850 newtons. The car engine is working at a constant rate of 8.5 kW. The car reaches a speed of $15 \, \text{m s}^{-1}$ after it has travelled 65 metres. Calculate the time taken.

6 A package of mass 800 grams is projected up a rough plane inclined at $20°$ to the horizontal. The speed of projection is $3.2 \, \text{m s}^{-1}$ and the resistance to motion is constant at 2.2 N. Calculate the speed of the package when it returns to its starting point.

7 An object of mass 1.8 kg is attached to the ends of two light elastic strings, both having the same modulus of elasticity. One of the strings has natural length 0.8 m and the other has a natural length of 1.1 m. The longer string is attached at A and the shorter string is attached at B on the same horizontal level. The object hangs 0.85 m below O, a point on the same level as A and B, 1.4 m from A and 0.8 m from B. Find the modulus of elasticity of the strings.

8 A light elastic string AB, of natural length 1.2 m, is fixed at point A on a rough plane inclined at $30°$ to the horizontal. The string has modulus of elasticity 115 N. A particle of mass 2 kg is attached to end B and the particle is released from rest to descend the plane from A to C. The particle descends 1.45 m from A.

a Show that the coefficient of friction between the particle and the inclined plane is approximately 0.456.

b Find the acceleration of the particle at C.

9 A car of mass 1500 kg moves along a straight horizontal road. The resistance to motion is constant, 750 N, and the car's engine is working at a constant rate of 19.5 kW.

a Find the acceleration of the car when the car's speed is $21.5 \, \text{m s}^{-1}$.

The road now ascends a constant slope inclined at $5°$ to the horizontal. The car's engine continues working at 19.5 kW and the resistance to motion remains at 750 N.

b Find the greatest steady speed of the car as it ascends the hill.

10 A car of mass 710 kg is ascending a hill inclined at $6°$ to the horizontal. The power exerted by the engine is 14 kW and the car has a constant speed of $18 \, \text{m s}^{-1}$. It is assumed that resistance to motion is kv N, where v is the car's speed and k is a constant value.

a Show that $k \approx 2.8$.

The power of the engine is now increased to 17.5 kW.

b Calculate the maximum speed of the car while it is ascending the hill.

✎ Checklist of learning and understanding

- For a variable force $f(x)$ that depends on displacement, x, work done is defined as $\int_{x_1}^{x_2} f(x) \, dx$.
- Hooke's law for an elastic string or spring is $T = kx$ or, alternatively, $T = \dfrac{\lambda x}{l}$.
- Work done against elasticity is $\dfrac{k}{2}(x_2^2 - x_1^2)$ or, alternatively, $\dfrac{\lambda}{2l}(x_2^2 - x_1^2)$.
- Elastic potential energy is $\dfrac{kx^2}{2}$ or, alternatively, $\dfrac{\lambda x^2}{2l}$.
- $\text{KE} + \text{GPE} + \text{EPE} = \text{constant}$.
- **A** Work done $= \text{force} \times \cos\theta \times \text{distance}$.

Mixed practice 5

In this exercise, unless otherwise instructed, use $g = 9.8\,\text{m s}^{-2}$, giving your final answers to an appropriate degree of accuracy.

A **1** A particle of mass 3.2 kg is placed on a smooth plane inclined at 18° to the horizontal. The particle, starting from rest, travels 10 metres down the plane from point P to point Q.

   a Find the potential energy lost as the particle descends from P to Q.

   b Find the kinetic energy gained and hence the speed gained by the particle as it descends from P to Q.

A **2** A sledge is being pulled along a smooth horizontal surface by a force of 45 newtons, acting at 40° to the horizontal. Calculate the work done as the sledge is moved 8.0 metres along the horizontal surface.

A **3** A water slide is modelled as a smooth plane of length 25 metres inclined at 30° to the horizontal. Samuel, with mass 72 kg, propels himself at a speed of 3.5 m s⁻¹ onto the top of the slide and descends to the splash pool.

   a Calculate Samuel's initial kinetic energy.

   b Calculate Samuel's loss of potential energy as he descends.

   c Calculate Samuel's kinetic energy and hence his speed as he enters the splash pool.

4 A vehicle of mass 950 kg moves along a horizontal road with driving force 525 newtons. It starts from rest and experiences a resistance to motion of $2.1x$ newtons. Find the speed of the vehicle after it has travelled 100 m.

5 An elastic string has one end attached to a point O, fixed on a horizontal table. The other end of the string is attached to a particle of mass 5 kilograms. The elastic string has natural length 2 metres and modulus of elasticity 200 newtons. The particle is pulled so that it is 2.5 metres from the point O and it is then released from rest on the table.

   a Calculate the elastic potential energy when the particle is 2.5 metres from the point O.

   b If the table is smooth, show that the speed of the particle when the string becomes slack is $\sqrt{5}\,\text{m s}^{-1}$.

   c The table is, in fact, rough and the coefficient of friction between the particle and the table is 0.4. Find the speed of the particle when the string becomes slack.

A **6** A light elastic string has one end attached to a point A fixed on a smooth plane inclined at 30° to the horizontal. The other end of the string is attached to a particle of mass 6 kg. The elastic string has natural length 4 metres and modulus of elasticity 300 newtons.

The particle is pulled down the plane in the direction of the line of greatest slope through A.

The particle is released from rest when it is 5.5 metres from A.

   a Calculate the elastic potential energy of the string when the particle is 5.5 metres from the point A.

   b Show that the speed of the particle when the string becomes slack is 3.66 m s⁻¹, correct to three significant figures.

   c Show that the particle will not reach point A in the subsequent motion.

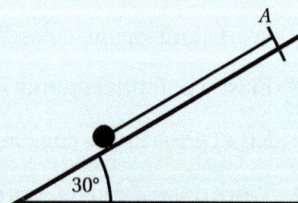

[© AQA 2008]

7 A truck of mass 32 tonnes experiences a resistance to motion of $2400x$ N. The truck is travelling at $45 \, \text{km h}^{-1}$ when the driver applies the brakes with a constant braking force of 9800 N. Find how far the truck travels before coming to rest.

8 An elastic string has natural length 1.5 metres and modulus of elasticity 120 newtons.

One end of the string is attached to a fixed point, A, on a rough plane inclined at 20° to the horizontal. The other end of the elastic string is attached to a particle of mass 4 kg. The coefficient of friction between the particle and the plane is 0.8.

The three points, A, B and C, lie on a line of greatest slope.

The point C is x metres from A, as shown in the diagram. The particle is released from rest at C and moves up the plane.

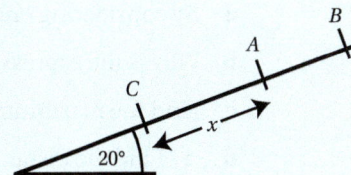

a Show that, as the particle moves up the plane, the frictional force acting on the particle is 29.5 N, correct to three significant figures.

b The particle comes to rest for an instant at B, which is 2 metres from A.

The particle then starts to move back towards A.

   i Find x.

   ii Find the acceleration of the particle as it starts to move back towards A.

[© AQA 2014]

9 Two particles, A and B, are connected by a light elastic string that passes through a hole at a point O in a rough horizontal table. The edges of the hole are smooth. Particle A has a mass of 8 kg and particle B has a mass of 3 kg.

The elastic string has natural length 3 metres and modulus of elasticity 60 newtons.

Initially, particle A is held 3.5 metres from the point O on the surface of the table and particle B is held at a point 2 metres vertically below O.

The coefficient of friction between the table and particle A is 0.4.

The two particles are released from rest.

a **i** Show that initially particle A moves towards the hole in the table.

   ii Show that initially particle B also moves toward the hole in the table.

b Calculate the initial elastic potential energy in the string.

c Particle A comes permanently to rest when it has moved 0.46 metres, at which time particle B is still moving upwards.

Calculate the distance that particle B has moved when it is at rest for the first time.

[© AQA 2013]

10 Carol, a bungee jumper of mass 70 kg, is attached to one end of a light elastic cord of natural length 26 metres and modulus of elasticity 1456 N. The other end of the cord is attached to a fixed horizontal platform which is at a height of 69 metres above the ground.

Carol steps off the platform at the point where the cord is attached and falls vertically. Hooke's law can be assumed to apply whilst the cord is taut.

Model Carol as a particle and assume air resistance to be negligible.

When Carol has fallen x m, her speed is $\tilde{v}$ m s^{-1}.

a By considering energy, show that $5v^2 = 306x - 4x^2 - 2704$ for $x \geqslant 26$.

b Why is the expression found in part **a** not true when x takes values less than 26?

c Find the maximum value of x.

d i Find the distance fallen by Carol when her speed is a maximum.

   ii Hence find Carol's maximum speed.

[© AQA 2015]

11 a An elastic string has natural length l and modulus of elasticity λ. The string is stretched from length l to length $l + e$. Show, by integration, that the work done in stretching the string is $\frac{\lambda e^2}{2l}$.

b A particle, of mass 5 kg, is attached to one end of a light elastic string. The other end of the string is attached to a fixed point O.

The string has natural length 1.6 m and modulus of elasticity 392 N.

   i Find the extension of the string when the particle hangs in equilibrium.

   ii The particle is pulled down to a point A, which is 2.2 m below the point O. Calculate the elastic potential energy in the string.

   iii The particle is released when it is at rest at the point A. Calculate the distance of the particle from the point A when its speed first reaches 0.8 m s^{-1}.

[© AQA 2013]

12 An elastic string has one end attached to a point O fixed on a rough horizontal surface. The other end of the string is attached to a particle of mass 2 kg. The elastic string has natural length 0.8 metres and modulus of elasticity 32 newtons.

The particle is pulled so that it is at the point A, on the surface, 3 metres from the point O.

a Calculate the elastic potential energy when the particle is at the point A.

b The particle is released from the rest at the point A and moves in a straight line towards O.

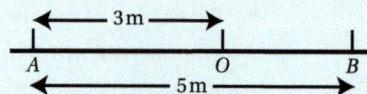

The particle is next at rest at the point B. The distance AB is 5 metres.

Find the frictional force acting on the particle as it moves along the surface.

c Show that the particle does not remain at rest at the point B.

d The particle next comes to rest at a point C with the string slack. Find the distance BC.

e Hence, or otherwise, find the total distance travelled by the particle after it is released from the point A.

[© AQA 2012]

13 **a** Hooke's law states that the tension in a stretched string of natural length l and modulus of elasticity λ is $\frac{\lambda x}{l}$ when its extension is x.

Using this formula, prove that the work done in stretching a string from an unstretched position to a position in which its extension is e is $\frac{\lambda e^2}{2l}$.

b A particle of mass 5 kg, is attached to one end of a light elastic string of natural length 0.6 metres and modulus of elasticity 150 N. The other end of the string is fixed to a point O.

i Find the extension of the elastic string when the particle hangs in equilibrium directly below O.

ii The particle is pulled down and held at the point P, which is 0.9 metres vertically below O. Show that the elastic potential energy of the string when the particle is in this position is 11.25 J.

iii The particle is released from rest at the point P. In the subsequent motion, the particle has speed v m s^{-1} when it is x metres above P.

Show that, while the string is taut, $v^2 = 10.4x - 50x^2$

iv Find the value of x when the particle comes to rest for the first time after being released, given that the string is still taut.

[© AQA 2008]

14 At a theme park, a light elastic rope is used to bring a carriage to rest at the end of a ride.

The carriage has mass 200 kg and is travelling at 8 m s^{-1} when the elastic rope is attached to the carriage as it passes over a point O. The other end of the elastic rope is fixed to the point O. The carriage then moves along a horizontal surface until it is brought to rest. The elastic rope is then detached so that the carriage remains at rest.

The elastic rope has natural length 6 m and modulus of elasticity 1800 N. The rope, once taut, remains horizontal throughout the motion.

a Calculate the elastic potential energy of the rope when the carriage is 10 m from O.

b A student's simple model assumes that there are no resistance forces acting on the carriage so that it is brought to rest by the elastic rope alone. Find the distance of the carriage from O when it is brought to rest.

c The student improves the model by also including a constant resistance force of 800 N while the carriage is in motion.

Find the distance of the carriage from O when it is brought to rest.

[© AQA 2011]

15 A van, of mass 1800 kg, travels at a constant speed of 20 m s^{-1} up a slope inclined at 2.5° to the horizontal. The van experiences constant resistance to motion of 7500 newtons. Find the power output of the van's engine.

A 16 A car, of mass 1200 kg, has a maximum speed of 25 m s^{-1} on a straight horizontal road. When the car travels at v m s^{-1}, it experiences a resistive force of 32 v newtons.

  a Show that the maximum power of the car is 20 000 watts.

The car is travelling along a straight horizontal road.

  b Find the maximum possible acceleration of the car when its speed is 20 m s^{-1}.

The car starts to climb a hill inclined at angle θ to the horizontal, where $\sin \theta = 0.05$.

  c Find the maximum possible constant speed of the van as it travels in a straight line up the hill.

A 17 A train, of mass 600 tonnes, travels at constant speed up a slope inclined at an angle θ to horizontal, where $\sin \theta = \dfrac{1}{40}$. The speed of the train is 24 m s^{-1} and it experiences total resistance forces of 200 000 N.

Find the power produced by the train, giving your answer in kilowatts.

[© AQA 2009]

A 18 When a car, of mass 1200 kg, travels at a speed of v m s^{-1}, it experiences a resistance force of magnitude 30 v newtons.

The car has a maximum constant speed of 48 m s^{-1} on a horizontal road.

  a Show that the maximum power of the car is 69 120 watts.

  b The car is travelling along a straight horizontal road.

   Find the maximum possible acceleration of the car when it is travelling at a speed of 40 m s^{-1}.

  c The car starts to descend a hill on a straight road which is inclined at an angle of 3° to the horizontal. Find the maximum possible constant speed of the car as it travels on this road down the hill.

[© AQA 2010]

A 19 A van, of mass 1400 kg, is accelerating at a constant rate of 0.2 m s^{-2} as it travels up a slope inclined at an angle θ to the horizontal.

The van experiences total resistance forces of 4000 N.

When the van is travelling at a speed of 20 m s^{-1}, the power output of the van's engine is 91.1 kW.

Find θ.

[© AQA 2015]

FOCUS ON … PROOF 1

Is there a connection between the equations for linear motion with constant acceleration in a straight line and motion in a circle involving angular equivalents of s, u, v and a? Can you prove an equivalent set of equations for constant angular acceleration?

The linear equations – sometimes known as the SUVAT equations – are:

1 $v = u + at$

2 $v^2 - u^2 = 2as$

3 $s = ut + \dfrac{1}{2}at^2$

4 $s = vt - \dfrac{1}{2}at^2$

5 $s = \dfrac{1}{2}(u+v)t$

> ⏮ **Rewind**
>
> You met these formulae in A Level Mathematics Student Book 1, Chapter 17.
> **These equations will be given in your formula book.**

You can obtain the first equation by applying calculus to basic definitions.

$$a = \frac{dv}{dt}$$

$$\int_0^t a\,dt = \int_u^v \frac{dv}{dt}\,dt$$

$$\therefore \left[at \right]_0^t = \left[v \right]_u^v$$

$$at - (a \times 0) = v - u$$

$$v = u + at$$

Angular displacement is usually represented by the symbol θ. Angular velocity is the rate of change of angle and is denoted by the symbol ω or $\dot{\theta}$. Angular acceleration, which is the rate of change of angular velocity, is denoted by $\ddot{\theta}$ (it is often given the symbol α to distinguish it from linear acceleration).

Again you can use the basic definition to obtain the equation. Use ω_0 for the initial angular velocity and ω_1 for the final angular velocity after the constant acceleration has been acting for time t.

$$\ddot{\theta} = \alpha$$

$$= \frac{d\omega}{dt}$$

$$\int_0^t \alpha\,dt = \int_0^t \frac{d\omega}{dt}\,dt$$

$$\alpha t = \left[\omega \right]_0^t$$

$$= \omega_1 - \omega_0$$

$$\omega_1 - \omega_0 = \alpha t$$

$$\omega_1 = \omega_0 + \alpha t$$

QUESTIONS

1 Show, by integration, that the equivalent of equation **3** for motion in a circle with constant acceleration is:

$$\theta = \omega_0 t + \frac{1}{2}\alpha t^2$$

2 Find the angular equivalents of equations **2**, **4** and **5**.

3 A particle P is moving with constant acceleration of 4 rad s^{-2}. Initially its angular velocity is 10 rad s^{-1}. What is its angular velocity after 10 seconds?

Although you distinguish between a velocity vector and its magnitude, which you call **speed**, you do not make the same distinction between an acceleration vector and its magnitude. You call them both acceleration and allow the context to identify whether you are referring to a scalar or vector quantity.

When you are dealing with Cartesian coordinates, the directions to which you relate the acceleration are obvious (x, y and z or **i**, **j** and **k**). When you refer to a particle moving in a circle with constant acceleration, you are referring to a scalar quantity, as the direction of the acceleration is changing so cannot be a constant vector relative to Cartesian coordinates. However, there are other ways of defining coordinates.

Radial and transverse, tangential and normal

If you are considering the non-linear motion of a body, instead of using Cartesian coordinates, you can define the motion in two ways.

- Use polar coordinates and look at radial and transverse components. 'Radial' means the direction along the line joining a fixed origin to the object in motion and 'transverse' is perpendicular to that direction.

It can be proved that the component of acceleration:

6 in the radial $\hat{\mathbf{r}}$ direction is $\ddot{r} - r\dot{\theta}^2$

7 in the transverse $\hat{\theta}$ direction is $\dfrac{1}{r}\dfrac{d(r^2\dot{\theta})}{dt}$.

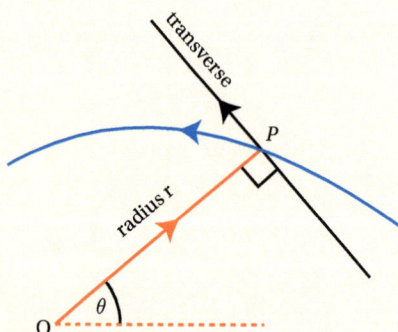

- Use tangential and normal components. 'Tangential' means along the tangent to the path of motion and 'normal' is the direction perpendicular to this.

It can be proved that the component of acceleration:

8   in the tangential $\hat{\mathbf{t}}$ direction is $\dfrac{\mathrm{d}v}{\mathrm{d}t}$

9   in the normal $\hat{\mathbf{n}}$ direction is $\dfrac{v^2}{\rho}$ where ρ is the radius of curvature at the point.

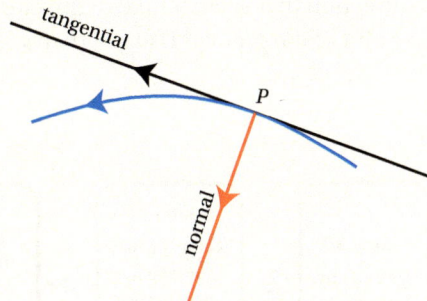

QUESTION

4 Show that if a particle P is moving in a circle, then statements **6** and **9** are equivalent, and statements **7** and **8** are also equivalent.

It is very easy to think of Mechanics in separate blocks, rather like the chapters in this book, but sometimes you have to use more than one principle to solve a problem in Mechanics. The best way to solve a Mechanics problem is to split the problem up into a series of logical steps. In this activity, you will look at problems involving more than one principle.

Consider this problem.

A small, smooth sphere, of mass 400 g is free to move in a smooth vertical groove, which is in the shape of a circle of radius 1 metre. At $t = 0$ the sphere is at rest at a point A at the lowest point of the groove when it is hit with a blow of impulse 3 N in a direction that is tangential to the circular groove at A. What is the speed of A when it reaches the highest point of the groove? Use $g = 10 \text{ m s}^{-2}$, giving your final answer to an appropriate degree of accuracy.

Look at the problem and make a plan!

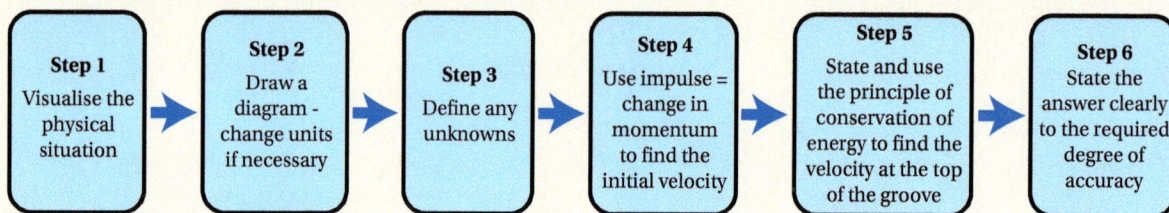

Step 1 Visualise the physical situation → **Step 2** Draw a diagram - change units if necessary → **Step 3** Define any unknowns → **Step 4** Use impulse = change in momentum to find the initial velocity → **Step 5** State and use the principle of conservation of energy to find the velocity at the top of the groove → **Step 6** State the answer clearly to the required degree of accuracy

Step 1: Visualise the physical situation

You need to have a clear picture in your mind of what is happening - not the mathematics but the actual physical situation. Without this picture you cannot represent what is happening on a diagram. You need to put as much relevant information as you can on the diagram so that it makes sense to you. You may need more than one diagram.

Consider the connections to find the principles needed. Remember that you may need to use more than one principle to solve a Mechanics problem.

You need to work out the connection between impulse, height and velocity. Impulse produces momentum and velocity so you need to use the impulse–momentum principle to find initial velocity. As the sphere rises, it slows down and the principle of conservation of energy will give you the relationship between velocity and height.

Step 2: Draw a diagram

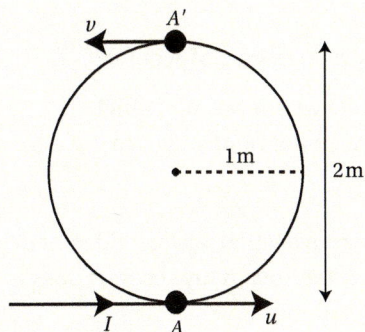

$400\,\text{g} = 0.4\,\text{kg}$

Step 3: Define any unknowns

Let u be the initial velocity of the particle.

Let v be the velocity of the particle at the highest point.

Step 4: Find the initial velocity

Impulse = change in momentum

$$= mu - 0$$

$$3 = 0.4u$$

$$u = 7.5\,\text{m s}^{-1}$$

Step 5: Find the velocity at the top of the groove

KE loss = PE gain

$$\frac{1}{2}mu^2 - \frac{1}{2}mv^2 = mgh$$

$$\frac{1}{2}mv^2 = \frac{1}{2}mu^2 - mgh$$

$$\frac{1}{2} \times 0.4v^2 = \frac{1}{2} \times 0.4 \times 7.5^2 - 0.4 \times 10 \times 2$$

$$v^2 = 16.25$$

$$v = 4.031\ldots$$

Step 6: State the answer clearly

The speed of A at the top of the groove is $4\,\text{m s}^{-1}$ (1 s.f.).

> 💡 **Tip**
>
> In the question the values are given to 1 s.f. so 1 s.f. is an appropriate degree of accuracy to use in your final answer.

QUESTIONS

1 In this question use $g = 10 \text{ m s}^{-2}$, giving your final answer to an appropriate degree of accuracy.

A particle of mass 2 kg is at rest on the edge of a smooth horizontal table which is 1 metre high. It is hit with an impulse of 10 N s in a horizontal direction away from the table and at right angles to the edge of the table. How far from the edge of the table does the particle land?

2 A particle of mass 600 g is at rest at a point A in a smooth, horizontal groove when it is hit with a blow of impulse 2 N s. The groove is in the shape of a circle of radius 1.5 m. After how many seconds does the particle return to A?

3 A particle of mass $2k$ kg is dropped from rest and falls a vertical distance of 4 m to the horizontal ground. The constant air resistance acting on the particle during the fall is 0.2 N. When it hits the ground, it rebounds with velocity v m s^{-1}. Given that the coefficient of restitution between the particle and the ground is 0.6, find the magnitude of v.

In a fairground game of 'test your strength' a player uses a hammer to hit one side of a platform that is balanced on a pivot. As the force of the hammer sends one side of the platform down, the other side rises up and sends a ball up a vertical tube towards a bell. If the ball hits the bell, then the player wins a prize.

In this section you will look at how to model this situation and at how you can then improve the model to make it more realistic.

Model 1

In this model, the ball is assumed to be a particle, so its mass acts at one point.

The impulse generated by the hammer is instantaneous and is 22 N s. All of the impulse is transmitted via the pivot to a ball, which is of mass 2 kg. The vertical tube is smooth and the bell is 3 m above the ground. Does the ball reach the bell?

Use $g = 9.8 \text{ m s}^{-2}$.

Let u be the initial velocity of the particle.

Use the impulse–momentum principle to find u and then energy equations to find the height, h, to which the ball rises.

$I = mv$:

$22 = 2u$

$u = 11 \text{ m s}^{-1}$

The final velocity of the particle is 0.

Loss in KE = gain in PE

$\frac{1}{2} \times 2 \times 11^2 = 2 \times 9.8 \times h$

$h = 6.2 \text{ m (2 s.f.)}$

The ball hits the bell.

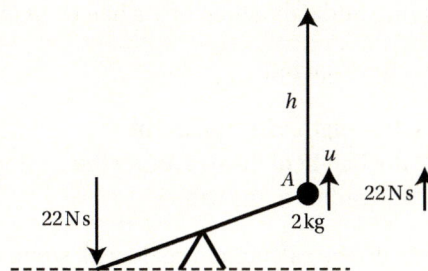

How can you make a better model?

How realistic is Model 1? What assumptions did you make? Which physical details did you leave out?

You have assumed that:

- the contact of the hammer is instant
- it takes no time for the platform to reach the ground
- the vertical tube is smooth
- the initial direction of the ball would be vertical if it were free to move.

You have left out:

- the length of the platform
- the height of the ball above the ground when it leaves the platform
- the radius of the ball.

Now do the calculation again with some changes.

Model 2

The platform is of length 1 m and is supported at its centre by a pivot of height 40 cm. The impulse transmitted to the ball is 22 N s and is at right angles to the platform. The ball is at the end of the platform at the base of the tube. The radius of the ball is 7.5 cm.

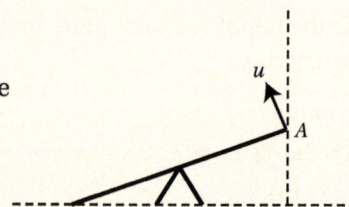

QUESTIONS

1 Find the component of the initial velocity of the ball in the vertical direction.

2 Work out the total height it now needs to rise to reach the bell.

3 Does the ball still reach the bell?

Model 3

To improve the model further, you need to look at the possibility of friction between the ball and the tube through which it moves. Frictional forces exist between most surfaces in contact and should be included to make this model more realistic.

QUESTION

4 A constant frictional force of 1 N acts on the ball while it is in the tube. Does the ball now reach the bell?

1 The terminal velocity of a falling object is reached when the upward force on the object – the drag – is equal to the weight of the object. The formula for the drag force is of the form:

$$\text{drag force} = \frac{C}{2}\rho^{\alpha}v^{\beta}A^{\gamma}$$

where C is a dimensionless constant, ρ is the density of the atmosphere, v is the terminal velocity and A is the exposed area of the falling object. Use dimensional analysis to find the values of α, β and γ and hence find a formula for v.

2 A small toy boat of mass 2 kg is sailing in a straight line with initial velocity $(\mathbf{i}+2\mathbf{j})\,\text{m s}^{-1}$. It is acted on by a constant wind with force $(3\mathbf{i}+2\mathbf{j})\,\text{N}$ for 10 seconds. What is its final velocity?

3 A group of children are playing on a playground roundabout which is spinning at a constant rate of 15 revolutions per minute. A small parcel of mass 4 kg is at rest on the roundabout at a distance of 1 m from the centre. If the parcel is at rest, what is the frictonal force acting on the parcel? You can model the roundabout as a horizontal disc and the parcel as a point mass.

A **4** In this question, use $g = 10\,\text{m s}^{-2}$, giving your final answer to an appropriate degree of accuracy.

A particle, A, of mass 500 grams is attached to one end of a light inextensible string of length 1 m. The other end of the string it attached to a fixed point B, directly above A.

A is hit with a blow of impulse 1.5 N s in a horizontal direction. Find the angle that the string makes with the vertical at the point when the particle first comes to rest, shown by A' in the diagram.

A **5** In this question, use $g = 10\,\text{m s}^{-2}$, giving your final answer to an appropriate degree of accuracy.

A car of mass 1500 kg is going up a hill at an angle θ to the horizontal, where $\sin\theta = 0.1$. The car is travelling against a constant frictional force of 300 N with a constant speed of $20\,\text{m s}^{-1}$. What is the power output of the car's engine as it goes up the hill?

6 Prove by induction that $\left[\dfrac{\text{d}^{n}x}{\text{d}t^{n}}\right] = \mathbf{LT}^{-n}$

A **7** An elastic string, of natural length 0.3 m, has a mass of 800 g attached to one end. The other end is attached to a fixed point, P. The mass is held in equilibrium at a point R by a horizontal force F and hangs at an angle of 60 to the vertical. QR is a horizontal line, as shown in the diagram. $PQ = 0.4\,\text{m}$. Find an expression, in terms of g, for the stiffness of the string.

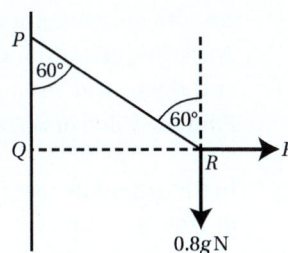

8   In this question, use $g = 9.8\,\text{m s}^{-2}$, giving your final answer to an appropriate degree of accuracy.

Two smooth spheres, A and B, both of mass 2 kg, are at rest on a smooth horizontal table which is 1.4 m high. The line joining A and B is at right angles to the edge of the table. A is 1.5 m from the edge of the table and B is 0.5 m from the edge of the table. A is projected towards B at $4\,\text{m s}^{-1}$. A is brought to rest by the collision and B subsequently moves to the edge of table and falls off it. What is the time from the collision to the moment that B hits the ground?

A 9   In this question, use $g = 9.8\,\text{m s}^{-2}$, giving your final answer to an appropriate degree of accuracy.

A conical pendulum consists of a particle A, of mass m kg, attached by a light inextensible string, of length 2 m to a point B. A describes horizontal circles of radius 1.5 m at a constant speed of $v\,\text{m s}^{-1}$ so that the string describes a cone. Find the value of v.

10   Brinell's test of hardness of materials evaluates the hardness of the material using a **Brinell hardness number** (BHN). The test involves forcing a steel or tungsten-carbide sphere into the material being tested and measuring the diameter of the indentation. The formula is $\text{BHN} = \dfrac{2P}{\pi D\left(D - \sqrt{D^2 - d^2}\right)}$

where P is the applied force, D is the diameter of the sphere and d is the diameter of the indentation.

a   Work out the dimensions of force.   **b**   What are the dimensions of BHN?

11   Two particles, A of mass 1 kg and B of mass 3 kg, are on a smooth horizontal plane. A is moving at $4\,\text{m s}^{-1}$ and B at $2\,\text{m s}^{-1}$. The particles collide and coalesce to form a new particle C which then hits a vertical wall at right angles. The coefficient of restitution between C and the wall is 0.8. What is the velocity of C as it leaves the wall?

12   In this question, use $g = 9.8\,\text{m s}^{-2}$, giving your final answer to an appropriate degree of accuracy.

Particles A and B, both of mass 3 kg, are joined by a light inextensible string of length 2 m. A is moving in circles on a smooth horizontal surface at a constant speed of $3.5\,\text{m s}^{-1}$. The string goes through a small, smooth hole in the table and B hangs at rest at a distance x m below the table. Find the value of x.

A 13   In this question, use $g = 10\,\text{m s}^{-2}$, giving your final answer to an appropriate degree of accuracy.

A conical pendulum consists of a particle A, of mass 2 kg, attached by a light inextensible string, of length 1.5 m to a point B. A describes horizontal circles at a constant speed of $5\,\text{m s}^{-1}$ so that the string sweeps out a cone. What is the volume of the cone?

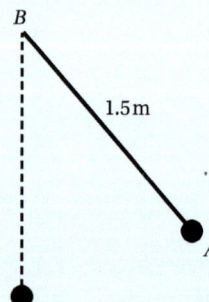

6 Momentum and collisions 2

In this chapter you will learn how to:

- find the impulse of a variable force
- apply the principles of impulse, conservation of momentum and Newton's experimental law in two dimensions using vector notation.

A If you are following the A Level course, you will also learn how to:

- calculate the result of oblique impacts with a fixed object.

Before you start...

Chapter 3	You should know the relationship between force, impulse and momentum.	1	A force of 3 N acts on a mass m kg for 3 seconds. What is the change in momentum of the mass during those 3 seconds?
Chapter 3	You should know the principle of conservation of momentum and Newton's experimental law.	2	A particle of mass m kg travelling in a straight line on a horizontal surface hits a vertical wall with speed u and rebounds with speed v. What is the coefficient of restitution between the wall and the particle?
A Level Mathematics Student Book 1, Chapter 15	You should understand how to combine vectors including drawing triangles to find the sum of two vectors.	3	Draw a sketch of a triangle to show the sum and difference of two vectors **a** and **b**.
A Level Mathematics Student Book 1, Chapter 15	You should be able to resolve a vector into two perpendicular components and be able to find the magnitude of a vector from its components.	4	The force F acts at 60° to the horizontal. What are the horizontal and vertical components of F?
		5	What is the magnitude of the vector $3\mathbf{i} - 6\mathbf{j}$?
A Level Mathematics Student Book 1, Chapter 14	You should be able to integrate simple functions and apply limits.	6	Find $\int_0^3 (3t^2 - 4t)\, dt$.

Variable forces and oblique impacts

In Chapter 3, you learnt about momentum and impulse involving constant forces and direct collisions. In reality, forces are rarely constant, for example, a wind does not blow at a constant speed but will rise and fall in strength. In this chapter, you will start to analyse more realistic situations, such as those involving variable forces or oblique impacts.

Section 1: Variable force and vector notation

If the variable force F is defined by more than one function over a given time you will need to integrate the functions separately.

▶ **Rewind**

In Chapter 3, you learned that:

- the impulse of a constant force F N acting for a time t s is Ft N s
- the impulse, I, of a variable force F acting for a time $t_1 \leqslant t \leqslant t_2$ is $I = \int_{t_1}^{t_2} F\, dt$
- the impulse of a force acting on a body is equal to the change in momentum.

WORKED EXAMPLE 6.1

A particle A, of mass 500 grams, is acted on by a variable force F N, which is defined, at t seconds, as:

$F = 0.3t^2 + 0.5t$ for $0 \leqslant t \leqslant 3$

$F = t + 1.2$ for $3 < t \leqslant 5$

Find the velocity of A after 4 seconds if its velocity is 2 m s^{-1} when $t = 0$.

	To find the increase in momentum of A you need to know the total impulse on A during the 4 seconds.
$500\,g = 0.5\,kg$	Change grams to kilograms.
Let the final velocity of A be v.	Define the unknown.
$I = \displaystyle\int_0^3 (0.3t^2 + 0.5t)\,dt + \int_3^4 (t+1.2)\,dt$	Integrate the force between $t = 0$ and $t = 4$ to find the total impulse on A in that time.

$= \left[0.3\dfrac{t^3}{3} + 0.5\dfrac{t^2}{2} \right]_0^3 + \left[\dfrac{t^2}{2} + 1.2t \right]_3^4$

$= \big[[2.7 + 2.25] - [0] \big] + \big[[8 + 4.8] - [4.5 + 3.6] \big]$

$= 4.95 + 4.7$

$= 9.65$

$I = mv - mu$	Solve for v.

$9.65 = 0.5v - (0.5 \times 2)$

$v = 21.3$ m s^{-1}. Hence the velocity of the particle after 4 seconds is 21.3 m s^{-1}.

EXERCISE 6A

1   Find the impulse generated by the forces shown by the solid lines between $t = 0$ and $t = 10$ seconds.

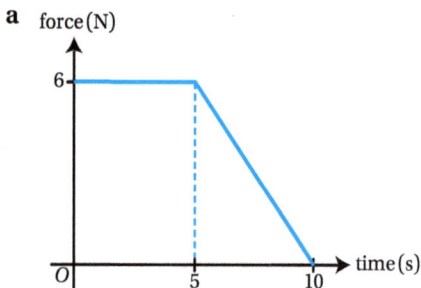

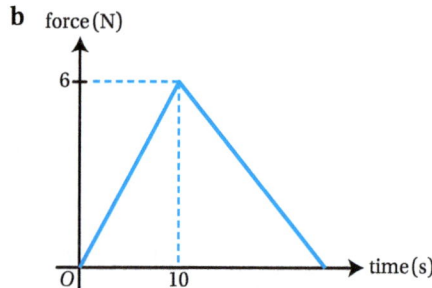

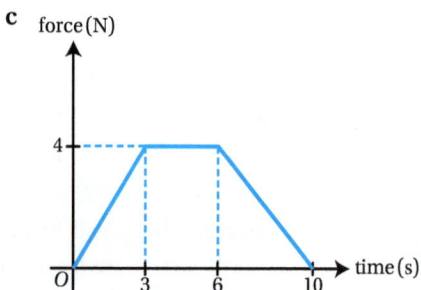

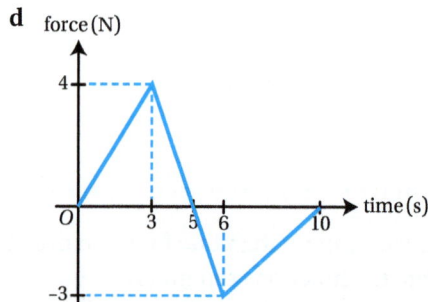

a

b

c

d

2 A particle of mass 4 kg is moving in a straight line on a smooth horizontal plane, when it is acted on by a force F N in the same straight line. Given that the speed of the particle is 6 m s^{-1} when $t = 0$ s, find the speed of the particle after 10 seconds for each of the forces shown in the diagrams in question 1.

3 Work out the quantities **a**-**e**.

Mass (kg)	Initial velocity (m s^{-1})	Final velocity (m s^{-1})	Constant force (N)	Time (s)
2	0	$8\mathbf{i} + 10\mathbf{j}$	**a**	5
1	$2\mathbf{i} - \mathbf{j}$	$14\mathbf{i} + 15\mathbf{j}$	$3\mathbf{i} + 4\mathbf{j}$	**b**
c	$-3\mathbf{i} + 5\mathbf{j}$	$-7\mathbf{i} + 11\mathbf{j}$	$-2\mathbf{i} + 3\mathbf{j}$	4
0.5	$2\mathbf{i} + 7\mathbf{j}$	**d**	$-\mathbf{i} + \mathbf{j}$	6
4	**e**	$1.5\mathbf{i} + 8\mathbf{j}$	$-2\mathbf{i} - 4\mathbf{j}$	5

4 A particle A, of mass 2 kg, is moving with velocity $(2\mathbf{i} + 3\mathbf{j})$ m s^{-1} when it collides with particle B, of mass 3 kg, which is moving with velocity $(\mathbf{i} + 2\mathbf{j})$ m s^{-1}. The particles coalesce during the collision. Find the velocity of the combined particle after the collision.

5 A particle A, of mass 2 kg, is moving with velocity $(2\mathbf{i} + 3\mathbf{j})$ m s^{-1} when it collides with particle B, of mass 3 kg, which is moving with velocity $(\mathbf{i} + 2\mathbf{j})$ m s^{-1}. The velocity of B after the collision is $(1.6\mathbf{i} + 2.6\mathbf{j})$ m s^{-1}. Find the velocity of A after the collision.

6 A particle, P, of mass 2.5 kg, moving in a straight line on a smooth horizontal plane, is acted on, in the same straight line, by a force F for 6 seconds.

a Given that $F = 2t$ N, find the total impulse of the force on P between $t = 0$ and $t = 6$ seconds.

b If the velocity of P is 4 m s^{-1} when $t = 0$ seconds, find the velocity of P when $t = 6$ seconds.

7 A particle A, of mass 3 kg, is moving with velocity $(2\mathbf{i} - 3\mathbf{j})$ m s^{-1} when it collides with particle B, also of mass 3 kg, which is moving with velocity $(\mathbf{i} + 4\mathbf{j})$ m s^{-1}. The two particles coalesce.

a Find the velocity of the combined particle after the collision.

b Calculate the loss in kinetic energy as a result of the collision.

8 A mass, A, of 10 kg, moving in a straight line on a smooth horizontal plane at 5 m s^{-1}, is acted on by a force F N along its line of motion. At time t s, F is defined as:

$F = 3t^2 + 1 \quad 0 \leq t \leq 2$

$F = 6t + 1 \quad t > 2$

a Find the magnitude of the total impulse on A:

    i between $t = 0$ and $t = 2$ seconds.

    ii between $t = 0$ and $t = 6$ seconds.

b Hence find the speed of A when $t = 6$ s.

9 At time $t = 0$, a particle P, of mass 5 kg, is moving in a straight line at a constant speed of 4 m s^{-1} on a smooth horizontal plane, when it is acted on by a force $F = (t^3 - 6t^2 + 8t) \text{ N}$ in the same straight line.

    a Find the total impulse on P:

        i between $t = 0$ and $t = 2$ seconds

        ii between $t = 0$ and $t = 4$ seconds.

    b Calculate the speed of P when $t = 4$ s.

10 At time $t = 0$ s, a particle P, of mass 4 kg, is moving in a straight line at a constant velocity of 4 m s^{-1} on a smooth horizontal plane when it is acted on by a force $F = (4t - 6) \text{ N}$, acting in the direction of motion. At time T seconds later, the particle is moving with velocity 6 m s^{-1}. Find the value of T.

Section 2: Oblique impacts and the impulse–momentum triangle

So far, you have considered direct impacts with objects moving along their line of centres or hitting walls at right angles. You will now look at **oblique impacts**.

Consider a particle travelling with velocity $\mathbf{u} = a\mathbf{i} + b\mathbf{j}$ that hits a wall that is parallel to the vector $\mathbf{i}$.

Since the impulse the wall exerts on the particle is perpendicular to the wall, the $\mathbf{i}$-component of the velocity will not be affected by the collision with the wall.

You can find the $\mathbf{j}$-component of the velocity after the collision using Newton's Experimental Law, exactly as you did in Chapter 3 where the particle hit the wall perpendicularly.

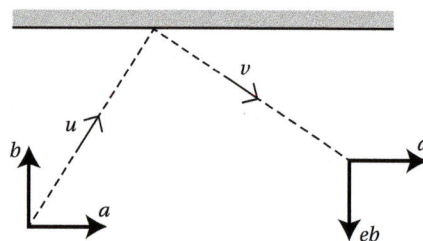

🔑 Key point 6.1

When a particle moving with speed $\mathbf{u} = a\mathbf{i} + b\mathbf{j}$ collides with a smooth, flat surface parallel to the vector $\mathbf{i}$, it rebounds with velocity $\mathbf{v} = a\mathbf{i} - eb\mathbf{j}$, where e is the coefficient of restitution between the particle and the surface.

⏪ Rewind

You met the coefficient of restitution in Chapter 3.

WORKED EXAMPLE 6.2

A smooth vertical wall is parallel to the positive $\mathbf{i}$ direction. A smooth sphere, of mass 3 kg, moving with velocity $(3\mathbf{i} + 5\mathbf{j}) \text{ m s}^{-1}$ on a smooth horizontal plane, collides with the wall and rebounds with velocity $(a\mathbf{i} + b\mathbf{j}) \text{ m s}^{-1}$. Given that the coefficient of restitution between the wall and the sphere is 0.75, find the values of a and b.

Velocity before collision $= 3\underline{i} + 5\underline{j}$

Rebound velocity $= a\underline{i} + b\underline{j}$

As the velocity is given as a vector, you are given the components of the velocity so there is no need to resolve.

Continues on next page

$a = 3$

There is no impulse parallel to the wall so there is no change of speed parallel to the wall.

$b = -5$
$eb = -5 \times 0.75$
$ = -0.375$

Perpendicular to the wall $v = -eu$.

$a = 3, b = -0.375$

You were asked for the values of a and b so you do not need to write the answer as a vector.

A If the velocity of the particle isn't given in vector form, but is instead given as a speed and an angle to the wall, then you will first need to resolve the velocity before and after into components parallel and perpendicular to the wall.

WORKED EXAMPLE 6.3

A sphere A, of mass 2 kg, is moving in a straight line at 5 m s^{-1} on a smooth horizontal surface when it collides with a wall. The line of motion of the sphere makes an angle of 40° with the wall. If the coefficient of restitution between the wall and the sphere is 0.6, find the speed and direction of the sphere when it rebounds from the wall. Give your speed correct to 2 decimal places and the angle correct to 1 decimal place.

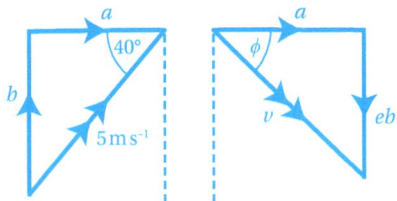

Draw a clear diagram showing the component of velocity parallel to the wall unchanged and the component of velocity perpendicular to the wall changed to $-eb$. You can write the components as a and b or 5 cos 40° and 5 sin 40°.

$a = 5 \cos 40°$

$b = 5 \sin 40°$

$eb = 0.6 \times 5 \sin 40°$

Resolve to find the values of a and b and work out eb.

Use Pythagoras' theorem to find v.

The rebound component perpendicular to the wall is $-eb$ which you show as $+eb$ away from the wall.

$v = \sqrt{(5 \cos 40°)^2 + (0.6 \times 5 \sin 40°)^2}$

$v = 4.29 \, \text{m s}^{-1}$

$\tan \phi = \dfrac{eb}{a}$

Use trigonometry to find the angle.

$ = \dfrac{0.6 \times 5 \sin 40°}{5 \cos 40°}$

$\phi = 26.7°$

Finding the impulse

In Worked example 6.3, the impulse on the sphere was acting perpendicular to the wall, as in this diagram.

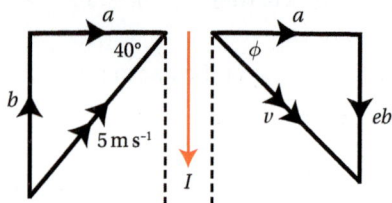

Taking the direction of the impulse as positive.

$$\text{Impulse} = \text{change in momentum}$$
$$= mv - mu$$
$$= meb - -mb$$
$$= meb + mb$$
$$mb = 2 \times 5 \sin 40°$$
$$meb = 2 \times 0.6 \times 5 \sin 40°$$
$$I = meb + mb$$
$$= 6 \sin 40° + 10 \sin 40°$$
$$= 10.3 \, \text{N s} \, (3 \, \text{s.f.})$$

There is no impulse parallel to the wall.

An alternative approach is to find I from an impulse–momentum triangle.

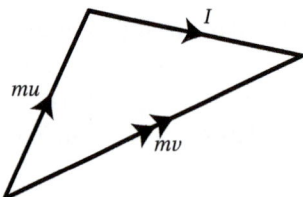

In Worked example 6.3, the mass of the sphere was 2 kg, and u was $5 \, \text{m s}^{-1}$ and you saw that $v = 4.29 \, \text{m s}^{-1}$ and $\phi = 26.7°$.

Therefore $mu = 2 \times 5 = 10 \, \text{kg m s}^{-1}$ and $mv = 2 \times 4.29 = 8.58 \, \text{kg m s}^{-1}$.

Using these values, the triangle would look like this:

and then $I = 10 \sin 40° + 8.58 \sin 26.7°$
$$= 10.3 \, \text{N s} \, (3 \, \text{s.f.})$$

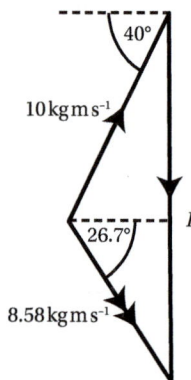

Tip

The easiest way to get the sides in the correct order is to draw the initial and final momentum from the same point and remember that the final momentum, mv, is the resultant of I and mu.

$$mu + I = mv$$

Tip

When you are dealing with a simple impact with a wall – when the impulse acts at right angles to the wall – then the method of splitting into components works best. However, when you are told that the impulse is not perpendicular to the wall, drawing the impulse–momentum triangle can be more efficient.

WORKED EXAMPLE 6.4

A small smooth sphere, of mass 600 grams, is moving at $60°$ to a smooth vertical wall when it collides with the wall. The speed of the sphere immediately before the collision is $10\,\text{m s}^{-1}$. The coefficient of restitution between the sphere and the wall is 0.7.

a Find the magnitude and direction of the sphere immediately after the collision.

b Find the impulse of the wall on the sphere, leaving your answer in surd form.

a $600\,g = 0.6\,\text{kg}$

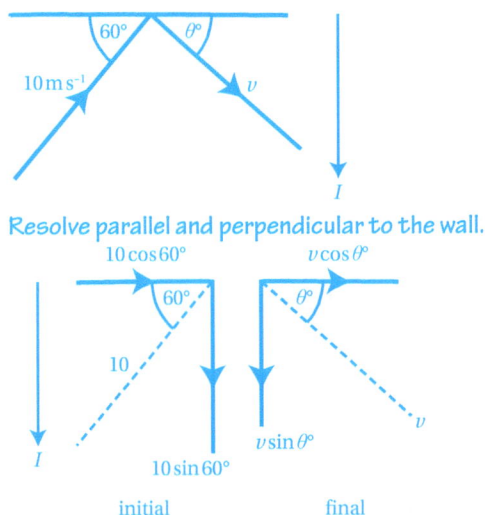

Convert grams to kilograms.

This is a simple oblique collision between an object moving horizontally and a vertical wall.

Resolve parallel and perpendicular to the wall.

initial   final

Draw clear diagrams with arrows showing the direction and values of the velocities before and after the collision split into their components parallel and perpendicular to the wall.

Let the velocity of the sphere after the collision be $v\,\text{m s}^{-1}$ at θ to the wall.

Define any unknown values.

$v \cos \theta = 10 \cos 60°$
$= 10 \times 0.5$
$= 5$

The component of the initial velocity parallel to the plane remains unchanged in the collision, as there is no impulse in that direction.

$v \sin \theta = -e \times 10 \sin 60°$
$= -0.7 \times 10 \times \dfrac{\sqrt{3}}{2}$
$= -3.5\sqrt{3}$

Find the component of the velocity perpendicular to the plane, using $v = -eu$.

$v^2 = 5^2 + (3.5\sqrt{3})^2$
$= 61.75$
$v = 7.858\,\text{m s}^{-1}$

Calculate the value of v from its components.

$\dfrac{v \sin \theta}{v \cos \theta} = \tan \theta$
$= \dfrac{3.5\sqrt{3}}{5}$
$\theta = 50.5°$

Find $\tan \theta$ and hence θ.

b Using impulse = change in momentum = $mv - mu$:
$I = mv \sin \theta - (-m10 \sin 60°)$
$= 0.6 \times 3.5\sqrt{3} - (-0.6 \times 5 \times \sqrt{3})$
$= 5.1\sqrt{3}\,\text{N s}$

Impulse only acts at right angles to the wall.

Decide on a direction to be positive – it is usually best to take away from the wall as positive – and substitute the values.

WORKED EXAMPLE 6.5

A ball, of mass 2 kg, is kicked against a rough wall. The ball is moving at an angle of 40° to the wall when it hits it at a speed of 5 m s^{-1}. As the wall is rough, the impulse of the wall on the ball is not perpendicular to the wall. The ball leaves the wall at an angle of 30° with a velocity of 4 m s^{-1}.

Find the magnitude and direction of the impulse of the wall on the ball.

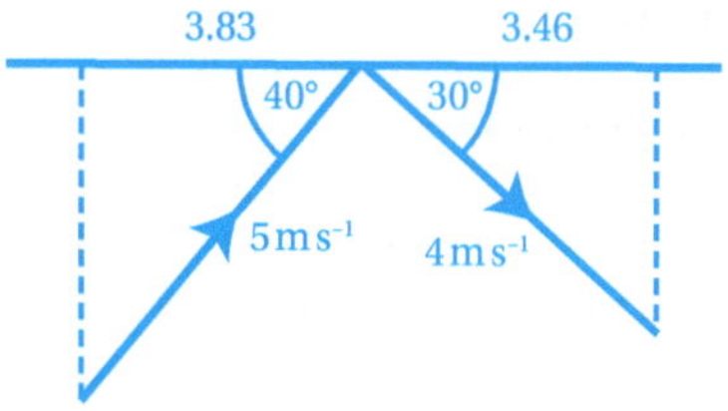

Draw a diagram of the velocities first. It is worth calculating the horizontal components to help when you are drawing the momentum–impulse triangle as it shows that mu reaches further horizontally than mv.

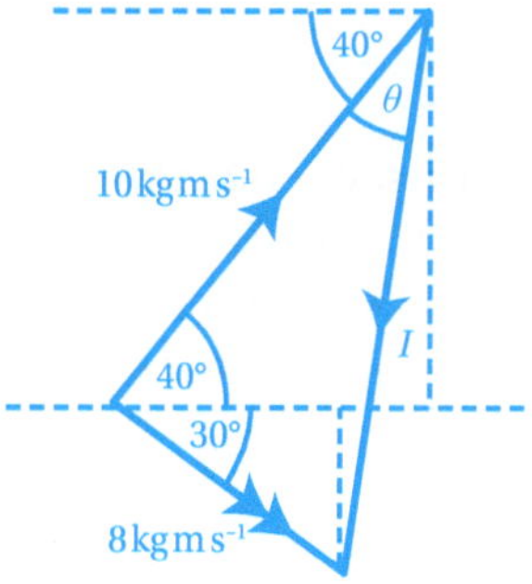

Sketch the impulse–momentum triangle. Remember that you are dealing with momentum and not speed so you must multiply by the mass.

$5 \times 2 = 10$ kg m s^{-1} and $4 \times 2 = 8$ kg m s^{-1}.

Make the triangle reasonably accurate and remember to draw mu and mv acting from the same starting point.

Using the cosine rule:

$I^2 = 100 + 64 - (2 \times 10 \times 8 \times \cos 70°)$

$\quad = 109.28 \text{ N s}$

$\quad I = 10.45 \text{ N s}$

Using the sine rule:

$\sin \theta = \dfrac{8 \sin 70°}{10.45}$

$\quad \theta = 46.0°$

The impulse makes an angle of $(40 + 46)° = 86°$ with the wall.

Give the angle with a direction. It does not matter which angle you use unless the question asks for a specific angle but make it clear which angle you are giving.

WORKED EXAMPLE 6.6

A cricket ball of mass 160 g is travelling horizontally at speed of 30 m s^{-1} when it is hit by a cricket bat. It leaves the bat, horizontally, at a speed of 40 m s^{-1} travelling at 40° to the line of its original path, as shown in the diagram. Work out the magnitude of the impulse of the bat on the ball.

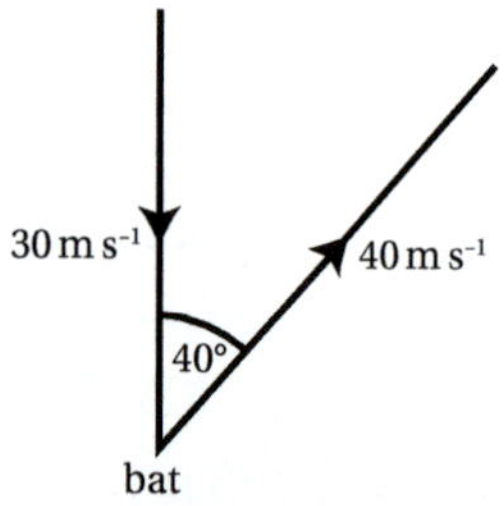

Continues on next page

$160\,g = 0.16\,kg$ .... Convert grams to kilograms.

$mu = 4.8\,kg\,m\,s^{-1}$ and $mv = 6.4\,kg\,m\,s^{-1}$ .... Calculate mu and mv.

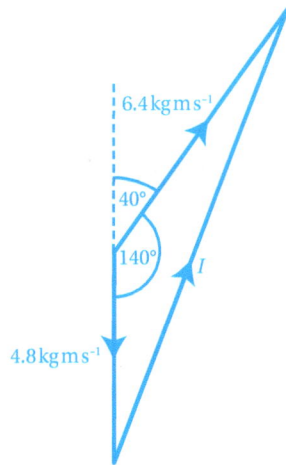

Draw a momentum–impulse triangle, remembering to keep the directions of the two velocities and to draw mu and mv acting from the same point and that $mu + I = mv$. You need to find the obtuse angle between mu and mv in the triangle.

Using the cosine rule:
$I^2 = 6.4^2 + 4.8^2 - (2 \times 6.4 \times 4.8 \times \cos 140°)$
$I^2 = 40.96 + 23.04 - (61.44 \times (-0.766))$
$\quad = 111.066$
$\quad I = 10.5\,N\,s\,(3\,s.f.)$

WORKED EXAMPLE 6.7

A sphere, of mass 5 kg, is moving with velocity 4 m s⁻¹ in the positive **i** direction when it is hit with a blow of impulse 15 N s in the positive **j** direction. Calculate the speed and direction of the sphere immediately after the impulse.

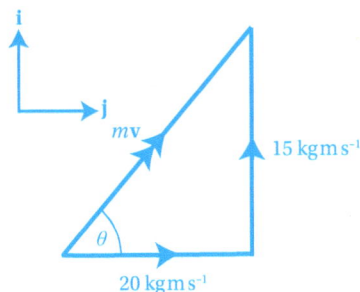

Draw the impulse–momentum triangle, remembering to multiply the velocity by the mass to get the momentum. You are given the magnitude and direction of the impulse and the magnitude and direction of mu. Remember to show mv and mu acting from the same point.

Using Pythagoras' theorem:
$(mv)^2 = 15^2 + 20^2$
$\quad mv = 25\,kg\,m\,s^{-1}$

Dividing by m:
$v = \dfrac{25}{5}$
$\quad = 5\,m\,s^{-1}$

Continues on next page

Using trigonometry:

$\theta = \tan^{-1}\left(\dfrac{15}{20}\right)$

$= 36.9°$

Immediately after the collision the sphere moves with speed 5 m s⁻¹ at 36.9° to the positive **i** direction.

State the final speed and direction of the sphere.

📷 **Focus on …**

You will use an impulse–momentum triangle to solve a problem involving conservation of energy in Focus on … Problem solving 2.

EXERCISE 6B

1 A smooth vertical wall is parallel to the positive **i** direction. A sphere, of mass 2 kg, moving with velocity $(4\mathbf{i}+7\mathbf{j})$ m s⁻¹ on a smooth horizontal plane collides with the wall and rebounds with velocity $(a\mathbf{i}+b\mathbf{j})$ m s⁻¹.

  a Given that the coefficient of restitution between the wall and the sphere is 0.6, find the values of a and b.

  b Find the magnitude of the velocity of the sphere when it rebounds from the wall.

2 A smooth vertical wall is parallel to the positive **i** direction. A sphere, of mass 4 kg, moving with velocity $(\mathbf{i}+6\mathbf{j})$ m s⁻¹ on a smooth horizontal plane collides with the wall and rebounds with velocity $(a\mathbf{i}+b\mathbf{j})$ m s⁻¹.

  a If the coefficient of restitution between the wall and the sphere is 0.8, find the values of a and b.

  b Calculate the loss of kinetic energy of the sphere as a result of its collision with the wall.

A **3** A particle A, of mass 4 kg, is moving in a straight line at 5 m s⁻¹ on a smooth horizontal surface when it collides with a wall. The line of motion of the particle makes an angle of 60° with the wall.

  a Calculate the component of the speed of the particle parallel to the wall.

  b Find the component of the speed of the particle perpendicular to the wall before the collision.

  c If the coefficient of restitution between the wall and the particle is 0.5, find the component of the speed perpendicular to the wall immediately after the collision.

  d Find the speed and direction of the particle when it rebounds from the wall. Give your speed correct to 2 decimal places and the angle correct to 1 decimal place.

4 A sphere, of mass 3 kg, is moving in a straight line at 5 m s⁻¹ on a smooth horizontal surface when it collides with a smooth, vertical wall. The line of motion of the sphere makes an angle of 30° with the wall. If the coefficient of restitution between the wall and the sphere is 0.4, find the speed and direction of the sphere when it rebounds from the wall. Give your speed correct to 2 decimal places and the angle correct to 1 decimal place.

5   A particle, of mass m kg, is moving in a straight line at u m s^{-1} on a smooth horizontal surface when it collides with a smooth, vertical wall. The line of motion of the sphere makes an angle of θ with the wall.

   a   Write down the component of the velocity of the particle, parallel to the wall, immediately before the collision.

   b   Write down the component of the velocity of the particle, parallel to the wall, immediately after the collision.

   c   Write down the component of the velocity of the particle, perpendicular to the wall, immediately before the collision.

   d   Given that the coefficient of restitution between the wall and the sphere is e, find the component of the velocity of the particle, perpendicular to the wall, immediately after the collision.

   e   Find the magnitude of the velocity of the particle immediately after the collision.

   f   Show that the loss in kinetic energy as a result of the collision is $\frac{1}{2}mu^2 \sin^2\theta(1-e^2)$.

6   A small smooth ball, of mass 800 grams, is moving in a straight line at 4 m s^{-1} on a smooth horizontal surface when it collides with a smooth, vertical wall. The line of motion of the ball makes an angle of 45° with the wall. If the coefficient of restitution between the wall and the sphere is 0.6, find:

   a   the speed and direction of the ball when it rebounds from the wall

   b   the impulse of the wall on the ball.

7   A sphere, of mass 2 kg, is moving in the positive $\mathbf{i}$ direction with speed 4 m s^{-1} when it receives a blow of impulse 6 N s acting in the negative $\mathbf{j}$ direction. Find the magnitude and direction of the velocity of the sphere immediately after the impact.

8   A sphere, of mass 6 kg, is moving in the positive $\mathbf{i}$ direction with speed 8 m s^{-1} when it receives a blow of impulse 10 N s acting in the $\mathbf{j}$ direction. Find the change in kinetic energy of the sphere as a result of the impulse.

9   A football, of mass 400 grams, is travelling horizontally at a speed of 20 m s^{-1} when it is kicked. It immediately moves, horizontally, at a speed of 25 m s^{-1}, travelling at 30° to the line of its original path, as shown in the diagram. Calculate the magnitude of the impulse of the kick.

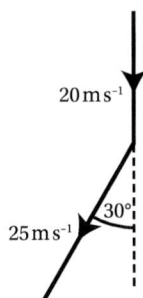

10 A snooker ball, of mass 160 grams, hits a vertical side cushion of a snooker table at a speed of $5\,\text{m s}^{-1}$, at an angle of $35°$ to the cushion, as shown in the diagram. The impulse of the cushion on the ball is perpendicular to the side of the table and the coefficient of restitution between the ball and the side cushion is 0.8.

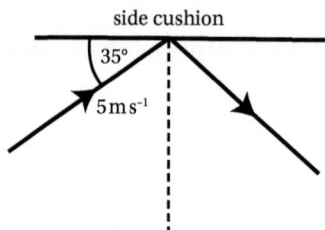

a Calculate the speed and angle to the side of the table at which the ball leaves the side cushion of the table.

b Find the kinetic energy lost by the snooker ball as a result of the collision.

11 A snooker ball, of mass 160 grams, hits a vertical side cushion of a snooker table at a speed of $u\,\text{m s}^{-1}$ at an angle of θ to the cushion, as shown in the diagram. The impulse of the cushion on the ball is perpendicular to the side of the table and the coefficient of restitution between the ball and the side cushion is 0.8. The ball then hits the side cushion at right angles to the original cushion. The coefficient of restitution between the ball and this side cushion is also 0.8. Work out the speed and angle to the side of the table at which the ball leaves the second side cushion of the table.

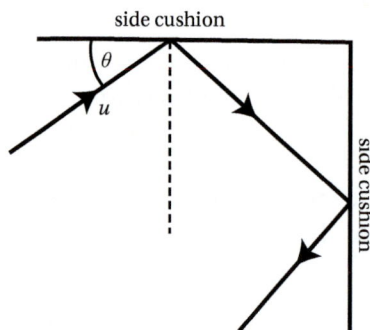

✏ Checklist of learning and understanding

- The impulse of a constant force F acting for a time t is Ft.
- The impulse, I, of a variable force F acting for a time t is $I = \displaystyle\int_{t_1}^{t_2} F\,\mathrm{d}t$.
- The impulse of a force acting on a body is equal to the change in momentum.
- When an object moving at speed u collides at an angle θ with a smooth, flat surface and rebounds:
  - the impulse acts at right angles to the surface and is equal to the change in momentum in that direction.
  - the component of the velocity parallel to the surface remains unchanged
  - the component of the velocity perpendicular to the surface is multiplied by $-e$, where e is the coefficient of restitution between the sphere and the surface.

Mixed practice 6

1 The diagram shows the force on a particle from $t = 0$ to $t = 6$ seconds. The mass of the particle is 2 kg and it is at rest when $t = 0$. Find the speed of the particle when $t = 6$. Choose from these options.

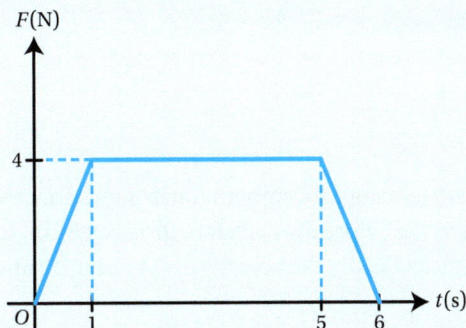

A $5\,\text{m s}^{-1}$ **B** $10\,\text{m s}^{-1}$ **C** $15\,\text{m s}^{-1}$ **D** $20\,\text{m s}^{-1}$

2 A smooth sphere of mass 2 kg, initially moving at a velocity of $(3\mathbf{i} - 2\mathbf{j})\,\text{m s}^{-1}$, is acted on by a force $(2\mathbf{i} + \mathbf{j})$ N for 3 seconds. Find the velocity of the sphere after 3 seconds. Choose from these options.

A $(12\mathbf{i} - \mathbf{j})\,\text{m s}^{-1}$ **B** $(12\mathbf{i} + 3.5\mathbf{j})\,\text{m s}^{-1}$ **C** $(6\mathbf{i} - 0.5\mathbf{j})\,\text{m s}^{-1}$ **D** $(6\mathbf{i} + 2.5\mathbf{j})\,\text{m s}^{-1}$

3 A smooth sphere is moving on a smooth horizontal surface when it strikes a smooth vertical wall and rebounds.

Immediately before the impact, the sphere is moving with speed 4 m s^{-1} and the angle between the sphere's direction of motion and the wall is α.

Immediately after the impact, the sphere is moving with speed v m s^{-1} and the angle between the sphere's direction of motion and the wall is 40°.

The coefficient of restitution between the sphere and the wall is $\frac{2}{3}$.

a Show that $\tan \alpha = \frac{3}{2} \tan 40°$.

b Find the value of v.

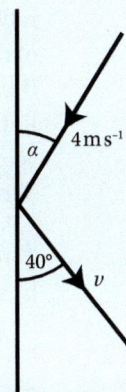

[© AQA 2010]

4 A ball of mass 0.2 kg is hit directly by a bat. Just before the impact, the ball is travelling horizontally with speed 18 m s^{-1}. Just after the impact, the ball is travelling horizontally with speed 32 m s^{-1} in the opposite direction.

a Find the magnitude of the impulse exerted on the ball.

b At time t seconds after the ball first comes into contact with the bat, the force exerted by the bat on the ball is $k(0.9t - 10t^2)$ newtons, where k is a constant and $0 \leq t \leq 0.09$. The bat stays in contact with the ball for 0.09 seconds.

Find the value of k.

[© AQA 2011]

5 A stone, of mass 2 kg, is moving in a straight line on a smooth horizontal sheet of ice under the action of a single force which acts in the direction of motion. At time t seconds, the force has magnitude $(3t+1)$ newtons, $0 \leqslant t \leqslant 3$.

When $t = 0$, the stone has velocity 1 m s^{-1}.

When $t = T$, the stone has velocity 5 m s^{-1}.

Find the value of T.

[© AQA 2013]

6 Two particles, A and B, are moving on a smooth horizontal surface when they collide. The mass of A is 6 kg and the mass of B is m kg. Before the collision, the velocity of A is $(5\mathbf{i} + 18\mathbf{j}) \text{ m s}^{-1}$ and the velocity of B is $(2\mathbf{i} - 5\mathbf{j}) \text{ m s}^{-1}$. After the collision, the velocity of A is $8\mathbf{i} \text{ m s}^{-1}$ and the velocity of B is $V\mathbf{j} \text{ m s}^{-1}$.

a Find m. **b** Find V.

[© AQA 2011]

7 The diagram shows part of a horizontal snooker table of width 1.69 m.

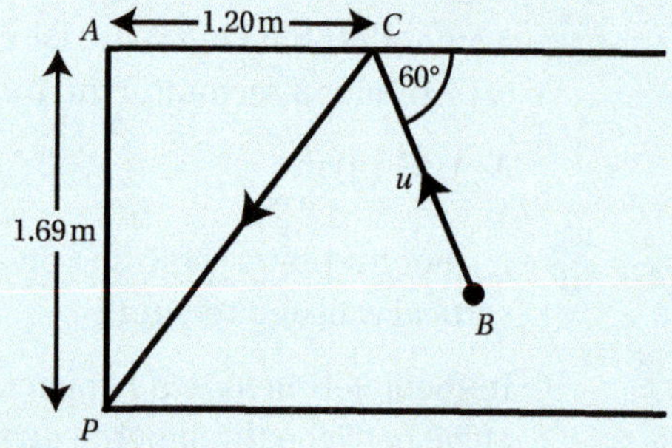

A player strikes the ball B directly, and it moves in a straight line. The ball hits the cushion of the table at C before rebounding and moving to the pocket at P at the corner of the table, as shown in the diagram. The point C is 1.20 m from the corner A of the table. The ball has mass 0.15 kg and, immediately before the collision with the cushion, it has velocity u in a direction inclined at $60°$ to the cushion. The **table** and the **cushion** are modelled as smooth.

a Find the coefficient of restitution between the ball and the cushion.

b Show that the magnitude of the impulse on the cushion at C is approximately $0.236u$.

c Find, in terms of u, the time taken between the ball hitting the cushion at C and entering the pocket at P.

d Explain how you have used the assumption that the cushion is smooth in your answers.

[© AQA 2012]

8 An ice-hockey player has mass 60 kg. He slides in a straight line at a constant speed of 5 m s^{-1} on the horizontal smooth surface of an ice rink towards the vertical perimeter wall of the rink, as shown in the diagram.

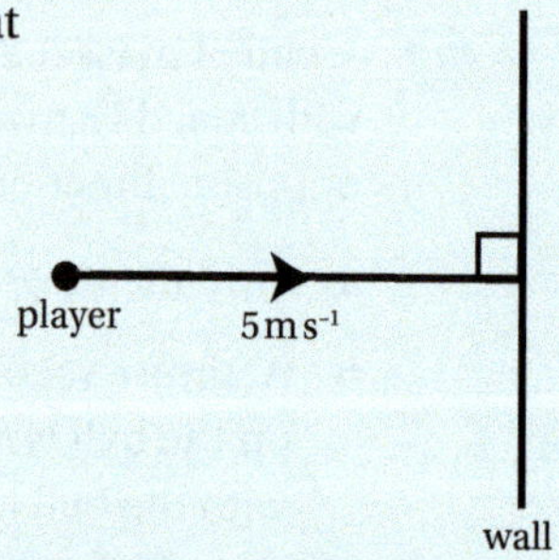

The player collides directly with the wall, and remains in contact with the wall for 0.5 seconds.

At time t seconds after coming into contact with the wall, the force exerted by the wall on the player is $4 \times 10^4 t^2 (1 - 2t)$ newtons, where $0 \leqslant t \leqslant 0.5$.

a Find the magnitude of the impulse exerted by the wall on the player.

b The player rebounds from the wall. Find the player's speed immediately after the collision.

[© AQA 2012]

9   A disc of mass 0.5 kg is moving with speed 3 m s^{-1} on a smooth horizontal surface when it receives a horizontal impulse in a direction **perpendicular to its direction of motion**. Immediately after the impulse, the disc has speed 5 m s^{-1}.

    a Find the magnitude of the impulse received by the disc.

    b Before the impulse, the disc is moving parallel to a smooth vertical wall, as shown in the diagram.

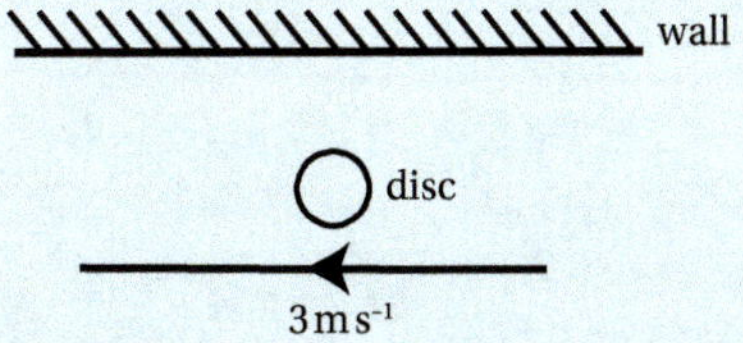

After the impulse, the disc hits the wall and rebounds with speed $3\sqrt{2}$ m s^{-1}.

Find the coefficient of restitution between the disc and the wall.

[© AQA 2015]

7 Circular motion 2

In this chapter you will learn how to:

- work with a particle moving in a circle with variable speed
- model the motion of a particle moving in a circle in a vertical plane
- use the principle of conservation of mechanical energy to solve problems involving a particle moving in a vertical circle
- solve problems involving moving particles where part of their path is a vertical circle.

Before you start...

Chapter 1	You should know the principle of conservation of mechanical energy (using kinetic energy and gravitational potential energy).	1	A cyclist is travelling at $4\,\mathrm{m\,s^{-1}}$ along a road when he reaches an incline making an angle of $5°$ with the horizontal. If the cyclist does not pedal to maintain his speed, assuming there is no resistance, how far along the road will he reach?
Chapter 4	You should be able to model motion in a horizontal circle.	2	A particle moves in a circular orbit of radius $3\,\mathrm{m}$ at a constant angular speed of $0.4\,\mathrm{rad\,s^{-1}}$. What is the linear speed of the particle?
A Level Mathematics Student Book 2, Chapter 17	You should be able to use the equations of motion for a particle moving under constant acceleration to model motion of a particle.	3	A ball is hit at an angle of $30°$ to the horizontal at a speed of $5\,\mathrm{m\,s^{-1}}$ from a height of $1\,\mathrm{m}$ above the ground. Calculate the maximum height above the ground reached by the ball.
A Level Mathematics Student Book 2, Chapter 18	You should be able to label the forces acting on a particle resting on a plane inclined at an angle θ to the horizontal.	4	A 2 kg particle is on the point of sliding down an inclined plane, inclined at $30°$ to the horizontal. Find the normal reaction between the particle and the inclined plane.

What is circular motion with variable speed?

If the speed of a particle is **not** constant but is a function of time, you will need to refine the model of circular motion that you developed in Chapter 4.

An important example of circular motion with variable speed is when a particle is moving in a vertical circle, with initial speed u and final speed v.

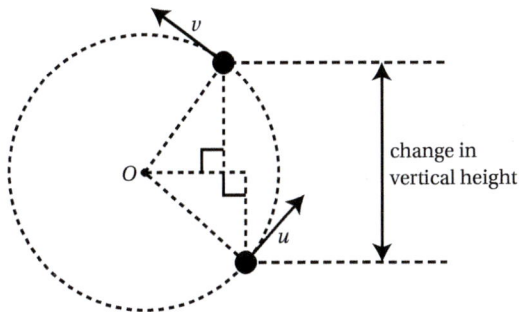

Section 1: Conservation of mechanical energy

Key point 7.1

You can use the principle of conservation of mechanical energy to determine the speed of a particle at any point in a vertical circular orbit.

Rewind

You learned about conservation of energy in Chapter 1.

WORKED EXAMPLE 7.1

A smooth bead of mass 50 grams is threaded onto a smooth circular wire of radius 2 m and centre O fixed in a vertical plane. The bead is projected from its lowest point A with speed 12 m s^{-1}.

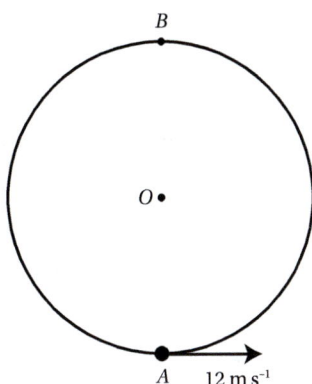

Find the speed of the bead when it reaches its highest point B in its motion.

Use $g = 9.8$ m s^{-2}, giving your final answer to an appropriate degree of accuracy.

Continues on next page

$u_A = 12\,\text{m s}^{-1}$ and vertical distance bead travels, AB, is 4 m.

Set the gravitational potential energy to equal zero at the horizontal line passing through the lowest point, A, of the vertical circle.

> Write down any information that may be helpful from the diagram. Include the zero level for gravitational potential energy.

At the point A:

$\text{GPE} + \text{KE} = mgh_A + 0.5mu_A^2$

$\qquad = 0.05 \times g \times 0 + 0.5 \times 0.05 \times 12^2$

$\qquad = 3.6$

> Calculate the gravitational potential energy and kinetic energy of the bead at A.

At the point B:

$\text{GPE} + \text{KE} = mgh_B + 0.5mu_B^2$

$\qquad = 0.05 \times g \times 4 + 0.5 \times 0.05 \times u_B^2$

$\qquad = 1.96 + 0.025u_B^2$

> Calculate the gravitational potential energy and kinetic energy of the bead at B.

Since energy is conserved:

$3.6 = 1.96 + 0.025u_B^2$

> By the principle of conservation of mechanical energy, the total energy at A is equal to the total energy at B.

Rearranging to make u_B the subject:

$0.025u_B^2 = 3.6 - 1.96$

$\qquad u_B^2 = 65.6$

$\qquad u_B = 8.1\,\text{m s}^{-1}\ (2.\text{s.f})$

You can also apply the principle of conservation of mechanical energy to calculate the speed of a particle following a more complex path.

WORKED EXAMPLE 7.2

In this question use $g = 9.8\,\text{m s}^{-2}$, giving your final answers to an appropriate degree of accuracy.

A bead is threaded onto a smooth wire that is fixed in a vertical plane as shown. The bead is projected from O with an initial speed of 3 m s^{-1}.

a Find the speed of the bead when it passes through:
  i the lowest point on the wire
  ii the point X.
b Will the bead have sufficient energy to reach the finishing point Y?
c Find the vertical height, measured from O, at which the bead first comes to rest.

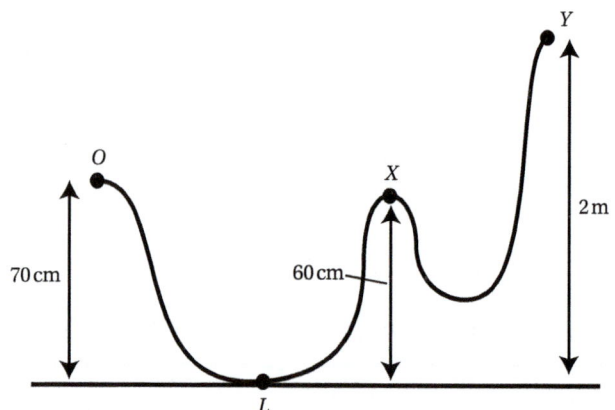

Continues on next page

a i $u = 3\,\text{m}\,\text{s}^{-1}$ and vertical distance OL is $0.7\,\text{m}$.
Set the gravitational potential energy to equal
zero at the horizontal line passing through L.

Write down any information that may be
helpful from the diagram. Include the zero
level for gravitational potential energy.

At the point O:
$$\text{GPE} + \text{KE} = mgh_O + 0.5mu^2$$
$$= mg \times 0.7 + 0.5 \times m \times 3^2$$

At the point L:
$$\text{GPE} + \text{KE} = mgh_L + 0.5mv^2$$
$$= mg \times 0 + 0.5mv^2$$

Since energy is conserved,
$$mg \times 0.7 + 0.5 \times m \times 3^2 = mg \times 0 + 0.5mv^2$$

By the principle of conservation of
mechanical energy, the total energy at O is
equal to the total energy at L.

Dividing through by m and rearranging to make
v^2 the subject:
$$9.8 \times 0.7 + 0.5 \times 3^2 = 0.5v^2$$
$$2 \times (6.86 + 4.5) = v^2$$
$$v^2 = 22.72$$
$$v = 4.8\,\text{m}\,\text{s}^{-1}\,(2\,\text{s.f.})$$

Only the positive solution is required since
the question specifically asks for speed.

ii The point X is $10\,\text{cm}$ below the point O.
$u = 3\,\text{m}\,\text{s}^{-1}$ and vertical distance OX is $0.1\,\text{m}$.
Set the gravitational potential energy to equal
zero at the horizontal line passing through X.

Write down any information that may be
helpful from the diagram. Include the zero
level for gravitational potential energy.

At the point O:
$$\text{GPE} + \text{KE} = mgh_O + 0.5mu^2$$
$$= mg \times 0.1 + 0.5 \times m \times 3^2$$

At the point X:
$$\text{GPE} + \text{KE} = mgh_X + 0.5mv^2$$
$$= mg \times 0 + 0.5mv^2$$

Since energy is conserved,
$$mg \times 0.1 + 0.5m \times 3^2 = mg \times 0 + 0.5mv^2$$

By the principle of conservation of
mechanical energy, the total energy at O is
equal to the total energy at X.

Dividing through by m and rearranging to make
v^2 the subject:
$$9.8 \times 0.1 + 0.5 \times 3^2 = 0.5 \times v^2$$
$$2 \times (0.98 + 4.5) = v^2$$
$$v^2 = 10.96$$
$$v = 3.3\,\text{m}\,\text{s}^{-1}\,(2\,\text{s.f.})$$

Again only the positive solution is
required.

b The point Y is $1.3\,\text{m}$ above the point O.
$u = 3\,\text{m}\,\text{s}^{-1}$ and vertical distance OY is $1.3\,\text{m}$.
Set the gravitational potential energy to equal
zero at the horizontal line passing through O.

Write down any information that may be
helpful from the diagram. Include the zero
level for gravitational potential energy.

Continues on next page

At the point O:
$$\text{GPE} + \text{KE} = mgh_O + 0.5mu^2$$
$$= mg \times 0 + 0.5 \times m \times 3^2$$

At the point Y:
$$\text{GPE} + \text{KE} = mgh_Y + 0.5mv^2$$
$$= mg \times 1.3 + 0.5 \times mv^2$$

Since energy is conserved:
$$mg \times 0 + 0.5 \times m \times 3^2 = mg \times 1.3 + 0.5 \times mv^2$$

> By the principle of conservation of mechanical energy, the total energy at O is equal to the total energy at Y.

Dividing through by m and rearranging to make v^2 the subject:
$$0.5 \times 3^2 = g \times 1.3 + 0.5 \times v^2$$
$$2 \times (4.5 - 12.74) = v^2$$
$$v^2 = -16.48$$

There are no real solutions for v. The particle will not have enough energy to reach Y.

> The amount of kinetic energy the bead has is less that than the gain in gravitational potential energy required to reach Y.

c   Let A be the point where the bead first comes to rest. $u = 3\,\text{m}\,\text{s}^{-1}$ and vertical distance OA is h_A m. Set the gravitational potential energy to equal zero at the horizontal line passing through O.

> Write down any information that may be helpful from the diagram. Include the zero level for gravitational potential energy.

At the point O:
$$\text{GPE} + \text{KE} = mgh_O + 0.5mu^2$$
$$= mg \times 0 + 0.5 \times m \times 3^2$$
$$= 4.5m$$

At the point A:
$$\text{GPE} + \text{KE} = mgh_A + 0.5mv^2$$
$$= mgh_A + 0.5 \times m \times 0^2$$
$$= 9.8mh_A$$

Since energy is conserved,
$$4.5m = 9.8mh_A$$

> By the principle of conservation of mechanical energy, the total energy at O is equal to the total energy at A.

Dividing through by m and rearranging to find h_A:
$$h_A = 0.46\,\text{m}\,(2\,\text{s.f.})$$

So the particle comes to rest at a height of
$$0.7 + 0.46 = 1.2\,\text{m}\,(2\,\text{s.f.})\text{ above the lowest point.}$$

Tip

An alternative approach to Worked example 7.2 would be to leave the zero level for GPE as the line through L (as in part **a i**) and then to solve the remaining parts by considering the change in GPE at each stage from this initial level. Using this approach, try to solve this question again.

If you want to find the forces acting on a particle as it moves in a vertical circle, you can use the principle of conservation of mechanical energy to find the speed at any point and then apply Newton's second law ($F = ma$).

Acceleration towards the centre of motion, known as **radial acceleration**, is $\frac{v^2}{r}$, so you can calculate the force towards the centre of the circular motion.

There is also a component of acceleration in the **tangential direction** but this is not included here.

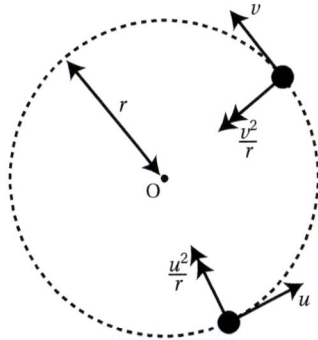

⏮ **Rewind**

You learned about Newton's second law in A Level Mathematics Student Book 1, Chapter 18.

◉ **Focus on ...**

In Focus on ... Problem solving 2 you will solve a problem involving the impulse–momentum principle as well as conservation of mechanical energy to find the speed of a particle moving in a vertical circular orbit.

WORKED EXAMPLE 7.3

A smooth bead of mass 50 grams is threaded onto a smooth circular wire of radius 200 cm and centre O fixed in a vertical plane. The bead is projected from its lowest point A with speed 12 m s^{-1}.

Calculate the magnitude of the normal reaction force of the wire on the bead when the bead is in the same horizontal line as the centre of the circle.

In this question use $g = 9.81 \text{ m s}^{-2}$, giving your final answer to an appropriate degree of accuracy.

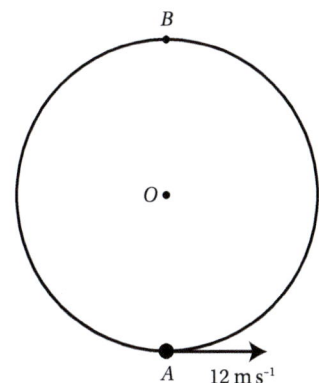

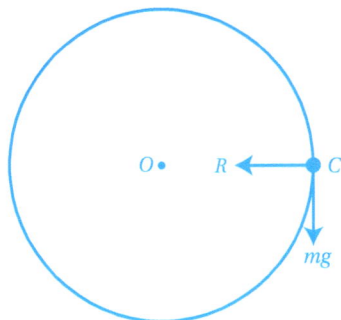

$u_A = 12 \text{ m s}^{-1}$ and the vertical distance the bead travels, AO, is 200 cm. Set the gravitational potential energy to equal zero at the horizontal line passing through the lowest point of the vertical circle A. Let C denote the position of the bead on the circular wire and R the normal reaction force of the wire on the bead.

Write down any information that may be helpful from the diagram. Include the zero level for gravitational potential energy. You first need to find the speed of the bead at the point C when the bead is in the same horizontal line as the centre of the circle.

Continues on next page

At the point A:

$$\text{GPE} + \text{KE} = mgh_A + 0.5mu_A^2$$
$$= 0.05 \times g \times 0 + 0.5 \times 0.05 \times 12^2$$
$$= 3.6$$

At the point C:

$$\text{GPE} + \text{KE} = mgh_C + 0.5mu_C^2$$
$$= 0.05 \times g \times 2 + 0.5 \times 0.05 \times u_C^2$$
$$= 0.981 + 0.025u_C^2$$

Since energy is conserved:

$$3.6 = 0.981 + 0.025u_C^2$$

> By the principle of conservation of mechanical energy, the total energy at A is equal to the total energy at C.

Rearranging to make u_C^2 the subject:

$$0.025u_C^2 = 3.6 - 0.981$$
$$u_C^2 = 104.76$$
$$u_C = 10 \, \text{m s}^{-1} \, (2 \, \text{s.f.})$$

Using $F = ma$ towards the centre O:

$$R = 0.05 \times a$$
$$= 0.05 \times \frac{v^2}{r}$$
$$= 0.05 \times \frac{104.76}{2}$$
$$R = 2.6 \, \text{N} \, (2 \, \text{s.f.})$$

> $\frac{mv^2}{r}$ is equal to the resultant force towards the centre of the circular motion. It is the normal reaction of the wire on the bead that provides this force.

> The value of g in this question is given to 3 s.f. However the question also contains information only given to 2 s.f. So 2 s.f. is an appropriate degree of accuracy for your final answer.

When the radius of the circular motion is at an angle to the horizontal, you also need to include the component of the weight towards the centre.

Key point 7.2

Once you know the speed of a particle at a particular point in a circular path, you can find the resultant force acting on the particle in the **radial direction** and use Newton's second law to find the acceleration towards the centre of the circle.

WORKED EXAMPLE 7.4

A particle of mass 0.2 kg is attached to one end of a light inextensible string of length 0.6 m. The other end of the string is attached to a fixed point O and is free to rotate in a vertical circle. The particle is hanging in equilibrium at its lowest point when it is projected with a horizontal speed of u m s^{-1}.

a   Find an expression for the tension in the string when it makes an angle of θ with the downward vertical through O.

b   Find the range of values of u for which the particle will perform a complete circle.
Use $g = 9.8$ m s^{-2}, giving your final answer to an appropriate degree of accuracy.

Continues on next page

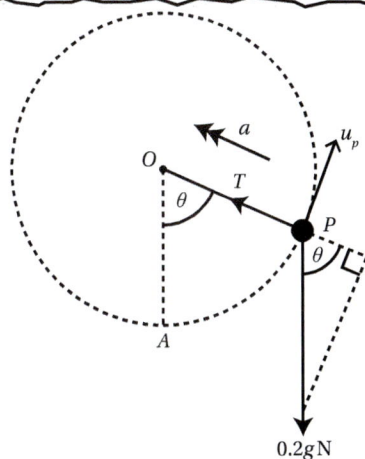

a Set the gravitational potential energy to equal zero at the horizontal line passing through the lowest point of the vertical circle. Call this point A.

Let the particle be at position P in its circular orbit when it makes an angle of θ with the downward vertical.

Write down any information that may be helpful from the diagram. Include the zero level for gravitational potential energy. Include any extra labels that might be helpful when trying to refer to position in the circular orbit. On the diagram shown, only the radial acceleration is marked since this is all you need to solve the problem but there will also be a tangential component.

At the point A:
$$\text{GPE} + \text{KE} = mgh_A + 0.5mu_A^2$$
$$= 0.2g \times 0 + 0.5 \times 0.2u^2$$
$$= 0.1u^2$$

At the point P:
$$\text{GPE} + \text{KE} = mgh_P + 0.5mu_P^2$$
$$= 0.2g \times 0.6(1 - \cos\theta) + 0.5 \times 0.2u_P^2$$
$$= 1.2(1 - \cos\theta) + 0.1u_P^2$$

Since energy is conserved:
$$0.1u^2 = 0.12g(1 - \cos\theta) + 0.1u_P^2$$
$$u_P^2 = u^2 - 1.2g(1 - \cos\theta)$$

By the principle of conservation of mechanical energy, the total energy at A is equal to the total energy at P.

$$a = \frac{v^2}{r}$$
$$= \frac{u^2 - 1.2g(1 - \cos\theta)}{0.6}$$

You now have an expression for acceleration using the formula from Chapter 4.

Using Newton's second law and resolving the forces in the radial direction of the circular motion:

Now resolve the forces in the same direction as the tension.

$$F = ma$$
$$T - 0.2g\cos\theta = 0.2 \times \frac{u^2 - 1.2g(1 - \cos\theta)}{0.6}$$

Rearranging to find an expression for tension in terms of u, g and θ:
$$T = \frac{1}{3}u^2 - \frac{2}{5}g + \frac{3}{5}g\cos\theta$$

Continues on next page

b For the particle to make a full circle the speed must be large enough so that the string has some tension in order to keep the string taut at the highest point in the circular motion.

Need $T > 0$ when $\theta = 180°$:

$$\frac{1}{3}u^2 - \frac{2}{5}g + \frac{3}{5}g\cos 180° > 0$$

$$\frac{1}{3}u^2 - \frac{2}{5}g - \frac{3}{5}g > 0$$

At the highest point in the movement the angle made with the downward vertical is 180°.

Rearranging to find u:

$$\frac{1}{3}u^2 > g$$

$$u^2 > 3g$$

$$u > \sqrt{3g}$$

So $u > 5.4 \text{ m s}^{-1}$ (2 s.f.) for there to be complete circles.

This gives a lower bound for the value that the initial speed can take in order for the particle to complete full circles.

🔑 Key point 7.3

If a particle connected to a light inextensible string moving in vertical circles is to complete full circles, the tension in the string must be greater than zero at the highest point of the circular orbit.

WORKED EXAMPLE 7.5

A particle of mass 0.1 kg is attached to one end of a light rod of length 0.4 m. The other end of the rod is attached to a fixed point O and is free to rotate in a vertical circle. The particle is hanging in equilibrium at its lowest point when it is projected with a horizontal speed of $u \text{ m s}^{-1}$. Find:

a an expression for the speed of the particle when the rod is at an angle of θ with the upward vertical through O

b the set of values of u for which the particle will perform a complete circle. Use $g = 9.8 \text{ m s}^{-2}$, giving your final answer to an appropriate degree of accuracy.

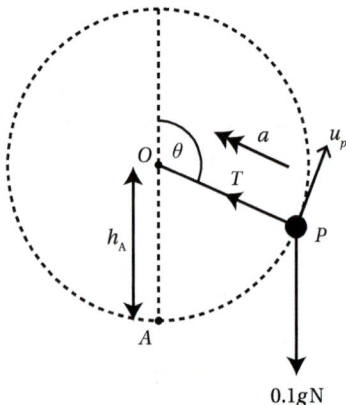

Continues on next page

In the diagram the vertical distance h is the vertical distance from the particle to the fixed point O. So, h_A denotes the vertical distance from the particle to the fixed point O when the particle is at point A.

Write down any information that may be helpful from the diagram. Include the zero level for gravitational potential energy. Also include any extra labels that might be helpful when trying to refer to position in the circular orbit. On the diagram shown, only the radial acceleration is marked since this is all you need to solve the problem but there will also be a tangential component.

a $m = 0.1$ kg, length of rod is 0.4 m and initial speed is u m s^{-1}.
Set the gravitational potential energy to equal zero at the horizontal line passing through the lowest point of the vertical circle. Call this point A.

Let the particle be at position P in its circular orbit when it makes an angle of θ with the upward vertical through O.

At the point A:
$$GPE + KE = mgh_A + 0.5mu^2$$
$$= 0.1 \times g \times 0 + 0.5 \times 0.1 \times u^2$$
$$= 0.05u^2$$

At the point P:
$$GPE + KE = mgh_P + 0.5mu_P^2$$
$$= 0.1 \times g \times 0.4(1 + \cos\theta) + 0.5 \times 0.1 \times u_P^2$$
$$= 0.04g(1 + \cos\theta) + 0.05u_P^2$$

Since energy is conserved:
$$0.05u^2 = 0.04g(1 + \cos\theta) + 0.05u_P^2$$
$$u_P^2 = u^2 - 0.8g(1 + \cos\theta)$$

By the principle of conservation of mechanical energy, the total energy at A is equal to the total energy at P.

b   For the particle to make a full circle the speed must be greater than zero when the particle is at the highest point in the circular orbit.

Unlike a string, a rod cannot go slack.

Need $u_P > 0$ when $\theta = 0°$:
$$u^2 - 0.8g(1 + \cos 0°) > 0$$
$$u^2 - 0.8g(1 + 1) > 0$$

At the highest point in the movement the angle made with the downward vertical is $0°$.

Rearrange to find u:
$$u^2 - 1.6g > 0$$
$$u^2 > 1.6g$$

$$u > \sqrt{1.6g}$$
So $u > 4.0$ m s^{-1} (2 s.f.) for there to be complete circles.

This gives a lower bound for the value that the initial speed can take in order for the particle to complete full circles.

Key point 7.4

If a particle connected to a light rod moving in vertical circles is to complete full circles, the speed of the particle must be greater than zero at the highest point of its circular orbit.

Tip

The same condition is true if the particle represents a bead threaded onto a smooth wire.

WORK IT OUT 7.1

A particle P of mass m kg is attached to one end of a light inextensible string of length r metres. The other end of the string is attached to a fixed point O. The particle hangs in equilibrium with the string taut at position O. The particle is then set in motion with a horizontal speed of u m s^{-1} so that the particle moves in a vertical circle. Which of these statements is correct?

Solution 1	Solution 2	Solution 3
The particle will complete vertical circles if the speed at the top of the circle is greater than zero.	The particle will complete vertical circles if the initial speed is $u = \sqrt{2gr}$ m s^{-1}.	The particle will complete vertical circles if the speed of the particle is enough to keep the string taut at the top of the circle.

EXERCISE 7A

In this exercise, unless otherwise instructed, use $g = 9.8$ m s^{-2}, giving your final answers to an appropriate degree of accuracy.

1 A particle P of mass m kg is attached to one end of a light inextensible string of length r metres. The other end of the string is attached to a fixed point O. The particle hangs in equilibrium with the string taut at position A. The particle is then set in motion with a horizontal speed of u m s^{-1} so that the particle moves in a vertical circle.

  a i Given that $r = 1$ and $u = 3$, find speed of the particle when angle AOP is $20°$.

     ii Given that $r = 3$ and $u = 9$, find speed of the particle when angle AOP is $110°$.

  b i Given that $r = 2.3$ and $u = 3.2$, find the acceleration towards centre O when angle AOP is $35°$.

     ii Given that $r = 0.75$ and $u = 5.3$, find the acceleration towards centre O when angle AOP is $70°$.

  c i Given that $r = 2$, $u = 4$ and $m = 2$, find the tension in the string when angle AOP is $30°$.

     ii Given that $r = 0.9$, $u = 6$ and $m = 1.2$, find the tension in the string when angle AOP is $130°$.

  d i Given that $r = 1.5$ and $u = 4$, find the angle made between OP and the downward vertical when the speed of the particle is 2 m s^{-1}.

     ii Given that $r = 0.75$ and $u = 3.2$, find the angle made between OP and the upward vertical when the speed of the particle is 0.8 m s^{-1}.

2 A smooth bead is threaded onto a smooth circular wire fixed in a vertical plane, with centre O and radius r metres. The bead is projected from the lowest point B with initial speed u m s^{-1}.

  a Given that $u^2 = 7gr$, find the speed of the bead when it passes through the general point A, where OA makes an angle of θ with the downward vertical.

  b Given that $u^2 = 2gr$, find the greatest height reached by the bead above the lowest point B of the circular wire.

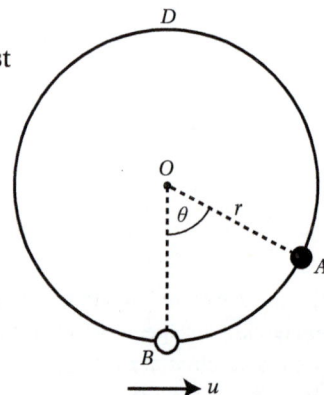

c Given that $u^2 = 5gr$, find the speed of the bead when it passes through the point C that is level with the centre O.

d Given that $u^2 = 9gr$, find the speed of the bead when it passes through the highest point D of the circular wire.

3 A smooth bead is threaded onto a smooth circular wire fixed in a vertical plane, with centre O and radius a metres. The bead is projected from the lowest point with initial speed u m s^{-1}. Will the bead make a full circle and, if not, find the maximum vertical height reached by the bead in each of these cases:

a $u^2 = ga$ 　　　　　　**b** $u^2 = \frac{2}{3}ga$ 　　　　　**c** $u^2 = 4ga$.

4 A particle of mass 0.5 kg is attached to one end of a light rod OA of length 0.4 m. The rod is free to rotate in a vertical plane about O. The particle is held at rest with OA horizontal and then released.

a Calculate the speed of the particle as it passes through the lowest point.

b Find the tension in the rod at this lowest point.

5 A particle of mass 0.5 kg is attached to one end of a light inextensible string OA of length 0.4 m. The particle is hanging in equilibrium at the lowest point B when it is set in motion with a speed of u m s^{-1}. Given that the string remains taut during the particle's motion, write an expression for the speed of the particle when OA makes an angle of θ with the downward vertical OB.

6 A bob B of mass 400 grams is attached to one end of a light inextensible string of length 30 cm. The other end of the string is attached to a fixed point O and the bob is hanging in equilibrium when it receives an impulse that sets the bob in motion with an initial speed of u m s^{-1}. By considering the tension in the string, describe the motion of the bob in each of these cases:

a $u^2 = 2g$ 　　　　　　**b** $u^2 = g$ 　　　　　　**c** $u^2 = 0.5g$.

7 A particle P of mass 1.2 kg is attached to one end of a light rod of length 1.5 m. The other end of the rod is attached to a fixed point O and it is free to rotate about O. The rod is hanging vertically with P below O when the particle is set in motion with a horizontal speed of u m s^{-1}. Find, in terms of the gravitational constant g, the minimum value of u for which the particle will perform a complete circle.

8 A light inextensible string of length r m has a particle P of mass m kg attached at one end. The other end is attached to a fixed point O and the particle P describes complete vertical circles, centre O. Given that the speed of the particle at the lowest point is twice the speed of the particle at its highest point, find the tension, T_H newtons, in the string when the particle is at the highest point. Give your answer in terms of m and the gravitational constant g.

9 A light inelastic string of length 2 m has one end attached to a fixed point O. A particle P of mass 0.5 kg is attached to the other end. The particle P is held with OP horizontal and the string taut.

a If the particle P is released from rest, what is the maximum speed and where will this occur in the circular orbit?

b If the particle P is projected vertically downwards with speed $\sqrt{2g}$ m s^{-1}, find the tension, T newtons, in the string when OP makes an angle of θ with the horizontal.

c Given that the string will break when the tension in the string is g N, find the angle between the string and the horizontal when the string breaks.

10   In this question use $g = 10 \text{ m s}^{-2}$, giving your final answers to an appropriate degree of accuracy.

A smooth hemispherical bowl centre O and of radius 15 cm is fixed on a horizontal surface such that the top of the bowl is parallel with the horizontal surface. A smooth marble P of mass 25 grams is held in place on the inner surface such that, for the plane containing the centre and the marble, the line OP makes an angle 60° with the downward vertical. The particle is released from rest.

a   Calculate the speed of the particle as it passes through the lowest point.

b   Calculate the normal reaction force acting on the marble when the marble passes through the lowest point.

Section 2: Problem solving situations

Leaving a circular path

Sometimes a particle will only follow a circular path for a short period of time. It will then need to be modelled as a particle moving freely under gravity.

▶▶❙ **Fast forward**

You will learn how to model the motion of a particle after it has left a circular orbit later in this chapter.

WORKED EXAMPLE 7.6

A smooth solid hemisphere with radius 4 m and centre O is resting on a horizontal table with its flat face in contact with the table. A particle P of mass 5 kg is resting on the hemisphere when it starts to slip from rest at the highest point A on the hemisphere.

a   If the hemisphere stays in a fixed position, find an expression for the normal reaction force of the particle to the surface of the hemisphere when the angle between OP and OA is θ.
b   Find the angle between OP and OA when the particle leaves the surface of the hemisphere.
c   Describe how you could model the subsequent movement of the particle, once it leaves the hemisphere.
d   Find the distance of the particle from the centre of the hemisphere when it first hits the ground.

In parts **b** and **d** use $g = 9.8 \text{ m s}^{-2}$, giving your final answers to an appropriate degree of accuracy.

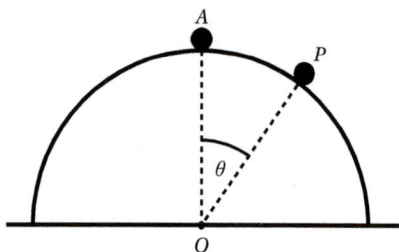

a $m = 5$ kg, radius $= 4$ m and initial speed $= 0 \text{ m s}^{-1}$.
Set the gravitational potential energy to equal zero at the horizontal line passing through the point O.

Write down any information that may be helpful from the diagram. Include where you will be measuring your gravitational potential energy from.

At the point A:
$\text{GPE} + \text{KE} = mgh_A + 0.5mu_A^2$
$\qquad = 5 \times g \times 4 + 0.5 \times 5 \times 0^2$
$\qquad = 20\,g$

At the point P:
$\text{GPE} + \text{KE} = mgh_P + 0.5mu_P^2$
$\qquad = 5 \times g \times 4\cos\theta + 0.5 \times 5 \times u_P^2$
$\qquad = 20\,g\cos\theta + 2.5u_P^2$

Continues on next page

Since energy is conserved:

$20g = 20g \cos \theta + 2.5 u_P^2$

$u_P^2 = 8g(1 - \cos \theta)$

By the principle of conservation of mechanical energy, the total energy at A is equal to the total energy at P.

Resolving perpendicularly to the surface of the hemisphere:

$R = mg \cos \theta - \dfrac{8mg(1 - \cos \theta)}{4}$

where $8mg(1 - \cos \theta)$ is the speed squared.

$R = 3mg \cos \theta - 2mg$

Now use Newton's second law and $a = \dfrac{v^2}{r}$ to find the normal reaction force R.

b   When the particle leaves the surface, $R = 0$.

$3mg \cos \theta - 2mg = 0$

So $\cos \theta = \dfrac{2}{3}$

$\theta = 48°$ (2 s.f.)

So the angle between OP and OA is $48°$ (2 s.f.).

At the instant when the particle leaves the surface, the normal reaction force between the particle and the surface is zero.

c   You can model the particle as a projectile falling freely under gravity.

When the particle is no longer moving in a circular path it is now free to move as if it were a projectile, falling freely under gravity.

d   The particle leaves the surface when $\theta = 48°$.

The horizontal distance between O and this point is given by:

$4 \sin(48.2°) = 3.0 \,\text{m}$ (2 s.f.)

Once the particle leaves the surface of the hemisphere it falls under gravity.

First, calculate the horizontal distance the particle travels before it leaves the surface of the hemisphere.

When the particle leaves the surface of the hemisphere it can now be modelled as a projectile.

Take A to O to be the positive vertical direction and take from O to the right to be the positive horizontal direction.

$\theta = 48°$

Initial vertical speed $= u_P \sin \theta$

$\qquad = \sqrt{8g(1 - \cos \theta)} \times \sin \theta$

$\qquad = 3.81 \,\text{m s}^{-1}$ (3 s.f.)

Horizontal speed $= u_P \cos \theta$

$\qquad = \sqrt{8g(1 - \cos \theta)} \times \cos \theta$

$\qquad = 3.4 \,\text{m s}^{-1}$ (2 s.f.)

You need to set up a direction for the horizontal and vertical components of the velocity and displacement for a projectile.

Continues on next page

Acceleration due to gravity $= 9.8\,\mathrm{m\,s^{-2}}$

Vertical height $= 4\cos\theta$

$$= 4 \times \frac{2}{3}$$

$$= 2.7\,\mathrm{m}\,(2\,\text{s.f.})$$

You can use the equations of motion for a particle moving with a constant acceleration to calculate horizontal and vertical components of velocity and displacement and the time of flight.

It is sensible to take the positive direction for the vertical movement in the same direction as the initial vertical component of the velocity.

See A Level Mathematics Student Book 2, Chapter 17, for a reminder of motion in two dimensions.

Using $s = ut + 0.5at^2$:

$2.67 = u_p t \sin\theta + 0.5 \times 9.8 \times t^2$

$2.67 = 3.81t + 4.9t^2$

$4.9t^2 + 3.81t - 2.67 = 0$

You have a quadratic equation in t and so can use the quadratic formula to find the positive value for t.

Using the quadratic formula:

$$t = \frac{-3.81 \pm \sqrt{3.81^2 - 4 \times 4.9 \times (-2.67)}}{9.8}$$

which gives $t = 0.45$ seconds or $t = -1.2$ seconds $(2\,\text{s.f.})$

Ignore the negative value for the time.

The horizontal distance travelled from the point where the particle leaves the surface of the hemisphere is given by $s = ut$:

$s = u_p \cos\theta + t$

$s = 3.4 \times 0.45$

$\quad = 1.5\,\mathrm{m}\,(2\,\text{s.f.})$

Total horizontal distance from O is given by:

$3.0 + 1.5 = 4.5\,\mathrm{m}\,(2\,\text{s.f.})$

Finally, you can combine the horizontal distances travelled by the particle before leaving the surface and after leaving the surface of the hemisphere.

Key point 7.5

When the normal reaction force between the particle and the surface is equal to zero, a particle loses contact with a surface.

Tip

After the particle loses contact with a surface, its movement can be modelled as a projectile and you can use the equations of motion under constant acceleration due to gravity to model the particle's movement.

WORKED EXAMPLE 7.7

A particle P of mass m kg is attached to one end of a light inextensible string of length l metres. The other end of the string is attached to a fixed point O such that the particle hangs in equilibrium directly below O at A. The particle is set in motion with a horizontal speed of $2\sqrt{gl}$ m s^{-1}.

a Find the vertical height of P above the starting position A at the point when the string first goes slack.

At the point when the string first goes slack, the particle is released from the string.

b Find the maximum height the particle reaches above its starting position.

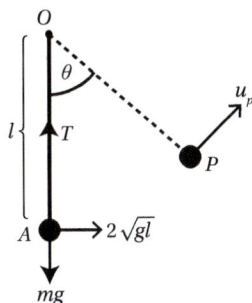

a Set the gravitational potential energy to equal zero at the horizontal line passing through the point A. Let θ be the angle formed between OP and the downward vertical OA. Let T be the tension in the string.

> Write down any information that may be helpful from the diagram. Include where you will be measuring your gravitational potential energy from. Include any extra labels that might be helpful when trying to refer to position in the circular orbit.

At the point A:
$$GPE + KE = mgh_A + 0.5mu_A^2$$
$$= mg \times 0 + 0.5 \times m \times (2\sqrt{gl})^2$$
$$= 2mgl$$

> Calculate the gravitational potential energy and kinetic energy of the particle at A.

At the point P:
$$GPE + KE = mgh_P + 0.5mu_P^2$$
$$= mg \times l(1 - \cos\theta) + 0.5 \times m \times u_P^2$$
$$= mgl(1 - \cos\theta) + 0.5mu_P^2$$

> Calculate the gravitational potential energy and kinetic energy of the particle at P.

Since energy is conserved:
$$2mgl = mgl(1 - \cos\theta) + 0.5\,mu_P^2$$
$$u_P^2 = 2lg(1 + \cos\theta)$$

> By the principle of conservation of mechanical energy, the total energy at A is equal to the total energy at P.

$$F = ma$$
$$T - mg\cos\theta = m\frac{v^2}{r}$$
$$T = mg\cos\theta + \frac{2mgl(1 + \cos\theta)}{l}$$
$$T = mg\cos\theta + 2mg(1 + \cos\theta)$$

> Once you have calculated the speed you can use Newton's second law and $a = \dfrac{v^2}{r}$ to find the tension T by resolving in the radial and tangential directions.

$$T = 0$$
So $mg\cos\theta + 2mg(1 + \cos\theta) = 0$

> When the string goes slack there is no tension in the string.

Continues on next page

Dividing through by mg and rearranging to make $\cos \theta$ the subject:

$\cos \theta + 2(1 + \cos \theta) = 0$

$\cos \theta + 2 + 2 \cos \theta = 0$

$\cos \theta = \dfrac{-2}{3}$

$\theta = 132°$

The vertical height above A where the string first becomes slack is:

$l(1 - \cos \theta) = l\left(1 - \dfrac{-2}{3}\right)$

$\qquad = \dfrac{5l}{3}$ m

> You can find the vertical height using $\cos \theta$.

b When the particle is released from the string and its circular path, the particle can now be modelled as a projectile.

For the motion of the particle you take the upward vertical as the positive direction to the projectile motion.

> This is an important modelling assumption.

Vertical speed $= u_p \sin \theta$

$\qquad = \sqrt{2gl(1 - \cos \theta)} \sin \theta$

$\qquad = \sqrt{\dfrac{2gl}{3}} \times \dfrac{\sqrt{5}}{3}$

$\qquad = \sqrt{\dfrac{10gl}{27}}$

The maximum height reached by the projectile is when the final vertical velocity equals zero.

Using $v^2 = u^2 + 2as$:

$0 = \dfrac{10gl}{27} - 2gs$

$s = \dfrac{5l}{27}$

Total distance $= \dfrac{5l}{3} + \dfrac{5l}{27} = \dfrac{49l}{27}$ m

> You can find the total vertical distance travelled by the particle by combining the projectile motion with the motion in its circular path.

WORK IT OUT 7.2

A smooth solid hemisphere with radius r m and centre O is placed in a fixed position on a horizontal plane with its flat face in contact with the horizontal plane. A particle P of mass m kg is resting on the hemisphere when it starts to move from rest from the highest point. When OP has turned through an angle of θ and the particle is still on the surface of the hemisphere, where the normal reaction force on the sphere on the particle is R N, which statement is true?

Solution 1	Solution 2	Solution 3
$R = mg(2 - \cos\theta)$	$R = mg(3\cos\theta - 2)$	$R = -mg(\cos\theta + 2)$
At P: $mgr = \frac{1}{2}mv^2 + mgr\cos\theta$ $v^2 = 2gr(1 - \cos\theta)$ $F = ma$ $R - g\cos\theta = \frac{mv^2}{r}$ $R = mg\cos\theta + \frac{m}{r}2gr(1 - \cos\theta)$ $R = mg\cos\theta + 2mg - 2mg\cos\theta$ $R = 2mg - mg\cos\theta$ $R = mg(2 - \cos\theta)$	At P: $mgr = \frac{1}{2}mv^2 + mgr\cos\theta$ $v^2 = 2gr(1 - \cos\theta)$ $F = ma$ $mg\cos\theta - R = \frac{mv^2}{r}$ $R = mg\cos\theta - \frac{m2gr(1 - \cos\theta)}{r}$ $R = mg\cos\theta - 2gm + 2gm\cos\theta$ $R = mg(3\cos\theta - 2)$	At P: $mgr = \frac{1}{2}mv^2 + mgr\cos\theta$ $v^2 = 2gr(1 + \cos\theta)$ $F = ma$ $mg\cos\theta - R = \frac{mv^2}{r}$ $R = mg\cos\theta - \frac{m2gr(1 + \cos\theta)}{r}$ $R = mg\cos\theta - 2mg - 2mg\cos\theta$ $R = -mg(\cos\theta + 2)$

EXERCISE 7B

In this exercise, unless otherwise instructed, use $g = 9.8$ m s^{-2}, giving your final answers to an appropriate degree of accuracy.

1. A smooth solid hemisphere with radius r metres and centre O is resting on a horizontal table with its flat face in contact with the table. A particle P of mass m kg is resting on the hemisphere when it is projected parallel with the horizontal surface at an initial speed of u m s^{-1} from point A on the hemisphere.

   a i Given that $u = 2$ and $r = 1$, find the speed of the particle if the angle between OP and OA is $10°$.

   ii Given that $u = 5$ and $r = 1.3$, find the speed of the particle if the angle between OP and OA is $22°$.

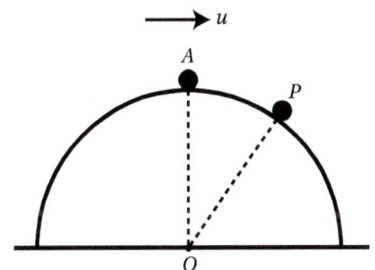

b **i** Given that $u = 2$, $r = 2.3$ and $m = 3$, find the normal reaction force acting on the particle at the surface of the hemisphere if the angle between OP and OA is $17°$.

   ii Given that $u = 5$, $r = 4.7$ and $m = 2.4$, find the normal reaction force acting on the particle at the surface of the hemisphere if the angle between OP and OA is $30°$.

c **i** Given that $u = 2$ and $r = 1.75$, find the angle between OP and OA when the particle leaves the surface of the hemisphere.

   ii Given that $u = 5$ and $r = 3$, find the angle between OP and the horizontal when the particle leaves the surface of the hemisphere.

d **i** Given that $u = 2$ and $r = 1.75$, find the speed of the particle when it leaves the surface of the hemisphere.

   ii Given that $u = 5$ and $r = 3$, find the speed of the particle when it leaves the surface of the hemisphere.

2 In this question use $g = 10 \text{ m s}^{-2}$, giving your final answers to an appropriate degree of accuracy.

A particle of mass 500 grams is released from rest at the top of a smooth track which forms a quarter of circle, centre O of radius 50 cm, followed by drop of 2 m to the ground.

a Calculate the speed of the particle as it leaves the quarter circle part of the track.

b What is the total horizontal distance that the particle travels before it hits the ground?

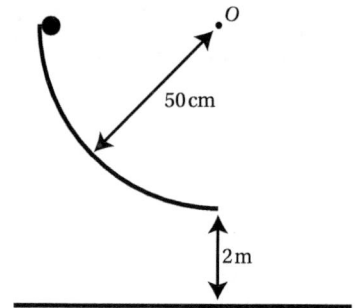

3 A smooth piece of track XY is constructed so that it is in the shape of a circular arc. The arc XY has a radius of 2 m and subtends an angle of $30°$ at its centre O_{XY}. The points X and O_{XY} are on a line that is parallel to a horizontal surface, which is vertically 5 m below the point Y. O_{XY}, X and Y all lie in the same vertical plane. A particle P is released from rest at X.

a Find the speed of the particle as it leaves the arc XY.

b Find the time taken for the particle to hit the ground after it has left Y.

c Find the horizontal distance that the particle P travels after it leaves the track before it hits the horizontal surface.

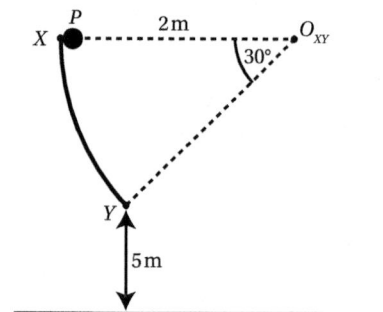

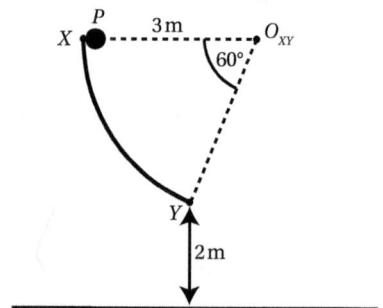

4 A smooth piece of track XY is constructed so that it is in the shape of a circular arc. The arc XY has a radius of 3 m and subtends an angle of $60°$ at its centre O_{XY}. The points X and O_{XY} are on a line that is parallel to a horizontal surface, which is vertically 2 m below the point Y. O_{XY}, X and Y all lie in the same vertical plane. A particle P is released from rest at X.

a Find the speed of the particle as it leaves the arc XY.

b Find the time taken for the particle to hit the ground after it has left Y.

c Find the horizontal distance that the particle P travels after it leaves the track before it hits the horizontal surface.

5   A smooth piece of track XY is constructed so that it is in the shape of
    a circular arc. The arc XY has a radius of 0.5 m and subtends an angle
    of 120° at its centre O_{XY}. The points X and O_{XY} are on a line that is that
    is parallel to a horizontal surface, which is vertically 4 m below the
    point Y. O_{XY}, X and Y all lie in the same vertical plane. A particle P
    is released from rest at X.

    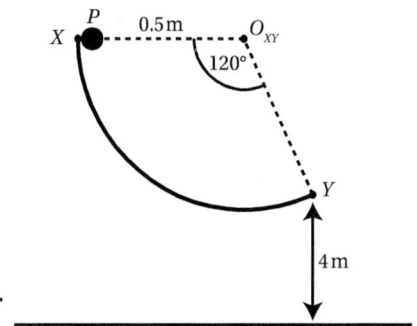

    a   Find the speed of the particle as it leaves the arc XY.

    b   Find the time taken for the particle to hit the ground after it has left Y.

    c   Find the horizontal distance the particle P travels after it leaves
        the track before it hits the horizontal surface.

6   A smooth piece of track XY is constructed so that it is in the shape
    of a circular arc. The arc XY has a radius of 0.3 m and subtends an
    angle of 90° at its centre O_{XY}. The points X and O_{XY} are on a line
    that is that is parallel to a horizontal surface, which is vertically 2 m
    below the point Y. O_{XY}, X and Y all lie in the same vertical plane.
    A particle P is released from rest at X.

    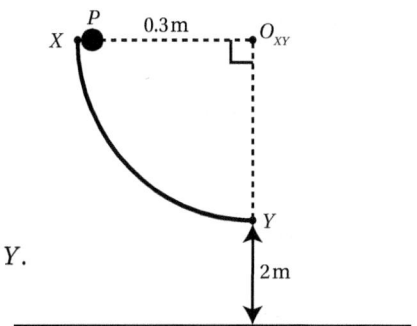

    a   Find the speed of the particle as it leaves the arc XY.

    b   Find the time taken for the particle to hit the ground after it has left Y.

    c   Find the horizontal distance the particle P travels after it leaves
        the track before it hits the horizontal surface.

7   A smooth solid hemisphere with centre O and radius 2 m is fixed with its flat surface in contact with a
    horizontal plane. A particle P is released from rest on the surface of the hemisphere, such that OP makes an
    angle of 5° with the upward vertical. The particle leaves the hemisphere at X. Find the angle between OX
    and the upward vertical.

8   A smooth sphere of centre O and radius 90 cm is fixed to a horizontal table. A particle P of mass 2 kg is
    released from rest at a point A on the surface of the sphere such that the acute angle formed between OA
    and the line perpendicular to the horizontal surface going through O is 25°. Find the speed of the particle
    when it leaves the surface of the sphere.

9   A light inextensible rope AB of length 4 m is attached at one end A to a horizontal beam 6 m above the
    horizontal ground and at the other end B to a seat. A platform sits 4 m above the horizontal ground where
    an acrobat P of mass 65 kg holds the rope taut whilst sitting on the seat attached to the rope. The acrobat
    is released from rest and follows a circular arc. After the acrobat has travelled through an angle of 90°,
    measured from the starting position, the acrobat releases themselves from the seat.

    a   What angle does the line AP make with the downward vertical?

    b   Calculate the tension in the rope when the acrobat is directly below A.

    c   Calculate the speed and direction of the acrobat as they leave the rope.

10 A marble P of mass 30 grams is attached to one end of a light inextensible string of length 60 cm. The other end of the string is attached to a fixed point O such that P hangs in equilibrium. The marble is set in motion with a horizontal speed of $3\,\mathrm{m\,s^{-1}}$. Let θ be the angle OP makes with the downward vertical at O. Given that the string does not become slack:

a find an expression for the speed of P

b find an expression for the tension in the string in terms of θ

c show that the marble does not make full circles.

11 A smooth rubbish chute is built in two sections, AB and BC, each in the shape of an arc of a circle. The arc AB has a radius of 3 m and subtends an angle of 60° at its centre O_{AB}. The arc BC has a radius 7 m and subtends an angle of 45° at its centre O_{BC}. The points O_{AB}, O_{BC}, and A, B and C all lie on a vertical line.

a If a bag containing rubbish of mass 3 kg is released from rest at A, calculate the speed at which the bag enters the arc BC.

A large container to collect the rubbish bags from the chute is positioned 2 m below C.

b Calculate the speed at which the rubbish bag reaches the large container below C.

c Determine whether or not the rubbish bag of mass 3 kg will lose contact with the chute before it reaches C.

✎ Checklist of learning and understanding

- For a particle moving in a circular path of radius r that does not move with constant angular speed you can find the velocity of the particle at any point in the path using the principle of conservation of mechanical energy. This is assuming that the particle is subject only to weight and a central force.
- The acceleration is directed towards the centre of the circular motion and you can use this to find the force in the same direction.
- If a particle connected to a light inextensible string moving in vertical circles is to complete full circles, then the tension in the string must be greater than zero throughout its circular orbit.
- If a particle connected to a light rod moving in vertical circles is to complete full circles, then the speed of the particle must be greater than zero throughout its circular orbit.
- When a particle loses contact with a surface, the normal reaction force between the particle and the surface becomes zero.

Mixed practice 7

In this exercise, unless otherwise instructed, use $g = 9.8$ m s^{-2}, giving your final answers to an appropriate degree of accuracy.

1 A particle P of mass 750 kg is attached to one end of a light inextensible rope of length 0.8 metres. The other end of the rope is attached to a fixed point O. The particle hangs in equilibrium with the rope taut at position A. The particle is then set in motion with a horizontal speed of 4 m s^{-1} so that the particle moves in a vertical circle. Find the maximum height the particle reaches above A. Choose from these options.

    A 18 cm   **B** 110 cm   **C** 82 cm   **D** 330 cm

2 A particle P of mass 200 grams is attached to one end of a light inextensible string of length 130 cm. The other end of the string is attached to a fixed point O. The particle hangs in equilibrium with the string taut at position A. The particle is then set in motion with a horizontal speed of 6 m s^{-1} so that the particle moves in a vertical circle. Find the tension in the string when the particle P is in the same horizontal line as the fixed point O. Choose from these options. The options are given to two significant figures.

    A 4.8 N   **B** 16 N   **C** 9.5 N   **D** 1.6 N

3 A smooth solid hemisphere with radius 115 cm and centre O is resting on a horizontal table with its flat face in contact with the table. A particle P of mass 720 grams is projected parallel with the horizontal surface at an initial speed of 3 m s^{-1}. Find the speed of the particle when OP makes an angle of 83° with the horizontal. Choose from these options. The options are given to two significant figures.

    A 5.1 m s^{-1} **B** 45 m s^{-1} **C** 5.4 m s^{-1} **D** 3.0 m s^{-1}.

4 In this question use $g = 10$ m s^{-2}, giving your final answers to an appropriate degree of accuracy. A particle of mass 0.4 kg is attached to one end of a light rod of length 2 m. The other end of the rod is attached to a fixed point O. The particle is hanging in equilibrium at its lowest point A when it is projected with a horizontal speed of 7 m s^{-1}. Using the principle of conservation of mechanical energy, find the speed of the particle when the angle that OP makes with downward vertical OA is 60°.

5 One end of a light inextensible rope of length 1 m is attached to ball B of mass 700 grams and the other end is attached to a fixed point A. The particle is hanging in equilibrium at C when it is set in motion with a horizontal speed of 5 m s^{-1}. Calculate the tension in the rope when AB makes an angle of 30° with the downward vertical AC.

6 A hollow circular cylinder is fixed with its axis horizontal. The inner surface of the cylinder is smooth and has a radius of 1.05 m. A particle P of mass 0.6 kg is resting on the inside of the cylinder when it is projected horizontally with speed 5 m s^{-1} from the lowest point A so that P moves in a vertical circle centre O, which is perpendicular to the axis of the cylinder. The angle AOP is θ.

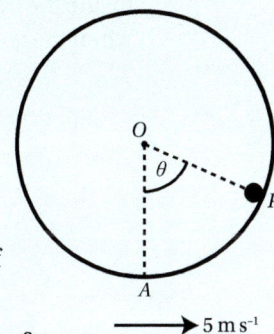

  a While P is in contact with the inner surface of the cylinder, the speed is v m s^{-1}. Find an expression for v^2 by using the principle of conservation of mechanical energy. You can give your answer in terms of g.

  b For what value of θ will the particle P leave the inner surface of the cylinder?

7 In this question use $g = 9.81$ m s^{-2}, giving your final answers to an appropriate degree of accuracy. A light inextensible string of length 3 m has one end attached to a fixed point O and the other end attached to a particle P of mass 400 grams. P moves in a vertical circle with centre O and radius 3 m. When P is at the highest point on the circle it has a speed of 7 m s^{-1}. Determine the tension in the string when P is at its lowest point in the circular orbit.

8 A light rod of length a metres is freely hinged to a fixed point O, while at the other end is attached to a particle P of mass m kg. The particle starts at rest from a point vertically below O and is projected horizontally with speed u m s^{-1}. Find the set of values of u, in terms of g and a, for which the particle moves in complete circles.

9 A smooth sphere of radius r metres and centre O has a particle of mass m kg sitting at rest at the highest point of the sphere. The particle P is projected horizontally with speed u m s^{-1}. The subsequent motion of P is down the sphere and it loses contact with the sphere when OP makes an angle of θ with the upward vertical.

    a Find an expression for $\cos \theta$ in terms of u, r and g (the acceleration due to gravity).

    b Determine the minimal value of u in terms of r and g for which P leaves the surface of the sphere the instant it is projected.

10 A light rod OP of length r metres has a particle of mass m attached at the point P. The rod is free to rotate in a vertical plane about a fixed point O. The greatest force acting along the rod is $10mg$.

    a At which point in the particle's circular orbit does the rod reach this greatest force?

    b Find the speed of the particle at the point where the rod has the greatest force.

    c Find the magnitude of the force, in terms of m and g, acting along the rod when the speed is $\sqrt{6rg}$.

11 In crazy golf, a golf ball is hit so that it starts to move in a vertical circle on the inside of a smooth cylinder.

Model the golf ball as a particle, P, of mass m. The circular path of the golf ball has radius a and centre O. At time t, the angle between OP and the horizontal is θ, as shown in the diagram.

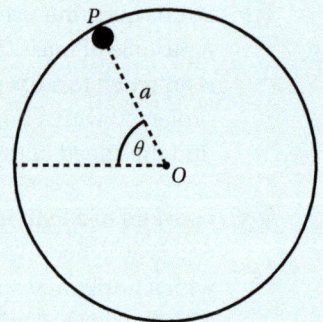

The golf ball has speed u at the lowest point of its circular path.

    a Show that, while the golf ball is in contact with the cylinder, the reaction of the cylinder on the golf ball is $\dfrac{mu^2}{a} - 3mg \sin \theta - 2\,mg$.

    b Given that $u = \sqrt{3ag}$, the golf ball will not complete a vertical circle inside the cylinder. Find the angle which OP makes with the horizontal when the golf ball leaves the surface of the cylinder.

[© **AQA 2009**]

12 A small bead, of mass m, is suspended from a fixed point O by a light inextensible string of length a. With the string taut, the bead is at the point B, vertically below O, when it is set into vertical circular motion with an initial horizontal velocity u, as shown in the diagram.

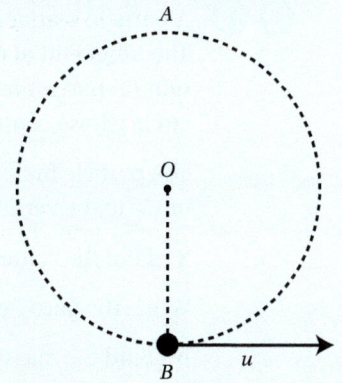

The string does not become slack in the subsequent motion.
The velocity of the bead at the point A, where A is vertically above O, is v.

a Show that $v^2 = u^2 - 4ag$.

b The ratio of the tensions in the string when the bead is at the two points A and B is $2 : 5$.

   i Find u in terms of g and a.   ii Find the ratio $u : v$.

[© AQA 2012]

13 Simon, a small child of mass 22 kg, is on a swing. He is swinging freely through an angle of 18° on both sides of the vertical. Model Simon as a particle, P, of mass 22 kg, attached to a fixed point, Q, by a light inextensible rope of length 2.4 m.

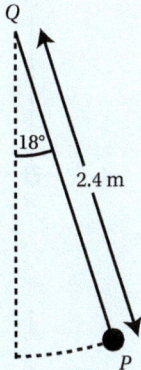

a Find Simon's maximum speed as he swings.

b Calculate the tension in the rope when Simon's speed is a maximum.

[© AQA 2012]

14 A particle P, of mass m kg, is placed at the point Q on the top of a smooth upturned hemisphere of radius 3 metres and centre O. The plane face of the hemisphere is fixed to a horizontal table. The particle is set into motion with an initial horizontal velocity of $2 \, \text{m s}^{-1}$. When the particle is on the surface of the hemisphere, the angle between OP and OQ is θ and the particle has speed $v \, \text{m s}^{-1}$.

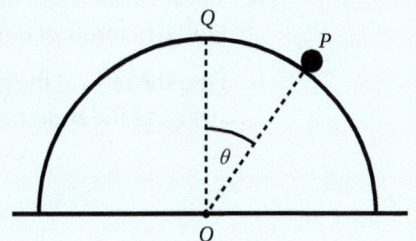

a Show that $v^2 = 4 + 6g(1 - \cos \theta)$.

b Find the value of θ when the particle leaves the hemisphere.

[© AQA 2006]

183

15 A particle is attached to one end of a light inextensible string of length 3 metres. The other end of the string is attached to a fixed point O. The particle is set into motion horizontally at point P with speed v, so that it describes part of a vertical circle whose centre is O. The point P is vertically below O.

The particle first comes momentarily to rest at the point Q, where OQ makes an angle of $15°$ to the vertical.

a Find the value of v.

When the particle is at rest at the point Q, the tension in the string is 22 newtons.

b Find the mass of the particle.

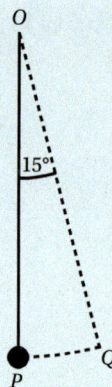

[© AQA 2010]

16 A small bead, of mass m, is suspended from a fixed point O by a light inextensible string, of length a. The bead is then set into circular motion with a string taut at B, where B is vertically below O, with a horizontal speed u.

a Given that the string does not become slack, show that the least value of u required for the bead to make complete revolutions about O is $\sqrt{5ag}$.

b In the case where $u = \sqrt{5ag}$, find, in terms of g and m, the tension in the string when the bead is at point C, which is at the same horizontal level as O, as shown in the diagram.

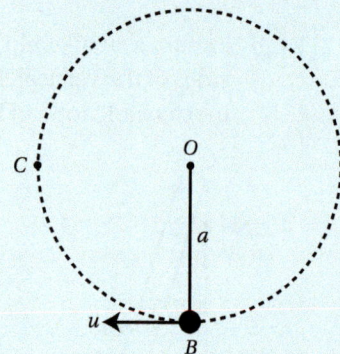

c State one modelling assumption that you have made in your solution.

[© AQA 2008]

17 A light inextensible string, of length a, has one end attached to a fixed point O. A small bead, of mass m, is attached to the other end of the string. The bead is moving in a vertical circle, centre O. When the bead is at B, vertically below O, the string is taut and the bead is moving with speed $5v$.

a The speed of the bead at the highest point of its path is $3v$. Find v in terms of a and g.

b Find the ratio of the greatest tension to the least tension in the string, as the bead travels around its circular path.

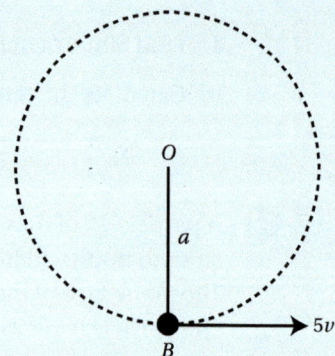

[© AQA 2011]

8 Centres of mass

This chapter is for A Level students only.

In this chapter you will learn how to:

- find the centre of mass of arrangements of particles, uniform rods and symmetrical uniform laminas
- find centres of mass of two- and three-dimensional objects of standard shape
- find centres of mass of composite bodies, including bent wires
- use integration to find centres of mass of uniform laminas and uniform solids of revolution
- apply your knowledge of centres of mass to problems of equilibrium. These will include suspension of a lamina and toppling or sliding of a lamina acted on by several forces.

Before you start…

GCSE	You should be able to add and subtract vectors and to multiply a vector by a scalar.	1 Evaluate: $1.5\begin{pmatrix} -1 \\ 3 \\ 2 \end{pmatrix} - 3\begin{pmatrix} 1 \\ 0 \\ -1 \end{pmatrix}$
A Level Mathematics Student Book 2, Chapter 11	You should be able to integrate functions of the type: $\int_{x_1}^{x_2} x\mathrm{f}(x)\,\mathrm{d}x$.	2 Evaluate: $\int_{1}^{3} x \ln x \,\mathrm{d}x$
A Level Mathematics Student Book 2, Chapter 19	You should understand the moment of a force and be able to calculate moments.	3 Find the moment of a force of $\begin{pmatrix} 0 \\ 3 \end{pmatrix}$ N acting at the point with position vector $\begin{pmatrix} 5 \\ 0 \end{pmatrix}$ metres about the point with position vector $\begin{pmatrix} 2 \\ 0 \end{pmatrix}$ metres.
A Level Mathematics Student Book 2, Chapter 18	You should be able to use the coefficient of friction and the inequality $F \leqslant \mu R$.	4 A point mass rests on a horizontal rough surface. Find the limiting value of friction, in terms of μ, given that the mass is 2 kg.

Where does mass act?

The particle model you have used in previous chapters assumes that mass is all located at a single point with no volume. This approximation works well for small objects. More complex objects may consist of two or more particles located in different places, or one-, two- or three-dimensional objects. For example, mass may be spread along a rod, throughout a two-dimensional shape such as a circular disc, or throughout a solid object such as a cube. For many purposes, a complex object can be modelled as though its mass is located at a single point, called the **centre of mass**. In this chapter, you will learn how to find the centre of mass of a range of different objects.

The location of the centre of mass of a complex object determines how it responds to forces that are applied to it, including its own weight. You will use your knowledge of the centre of mass, together with your knowledge of moments, to work out angles when objects are suspended in space. You will also work out whether objects placed on an inclined surface will rest in equilibrium, or topple over or slide.

Section 1: Centre of mass of a system of point masses

Centre of mass of two particles

The centre of mass of two identical particles lies at the midpoint of a straight line drawn between them.

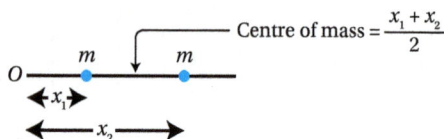

If the masses of the particles are different, then the centre of mass does not lie at the midpoint. It is closer to the larger mass. You find the centre of mass, $\bar{x}$, by calculating a weighted average:

$$\bar{x} = \frac{m_1 x_1 + m_2 x_2}{m_1 + m_2}$$

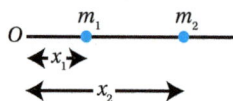

For example, if $m_1 = 2$ kg, $m_2 = 3$ kg, $x_1 = 0$ and $x_2 = l$, then $\bar{x}$ is $\frac{2 \times 0 + 3 \times l}{5}$ $= \frac{3l}{5}$. The centre of mass divides the straight line joining the particles in the ratio $m_2 : m_1$.

Several particles arranged in a straight line

You can now extend the formula for two masses to n masses.

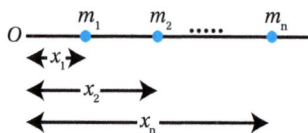

$$\bar{x} = \frac{m_1 x_1 + m_2 x_2 + \ldots + m_n x_n}{m_1 + m_2 + \ldots + m_n}$$

If you write M instead of $m_1 + m_2 + \ldots + m_n$, you can alternatively write the formula as shown in Key point 8.1.

Rewind

You met moments in A Level Mathematics Student Book 2, Chapter 19. The formula given in Key point 8.1 equates the sum of the moments of mass of n particles with the moment of mass of a combined particle acting at the centre of mass.

Key point 8.1

A combination of n particles having masses $m_1, m_2, \ldots, m_n$ arranged in a straight line, at positions $x_1, x_2, \ldots, x_n$, can be modelled as a single object of mass M, with position $\bar{x}$ where:

$$M\bar{x} = m_1 x_1 + m_2 x_2 + \ldots + m_n x_n$$

WORKED EXAMPLE 8.1

Three point masses are attached to a light bar AB of length 0.5 metres. These have mass 150 grams, 250 grams and 350 grams and are attached at the bar at A, the midpoint of the bar, and B, respectively. Find the distance of the centre of mass from A.

Draw a diagram with masses and lengths from A in standard units.

The modelling assumption that the bar is 'light' means that you do not need to include its mass.

$$M\bar{x}_A = 0.15 \times 0 + 0.25 \times 0.25 + 0.35 \times 0.5$$

Use the formula for an arrangement of particles.

M is the total mass.

The distance of the 150 gram mass from A is zero.

$$0.75\bar{x}_A = 0.0625 + 0.175$$
$$0.75\bar{x}_A = 0.2375$$
$$\bar{x}_A = 0.317\,\text{m}$$

In Worked example 8.1 the centre of mass is 0.317 m from A. The system of three particles has the same moment of mass as a single particle of mass 750 grams placed at the centre of mass.

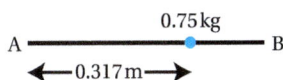

WORKED EXAMPLE 8.2

A light rod AB of length 3.5 metres, has three masses attached to it. A 2 kg mass is attached 1 metre from A. A 1.5 kg mass is attached 2 metres from A, and an unknown mass, m kg, is attached at end B. Find the value of m given that the centre of mass of the system is 1.5 metres from point A.

Total mass $= (2 + 1.5 + m)\,\mathrm{kg} = (3.5 + m)\,\mathrm{kg}$	Start by calculating the total mass.
$(3.5 + m) \times 1.5 = 2 \times 1 + 1.5 \times 2 + m \times 3.5$ $5.25 + 1.5\,m = 5 + 3.5\,m$ $\Rightarrow m = 0.125$	Use the formula for point masses arranged in a straight line. $M\bar{x} = m_1 x_1 + m_2 x_2 + \ldots + m_n x_n$

Particles arranged in a plane

If particles are arranged in a plane, you can find the centre of mass separately for x and y. Vectors give you a nice way of combining these calculations.

🔑 Key point 8.2

If you have n particles with masses $m_1, m_2, \ldots, m_n$, at position vectors

$\begin{pmatrix} x_1 \\ y_1 \end{pmatrix}, \begin{pmatrix} x_2 \\ y_2 \end{pmatrix}, \ldots, \begin{pmatrix} x_n \\ y_n \end{pmatrix}$, you can model these as a single mass M,

with position vector $\begin{pmatrix} \bar{x} \\ \bar{y} \end{pmatrix}$.

$$M \begin{pmatrix} \bar{x} \\ \bar{y} \end{pmatrix} = m_1 \begin{pmatrix} x_1 \\ y_1 \end{pmatrix} + m_2 \begin{pmatrix} x_2 \\ y_2 \end{pmatrix} + \ldots + m_n \begin{pmatrix} x_n \\ y_n \end{pmatrix}$$

WORKED EXAMPLE 8.3

Three particles are arranged in a plane. Particle A has mass 5 kg and is placed at $(6, 2)$. Particle B has mass 3 kg and is placed at $(7, 7)$. Particle C has mass 4 kg and is placed at $(2, 6)$.

Find the x- and y-coordinates of the centre of mass.

Total mass $= 12$ kg	Start by calculating the total mass.
$12 \begin{pmatrix} \bar{x} \\ \bar{y} \end{pmatrix} = 4 \begin{pmatrix} 2 \\ 6 \end{pmatrix} + 5 \begin{pmatrix} 6 \\ 2 \end{pmatrix} + 3 \begin{pmatrix} 7 \\ 7 \end{pmatrix}$	Use the formula for point masses in a plane. Multiply the position vector of each point mass by the mass placed there: $m_1 \begin{pmatrix} x_1 \\ y_1 \end{pmatrix} + m_2 \begin{pmatrix} x_2 \\ y_2 \end{pmatrix} + \ldots + m_n \begin{pmatrix} x_n \\ y_n \end{pmatrix}$.

Continues on next page

$$\begin{pmatrix} \bar{x} \\ \bar{y} \end{pmatrix} = \frac{1}{12}\begin{pmatrix} 59 \\ 55 \end{pmatrix}$$

.... Divide the result by the total mass.

$$= \begin{pmatrix} 4.92 \\ 4.58 \end{pmatrix} \text{(3 s.f.)}$$

EXERCISE 8A

1. A light rod AB of length 2 m has a mass of 2 kg placed 40 cm from A and a mass of 4.5 kg placed at B. Find the distance of the centre of mass from A.

2. A light rod of length 1.5 m has a mass of 1.8 kg placed at one end A. A mass m kg is placed 30 cm from the other end B, and the centre of mass lies in the middle of the rod. Find m.

3. A light rod has masses 4 kg and 5 kg placed at each end, and the centre of mass lies 40 cm from the 4 kg mass. Find the length of the rod.

4. Masses m kg, $2m$ kg and $3m$ kg are placed $2x$ cm, $3x$ cm and $4x$ cm from one end, O, of a light rod. The centre of mass lies 25 cm from O. Find the value of x.

5. Three point masses have position vectors in the x–y plane, as shown in the diagram. Calculate the position of the centre of mass of the three masses combined.

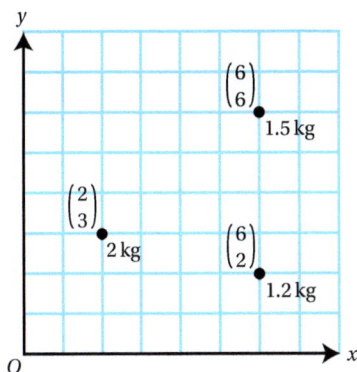

6. Four point masses have position vectors in the x–y plane as shown in the diagram. Calculate the position of the centre of mass of the four masses combined.

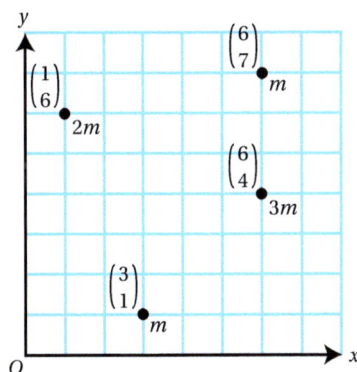

7 Four point masses have position vectors in the x–y plane as shown in the diagram. Calculate the position of the centre of mass of the four masses combined.

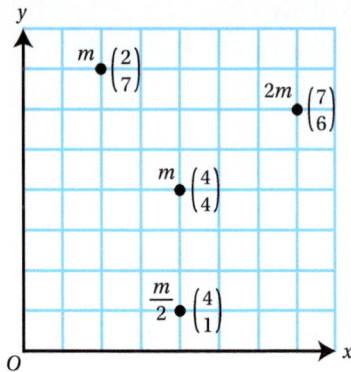

8 Three point masses, 1.5 kg, 2.5 kg and 2 kg are placed in a plane at $\begin{pmatrix} 1 \\ 2 \end{pmatrix}$ cm, at $\begin{pmatrix} -6 \\ 5 \end{pmatrix}$ cm and at $\begin{pmatrix} 3 \\ -1 \end{pmatrix}$ cm

respectively from an origin at $\begin{pmatrix} 0 \\ 0 \end{pmatrix}$ cm. Find the position vector of the centre of mass relative to $\begin{pmatrix} 0 \\ 0 \end{pmatrix}$ cm.

9 Three point masses, 1.2 kg, 2.8 kg and 0.8 kg are placed in a plane at $\begin{pmatrix} -1 \\ 3 \end{pmatrix}$ cm, at $\begin{pmatrix} 2 \\ 6 \end{pmatrix}$ cm and at $\begin{pmatrix} x \\ y \end{pmatrix}$ cm

respectively from an origin at $\begin{pmatrix} 0 \\ 0 \end{pmatrix}$ cm. The centre of mass is at $\begin{pmatrix} 1.75 \\ 4.75 \end{pmatrix}$ cm. Find the values of x and y.

Section 2: Centres of mass of standard shapes

Centre of mass of a uniform rod

An inflexible body with its mass spread along a straight line is called a rod. Its shape is defined by its length; its cross-sectional area is zero. A uniform rod has constant mass per unit length (kilograms per metre, kg m^{-1}, in standard units).

Rewind

You learned to work with uniform rods in A Level Mathematics Student Book 2, Chapter 19.

> **Key point 8.3**
>
> The centre of mass of a uniform rod lies at its midpoint.

Centre of mass of a uniform lamina of standard shape

A **lamina** is a two-dimensional object that lies in a plane. An important modelling assumption, used in calculations, is that the lamina has zero thickness. A **uniform lamina** has constant mass per unit area (kilograms per square metre, kg m^{-2}, in standard units).

A compact disc is close in shape to what is meant by a lamina, as its cross-sectional area is much greater than its thickness.

Key point 8.4

The centre of mass of a symmetrical uniform lamina lies on any axis of symmetry.

If there is more than one axis of symmetry, then the centre of mass lies at the intersection of these.

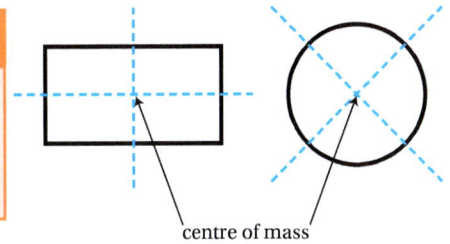

centre of mass

WORKED EXAMPLE 8.4

Calculate the coordinates of the centre of mass of the rectangular lamina with vertices at $(2, 3)$, $(6, 1)$, $(9, 7)$ and $(5, 9)$.

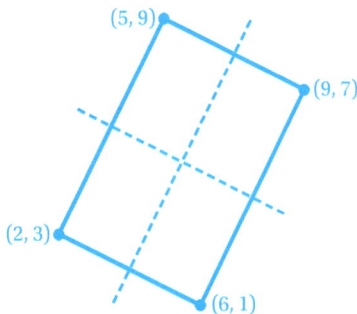

Draw a sketch.

The centre of mass lies at the intersection of the lines of symmetry shown.

$$\begin{pmatrix} \bar{x} \\ \bar{y} \end{pmatrix} = \begin{pmatrix} \dfrac{2+6+9+5}{4} \\ \dfrac{3+1+7+9}{4} \end{pmatrix}$$

$$= \begin{pmatrix} 5.5 \\ 5 \end{pmatrix}$$

A quick way to find the centre of the rectangle is:

$$\left(\frac{x_1 + x_2 + x_3 + x_4}{4}, \frac{y_1 + y_2 + y_3 + y_4}{4} \right)$$

The centre of mass of a triangular lamina lies at the intersections of the medians.

In the case of a lamina in the shape of an equilateral triangle, the medians are all axes of symmetry.

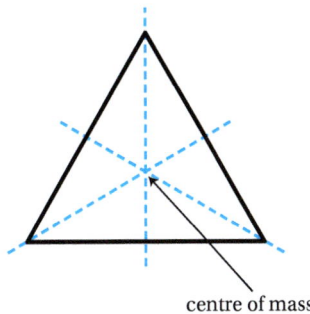

centre of mass

> **Tip**
>
> A **median** of a triangle joins a vertex to the midpoint of the opposite side.

In any triangle, all three medians intersect at the same place, even when they are not axes of symmetry. This intersection is the location of the centre of mass of a uniform triangular lamina.

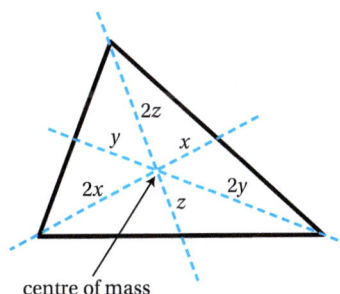

centre of mass

191

🔑 Key point 8.5

The medians of a triangle intersect at $\left(\dfrac{x_1 + x_2 + x_3}{3}, \dfrac{y_1 + y_2 + y_3}{3} \right)$, where $(x_1, y_1), (x_2, y_2), (x_3, y_3)$ are the vertices of the triangle.

🔑 Key point 8.6

Centre of gravity of a triangular lamina: $\dfrac{2}{3}$ along the median from the vertex.

This will be given in your formula book.

📷 Focus on ...

You will prove the formula for the centre of mass of a uniform triangular lamina in Focus on ... Proof 2.

WORKED EXAMPLE 8.5

Find the distance of the centre of mass of the triangular lamina from AB.

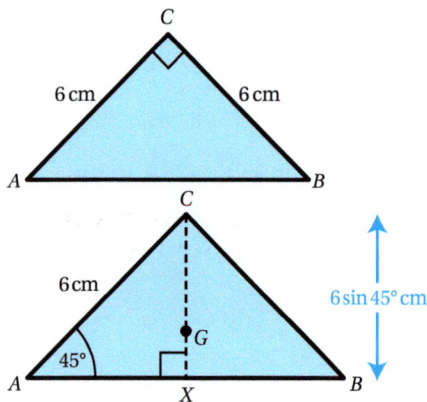

The shape is an isosceles triangle with angles $90°$, $45°$, $45°$.

Drop a perpendicular from C meeting AB at X.

Calculate the height of the triangle, XC.

$XC = 6 \sin 45°$

The required distance is XG.

The centre of mass, G, divides the median XC in the ratio $1:2$.

$XG = \dfrac{1}{3} \times 6 \sin 45°$

$\quad = \sqrt{2}$

$\quad = 1.4 \text{ cm} \ (2 \text{ s.f.})$

WORKED EXAMPLE 8.6

Calculate the coordinates of the centre of mass $\begin{pmatrix} \bar{x} \\ \bar{y} \end{pmatrix}$ of the uniform triangular lamina having vertices at $(2, 5)$, $(10, 3)$ and $(7, 9)$.

$\begin{pmatrix} \bar{x} \\ \bar{y} \end{pmatrix} = \begin{pmatrix} \dfrac{2+10+7}{3} \\ \dfrac{5+3+9}{3} \end{pmatrix} = \begin{pmatrix} \dfrac{19}{3} \\ \dfrac{17}{3} \end{pmatrix}$

Use the coordinates of the vertices.

WORKED EXAMPLE 8.7

Calculate the coordinates of the centre of mass $\begin{pmatrix} \bar{x} \\ \bar{y} \end{pmatrix}$ of the uniform triangular lamina.

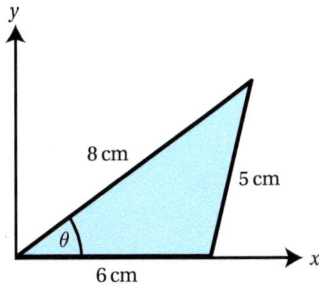

Vertices are at: $(0,0)$, $(6,0)$ and $(8\cos\theta, 8\sin\theta)$. — Use the coordinates of the vertices.

Using the cosine rule:

$\theta = \cos^{-1}\left(\dfrac{8^2+6^2-5^2}{96}\right)$

$\approx 38.62°$

Substituting the value of θ into the coordinates of the vertex:

$(8\cos\theta, 8\sin\theta) \approx (6.250, 4.994)$ — Give your values here to at least four significant figures so that you can give the final coordinates to three significant figures.

$\begin{pmatrix} \bar{x} \\ \bar{y} \end{pmatrix} = \begin{pmatrix} \dfrac{0+6+6.250}{3} \\ \dfrac{0+0+4.994}{3} \end{pmatrix}$

$= \begin{pmatrix} 4.08 \\ 1.66 \end{pmatrix}$ (3 s.f.)

You can find the centre of mass of a lamina that is in the shape of a sector of a circle. This includes half and quarter discs.

Key point 8.7

The centre of mass of a sector of a circle, with radius r and angle 2α radians at the centre of the circle, is $\dfrac{2r\sin\alpha}{3\alpha}$ from the centre of the sector, on the axis of symmetry.

This will be given in your formula book.

Common error

The angle in Key point 8.7 is α, which is half the angle at the centre of the sector. Make sure you know that the angle at the centre of the sector is 2α. Remember to halve the angle at the centre of the sector before using the formula.

WORKED EXAMPLE 8.8

Find the centre of mass of a quarter disc of radius 5 cm. Find the distance OG, where O is at the centre of the quadrant and G is the centre of mass.

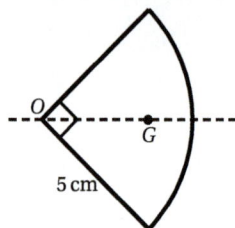

$2\alpha = \dfrac{\pi}{2} \Rightarrow \alpha = \dfrac{\pi}{4}$ .... The angle at the centre of the sector is $\dfrac{\pi}{2}$.

$OG = \dfrac{2r\sin\alpha}{3\alpha}$ .... The formula requires that the angle at the centre is 2α.

$OG = \dfrac{10\sin\dfrac{\pi}{4}}{\dfrac{3\pi}{4}}$ .... Use the standard formula: $\dfrac{2r\sin\alpha}{3\alpha}$.

.... Work in radians.

$\qquad = \dfrac{20\sqrt{2}}{3\pi}$

$\qquad = 3.00\ cm\ (3\ s.f.)$

Centre of mass of a uniform wire

A wire is a one-dimensional but flexible solid object. The centre of mass of a uniform straight wire lies at its midpoint.

> ⚠ **Common error**
>
> As with a sector of a circle 2α is the angle at the centre, measured in radians, so you must halve this angle before using the formula.

🔑 **Key point 8.8**

The centre of mass of a uniform wire bent to form an arc of a circle, with radius r and angle 2α radians at the centre of the circle, is $\dfrac{r\sin\alpha}{\alpha}$ from the centre of the sector.

This will be given in your formula book.

WORKED EXAMPLE 8.9

A 5 cm length of uniform wire is bent to form an arc of a circle of radius 8 cm. Find the angle, θ, made by the arc at the centre of the circle, and the distance of the centre of mass, G, from O, the centre of the circle.

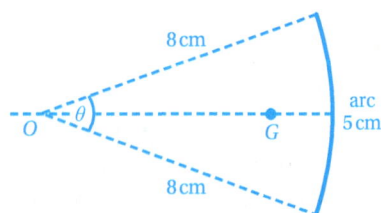

.... Draw a diagram.

Continues on next page

Using the formula for arc length:

$\text{Arc length} = \text{radius} \times \theta$

$5 = 8 \times \theta$

$\theta = 0.625 \text{ radians}$

$2\alpha = 0.625 \text{ radians}$

$\alpha = 0.3125 \text{ radians}$

$OG = \dfrac{r \sin \alpha}{\alpha}$

$\quad = \dfrac{8 \sin 0.3125}{0.3125}$

$\quad = 7.87 \text{ cm } (3 \text{ s.f.})$

You met the formula for arc length in A Level Mathematics Student Book 2, Chapter 7.

Remember to halve the angle to get α.

Work in radians and use the formula.

EXERCISE 8B

1 A uniform rectangular lamina has vertices at $(7, 2)$, $(8, 4)$, $(4, 6)$ and $(3, 4)$. Find the coordinates of the centre of mass of the lamina.

2 A uniform square lamina has three of its vertices at $(1, 3)$, $(4, 1)$ and $(6, 4)$. Calculate the coordinates of the centre of mass.

3 A uniform lamina is in the shape of an equilateral triangle of side length 3 cm. It is placed with one vertex at $(0, 0)$ and one edge along the x-axis. Calculate the coordinates of the centre of mass.

4 Find the centres of mass of the uniform triangular laminas with vertices as given.

    a $(1, 1)$, $(6, 2)$ and $(2, 3)$ **b** $(-1, 3)$, $(3, 7)$ and $(4, 2)$ **c** $(3, 2)$, $(-5, -2)$ and $(4, 5)$

    d $(-2, -6)$, $(1, 4)$ and $(0, 3)$ **e** $(2, -4)$, $(-8, 1)$ and $(-3, 2)$

5 A uniform semicircular lamina has radius 5 cm. Find the distance from the centre of the lamina to the centre of mass.

6 Find the coordinates of the centres of mass of each uniform triangular lamina by first finding the coordinates of the vertices.

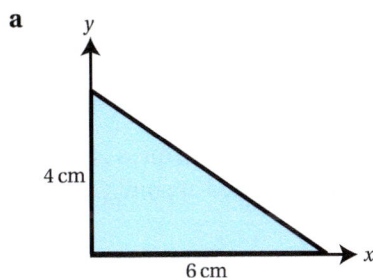

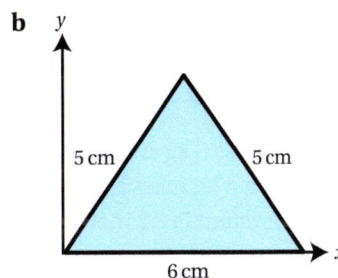

    a

    b

c

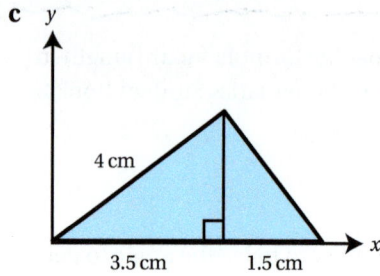

d

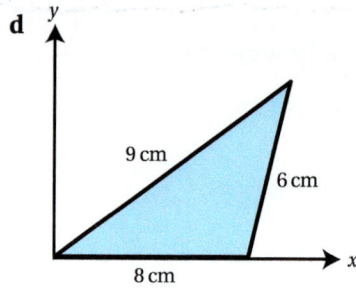

7   A length of uniform wire is bent to form an arc of a circle. The radius of the corresponding circle is 10 cm and the arc makes an angle of $\frac{\pi}{4}$ at its centre. Find the distance of the centre of mass from the centre of the circle.

8   A length of uniform wire is bent to form an arc of a circle. The arc is of length 5 cm, and makes an angle at the centre of the corresponding circle of $\frac{\pi}{6}$. Find the distance of the centre of mass from the centre of the circle.

9   The centre of mass of a length of uniform wire bent to form an arc of a circle is $0.9r$ from the centre of the circle. Use a numerical method to find the angle made by the arc at the centre of the circle, giving your answer in radians to 2 decimal places.

Section 3: Centres of mass of composite bodies

Key point 8.9

For a **composite body:**

$$M\begin{pmatrix} \bar{x} \\ \bar{y} \end{pmatrix} = m_1\begin{pmatrix} \bar{x}_1 \\ \bar{y}_1 \end{pmatrix} + m_2\begin{pmatrix} \bar{x}_2 \\ \bar{y}_2 \end{pmatrix} + \ldots + m_n\begin{pmatrix} \bar{x}_n \\ \bar{y}_n \end{pmatrix}, \ M = m_1 + m_2 + \ldots + m_n$$

You have already used this formula to find an equivalent centre of mass of a system of particles.

You can apply the same approach to calculating the centre of mass of a composite body made from any combination of the shapes you have worked with so far. This time you work from the centres of mass of the component parts $\begin{pmatrix} \bar{x}_i \\ \bar{y}_i \end{pmatrix}$.

WORKED EXAMPLE 8.10

A uniform rod AB, of mass 5 kg and length 4 metres, has three masses attached to it. A 3 kg mass is attached 0.5 metres from A and a 4 kg mass is attached 0.5 metres from B. A 2 kg mass is attached at point C. The centre of mass of the system is 2.2 metres from A. Find the length AC.

For the uniform rod $\bar{x} = 2$ metres   As the rod is uniform its centre of mass is at its midpoint.

Continues on next page

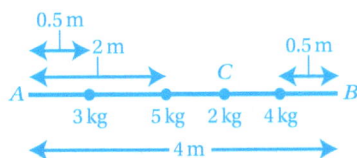

$$14 \times 2.2 = 5 \times 2 + 3 \times 0.5 + 4 \times 3.5 + 2 \times AC$$
$$AC = 2.65 \text{ metres}$$

Measure distances from A and use:

$$M\begin{pmatrix} \bar{x} \\ \bar{y} \end{pmatrix} = m_1 \begin{pmatrix} \bar{x}_1 \\ \bar{y}_1 \end{pmatrix} + m_2 \begin{pmatrix} \bar{x}_2 \\ \bar{y}_2 \end{pmatrix} + \cdots + m_n \begin{pmatrix} \bar{x}_n \\ \bar{y}_n \end{pmatrix}$$

WORKED EXAMPLE 8.11

A composite body is made from a uniform rectangular lamina of mass $2m$ kg with side lengths 25 cm and 40 cm placed with one vertex at $(0, 0)$ and one of its longer sides along the y-axis. Point masses, m kg, $2m$ kg and $3m$ kg are added at $(20, 38)$, $(10, 25)$ and $(22, 8)$, respectively. Find the centre of mass of the composite body.

For the uniform rectangular lamina:

$$\bar{x} = \begin{pmatrix} 12.5 \\ 20 \end{pmatrix}$$

As the rectangular lamina is uniform its centre of mass is at its geometric centre.

Total mass $= 8m$ kg

Find the total mass.

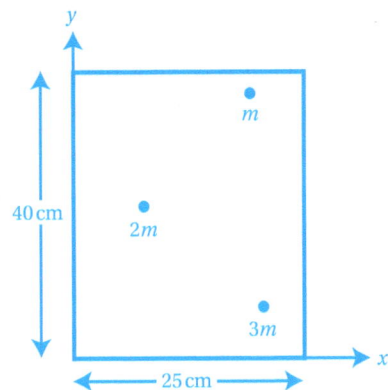

$$8m\begin{pmatrix} \bar{x} \\ \bar{y} \end{pmatrix} = 2m\begin{pmatrix} 12.5 \\ 20 \end{pmatrix} + m\begin{pmatrix} 20 \\ 38 \end{pmatrix}$$
$$+ 2m\begin{pmatrix} 10 \\ 25 \end{pmatrix} + 3m\begin{pmatrix} 22 \\ 8 \end{pmatrix}$$

$$\begin{pmatrix} \bar{x} \\ \bar{y} \end{pmatrix} = \begin{pmatrix} 16.4 \\ 19 \end{pmatrix} cm$$

Use:

$$M\begin{pmatrix} \bar{x} \\ \bar{y} \end{pmatrix} = m_1 \begin{pmatrix} \bar{x}_1 \\ \bar{y}_1 \end{pmatrix} + m_2 \begin{pmatrix} \bar{x}_2 \\ \bar{y}_2 \end{pmatrix} + \ldots + m_n \begin{pmatrix} \bar{x}_n \\ \bar{y}_n \end{pmatrix}$$

WORKED EXAMPLE 8.12

A composite body consists of a uniform rectangular lamina $ABCD$ with dimensions 30 cm by 20 cm and a uniform circular lamina, centre O, with diameter 20 cm joined to a shorter side. A diameter of the circular lamina coincides with edge BC of the rectangle. The mass density per unit area is the same for the rectangular and circular laminas. Find the distance of the centre of mass of the composite lamina from AB and AD.

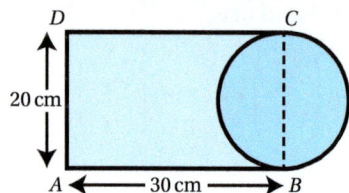

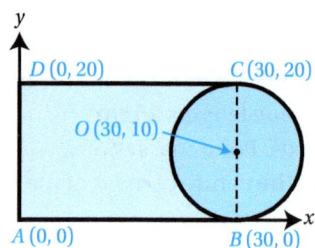

In this question you are not given the coordinates of the vertices. You can introduce the coordinate system with the origin at A and the axes along AB and AD.

For the composite body, $\bar{y} = 10$ cm

The centre of mass lies on the axis of symmetry at $y = 10$ cm.

Using the composite body formula:

$M\bar{x} = m_1\bar{x}_1 + m_2\bar{x}_2$

Area of rectangular lamina $A_1 = 600$ cm^2
Area of circular lamina $A_2 = \pi \times 10^2$ cm^2

As the composite lamina is uniform, mass is directly proportional to area so you can work with areas.

$(600 + 100\pi)\bar{x} = 600 \times 15 + 100\pi \times 30$
$914.2\bar{x} = 9000 + 9424.8$
$\bar{x} = 20.2$ cm (3 s.f.)

The centre of mass of the composite body is 10 cm from AB and 20.2 cm from AD.

Check that the x-coordinate of the centre of mass is sensible.

When part of a larger shape has been cut out, you can use the usual formula for a composite lamina. This time m_2 is the mass of the original lamina before removal of the lamina of mass m_1 and $M = m_2 - m_1$.

$$M\begin{pmatrix} \bar{x} \\ \bar{y} \end{pmatrix} = m_2 \begin{pmatrix} x_2 \\ y_2 \end{pmatrix} - m_1 \begin{pmatrix} x_1 \\ y_1 \end{pmatrix}, M = m_2 - m_1$$

WORKED EXAMPLE 8.13

The rectangular uniform lamina *ABCD* has had a 2 cm square cut out of it. Find the distance of the centre of mass of the composite lamina from *AB* and *AD*.

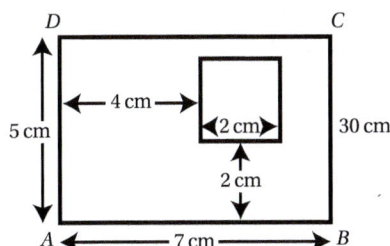

Let *AB* be the *x*-axis and *AD* be the *y*-axis.

Let *A* be $(0,0)$.

Using the rearranged formula for composite bodies:

Area of lamina = area of rectangle ABCD − area of square

Area of lamina = $35 - 4$

$\qquad\qquad = 31\,\text{units}^2$

The mass of the lamina and the square cut-out are directly proportional to area, so you can work with areas.

$$31\begin{pmatrix}\bar{x}\\\bar{y}\end{pmatrix} = 35\begin{pmatrix}3.5\\2.5\end{pmatrix} - 4\begin{pmatrix}5\\3\end{pmatrix}$$

$$\begin{pmatrix}\bar{x}\\\bar{y}\end{pmatrix} = \begin{pmatrix}3.31\\2.44\end{pmatrix}\text{units (3 s.f.)}$$

Check the diagram to make sure that the centre of mass looks sensible.

When a wire is bent into several straight sections, you can combine the sections as though there are point masses at the centre of each section.

WORKED EXAMPLE 8.14

A uniform wire of length 120 cm is bent to form three sides, *AB*, *BC* and *CD* of a rectangle, as shown. Find the distance of the centre of mass from the straight line passing through *AD*.

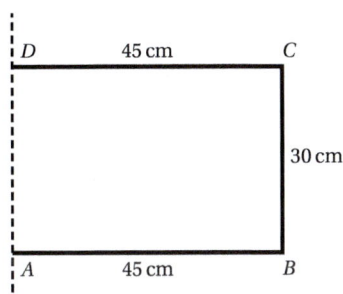

Let *AB* be the *x*-axis and *AD* be the *y*-axis.

Let *A* be $(0,0)$.

The centres of mass of *AB* and *DC* are 22.5 cm from *AD*.

As the sections of wire are uniform, the centres of mass are at the midpoints.

Continues on next page

Using the composite body formula:

$120\bar{x} = (45 \times 22.5) + (30 \times 45) + (45 \times 22.5)$

As the wire is uniform, its mass is directly proportional to length.

$\bar{x} = 28.1\,cm\ (3\ s.f.)$

The centre of mass is 28.1 cm from the straight line passing through AD.

The centre of mass of the wire does not lie on the wire itself.

WORKED EXAMPLE 8.15

A uniform wire is bent into a framework consisting of a semicircular arc AB of radius 3 cm, together with the diameter joining AB. Find the distance of the centre of mass from AB.

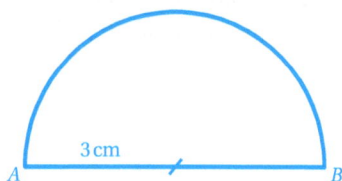

Take AB as the x-axis.

Let the y-axis pass through the midpoint of AB.

Total length of framework $= (6 + 3\pi)\,cm$

As the wire is uniform, mass is proportional to length.

Using $\dfrac{r \sin \alpha}{\alpha}$, where $r = 3$ and $\alpha = \dfrac{\pi}{2}$:

Use the formula for the centre of mass of a uniform arc of wire.

$$\frac{r \sin \alpha}{\alpha} = \frac{3 \sin \dfrac{\pi}{2}}{\dfrac{\pi}{2}}$$

$$= \frac{6}{\pi}$$

The centre of mass of the arc is $\dfrac{6}{\pi}$ from AB.

Use the formula for the centre of mass of an arc of wire: $\bar{r} = \dfrac{r \sin \alpha}{\alpha}$.

Using the composite body formula:

$(3\pi + 6)\bar{y} = 3\pi \times \dfrac{6}{\pi} + 6 \times 0$

Combine the straight edge and the arc.

$\therefore \bar{y} = 1.17\,cm\ (3\ s.f.)$.

$\therefore$ the centre of mass is 1.17 cm from AB.

Centre of mass of standard 3-dimensional figures

You need to know how to use formulae for centres of mass of a solid hemisphere, hemispherical shell, solid cone or pyramid and conical shell.

Key point 8.10

The centres of mass of a solid hemisphere, hemispherical shell, solid cone or pyramid and conical shell are:

Solid hemisphere, radius r	$\frac{3}{8}r$ from centre
Hemispherical shell, radius r	$\frac{1}{2}r$ from centre
Solid cone or pyramid of height h	$\frac{1}{4}h$ above the base on the line from centre of base to vertex
Conical shell of height h	$\frac{1}{3}h$ above the base on the line from centre of base to vertex

These will be given in your formula book.

Fast forward

In Section 4, you will learn how to find the centre of mass of a solid hemisphere and a solid cone by integration.

Did you know?

The design of the folding mechanism of a bed that can be folded up by hand into a wall cupboard when not in use means that little lifting force is needed. This is remarkable when you consider the significant weight of the bed, including the mattress and bedding. How is it possible to achieve this? The answer lies in 'counter-weighting', which enables the bed to be fairly well balanced in all positions. Counter-weighting relies on an understanding of how mass is spread over the object to be lifted and a means of counteracting its weight in all positions. To start with, you would need to know the location of the centre of mass of the object to be lifted.

WORKED EXAMPLE 8.16

A uniform conical shell of perpendicular height 24 cm and radius 10 cm is joined to a uniform disc of radius 10 cm. The mass per unit area of the shell and the circular base are the same.

Find the distance of the centre of mass of the composite shell from the base.

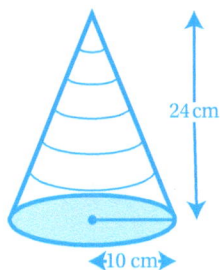

Slant height of cone $= \sqrt{24^2 + 10^2} = 26$ cm

Curved surface area $= \pi \times 10 \times 26$

$= 260\pi$

Area of base $= \pi \times 10^2$

$= 100\pi$

Draw a diagram.

Let the centre of the circular base be $(0, 0)$.

Let the main axis of the cone be the y-axis.

As the shell and base are uniform and have the same mass per unit area, mass is proportional to surface area.

Curved surface area of cone $= \pi \times r \times l$

Continues on next page

Using the formula for a conical shell:

$(260\pi + 100\pi)\bar{y} = (260\pi \times 8) + (100\pi \times 0)$ .... The centre of mass of a conical shell is $\frac{1}{3}h$ above the base on the line from the centre of the base to the vertex.

Cancel π and simplify:

$36\bar{y} = 26 \times 8 \Rightarrow \bar{y} = 5.78$ cm (3 s.f.)

WORKED EXAMPLE 8.17

A solid hemisphere of radius r is joined to a solid cone of radius r and height $3r$. Both solids are uniform with the same mass per unit volume. The base of the cone coincides with the base of the hemisphere.

Show that the centre of mass is $\frac{27r}{10}$ from the vertex of the cone.

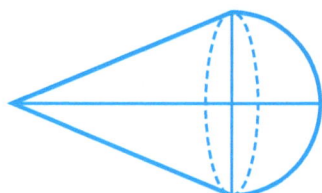

Draw a diagram.

Let the vertex of the cone be $(0, 0)$.

Let the main axis of the cone be the x-axis.

Volume of cone $= \frac{1}{3}\pi r^2 \times 3r = \pi r^3$ .... As the solids are uniform, mass is proportional to volume.

Volume of hemisphere $= \frac{2}{3}\pi r^3$

Total volume of composite shape $= \frac{5}{3}\pi r^3$

For the cone:

$\bar{x} = \frac{3}{4} \times 3r$

$= \frac{9r}{4}$

The centre of mass of a uniform solid cone is $\frac{h}{4}$ from the centre of its base.

For the hemisphere:

$\bar{x}_2 = 3r + \frac{3r}{8}$

$= \frac{27r}{8}$

The centre of mass of a uniform hemisphere is $\frac{3r}{8}$ from the centre.

$\frac{5}{3}\pi r^3 \bar{x} = \left(\pi r^3 \times \frac{9r}{4}\right) + \left(\frac{2}{3}\pi r^3 \times \frac{27r}{8}\right)$ .... Use:

$$M\begin{pmatrix} \bar{x} \\ \bar{y} \end{pmatrix} = m_1 \begin{pmatrix} \bar{x}_1 \\ \bar{y}_1 \end{pmatrix} + m_2 \begin{pmatrix} \bar{x}_2 \\ \bar{y}_2 \end{pmatrix} + \ldots + m_n \begin{pmatrix} \bar{x}_n \\ \bar{y}_n \end{pmatrix}$$

Cancelling πr^3 and simplifying:

$\bar{x} = \frac{27r}{20} + \frac{27r}{20}$

$= \frac{27r}{10}$

as required.

WORK IT OUT 8.1

A brooch is modelled as a lamina in the shape of a sector of a circle, together with an arc of wire on the circumference of the sector with radius r cm, as shown. The angle at the centre of the sector is $\frac{\pi}{3}$ radians, the mass of the sector is 200 grams and the mass of the arc of wire is 300 grams.

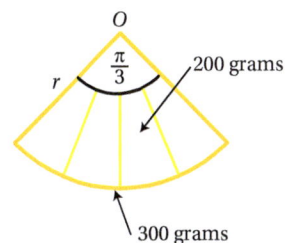

Which of these equations could be used to find the distance of the centre of mass of the brooch, $\bar{r}$, from O?

Solution 1	Solution 2
$500\bar{r} = 300 \times \dfrac{2r \sin \frac{\pi}{3}}{3 \times \frac{\pi}{3}} + 200 \times \dfrac{r \sin \frac{\pi}{3}}{\frac{\pi}{3}}$	$500\bar{r} = 200 \times \dfrac{2r \sin \frac{\pi}{3}}{3 \times \frac{\pi}{3}} + 300 \times \dfrac{r \sin \frac{\pi}{3}}{\frac{\pi}{3}}$

Solution 3	Solution 4
$500\bar{r} = 300 \times \dfrac{2r \sin \frac{\pi}{6}}{3 \times \frac{\pi}{6}} + 200 \times \dfrac{r \sin \frac{\pi}{6}}{\frac{\pi}{6}}$	$500\bar{r} = 200 \times \dfrac{2r \sin \frac{\pi}{6}}{3 \times \frac{\pi}{6}} + 300 \times \dfrac{r \sin \frac{\pi}{6}}{\frac{\pi}{6}}$

EXERCISE 8C

1 Calculate the centres of mass of the uniform laminas in these diagrams.

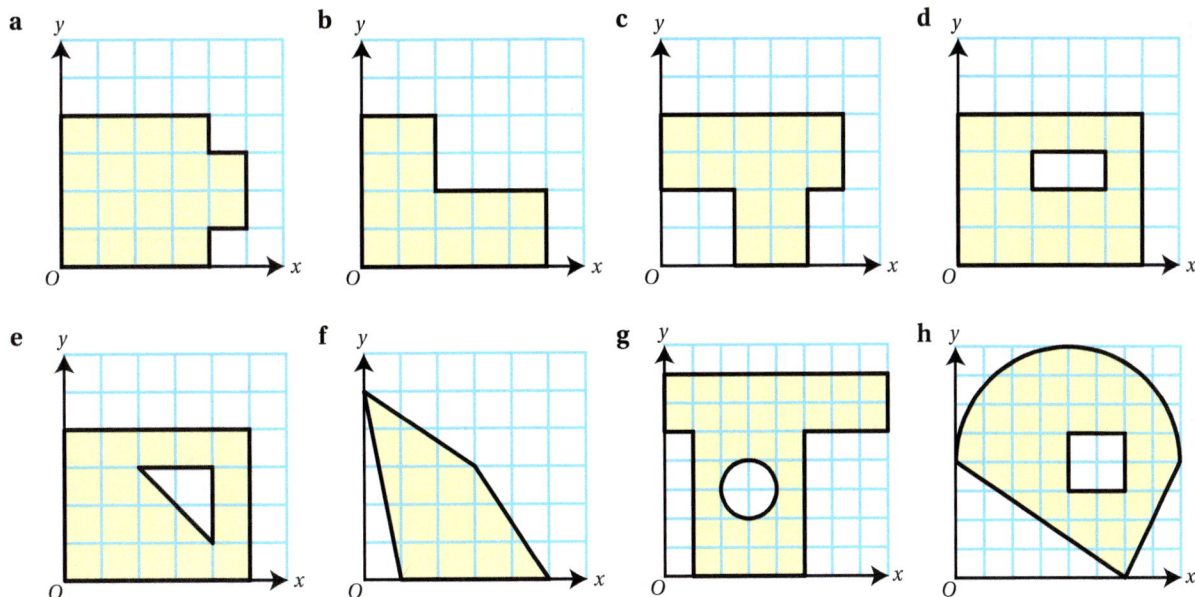

a

b

c

d

e

f

g

h

2 A composite body is made from a uniform rod AB of mass 2.5 kg and length 1.2 metres with three point masses, X, Y and Z attached to it. X has mass 1.2 kg and AX is 0.2 metres. Y has mass 0.8 kg and AY is 1.1 metres. Z has mass 1.8 kg and AZ is 0.7 metres. Find the distance of the centre of mass of the composite body from A.

3 A composite body is made from a rectangular lamina $ABCD$ of mass 1 kg with side lengths 30 cm and 20 cm together with point masses, 2.5 kg each, added at X and Y, as shown. Find the distance of the centre of mass of the composite body from AB and AD.

4 When a point mass of 1 kg is added to a uniform rod XY of mass 2.5 kg and length a metres, it moves the position of the centre of mass. Find where the additional mass must be added to move the centre of mass to $\frac{5a}{12}$ metres from X. Give your answer in terms of a.

5 A composite body is made from a rod AB of length 80 cm and mass 2.5 kg that has a disc of mass 1 kg attached to end B, with its centre placed at the end of the rod. A mass of m kg is attached to end A of the rod. Find the value of m if the centre of mass is to be 20 cm from A.

6 A length of uniform wire is bent to form three sides of a rectangle $ABCD$, $AB = CD = 10$ cm and $BC = 8$ cm. Find the distance of the centre of mass from AD.

7 Three uniform rods are joined together to make a right-angled triangular framework. Edge AB is of length 12 cm, edge BC is of length 13 cm and edge AC is of length 5 cm. The rods have equal mass density per unit length. Calculate the distance of the centre of mass from AB and AC.

8 A uniform triangular lamina of mass 2.5 kg has vertices at $A(0, 0)$, $B(7, 2)$ and $C(4, 6)$. A 3 kg mass is attached to the lamina at $(4, 5)$ and a 2 kg mass is attached at $(4, 2)$. Find the coordinates of the centre of mass of the composite body.

9 A uniform composite lamina consists of a rectangle $ABCD$ and a semicircular lamina. AB is of length 30 cm and AD is of length 20 cm. The rectangular lamina and the semicircular lamina have the same mass per unit area. The semicircular lamina has diameter 20 cm and is joined on so its diameter coincides with BC (see diagram). Find the distance of the centre of mass from AD.

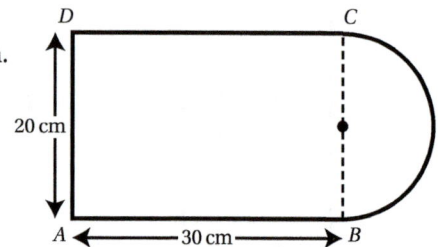

10 A shop sign consists of a uniform horizontal rod AB together with a lamina in the shape of a trapezium, as shown in the diagram. The rod is 1.5 metres in length and has a mass of 4.5 kg. The lamina has a mass of 3 kg and hangs with BC vertical. Find the distance of the centre of mass of the shop sign from edges AB and BC.

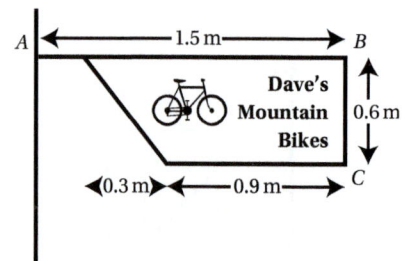

11 A garden ornament is made from a solid cylinder with a solid hemisphere placed on top. The radius of the cylinder is 5 cm, its height is 20 cm, and it mass is 4 kg. The hemisphere has radius 8 cm and mass 2 kg. The main axis of the cylinder passes through the centre of the hemisphere. The ornament is placed on level ground with the hemispherical part uppermost. Find the height of the centre of mass of the ornament above the ground.

12 A solid uniform frustum of a cone has been made from a solid cone of base radius 15 cm and height 50 cm. A cone of height 30 cm has been removed from the vertex end, as shown in the diagram. Calculate the distance of the centre of mass of the frustum from the base.

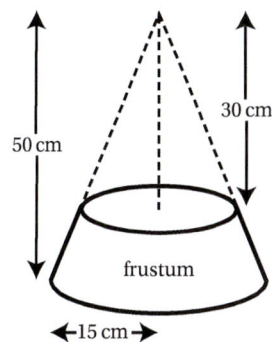

13 A hat is modelled as a conical shell together with a brim both made of the same uniform fabric. The conical shell has a radius of 9.45 cm and a slant height of 33.75 cm. The brim is an annulus with inner radius 9.45 cm and outer radius 14.5 cm. The diagram shows the shape of the hat. Find the vertical distance of the centre of mass of the hat above its brim.

> **Tip**
>
> An annulus is a plane figure made by cutting out a concentric disc from a larger disc.

14 A uniform solid is made from a solid hemisphere and a solid cone. The hemisphere and cone have the same base radius and the centre of the circular plane face of the hemisphere coincides with the centre of the circular base of the cone. The centre of mass of the composite solid lies in the plane of the join. Show that the height of the cone is given by $h = \sqrt{3}r$.

Section 4: Centres of mass by integration

You can find the centre of mass of an object by integration.

- When a lamina has a shape that can be expressed as a function $f(x)$ you can use integration to find the centre of mass.
- You can also use integration to find the centre of mass of a symmetrical solid of revolution defined by function $f(x)$. The centre of mass will lie on the axis of revolution.

> **Tip**
>
> It is usually better to use standard results, where possible. If the shapes are non-standard, or the mass density is not uniform, you need to use integration. You will also be expected to use integration to derive some of the standard results.

Centre of mass of a uniform lamina defined by a function, f(x)

If a lamina is not a standard shape you may be able to use a mathematical function to model the shape.

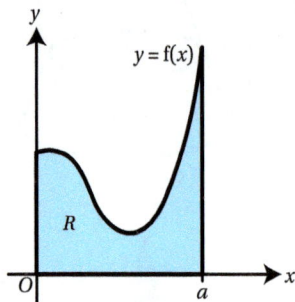

In this example, the region R represents a uniform lamina. R is the area defined by the function f(x) and the lines $x = a$, $y = 0$ and $x = 0$.

Key point 8.11

The coordinates of the centre of mass of a uniform lamina defined by f(x) and the lines $x = a$, $y = 0$ and $x = 0$, are given by integration:

$$\bar{x} = \frac{\int_0^a x\,f(x)\,dx}{\int_0^a f(x)\,dx} \qquad \bar{y} = \frac{\frac{1}{2}\int_0^a (f(x))^2\,dx}{\int_0^a f(x)\,dx}$$

It is often convenient to use these rearrangements of the formulae:

- $A\bar{x} = \displaystyle\int_0^a x\,f(x)\,dx$

- $A\bar{y} = \dfrac{1}{2}\displaystyle\int_0^a (f(x))^2\,dx$

where A is the area of the lamina.

WORKED EXAMPLE 8.18

A lamina has three straight edges along the lines $x = 0$, $x = 2$ and $y = 0$.

The fourth edge is a curve modelled by f(x) = $x^2 + 4$, as shown in the diagram.

Find the coordinates of the centre of mass of the lamina.

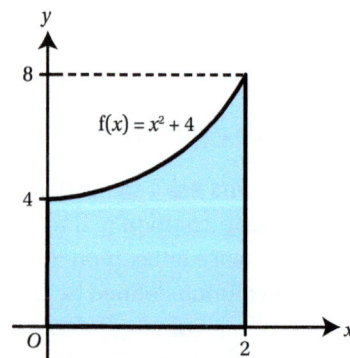

Continues on next page

$$\bar{x} = \frac{\int_0^a x\,f(x)\,dx}{\int_0^a f(x)\,dx}$$

Use the formula for the x-coordinate of the centre of mass.

$$\bar{x} = \frac{\int_0^2 (x^3 + 4x)\,dx}{\int_0^2 (x^2 + 4)\,dx}$$

Evaluating the numerator and denominator:

$$\bar{x} = \frac{\left[\frac{x^4}{4} + 2x^2\right]_0^2}{\left[\frac{x^3}{3} + 4x\right]_0^2}$$

$$= \frac{12}{10\frac{2}{3}}$$

$$= 1\frac{1}{8}$$

Check that the value of $\bar{x}$ looks sensible.

$$\bar{y} = \frac{\int_0^2 \frac{1}{2}(x^2 + 4)^2\,dx}{10\frac{2}{3}}$$

Use the formula for the y-coordinate of the centre of mass. Use the value of $10\frac{2}{3}$ already calculated for the area of the lamina.

$$= \frac{\int_0^2 x^4 + 8x^2 + 16\,dx}{21\frac{1}{3}}$$

$$= \frac{\left[\frac{x^5}{5} + 8\frac{x^3}{3} + 16x\right]_0^2}{21\frac{1}{3}}$$

$$= 2.8$$

Check that the value of $\bar{y}$ looks sensible.

The coordinates of the centre of mass are $(1.125, 2.8)$.

You already know how to calculate the centre of mass of a uniform triangular lamina from the coordinates of its vertices and the fact that the centre of mass lies at the intersection of its medians.

You can use integration to find the centre of mass of a right-angled isosceles triangle.

WORKED EXAMPLE 8.19

Use integration to find the centre of mass of this uniform triangular lamina.

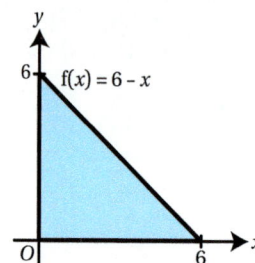

$\bar{x} = \bar{y}$

The lamina is in the shape of an isosceles triangle so the centre of mass lies on its axis of symmetry.

Using the formula for the centre of mass of a lamina by integration:

$$\bar{x} = \frac{\displaystyle\int_0^a x\,\mathrm{f}(x)\,\mathrm{d}x}{\displaystyle\int_0^a \mathrm{f}(x)\,\mathrm{d}x}$$

$$= \frac{\displaystyle\int_0^6 (6x - x^2)\,\mathrm{d}x}{\displaystyle\int_0^6 (6 - x)\,\mathrm{d}x}$$

Integrating the numerator and denominator:

$$\therefore \bar{x} = \frac{\left[3x^2 - \dfrac{x^3}{3} \right]_0^6}{\left[6x - \dfrac{x^2}{2} \right]_0^6}$$

The centre of mass of a triangular lamina lies at the intersection of its medians.

$$\bar{x} = \frac{36}{18} = 2$$

$$\begin{pmatrix} \bar{x} \\ \bar{y} \end{pmatrix} = \begin{pmatrix} 2 \\ 2 \end{pmatrix}$$

WORKED EXAMPLE 8.20

In the right-angled uniform triangular lamina ABC, angle $BCA = 90°$, $CB = a$ and $CA = b$.

Use integration to find the centre of mass of the lamina. State the distances of the centre of mass from CB and CA.

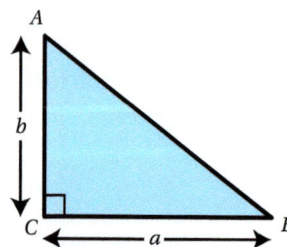

Continues on next page

For the edge AB:

gradient $= -\dfrac{b}{a}$

$\Rightarrow y = -\dfrac{b}{a}x + b$

$A\bar{x} = \displaystyle\int_0^a x\left(-\dfrac{b}{a}x + b\right)\mathrm{d}x$

$A\bar{x} = \displaystyle\int_0^a \left(-\dfrac{b}{a}x^2 + bx\right)\mathrm{d}x$

$A\bar{x} = \left[-\dfrac{bx^3}{3a} + \dfrac{bx^2}{2}\right]_0^a$

$A\bar{x} = -\dfrac{ba^3}{3a} + \dfrac{ba^2}{2}$

$\quad = \dfrac{ba^2}{6}$

$A\bar{y} = \dfrac{b^2 a}{6}$

Using the formula for the area of a triangle:

$A = \dfrac{1}{2}b \times a$

$\Rightarrow \begin{pmatrix} \bar{x} \\ \bar{y} \end{pmatrix} = \begin{pmatrix} \dfrac{a}{3} \\ \dfrac{b}{3} \end{pmatrix}$

The centre of mass lies $\dfrac{b}{3}$ from CB and $\dfrac{a}{3}$ from CA.

Let CB be the x-axis and CA be the y-axis.

Find the equation of edge AB.

Use $A\bar{x} = \displaystyle\int_0^a x\,\mathrm{f}(x)\,\mathrm{d}x$

Put $\mathrm{f}(x)$ in the formula.

Integrate from $x = 0$ to $x = a$.

Substitute limits to find $A\bar{x}$.

You could use integration to find $A\bar{y}$ but, in this case, consider that you could have chosen CA to be the x-axis and CB the y-axis, then a and b would be swapped over.

There is no need for integration here.

You can use the coordinates of the vertices to check this result.

Centre of mass of a uniform solid of revolution

Key point 8.12

The centre of mass of a uniform solid of revolution with radius defined by $\mathrm{f}(x)$ is:

$$\bar{x} = \dfrac{\displaystyle\int_0^a \pi x y^2\,\mathrm{d}x}{\displaystyle\int_0^a \pi y^2\,\mathrm{d}x}$$

where $\displaystyle\int_0^a \pi y^2\,\mathrm{d}x$ is the volume of the solid of revolution.

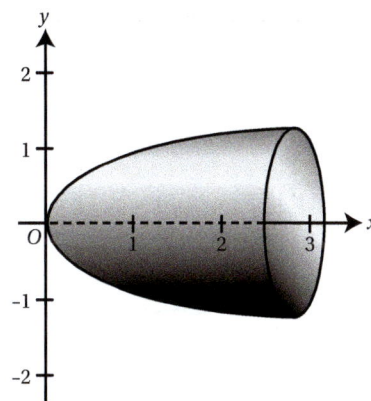

The centre of mass lies on the axis of revolution.

The formula can be derived by imagining the solid to be divided into many small discs and summing along the x-axis.

It can be more convenient to use the formula in the form:

$V\bar{x} = \int_0^a \pi x y^2 \, dx$, where V is the volume of the solid.

> **Tip**
>
> Since the solid is uniform, you can work with volume rather than mass.

> **ⓘ Did you know?**
>
> You can use polar integration to find the centre of mass of a surface of revolution.

> **⏮ Rewind**
>
> In Further Mathematics Student Book 1, Chapter 6, you will have learnt about polar coordinates and practised finding the volume of a solid of revolution.

WORKED EXAMPLE 8.21

The region R is bounded by the curve $y = \sqrt{4 - x^2}$ for $0 \leqslant x \leqslant 2$ and the x-axis and y-axis.

R is rotated through 2π radians about the x-axis to produce a solid of revolution. Show by integration that the centre of mass of the solid has x-coordinate $\frac{3}{4}$.

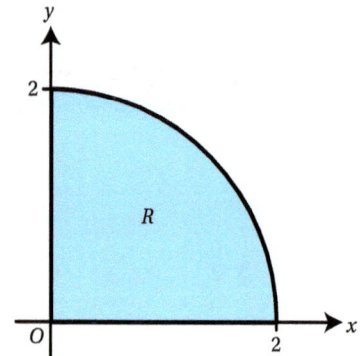

Using the formula for the centre of mass of a volume of revolution by integration:

$$\bar{x} = \frac{\displaystyle\int_0^2 \pi x (4 - x^2) \, dx}{\displaystyle\int_0^2 \pi (4 - x^2) \, dx}$$

The region is a quarter disc of radius 2, centre $(0, 0)$, $0 \leqslant x \leqslant 2$.

The solid of revolution is a hemisphere.

The formula book gives a formula for the centre of mass of a hemisphere, but you are required to 'show by integration...' so you cannot just quote this result.

$$\bar{x} = \frac{\displaystyle\int_0^2 (4x - x^3) \, dx}{\displaystyle\int_0^2 (4 - x^2) \, dx}$$

Cancel π and expand the brackets in the numerator.

Continues on next page

$$\bar{x} = \dfrac{\left[2x^2 - \dfrac{x^4}{4}\right]_0^2}{\left[4x - \dfrac{x^3}{3}\right]_0^2}$$

Write down the integrals and substitute the limits.

$$\Rightarrow \bar{x} = \dfrac{2 \times 2^2 - \dfrac{2^4}{4}}{4 \times 2 - \dfrac{2^3}{3}}$$

$$= \dfrac{4}{\dfrac{16}{3}}$$

$$\Rightarrow \bar{x} = \dfrac{3}{4} \text{ as required.}$$

> **Tip**
>
> The formula book gives $\bar{x} = \dfrac{3R}{8}$ as the distance of the centre of mass from the centre of a hemisphere.

WORKED EXAMPLE 8.22

Use integration to show that the centre of mass of a uniform solid right circular cone of height h lies $\dfrac{h}{4}$ from its base.

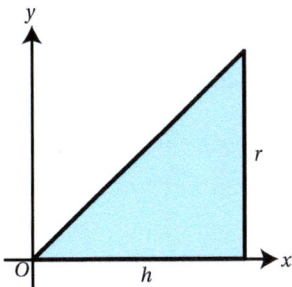

Let r be the radius of the cone.

You can generate the solid cone by rotating a right-angled triangular region about the x-axis.

Gradient $= \dfrac{r}{h} \Rightarrow y = \dfrac{r}{h}x$

Find the equation of the hypotenuse.

Using the formula for the centre of mass of a solid of revolution.

$$\bar{x} = \dfrac{\displaystyle\int_0^h \pi x \times \left(\dfrac{rx}{h}\right)^2 dx}{\displaystyle\int_0^h \pi \left(\dfrac{rx}{h}\right)^2 dx}$$

Continues on next page

$$\bar{x} = \frac{\int_0^h x^3 \, dx}{\int_0^h x^2 \, dx}$$

Cancel $\pi \times \left(\dfrac{r}{h}\right)^2$.

$$\bar{x} = \frac{\left[\dfrac{x^4}{4}\right]_0^h}{\left[\dfrac{x^3}{3}\right]_0^h}$$

Integrate and substitute limits.

$$= \frac{h^4}{4} \times \frac{3}{h^3}$$

$$\bar{x} = \frac{3h}{4}$$

Simplify.

The centre of mass is $\dfrac{3h}{4}$ from the vertex.

So the centre of mass is $\dfrac{h}{4}$ from the base of the cone.

In Worked example 8.22, you could have used $f(x) = r - \dfrac{r}{h} x$ to generate the cone as a solid of revolution.

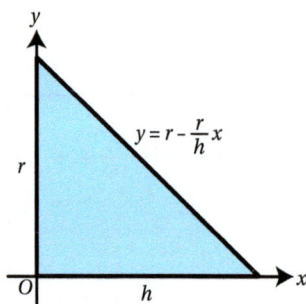

This would have led directly to $\dfrac{h}{4}$ but the integration would have required more steps.

WORKED EXAMPLE 8.23

The region R is bounded by the line $y = \dfrac{1}{2} x + 3$ for $0 \leqslant x \leqslant 4$ and the x-axis and y-axis.

R is rotated through 2π radians about the x-axis to produce a solid of revolution. Calculate the x-coordinate of the centre of mass of the solid.

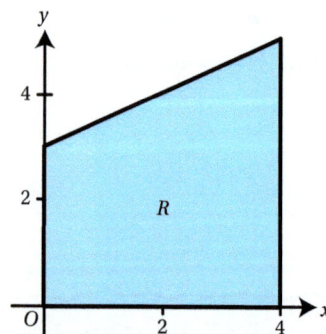

Continues on next page

Using the formula for the centre of mass of a
volume of revolution by integration:

$$\bar{x} = \frac{\displaystyle\int_0^4 \pi x \times \left(\frac{1}{2}x + 3\right)^2 dx}{\displaystyle\int_0^4 \pi \left(\frac{1}{2}x + 3\right)^2 dx}$$

The solid formed is a frustum of a cone.

$$= \frac{\displaystyle\int_0^4 \left(\frac{x^3}{4} + 3x^2 + 9x\right) dx}{\displaystyle\int_0^4 \left(\frac{x^2}{4} + 3x + 9\right) dx}$$

Cancel π and expand the brackets in the numerator.

$$= \frac{\left[\dfrac{x^4}{16} + x^3 + \dfrac{9x^2}{2}\right]_0^4}{\left[\dfrac{x^3}{12} + \dfrac{3x^2}{2} + 9x\right]_0^4}$$

Write down the integrals and substitute the limits.

$$= \frac{152}{\dfrac{196}{3}}$$

$$\bar{x} \approx 2.33 \ (3 \text{ s.f.})$$

When integrating to find the centre of mass you may need to use any of the
integration techniques you have already learned.

> **Tip**
>
> Worked example 8.24 uses integration by parts and a trigonometric
> identity.

> **◄◄ Rewind**
>
> See A Level Mathematics
> Student Book 2 for revision on
> integration techniques.

WORKED EXAMPLE 8.24

The region R is bounded by the curve $y = \sin x$, $y = 0$ and $0 \leqslant x \leqslant \dfrac{\pi}{2}$.

R is rotated through 2π radians about the x-axis. Find the x-coordinate of the centre of mass of the solid
formed.

Using the formula for the centre of mass of a
volume of revolution:

$$\bar{x} = \frac{\displaystyle\int_0^{\frac{\pi}{2}} x \sin^2 x \, dx}{\displaystyle\int_0^{\frac{\pi}{2}} \sin^2 x \, dx}$$

You need to express $\sin^2 x$ in terms of a double angle
identity:

$$\cos 2x = 1 - 2\sin^2 x$$

$$\therefore \sin^2 x = \frac{1}{2} - \frac{1}{2}\cos 2x$$

Continues on next page

$$\bar{x} = \frac{\int_0^{\frac{\pi}{2}} \left(\frac{1}{2}x - \frac{x}{2}\cos 2x\right) dx}{\int_0^{\frac{\pi}{2}} \left(\frac{1}{2} - \frac{1}{2}\cos 2x\right) dx}$$

Substitute for $\sin^2 x$.

You need to integrate $\frac{x}{2}\cos 2x$ by parts.

Integrating numerator and denominator using integration by parts:

$$\bar{x} = \frac{\left[\dfrac{x^2}{4}\right]_0^{\frac{\pi}{2}} - \left[\dfrac{x\sin 2x}{4}\right]_0^{\frac{\pi}{2}} - \displaystyle\int_0^{\frac{\pi}{2}} \dfrac{\sin 2x}{4}\,dx}{\left[\dfrac{x}{2} - \dfrac{\sin 2x}{4}\right]_0^{\frac{\pi}{2}}}$$

Be careful with $+$ and $-$ signs.

$$\bar{x} = \frac{\left[\dfrac{x^2}{4}\right]_0^{\frac{\pi}{2}} - \left[\dfrac{x\sin 2x}{4}\right]_0^{\frac{\pi}{2}} - \left[\dfrac{\cos 2x}{8}\right]_0^{\frac{\pi}{2}}}{\left[\dfrac{x}{2} - \dfrac{\sin 2x}{4}\right]_0^{\frac{\pi}{2}}}$$

$$\bar{x} = \frac{\dfrac{\pi^2}{16} - \left(-\dfrac{1}{8} - \dfrac{1}{8}\right)}{\dfrac{\pi}{4}}$$

Substitute limits.

$$\bar{x} = 1.10 \text{ radians (3 s.f.)}$$

Check your solution, using your calculator, if possible.

EXERCISE 8D

1 A uniform triangular lamina is in the shape of a right-angled triangle ABC, with angle $BAC = 90°$, $AB = 8$ cm and $AC = 5$ cm.

a Find the equation of the line passing through CB.

b Use integration to find the coordinates of the centre of mass of the lamina.

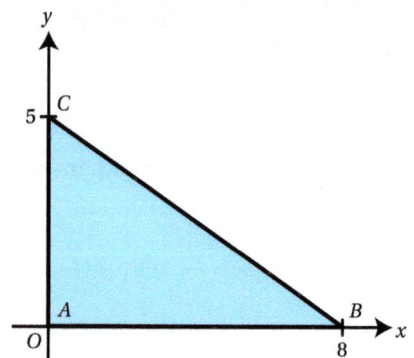

2 Use integration to find the centre of mass of a uniform lamina bounded by $y = 2\sqrt{x}$, $y = 0$ and $x = 1$.

3 Use integration to show that the distance of the centre of mass of a uniform solid cone of height $3r$ metres and base radius r metres is $\frac{9r}{4}$ from its vertex.

4 A uniform triangular lamina is bounded by the line $y = 8 - x$ and the positive x- and y-axes. Use integration to find the centre of mass of the triangular lamina.

5 The shape of a solid toy can be modelled by rotating the graph of $y = x\sqrt{5-x}$, $0 \le x \le 5$, where x is measured in centimetres, through $360°$ about the x-axis.

Assuming the solid formed is uniform, find the centre of mass of the toy.

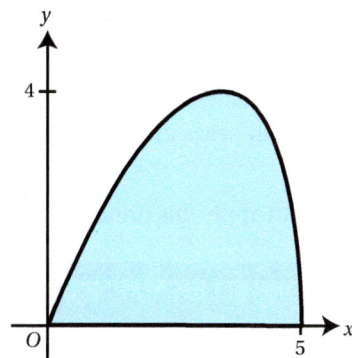

6 The region bounded by the line $y = x + 6$, $y = 0$ and $0 \le x \le 4$ is rotated though $360°$ about the x-axis to form a truncated cone (frustum). Use integration to find the centre of mass of the frustum.

7 A uniform lamina is bounded by the curve $y = kx^2$, the line $x = 3$ and the x-axis. Find:

a the area of the lamina, in terms of k

b the x-coordinate of the centre of mass of the lamina

c the y-coordinate of the centre of mass of the lamina, in terms of k.

8 A uniform lamina is bounded by the curve $y = 9 - x^2$ and the x-axis, $-3 \le x \le 3$. Find the y-coordinate of the centre of mass of the lamina.

9 A uniform lamina is defined by the positive x-axis, the positive y-axis and the curve with equation $y = \sqrt{R^2 - x^2}$.

Use integration to find the position of the centre of mass of the lamina, in terms of R.

10 The region bounded by the line $y = \cos x$, $y = 0$ and $0 \le x \le \dfrac{\pi}{2}$ is rotated though 2π radians about the x-axis to form a solid figure. Use integration to find the x-coordinate of the centre of mass of the solid.

Section 5: Equilibrium of a rigid body

A **rigid body** is a single or composite object consisting of particles, rods, wires, laminas and solids that are fixed in shape. A rigid body is in equilibrium if the resultant force acting on the body is zero and the resultant moment acting on the body is also zero.

Suspension of a lamina from a point

The moment of weight and reaction about the point of suspension are both zero as the line of action of both forces passes through the point of suspension.

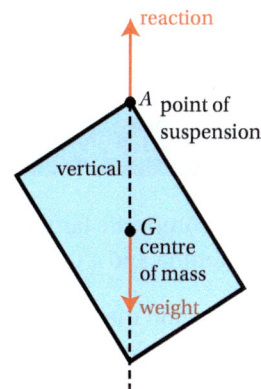

215

🔑 Key point 8.13

If a rigid body is freely suspended, it will hang with its centre of mass vertically below the point of suspension.

You can apply this principle to solve problems.

WORKED EXAMPLE 8.25

A uniform lamina has its centre of mass G at the point $(5, 8)$. A is a point on the edge of the lamina at $(2, 12)$. Find the angle between the line $y = 8$ and the vertical when the lamina is freely suspended from A.

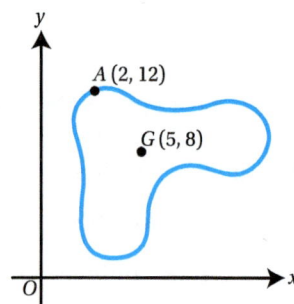

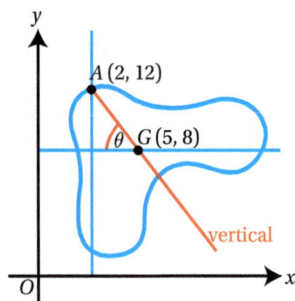

The lamina will hang with the centre of mass G vertically below A.

Draw a line through A and G together with the line $y = 8$. The line AG will hang vertical. You might find it helpful to rotate the page.

Let the angle between AG and $y = 8$ be θ.

Using trigonometry:

$$\tan \theta = \frac{12 - 8}{5 - 2}$$

$$= \frac{4}{3}$$

$$\therefore \theta \approx 53.1° \text{ (3 s.f.)}$$

WORKED EXAMPLE 8.26

A composite lamina of mass M kg is made from a uniform rectangular lamina and a uniform isosceles triangular lamina joined together.

a Find the distance of the centre of mass from AB and from AE.
The lamina is freely suspended from D.

b Find the angle between DB and the vertical.
The lamina remains suspended from D but now has a point mass kM kg attached at C. The lamina now hangs with AB horizontal.

c Find the exact value of k.

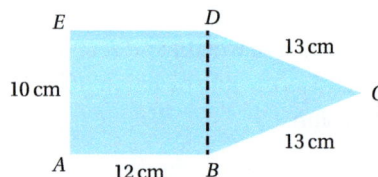

Continues on next page

If a perpendicular is drawn from C to DB it makes two $5:12:13$ triangles.

a Area of rectangular lamina $= 120 \text{ cm}^2$

Area of triangular lamina $= 60 \text{ cm}^2$

Using the composite body formula:

The mass of each component is directly proportional to area, so you can work with area.

$$(120 + 60)\begin{pmatrix} \bar{x} \\ \bar{y} \end{pmatrix} = 120 \begin{pmatrix} 6 \\ 5 \end{pmatrix} + 60 \begin{pmatrix} 16 \\ 5 \end{pmatrix}$$

Let the x-axis pass through AB and the y-axis pass through AE.

$$\begin{pmatrix} \bar{x} \\ \bar{y} \end{pmatrix} = \begin{pmatrix} 9\frac{1}{3} \\ 5 \end{pmatrix}$$

Let vertex A be $(0, 0)$.

b

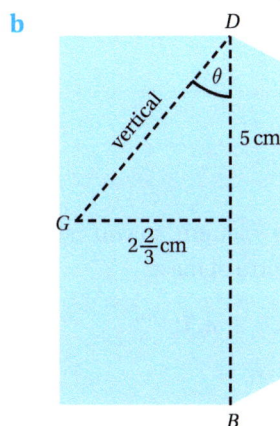

Draw in the vertical through D, which passes through the centre of mass G.

Using trigonometry:

$$\tan \theta = \frac{2\frac{2}{3}}{5}$$

Calculate θ.

$$\Rightarrow \theta \approx 28.1°$$

c

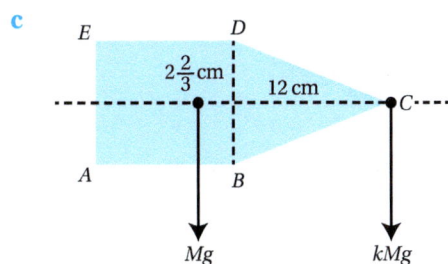

Taking moments about the midpoint of DB:

$$2\frac{2}{3}Mg - 12kMg = 0$$

As the lamina is hanging in equilibrium the resultant moment is zero.

$$k = \frac{2}{9}$$

217

WORKED EXAMPLE 8.27

A piece of uniform wire AB of length 20 cm is bent to form three sides of a rectangle, 1 cm, 18 cm and 1 cm, and then suspended freely from A. Calculate the angle between AB and the vertical.

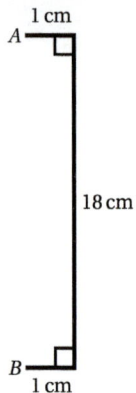

Let the midpoint of AB be $O(0, 0)$, and the centre of mass be at G.

Using the composite body formula:

The wire is symmetrical so $\bar{y} = 0$.

$20 \times OG = 1 \times 0.5 + 18 \times 1 + 1 \times 0.5$

Since the wire is uniform, mass $\propto$ length, so you can work with length to find the centre of mass.

Calculate $\bar{x}$, OG, using $M\bar{x} = m_1\bar{x}_1 + m_2\bar{x}_2$.

$\Rightarrow OG = \dfrac{19}{20} = 0.95 \text{ cm}$

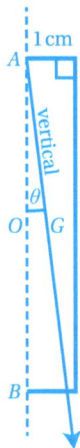

Draw a line through A and G. The line AG will be vertical. You may find it helpful to rotate the page.

Let θ be the angle between AB and the vertical.

Using trigonometry:

$\tan \theta = \dfrac{OG}{OA}$

$\quad = \dfrac{0.95}{9}$

$\Rightarrow \theta = 6.03° \text{ (3 s.f.)}$

WORKED EXAMPLE 8.28

A composite lamina of mass M kg is made from two rectangular laminas joined together. There is an axis of symmetry passing between the midpoints of AF, BE and CD.

a Find the distance of the centre of mass from AB and from AF.

The lamina is freely suspended from E.

b Find the angle between EB and the vertical.

The lamina remains suspended from E but now has a point mass kM kg attached at C. The lamina now hangs with AB horizontal.

c Find the exact value of k.

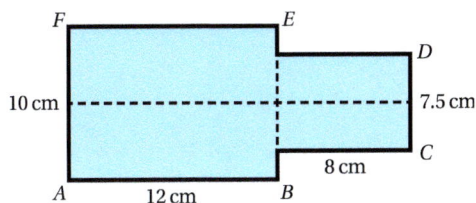

a Area of larger rectangular lamina = 120 cm²

Area of smaller rectangular lamina = 60 cm²

Using the composite body formula:

$$(120 + 60)\begin{pmatrix} \bar{x} \\ \bar{y} \end{pmatrix} = 120 \begin{pmatrix} 6 \\ 5 \end{pmatrix} + 60 \begin{pmatrix} 16 \\ 5 \end{pmatrix}$$

$$\begin{pmatrix} \bar{x} \\ \bar{y} \end{pmatrix} = \begin{pmatrix} 9\frac{1}{3} \\ 5 \end{pmatrix}$$

> The mass of each component is directly proportional to area so you can work with area.
>
> Work out the distances of the centres of mass of each rectangle from AB and AF, using
>
> $$M\begin{pmatrix} \bar{x} \\ \bar{y} \end{pmatrix} = m_1 \begin{pmatrix} \bar{x}_1 \\ \bar{y}_1 \end{pmatrix} + m_2 \begin{pmatrix} \bar{x}_2 \\ \bar{y}_2 \end{pmatrix}, \text{taking vertex } A$$
>
> as $(0, 0)$.

b

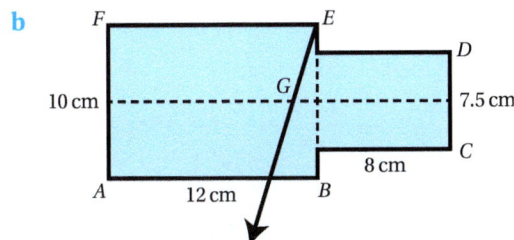

> The centre of mass G will be vertically below E when the lamina is suspended. Draw in the vertical through E, which passes through G.

Using trigonometry:

$$\tan \angle GEB = \frac{12 - 9\frac{1}{3}}{5}$$

$$= \frac{2\frac{2}{3}}{5}$$

$\therefore \angle GEB = 28.1°$ (3 s.f.)

Taking moments about the midpoint of EB:

c $2\frac{2}{3} Mg = 8kMg$

> The weight of the lamina acts at G.

$$\Rightarrow k = \frac{1}{3}$$

Toppling of a lamina when there is sufficient friction to prevent sliding

If a lamina is placed on a rough inclined plane, it may slide down the plane or it may topple over.

A lamina will be in stable equilibrium if a vertical line through the centre of mass of the lamina lies within its line of contact with the plane. It will not topple.

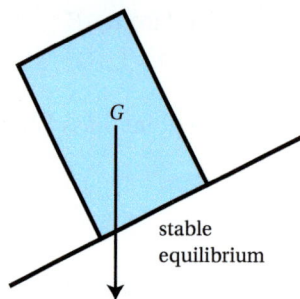

stable equilibrium

A lamina will be in limiting equilibrium if its centre of mass lies vertically above the end of its line of contact with the plane. It is about to topple.

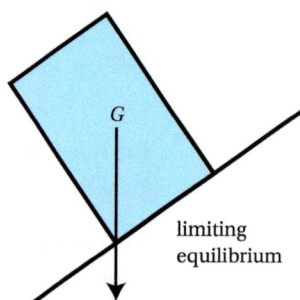

limiting equilibrium

A lamina will topple if its centre of mass lies vertically above a point on the inclined plane outside its line of contact with the plane.

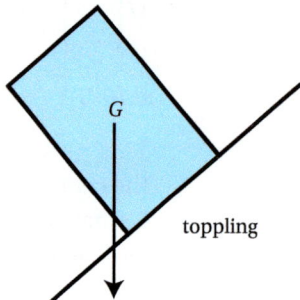

toppling

🔑 Key point 8.14

If there is sufficient friction at the surface to prevent sliding, a lamina topples if its centre of mass lies vertically above a point on the inclined plane outside its line of contact with the plane.

💡 Tip

Use a diagram to find the position of the centre of mass of the lamina above its line of contact with the inclined plane.

WORKED EXAMPLE 8.29

A rectangular lamina measures 10 cm by 8 cm. It rests with one of its shorter sides on an inclined plane. Friction between the lamina and the inclined plane is sufficiently large to prevent sliding. Find the maximum inclination of the plane to the horizontal that will allow the lamina to rest in equilibrium.

Draw a sketch, showing the locations of the angle between the plane and the horizontal.

When the lamina is in limiting equilibrium with its centre of mass above its line of contact with the plane, the inclination of the plane is maximised.

Using trigonometry:

$\theta \leqslant \tan^{-1} \dfrac{4}{5}$

$\therefore \theta \leqslant 38.7°$ (3 s.f.)

The inclination of the plane must be no more than $38.7°$.

WORKED EXAMPLE 8.30

A rectangular lamina, measuring 15 cm by 7.5 cm, has a square removed from one corner.

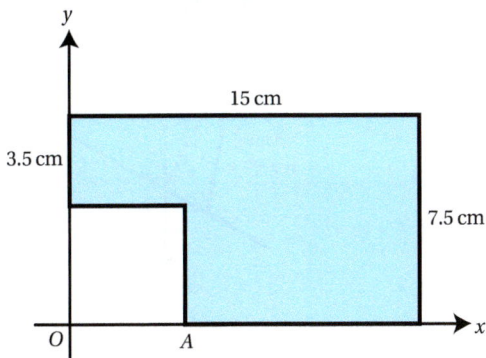

a Find the centre of mass of the lamina.

The lamina is placed on a rough inclined plane and rests in limiting equilibrium on the point of toppling about A.

b Find the angle of inclination of the plane to the horizontal.

a The centre of mass of the missing square lies at $\begin{pmatrix} 2 \\ 2 \end{pmatrix}$ cm.

Area of lamina $= 15 \times 7.5 - 16 \, cm^2$

$= 96.5 \, cm^2$

Continues on next page

Using the composite body formula:

$$96.5 \begin{pmatrix} \bar{x} \\ \bar{y} \end{pmatrix} = 112.5 \begin{pmatrix} 7.5 \\ 3.75 \end{pmatrix} - 16 \begin{pmatrix} 2 \\ 2 \end{pmatrix}$$

$$\begin{pmatrix} \bar{x} \\ \bar{y} \end{pmatrix} = \begin{pmatrix} 8.41 \\ 4.04 \end{pmatrix} \text{cm (3 s.f.)}$$

Find the area of the lamina by subtraction.

Use $M \begin{pmatrix} \bar{x} \\ \bar{y} \end{pmatrix} = m_1 \begin{pmatrix} \bar{x}_1 \\ \bar{y}_1 \end{pmatrix} - m_2 \begin{pmatrix} \bar{x}_2 \\ \bar{y}_2 \end{pmatrix}$ to find the

centre of mass of the composite lamina.

b

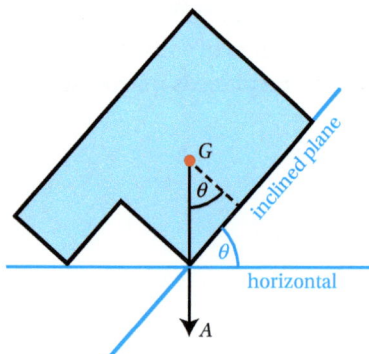

Draw a sketch.

The centre of mass is resting above A. The lamina is in limiting equilibrium.

Using trigonometry:

$$\theta = \tan^{-1}\left(\frac{8.41 - 4}{4.04} \right)$$

$$\Rightarrow \theta = 47.5° \text{ (3 s.f.)}$$

Toppling or sliding of an object on an inclined plane

If a force is applied to an object resting on a rough surface, the turning moment may cause the object to topple before it slides. In other cases, the resultant force may be sufficient to cause the object to slide before it topples.

Consider the forces acting on an object resting in stable equilibrium on a rough inclined plane.

The weight acts vertically downwards through G, the centre of mass. The normal reaction and friction act at the point on the inclined plane that the weight passes through.

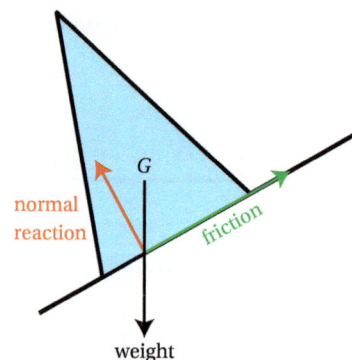

⏮ Rewind

Recall from A Level Mathematics Student Book 2, Chapter 18: $F \leqslant \mu R$

In the limiting case where the object is about to slide, $F = \mu R$.

💡 Tip

If the object is about to topple, its centre of mass lies vertically above the end of its line of contact with the plane: the normal reaction and frictional force both act at the point that the object would topple about.

WORKED EXAMPLE 8.31

A uniform solid cylinder is resting in equilibrium with one end on a rough plane inclined at a variable angle α to the horizontal. The cylinder has diameter 0.6 metres and height 1.8 metres.

a Assuming the plane is sufficiently rough to prevent sliding, find the maximum value of α that would allow the cylinder to continue to rest in equilibrium.

The coefficient of friction between the cylinder and the plane is $\frac{2}{9}$.

b As α is increased, show that the cylinder will slide before it topples.

a

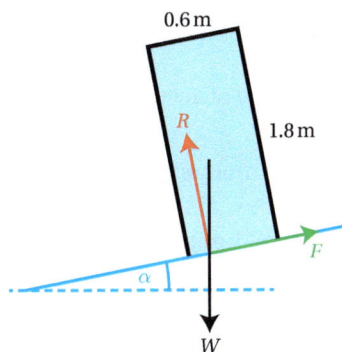

Draw a diagram showing the forces.

Using trigonometry:

$\tan \alpha = \dfrac{0.3}{0.9}$

$\Rightarrow \alpha = 18.4°$ (3 s.f.)

When the cylinder is in limiting equilibrium, its centre of mass lies directly above the outer edge of its base.

The centre of mass of the cylinder lies on its axis of symmetry at a height of 0.9 m above the base.

b The cylinder slides down the plane if:

$W \sin \alpha > \mu R$

and $R = W \cos \alpha$

$\therefore W \sin \alpha > \dfrac{2}{9} W \cos \alpha$

so $\tan \alpha > \dfrac{2}{9} \Rightarrow \alpha > 12.5°$ (3 s.f.)

Consider the component of the weight acting parallel to the plane. Sliding will occur if friction exceeds its limiting value.

Resolve perpendicular to the plane to find the magnitude of R in terms of W.

Use $\dfrac{\sin \alpha}{\cos \alpha} = \tan \alpha$.

So the cylinder starts to slide when α exceeds $12.5°$ but does not topple until α exceeds $18.4°$.

This is the condition for sliding.

An object resting on a horizontal plane will topple over if an applied force causes a resultant turning moment.

WORKED EXAMPLE 8.32

A cardboard box in the form of a cuboid and its contents, with a combined mass of 0.35 kg, rests in equilibrium on a rough horizontal plane. The contents of the box are evenly distributed and the centre of mass of the box lies at its geometric centre. The diagram shows a vertical cross-section through the centre of the box, $WXYZ$.

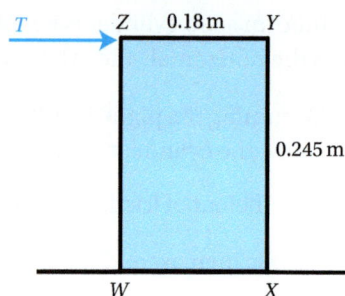

A horizontal force of magnitude T newtons acts on a horizontal line through Z. The coefficient of friction between the box and the plane is μ. As T gradually increases from zero, the box slides before it topples if $\mu < k$. Show that $k = \dfrac{18}{49}$.

In this question use $g = 9.8 \text{ m s}^{-2}$, giving your final answers to an appropriate degree of accuracy.

Taking moments about X:	The box will topple about X if the moment of T exceeds the moment of the weight of the box. At the point of toppling the normal reaction from the surface acts through X.
$T \times 0.245 - 0.35g \times 0.09 > 0$	
$T > 1.26 \text{ N}$	

Considering forces $\parallel$ to WX:	The box will slide if there is a resultant force parallel to the plane surface.
$T - \mu R > 0$ and $R = 0.35g$ N	
$\therefore T > 0.35g\mu$ N	
$T > 3.43\mu$ N	
$\therefore 3.43\mu < 1.26$	The box will slide before it topples if $3.43\mu < T \leqslant 1.26$.
$\mu < \dfrac{18}{49}$	
So $k = \dfrac{18}{49}$ as required.	

WORKED EXAMPLE 8.33

A uniform solid cube, of side 10 metres and mass m kg, rests on a rough horizontal plane. The diagram shows a vertical cross-section $PQRS$ through the centre of mass of the cube. A force, W newtons, is applied at the midpoint of RS, acting at an angle of θ above the horizontal as shown, where $\theta < 45°$.

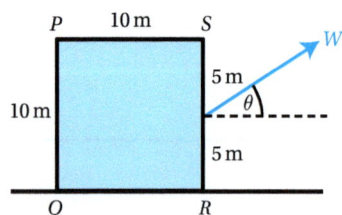

a Assuming that the cube would not slide but is on the point of toppling about R, find an expression for W in terms of m, g and θ.

b Assuming that the cube would not topple but is on the point of sliding along the plane, show that
$W = \dfrac{\mu mg}{\cos\theta + \mu \sin\theta}$, where μ is the coefficient of friction between the cube and the plane.

c Find an inequality for μ if the cube is to slide before it topples.

Continues on next page

a Taking moments about R:

$mg \times h = W \cos \theta \times 5$

$\therefore W = \dfrac{mg}{\cos \theta}$

The cube will topple about R if the moment of T exceeds the moment of the weight of the box. At the point of toppling the normal reaction from the surface acts through R.

b Resolving perpendicular to the surface, letting the normal reaction at the surface be N:

$W \sin \theta + N = mg$

$\therefore N = mg - W \sin \theta$

Resolving parallel to the surface:

$W \cos \theta = \mu R$

$\therefore W \cos \theta = \mu(mg - W \sin \theta)$

Rearranging to make W the subject:

$W \cos \theta + \mu W \sin \theta = \mu mg$

$\therefore W = \dfrac{\mu mg}{\cos \theta + \mu \sin \theta}$

The cube is on the point of sliding if the resultant force parallel to the plane surface is zero and friction takes its limiting value, μR newtons.

c $\dfrac{\mu mg}{\cos \theta + \mu \sin \theta} < \dfrac{mg}{\cos \theta}$

$\mu \cos \theta < \cos \theta + \mu \sin \theta$

$\mu(\cos \theta - \sin \theta) < \cos \theta$

$\mu < \dfrac{\cos \theta}{\cos \theta - \sin \theta}$

The cube will slide before it topples if

$\dfrac{\mu mg}{\cos \theta + \mu \sin \theta} < W < \dfrac{mg}{\cos \theta}$

⏮ Rewind

You learned how to resolve a force into two perpendicular directions in A Level Mathematics Student Book 2, Chapter 18.

EXERCISE 8E

In questions 1–4 the x-axis lies in a horizontal plane and the y-axis in a vertical plane.

1 A lamina with centre of mass at the point $G(5, 8)$ is freely suspended from the point $X(10, 10)$. Find the angle between GX and the line $y = 10$.

2 A lamina with centre of mass at the point $G(4, 4)$ is freely suspended from the point $X(12, 16)$. Find the angle between GX and the line $y = 16$.

3 A lamina with centre of mass at the point $G(7, 1)$ is freely suspended from the point $X(3, 5)$. Find the angle between GX and the line $y = 5$.

4 A lamina with centre of mass at the point $G(25, 10)$ is freely suspended from the point $X(20, 15)$. Find the angle between GX and the line $y = 15$.

5 A uniform rectangular lamina with side lengths 15 cm and 10 cm is freely suspended from one vertex. Find the angle between the longer side and the vertical.

6 A uniform rectangular lamina with side lengths 18 cm and 25 cm is freely suspended from one vertex. Find the angle between the shorter side and the vertical.

7 A uniform lamina in the shape of an equilateral triangle ABC of side 25 cm has an equilateral triangle of side 10 cm removed from vertex C.

  a Find the distance of the centre of mass from AB.

  The lamina is freely suspended from A.

  b Find the angle between AB and the vertical.

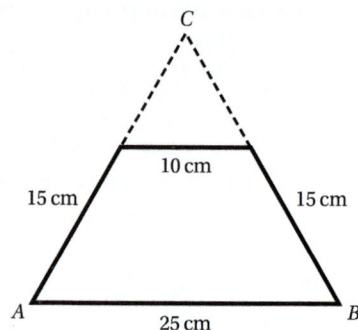

8 A rectangular lamina, measuring 15 cm by 7.5 cm, has a quarter disc removed from one corner.

  a Find the distance of the centre of mass of the lamina from AB and DE.

  The lamina is placed on an inclined plane and rests with its centre of mass above the point A and rests in equilibrium.

  b Find the inclination of the plane to the horizontal.

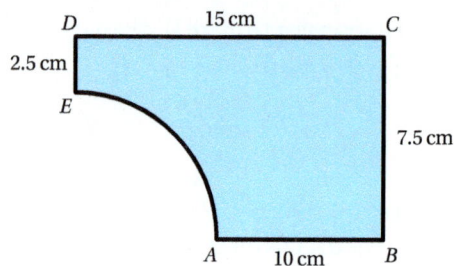

9 A uniform rectangular lamina $ABCD$ has mass 10 kg. The side AB measures 60 cm and the side BC measures 40 cm. A uniform circular lamina, of mass 5 kg, and radius 10 cm, is fixed to the rectangular lamina to form a sign. The centre of the circular lamina is 20 cm from AB and BC.

  a Find the distances of the centre of mass from AB and AD.

  The sign is freely suspended from P, the midpoint of DC.

  b Calculate the angle between AD and the vertical when the sign hangs in equilibrium.

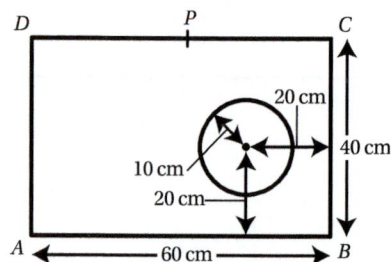

10 A uniform solid cylinder of height 0.5 metres and radius 0.1 metres rests with one of its plane faces on a rough plane inclined at θ to the horizontal. There is sufficient friction between the cylinder and the plane to prevent sliding. Calculate the value of θ if the cylinder is on the point of toppling.

11 A solid cone of base radius r cm and height $5r$ cm rests with its circular base on a rough plane inclined at $\theta°$ to the horizontal. There is sufficient friction between the cone and the plane to prevent sliding. Calculate the value of θ if the cone is on the point of toppling.

12 A solid cone of base radius 50 cm and height h metres rests with its circular base on a rough plane inclined at 30° to the horizontal. There is sufficient friction between the cone and the plane to prevent sliding. Calculate the exact value of h, given the cone is on the point of toppling.

13 A piece of wire AB of length 20 cm is bent to form an arc of a quarter-circle, and then suspended freely from A.

   a Calculate the angle between AB and the vertical.

The arc of wire remains in suspension at A when a force, F, is applied to the arc at its midpoint along a tangent, upwards. The mass of the arc of wire is 200 grams.

   b Find the magnitude of the force required to maintain the arc of wire in equilibrium with AB vertical.

14 A uniform rectangular lamina $ABCD$ of mass m kg rests with AB on a horizontal plane, which is rough enough to prevent slipping. AB measures 30 cm and BC measures 20 cm. A force, F N, is applied to the lamina at C at an angle of $30°$ below the horizontal. Find the magnitude of F, in terms of m, if the lamina is on the point of toppling about B.

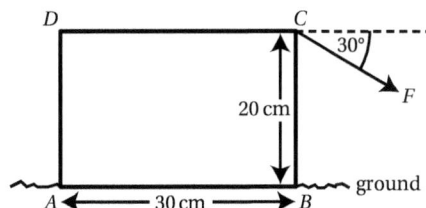

15 A uniform rectangular lamina $ABCD$ of mass 10 kg rests with AB on a horizontal rough plane. AB measures 25 cm and AD measures 50 cm. The coefficient of friction between the plane and the block is 0.2. A horizontal force, F N, is applied to the lamina at C.

   a Find the value of F if the lamina is on the point of sliding along the plane.

   b Find the value of F if the lamina is on the point of toppling about B.

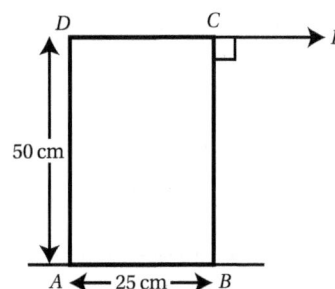

16 A box of breakfast cereal, of total mass 0.4 kg, rests on a rough horizontal plane. It can be assumed that the centre of mass of the box with its contents is on a vertical line through the centre of the box. The diagram shows a vertical cross-section $ABCD$ through the centre of mass of the box and its contents, where $AB = 0.2$ m and $BC = 0.28$ m. A horizontal force of magnitude P is applied at A, in the direction AB.

The coefficient of friction between the box and the plane is μ. As P is gradually increased from zero, the box slides before it topples if, and only if, $\mu < k$. Find the value of k.

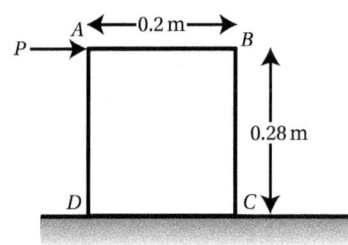

[© AQA 2013]

Checklist of learning and understanding

- A combination of n point masses $m_1, m_2, \ldots m_n$, arranged on a straight line at $x_1, x_2, \ldots x_n$, can be modelled as a single mass $M = m_1 + m_2 + \cdots + m_n$, with position $\bar{x}$, where:

  $M\bar{x} = m_1 x_1 + m_2 x_2 + \cdots + m_n x_n$

- A combination of n point masses $m_1, m_2, \ldots m_n$, arranged in a plane, at positions $\begin{pmatrix} x_1 \\ y_1 \end{pmatrix}, \begin{pmatrix} x_2 \\ y_2 \end{pmatrix}, \ldots, \begin{pmatrix} x_n \\ y_n \end{pmatrix}$,

  can be modelled as a single mass $M = m_1 + m_2 + \cdots + m_n$, with position vector $\begin{pmatrix} \bar{x} \\ \bar{y} \end{pmatrix}$, where:

  $M\begin{pmatrix} \bar{x} \\ \bar{y} \end{pmatrix} = m_1 \begin{pmatrix} x_1 \\ y_1 \end{pmatrix} + m_2 \begin{pmatrix} x_2 \\ y_2 \end{pmatrix} + \cdots + m_n \begin{pmatrix} x_n \\ y_n \end{pmatrix}.$

- The centre of mass of a uniform rod lies at its midpoint.
- The centre of mass of a symmetrical uniform lamina lies on any axis of symmetry. If there is more than one axis of symmetry the centre of mass lies at the intersection of these.
- The centre of mass of a uniform triangular lamina lies at the intersection of its medians. The medians

  intersect at $\left(\dfrac{x_1 + x_2 + x_3}{3}, \dfrac{y_1 + y_2 + y_3}{3} \right)$, where (x_1, y_1), (x_2, y_2) and (x_3, y_3) are the vertices of the triangle.

- The centre of mass of a uniform sector of a circle, having radius r and angle 2α radians at the centre of the

  circle is $\dfrac{2r \sin \alpha}{3\alpha}$ from the centre of the sector.

- The centre of mass of a uniform wire bent to form an arc of a circle, having radius r and angle 2α radians at

  the centre of the circle is $\dfrac{r \sin \alpha}{\alpha}$ from the centre of the circle.

- The rule for a combination of point masses may be extended to composite bodies comprising point masses, wires, and laminas.

  $M\begin{pmatrix} \overline{x} \\ \overline{y} \end{pmatrix} = m_1 \begin{pmatrix} \overline{x_1} \\ \overline{y_1} \end{pmatrix} + m_2 \begin{pmatrix} \overline{x_2} \\ \overline{y_2} \end{pmatrix} + \ldots + m_n \begin{pmatrix} \overline{x_n} \\ \overline{y_n} \end{pmatrix}$, where $M = m_1 + m_2 + \ldots + m_n$.

- The centre of mass of a uniform lamina with shape defined by $f(x)$ is found by integration: $\bar{x} = \dfrac{\displaystyle\int_0^a x\, f(x)\, dx}{\displaystyle\int_0^a f(x)\, dx}$

- The centre of mass of a uniform solid of revolution is found by integration: $\bar{x} = \dfrac{\displaystyle\int_0^a \pi x y^2\, dx}{\displaystyle\int_0^a \pi y^2\, dx}$

- If a rigid body is freely suspended, it will hang with its centre of mass vertically below the point of suspension.
- If there is sufficient friction at the surface to prevent sliding, the position of the centre of mass of a lamina above its line of contact with the inclined plane allows you to work out whether it will topple.
- You can use your knowledge of friction and moments to determine whether a body placed on a rough surface will slide or topple.

Mixed practice 8

1 A uniform rod AB, of mass 3 kg and length 4.5 metres, has three masses attached to it. A 4.5 kg mass is attached at the end A and a 7.5 kg mass is attached at the end B. A 5 kg mass is attached at a point C on the rod.

Find the distance AC if the centre of mass of the system is 2.5 m from point A.

2 Three particles are attached to a light rectangular lamina $OABC$. Take OA as the x-axis and OC as the y-axis, as shown.

Particle P has mass 1.5 kg and is attached at $(10, 12)$.

Particle Q has mass 3.5 kg and is attached at $(14, 8)$.

Particle R has mass 2 kg and is attached at $(5, 4)$.

Find the coordinates of the centre of mass of the system.

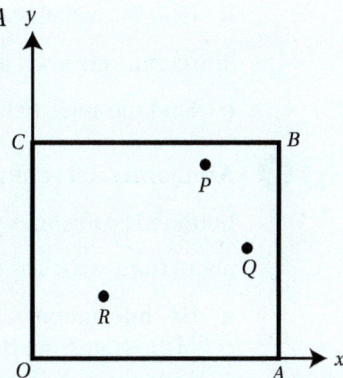

3 Four tools are attached to a board. The board is to be modelled as a uniform lamina and the four tools as four particles. The diagram shows the lamina, the four particles A, B, C and D, and the x- and y-axes.

The board has mass 4 kg and its centre of mass is at the point $(6, 4)$.

Particle A has mass 3 kg and is at the point $(10, 7)$.

Particle B has mass 2 kg and is at the point $(1, 5)$.

Particle C has mass 1 kg and is at the point $(4, 6)$.

Particle D has mass 5 kg and is at the point $(8, 1)$.

Find the coordinates of the centre of mass of the system of board and tools.

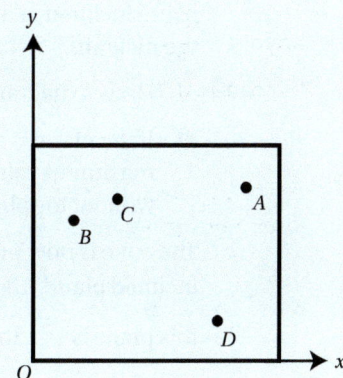

4 The diagram shows a uniform lamina in the shape of two rectangles, $AWEF$ and $WBCD$, attached together. AF measures 4 cm, AW measures 5 cm, WB measures 4 cm and BC measures 7 cm.

a Find the position of the centre of mass from AB and from AF.

The lamina is freely suspended from C.

b Find the angle between BC and the vertical when the lamina is in equilibrium.

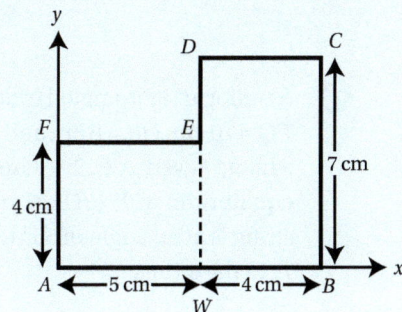

5 A uniform rectangular lamina $ABCD$ has mass 2.2 kg. AB is 10 cm long and BC is 8 cm long. A uniform square lamina of mass 1.6 kg and side length 4 cm is attached onto the rectangular lamina with one edge along the middle of the shorter side of the rectangular lamina. The diagram shows the system.

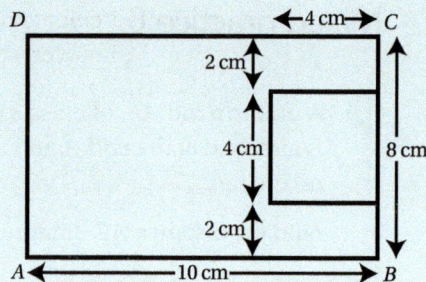

a Explain why the centre of mass is 4 cm from AB.

b Find the distance of the centre of mass from AD.

The composite body is freely suspended from D.

c Find the angle between DC and the vertical when the body hangs in equilibrium.

6 A uniform solid cone is formed by rotating the finite region bounded by the lines $y = \frac{1}{8}x$, $y = 0$ and $x = 8h$ through 2π radians about the x-axis. The cone is shown in the diagram.

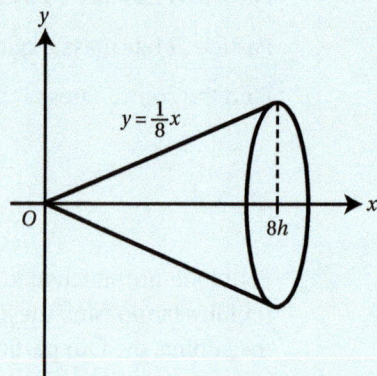

a Use integration to show that the distance of the centre of mass of the cone from the origin is $6h$.

b The cone rests in equilibrium with its plane face on a rough plane inclined at an angle θ to the horizontal, as shown in the diagram.

  i Draw a diagram showing all the forces acting on the cone.

  ii If the plane is sufficiently rough to prevent sliding, find the maximum value of θ for the cone to remain in equilibrium without toppling.

c The cone is now placed with its plane face on another rough inclined plane. The coefficient of friction between the cone and this plane is $\frac{6}{13}$. The angle α between the inclined plane and the horizontal is gradually increased from $\alpha = 0°$.

Determine whether the cone will topple first or slide first.

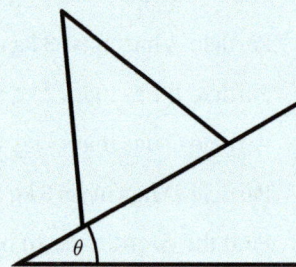

[© AQA 2011]

7 A uniform right-angled triangular lamina PQR with sides $PQ = 10$ cm, $QR = 6$ cm and $RP = 8$ cm is freely suspended from a hinge at vertex P. The lamina has mass 2.5 kg and is held in equilibrium with PR horizontal by a string attached to R. The string is at an angle of 50° to the horizontal. Calculate the tension, T, in the string.

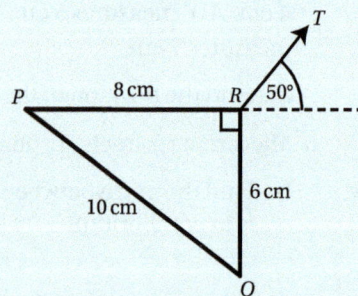

8 A uniform semi-circular arc of wire ACB is freely pivoted at A. The arc has mass 0.4 kg and diameter 5 cm. The arc is held in equilibrium, with AB vertical, by a horizontal force at B of X newtons. Find the value of X.

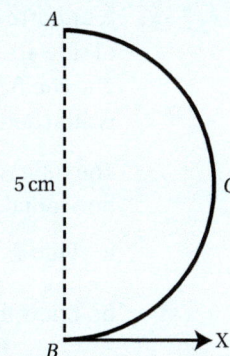

9 A uniform triangular lamina is bounded by the line $y = a - x$ and the positive x- and y-axes, as shown in the diagram.

a **i** Explain why the centre of mass of the lamina lies on the line $y = x$.

   ii By using integration, find the coordinates of the centre of mass of the lamina.

b A lamina is in the shape of an isosceles right-angled triangle, ABC, with its equal sides AB and BC of length a. The lamina has weight W. It rests in a vertical plane with the side BC on a rough horizontal surface. The coefficient of friction between the lamina and the surface is μ. A force of magnitude P acts at A in the direction parallel to CA, as shown in the diagram. The magnitude of the force is gradually increased.

   i Show that when the lamina is on the point of toppling about B, $P = \dfrac{W\sqrt{2}}{3}$.

   ii The lamina slides before it topples if and only if $\mu < k$. Determine the value of k.

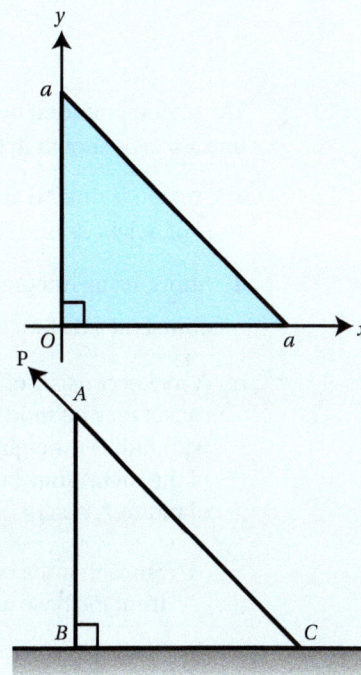

[© AQA 2015]

10 A uniform cube, of side $2a$ and mass m, rests on a rough horizontal plane. The diagram shows a vertical cross-section $ABCD$ through the centre of mass of the cube.

A force, of magnitude P, is applied at the midpoint of BC. This force acts in the plane $ABCD$ and makes an angle θ with the horizontal. The coefficient of friction between the cube and the plane is μ.

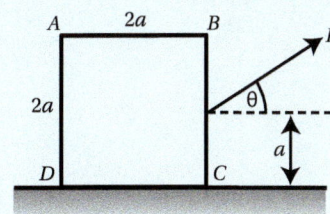

a In the case where the cube does not slide but is on the point of toppling about the edge through C, find an expression for P in terms of m, g and θ.

b In the case where the cube remains upright but is on the point of sliding along the plane, show that
$$P = \frac{\mu m g}{\cos\theta + \mu \sin\theta}.$$

c Find an inequality that μ must satisfy if the cube slides before it topples.

d Would your answer in part **c** change if the mass of the cube were doubled? Explain why.

[© AQA 2010]

11 A uniform block in the shape of a cuboid has weight W, a square base of side $4a$, a height of $8a$ and stands on a rough horizontal surface. The coefficient of friction between the block and the surface is μ. A rope is attached to the point M, the midpoint of a top edge of the block.

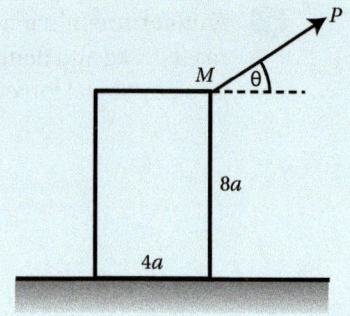

The rope is pulled with a force P, which acts at an angle of θ above the horizontal and is perpendicular to the top edge.

a Find P, in terms of W and θ, if the block is on the point of toppling.

b Show that $P = \dfrac{\mu W}{\cos\theta + \mu \sin\theta}$ if the block is on the point of sliding.

c Given that $\tan\theta = 1$, find an inequality that μ must satisfy if the block slides before it topples.

[© AQA 2007]

12 The region bounded by the line $y = \frac{1}{2}x$, the x-axis and the line $x = 2r$ is shown in the diagram.

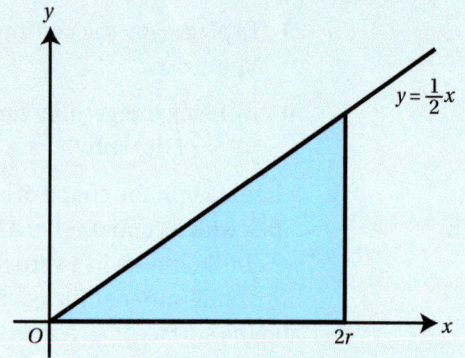

The region is rotated about the x-axis to form a uniform solid cone of height $2r$ and radius r.

a Show, using integration, that the centre of mass of the cone is at a distance of $\dfrac{3r}{2}$ from the origin.

b A rocket consists of two parts. The lower part of the rocket may be modelled as a uniform solid cylinder with radius r, height $2r$ and density ρ. The upper part of the rocket may be modelled as a uniform solid cone of radius r, height $2r$ and density $k\rho$, as shown in the diagram.

i Show that the centre of mass of the rocket is at a distance of $\left(\dfrac{6+5k}{6+2k}\right)r$ from the base of the rocket.

ii The rocket is now placed on a rough plane, which is inclined at an angle of θ to the horizontal, where $\tan\theta = \frac{2}{3}$.

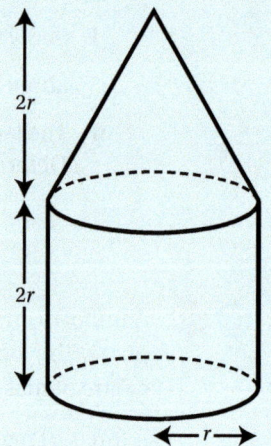

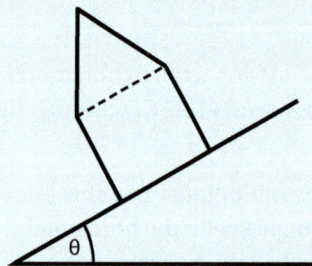

Given that the rocket does **not** slide and is just on the point of toppling, find the value of k.

[© AQA 2008]

13 The region bounded by the line $y = x + 3r$, the y-axis, the x-axis and the line $x = 2r$ is shown in the diagram.

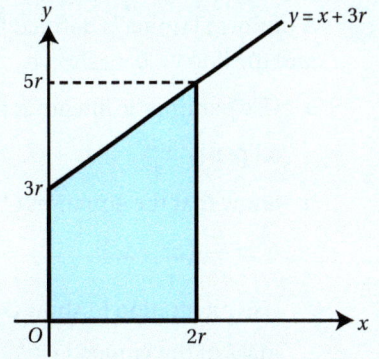

This region is rotated about the x-axis to form a frustum, of volume $\frac{98\pi r^3}{3}$, of a uniform solid cone.

a Using integration, find the distance of the centre of mass of the frustum of the cone from O.

b The frustum of a uniform solid cone with radii $3r$ and $5r$ and height $2r$ has weight W. The frustum stands on a horizontal surface. The diagram shows a cross-section, $ABCD$, which includes the axis of symmetry, of this frustum. A force P is applied to the point B and acts in the same plane as this cross-section at an angle of θ below the horizontal.

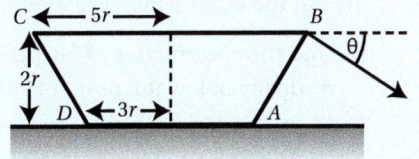

The frustum does not slide and is about to topple about A.

  i Show that

$$P = \frac{3W}{2(\cos\theta + \sin\theta)}$$

  ii Find, in terms of W, the minimum possible value of P.

  iii State the value of θ for which P is a minimum.

[© AQA 2012]

14 a A uniform semicircular lamina of radius r has its centre at the origin and its axis of symmetry along Ox. The position of its centre of mass has coordinates $(\bar{x}, 0)$.

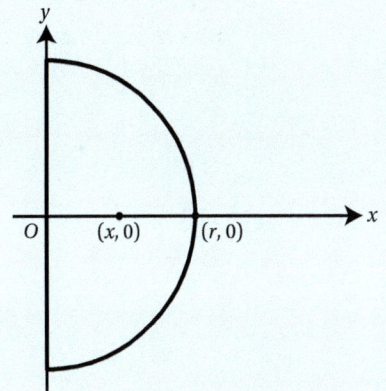

  i Show that $\frac{1}{2}\pi r^2 \bar{x} = \int_0^r 2x\sqrt{r^2 - x^2}\,\mathrm{d}x$.

  ii Hence prove that $\bar{x} = \frac{4r}{3\pi}$.

b The diagram shows a uniform lamina, used as an advertising feature in a local supermarket to promote ice cream. It consists of a semicircle, of diameter $AB = 1\,\text{m}$, and an isosceles triangle ABC, where C is at a distance $1.2\,\text{m}$ from AB.

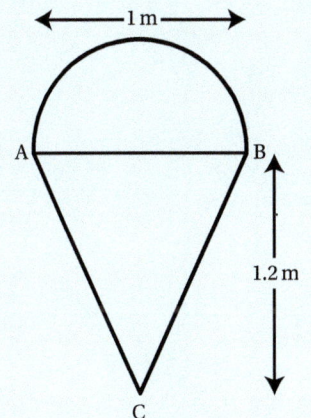

  i State the distance of the centre of mass of the triangle from C.

  ii Show that the distance of the centre of mass of the semicircle from C is approximately $1.41\,\text{m}$.

  iii Find the distance of the centre of mass of the complete lamina from C.

c The lamina is freely suspended from A. Find the angle that AB makes with the vertical through A, giving your answer to the nearest degree.

[© AQA 2006]

15 A uniform lamina is defined by the ellipse $\frac{x^2}{a^2} + \frac{y^2}{b^2} = 1$, the line $x = 0$ and the line $y = 0$, as shown.

a Use parametric integration to show that the area of the quarter ellipse is $\frac{\pi ab}{4}$.

b Show that the equation of the curved edge can be written as $y^2 = \frac{b^2}{a^2}(a^2 - x^2)$.

c Use integration to show that the x-coordinate of the centre of mass of the lamina is $\frac{4a}{3\pi}$.

The lamina is to be freely suspended from $(0, 0)$.

d Find the coordinates of the point on the curved edge that lies vertically below the point of suspension.

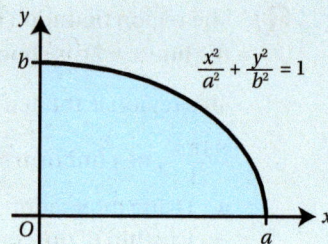

Tip

The y-coordinate of the centre of mass of the quarter ellipse is $\frac{4b}{3\pi}$.

9 Moments and couples

Before you start...

A Level Mathematics Student Book 2, Chapter 18	You should be able to resolve forces.	1	Find the component of the weight of a 5 kg block sitting on a ramp inclined at 25° to the horizontal parallel to the ramp.
A Level Mathematics Student Book 2, Chapter 19	You should understand how to calculate moments for forces acting perpendicular.	2	Calculate the moment about A for this system of forces.
Chapter 8	You should know where the centre of mass of a uniform rod or lamina is.	3	Find the centre of mass of a rectangular lamina with side lengths 3 cm and 6 cm.
Further Mathematics Student Book 2	You should know how to calculate the cross product.	4	Calculate the cross product $\mathbf{a} \times \mathbf{b}$ where $\mathbf{a} = 3\mathbf{i} - 2\mathbf{j} + \mathbf{k}$ and $\mathbf{b} = \mathbf{i} - 6\mathbf{k}$.

Moments and couples

In A Level Mathematics Student Book 2, Chapter 19, you saw that the moment (turning effect) depended upon both the force applied and the perpendicular distance from the pivot point.

In this chapter, you will consider forces where the lines of action are not necessarily acting perpendicular to a point P.

Section 1: Moments

> 🔑 **Key point 9.1**
>
> The moment of a force F about a point P is:
>
> $$\text{moment} = Fd \sin \theta$$
>
> where d is any distance between the line of action of the **force** F and the **point** P and θ is the **angle**, as shown.
>
> The units of moment are **newton metres** (N m).

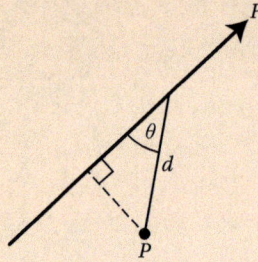

The moment will either cause a clockwise or an anticlockwise rotation about the point.

There are many situations involving forces that cause a rotation and you will need a way to model each situation depending on the shapes or objects involved, which may include:

- a uniform lamina
- a uniform rod
- a non-uniform rod.

> ⏪ **Rewind**
>
> You learnt how to calculate the centre of mass of an object in Chapter 8.

WORKED EXAMPLE 9.1

Find the moment about the point A.

$$\text{moment} = Fd \sin \theta$$

$$\text{moment} = 15 \times 10 \times \sin 30°$$

$$\text{moment} = 75 \, \text{N m}$$

The diagram does not give the perpendicular distance so you need to calculate it using $d \sin \theta$.

In some diagrams it may not be clear which angle you should use to calculate the perpendicular distance to the line of action of the force.

WORKED EXAMPLE 9.2

Find the moment about the point A.

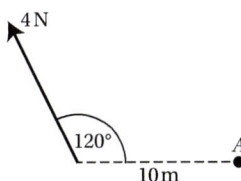

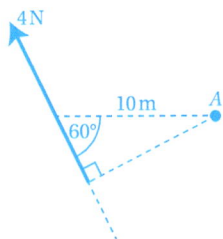

The diagram provided makes it difficult to see which angle you need, so you might find it helpful to redraw the diagram.

moment $= Fd \sin \theta$

moment $= 4 \times 10 \times \sin 60°$

The angle you need is $180° - 120° = 60°$.

moment $= 20\sqrt{3}$

moment $= 35\,\text{N}\,\text{m}\,(2\,\text{s.f.})$

Round to an appropriate degree of accuracy, given the information in the question.

Key point 9.2

To find the resultant moment about a point, find the sum of the clockwise moments and the sum of the anticlockwise moments separately.

The resultant moment will be the difference between the two sums, in the direction of the larger moment.

Tip

Remember, if an object is in equilibrium there is a zero resultant force and a zero resultant moment about any point.

When considering the moments about a point on a rod, instead of finding the perpendicular distance from the point to the line of action of the force, you can consider the components of the force acting perpendicular to the rod.

WORKED EXAMPLE 9.3

A uniform rod AB of mass 3000 grams is pivoted at A and held in equilibrium at an angle of $60°$ to the vertical by a force F applied at B, perpendicular to AB. Find the force F.

Use $g = 9.8\,\text{m}\,\text{s}^{-2}$, giving your final answer to an appropriate degree of accuracy.

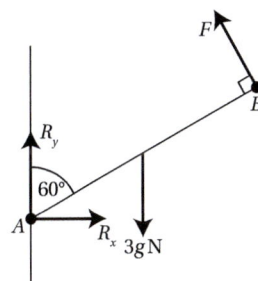

Continues on next page

Let the length of the rod be 2*x*.

Since you are not given the length of the rod in the question, introduce a length for your calculations involving moments. Choosing 2*x* is sensible since the rod is uniform.

Taking anticlockwise moments about *A*:

Since you don't know what the reaction forces are at the pivot, taking moments about *A* removes the need to consider them in your calculations involving moments.

$3g \times \cos 30° - F \times 2x = 0$

$F = \dfrac{3g \cos 30°}{2}$

$F = 12.730\,573\,44\ldots$

You can resolve the weight of the rod perpendicular to the rod. The component of the rod's weight that acts parallel to the rod will have no effect on the moment. You must convert the mass of the rod into kg.

$F = 13\,\text{N}$ (2 s.f.)

Since the value of *g* is given to 2 significant figures, 2 significant figures is an appropriate degree of accuracy to use in your final answer.

🔑 Key point 9.3

When considering the moments about a point on a rod, you can find the components of the forces acting perpendicularly to the rod, instead of finding the perpendicular distance from the point to the line of action of each force.

The component acting parallel to the rod will have no effect on the moments, since each parallel component will act through the point about which the moments are being calculated.

WORKED EXAMPLE 9.4

A uniform rectangular lamina *ABCD* of mass 15 kg is held in equilibrium by a horizontal force *F* applied at the *C*. *A* rests on the ground. Given *AB* = 30 cm, *BC* = 40 cm and *AD* makes an angle of 35° to the horizontal, find the magnitude of *F*.

Use $g = 9.8\,\text{m s}^{-2}$, giving your final answer to an appropriate degree of accuracy.

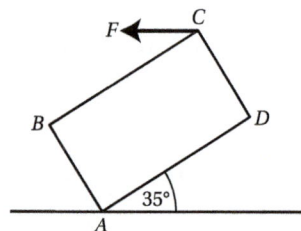

Continues on next page

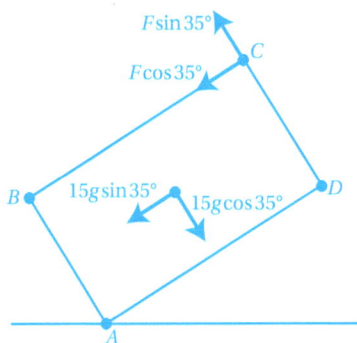

Redraw the diagram to show the forces acting.

Taking anticlockwise moments about A:

Since you don't know what the reaction forces are at the corner A, taking moments about A removes the need to consider them in your calculation involving moments.

$F \sin 35° \times 0.4 + F \cos 35° \times 0.3 - 15g \cos 35° \times 0.2$

$+ 15g \sin 35° \times 0.15 = 0$

From your diagram, you can see which components of each force (F and weight) act in which direction.

$F = \dfrac{15g \cos 35° \times 0.2 - 15g \sin 35° \times 0.15}{\sin 35° \times 0.4 + \cos 35° \times 0.3}$

$F = 24 \text{ N (2 s.f.)}$

Since the value of g is given to 2 significant figures, 2 significant figures is an appropriate degree of accuracy to use in your final answer.

WORK IT OUT 9.1

Find the sum of the moments about A of the forces shown.

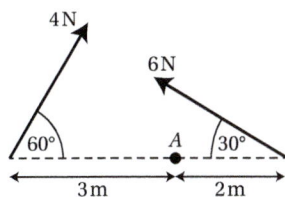

Which is the correct solution? Identify the errors made in the incorrect solutions.

Solution 1	Solution 2	Solution 3
$4 \times 3 \sin 60° - 6 \times 2 \sin 30°$ $= 4 \text{ N m (1 s.f.)}$ Moment of 4 N m.	Taking moments anticlockwise about A: $6 \times 2 - 4 \times 3 = 0 \text{ N m}$ No moment about A.	Taking moments anticlockwise about A: $6 \times 2 \sin 60° - 4 \times 3 \sin 30°$ $= -4 \text{ N m (1 s.f.)}$ Moment of 4 N m clockwise.

EXERCISE 9A

In this exercise, unless instructed otherwise, use $g = 9.8\ \mathrm{m\,s^{-2}}$, giving your final answers to an appropriate degree of accuracy.

1 Find the moment about the point P of the weight of each uniform rod.

a i

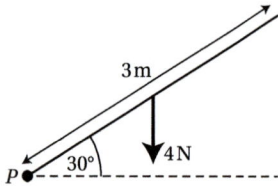

ii

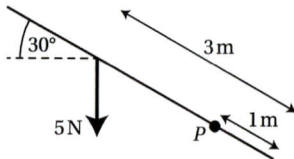

b i

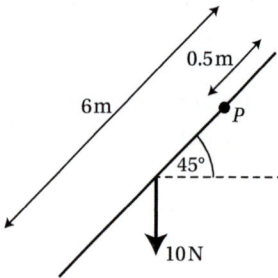

ii

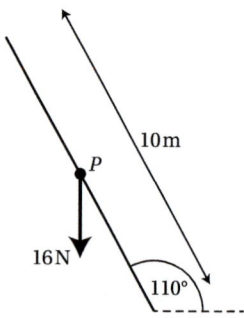

c i

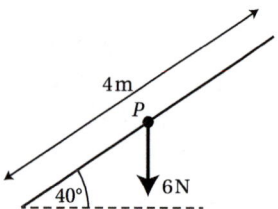

ii

2 Find the moment about P of the weight of each uniform lamina.

a i

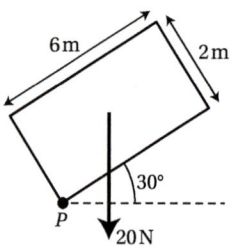

ii

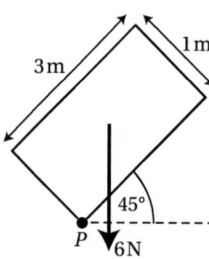

b i

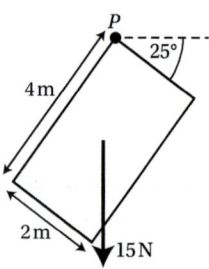

ii

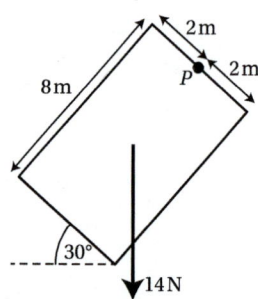

3 A 4 m long uniform rod has weight 50 N. Find the net moment about the point P in each situation.

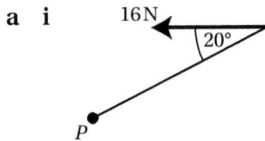

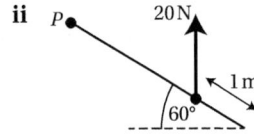

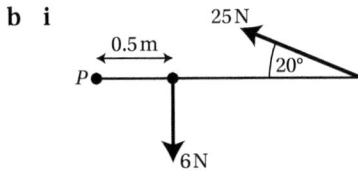

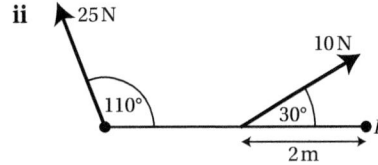

a **i**

ii

b **i**

ii

4 A 4 m by 6 m uniform rectangular lamina weighs 150 N. Find the net moment about the point P in each situation, given that the lamina is in a vertical plane.

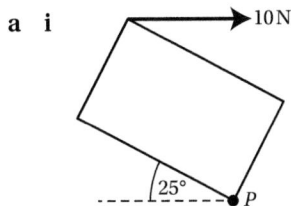

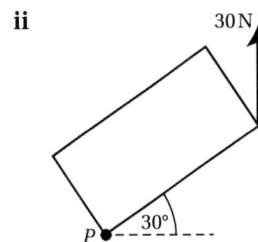

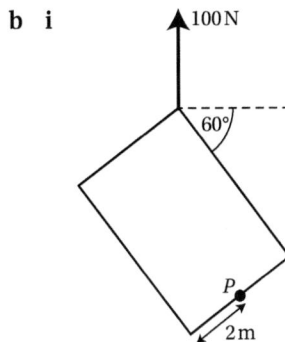

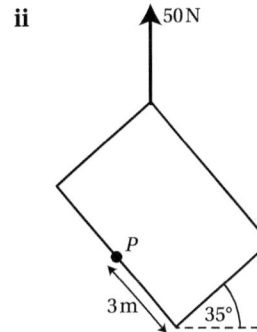

a **i**

ii

b **i**

ii

5 The diagram shows a uniform rod of mass 5 kg and length 4 m which is freely hinged at the point X and is resting horizontally in equilibrium. Find the magnitude of the force F.

6 A pendulum consisting of a light string of length 50 cm has one end freely joined at A and the other end attached to a particle of 500 grams, as shown. The pendulum is held in equilibrium by a force at the particle acting perpendicularly to the string. Find the magnitude of the force F.

7 A non-uniform rod AB of length 10 m is held horizontally in equilibrium when a 5 N force (making an angle of 30° to the horizontal) and a horizontal force F N acting along the line AB are attached at A and a force of 10 N (making an angle of 60° to the horizontal) is attached at B. Find the mass of the rod and the distance from A of the centre of mass of the rod.

8 The lower end A of a uniform beam AB of mass m and length $2x$ is resting on a rough horizontal floor. The beam is kept in equilibrium at an angle of 45° to the horizontal by a string attached at B. If the string makes an angle of 60° with BA, find the tension in the string in terms of m and g.

9 When finding the moment of a force about a point it is sometimes helpful to resolve the force into components first. For this diagram, justify the statement that calculating the moment about the point A (using the component of the force F perpendicular to the light rod) is equivalent to finding the perpendicular distance from A to the line of action of F.

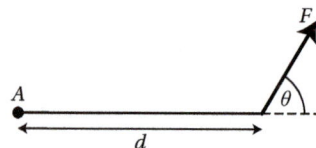

Section 2: An introduction to couples

Sometimes when two forces of the same magnitude act in opposite directions along different lines of action, they have a zero resultant force but do have a turning effect.

Forces that are parallel and act in the same direction are said to be **like forces** and those that are parallel and act in the opposite direction are said to be **unlike forces**.

Two unlike forces of equal magnitude, not acting along the same line of action, are said to form a **couple**.

Key point 9.4

A couple has a turning effect but cannot produce a translation effect (the resultant force is zero).

The effect of a couple on a rigid body is to cause it to rotate.

The turning effect of a couple is independent of the point about which the turning takes place.

Did you know?

The resultant moment of a couple is called a torque and acts perpendicular to the plane of forces.

WORKED EXAMPLE 9.5

Two 10 N forces are applied to the ends A and B of a rod of length 4 m. The forces are parallel but act in opposite directions.

a Find the sum of the moments of the forces about the centre of the rod.
b Describe the motion of the rod.

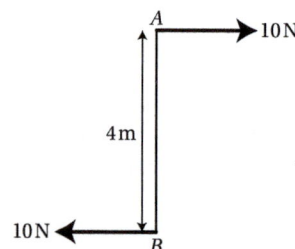

Continues on next page

a   Taking clockwise moments about the centre of the rod:

$10 \times 2 + 10 \times 2 = 40\,\text{N}\,\text{m}$

> The directions of both forces are clockwise about the centre of the rod.

b   The two forces form a couple with magnitude 40 N m and the rod will rotate in a clockwise direction about the centre of the rod.

> Since the forces are equal in magnitude and in opposite directions, they have no translational effect but do have a turning effect.

It is also possible for three or more parallel forces to form a couple.

WORKED EXAMPLE 9.6

Show that the system of forces given in this diagram forms a couple and find the magnitude of the moment of this couple.

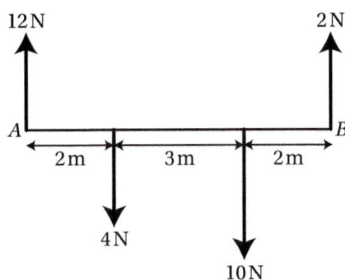

Resolving forces in a direction parallel to the 12 N force:

$12 + 2 - 4 - 10 = 0$

> To prove that the forces form a couple you must resolve the forces to show that the resultant force is zero.

The forces are balanced.

Taking clockwise moments about A:

> You can take moments about any point to determine if the forces form a couple, or the moments are balanced and there is no turning effect.

$4 \times 2 + 10 \times 5 - 2 \times 7 = 44\,\text{N}\,\text{m}$

The magnitude of the couple is 44 N m.

> **Tip**
>
> The direction of a couple is also referred to as the **sense** of the couple.

EXERCISE 9B

In this exercise, unless instructed otherwise, use $g = 9.8 \text{ m s}^{-2}$, giving your final answers to an appropriate degree of accuracy.

1 Determine in each case if the system of forces forms a couple. When a couple is formed, calculate the magnitude of the moment of the couple and state its direction.

a **i**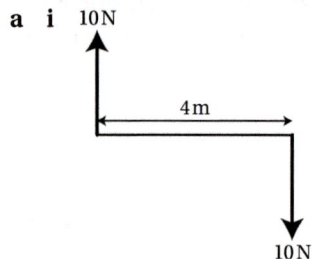

ii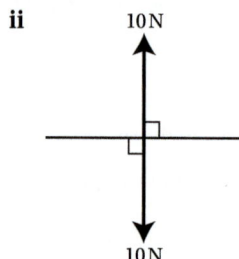

b **i**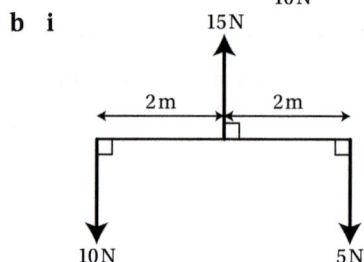

ii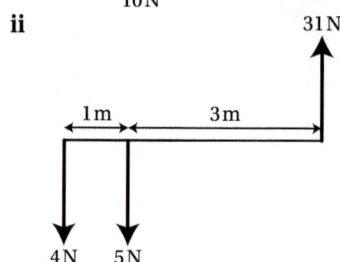

c **i**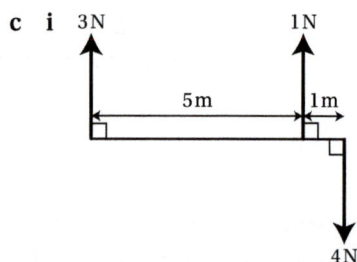

ii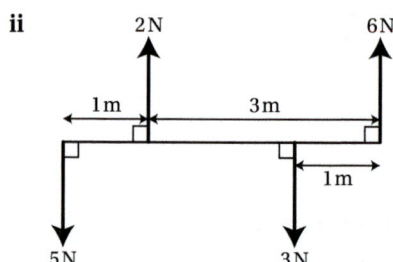

2 These diagrams show light rectangular frames with the forces acting along the edges as indicated. Determine in each case if the system of forces forms a couple. When a couple is formed, calculate the magnitude of the moment of the couple and state its direction.

a **i**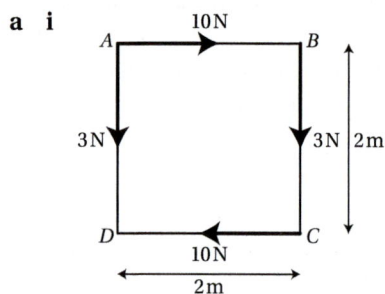

ii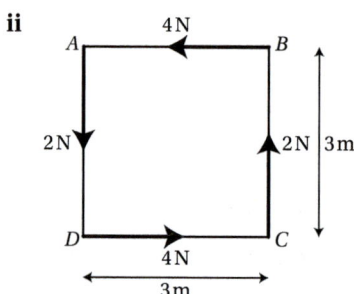

b **i**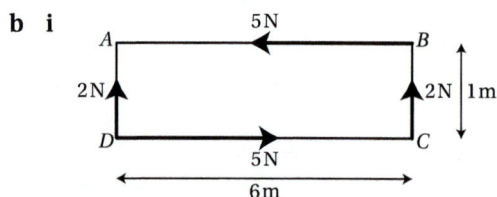

ii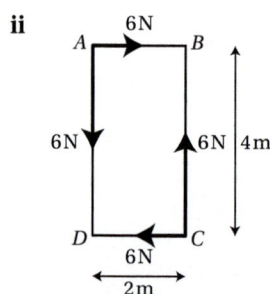

3 A rectangular lamina $ABCD$, with side lengths $AD = X$ m and $DC = Y$ m, has two forces of F N attached so that a couple M N m anticlockwise about its centre is produced. Draw a diagram to indicate the lines of action of the forces if:

a $X = 3, Y = 4, F = 50$, and

   i $M = 150$ **ii** $M = -200$

b $X = 2, Y = 8, F = 400$, and

   i $M = -800$ **ii** $M = 800$

c $X = 4, Y = 4, F = 25$, and

   i $M = 100$ **ii** $M = 0$.

4 Show that the system of forces in the diagram forms a couple and find the magnitude of the moment of this couple.

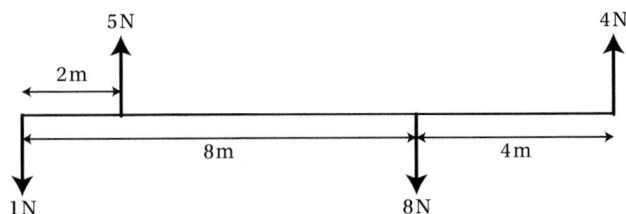

5 The diagram shows the forces that act on a 40 cm by 20 cm lamina. The lamina rotates about its centre but does not move. Find the magnitude of the forces X and Y, and show that the system of forces is equivalent to a couple at the centre of the lamina.

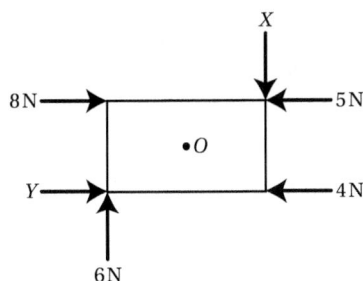

6 A light rod of length X m lies on a horizontal table. The ends of the rod are each held by a clamp. The rod is acted upon by a couple of magnitude M N m causing it to rotate on the table. What force perpendicular to the rod must each clamp exert to prevent the rotation? Give your answer in terms of X and M.

7 The diagram shows the forces acting on each wheel of a car. These forces are equivalent to a couple (a turning effect) and a single force (a translation effect) acting at the centre of the car. Find the magnitude of the force and of the couple.

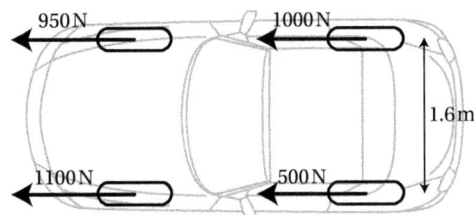

Section 3: Vector methods

You can use vectors to describe forces and apply the ideas from sections 1 and 2.

WORKED EXAMPLE 9.7

A force of $(3\mathbf{i} + 2\mathbf{j})$ N acts at the point with position vector $(5\mathbf{i} + \mathbf{j})$ m and a force of $(\mathbf{i} - \mathbf{j})$ N acts at the point with position vector $(2\mathbf{i} + \mathbf{j})$ m. Find the net moment of these forces about the point P with position vector $\mathbf{i} + 3\mathbf{j}$.

Draw a diagram of the situation.

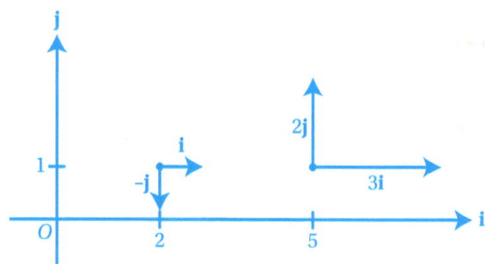

Taking anticlockwise moments about P:

$2 \times 1 - 1 \times 1 + 3 \times 2 + 2 \times 4 = 15\,\text{N m}$

Net moment is $15\,\text{N m}$ anticlockwise

WORKED EXAMPLE 9.8

A force of $(3\mathbf{i} - 5\mathbf{j})$ N acts at the point with position vector $(6\mathbf{i} + \mathbf{j})$ m, and a force of $(-3\mathbf{i} + 5\mathbf{j})$ acts at the point that has position vector $(4\mathbf{i} + \mathbf{j})$ m. Show that these forces reduce to a couple, and find the moment of the sense of the couple.

Draw a diagram of the situation.

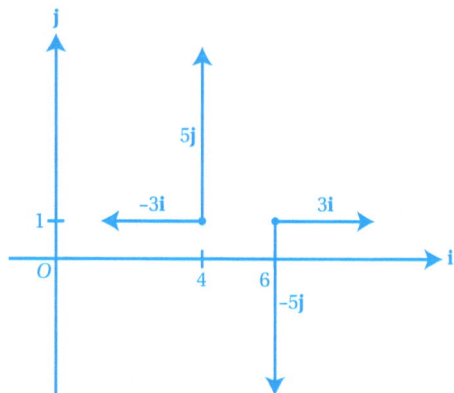

Resolving forces in the direction of $\mathbf{i}$:

$-3\mathbf{i} + 3\mathbf{i} = 0$

Resolving forces in the direction of $\mathbf{j}$:

$5\mathbf{j} - 5\mathbf{j} = 0$

To show that the forces reduce to a couple the resultant force must be zero but the net moment must be non-zero.

The resultant force is zero. There is no translation effect.
For a couple, you need a non-zero moment.

Continues on next page

Taking anticlockwise moments about the origin, O:

$1 \times 3 - 1 \times 3 + 4 \times 5 - 6 \times 5 = -10 \, \text{N m}$

The couple has a moment of $10 \, \text{N m}$ clockwise. .... State the moment and sense of the couple.

The moment of a force about an arbitrary centre O can also be described by the vector equation:

$$\mathbf{M} = \mathbf{r} \times \mathbf{F}$$

where $\mathbf{r}$ is the position vector measured from O to any point along the line of action of the force vector $\mathbf{F}$ and $\times$ indicates the vector cross-product. When there is more than once force acting, you can take a linear combination of the cross products.

Key point 9.5

The **resultant moment** $\mathbf{M}$ is the sum of the individual moments $\mathbf{M}_i$ for the forces $\mathbf{F}_i$ about an arbitrary centre O:

$$\sum \mathbf{M}_i = \sum (\mathbf{r}_i \times \mathbf{F}_i)$$

where $\mathbf{r}_i$ is the position vector measured from O to any point along the line of action of the force vector $\mathbf{F}_i$.

Rewind

The cross product or vector product is covered in Further Mathematics Student Book 2.

WORKED EXAMPLE 9.9

A force $(3\mathbf{i} + 4\mathbf{j} - \mathbf{k})$ N is directed along a line passing through $(2, 1, 4)$. Calculate the moment of this force about the origin.

A position vector of a point acting a long the line of action of the force is $2\mathbf{i} + \mathbf{j} + 4\mathbf{k}$. .... You need the position vector measured from the point where the moment will be calculated about.

$\mathbf{M} = \mathbf{r} \times \mathbf{F}$

$$\mathbf{M} = \begin{pmatrix} 2 \\ 1 \\ 4 \end{pmatrix} \times \begin{pmatrix} 3 \\ 4 \\ -1 \end{pmatrix} = \begin{pmatrix} -17 \\ 14 \\ 5 \end{pmatrix} \, \text{N m}$$

WORKED EXAMPLE 9.10

Forces $2\mathbf{i} - 3\mathbf{j} + \mathbf{k}$, $\mathbf{i} - 4\mathbf{j}$ and $-2\mathbf{i} + 3\mathbf{j} - 2\mathbf{k}$ are acting at the points $(-1, 3, 0), (2, 1, 1)$ and $(4, 0, 1)$ respectively. Calculate the magnitude of the resultant moment produced by these forces about the point $P(2, 3, 1)$.

A displacement vector of a point acting along the line of action of the force $2\mathbf{i} - 3\mathbf{j} + \mathbf{k}$ from P is $-3\mathbf{i} - \mathbf{k}$.

A displacement vector of a point acting along the line of action of the force $\mathbf{i} - 4\mathbf{j}$ from P is $-2\mathbf{j}$.

A displacement vector of a point acting along the line of action of the force $2\mathbf{i} + 3\mathbf{j} - 2\mathbf{k}$ from P is $2\mathbf{i} - 3\mathbf{j}$.

> You need the position vector measured from the point about which the moment will be calculated for each force.

$$\sum M_i = \sum (r_i \times F_i)$$

$$M = \begin{pmatrix} -3 \\ 0 \\ -1 \end{pmatrix} \times \begin{pmatrix} 2 \\ -3 \\ 1 \end{pmatrix} + \begin{pmatrix} 0 \\ -2 \\ 0 \end{pmatrix} \times \begin{pmatrix} 1 \\ -4 \\ 0 \end{pmatrix} + \begin{pmatrix} 2 \\ -3 \\ 0 \end{pmatrix} \times \begin{pmatrix} 2 \\ 3 \\ -2 \end{pmatrix}$$

$$M = \begin{pmatrix} 9 \\ 9 \\ 23 \end{pmatrix}$$

$$|M| = \sqrt{9^2 + 9^2 + 23^2} = 26.28687885\ldots$$

> You need the magnitude for the moment.

$$|M| = 26 \,\text{Nm} \,(2\,\text{s.f.})$$

> Give your final answer to an appropriate degree of accuracy.

In Worked example 9.10 you were asked to calculate the resultant moment about a certain point P. If you calculated the moment about the origin you would obtain a different value. If the system of forces forms a couple then, by Key point 9.4, the moment of the couple is independent of the point about which the turning is taking place.

WORKED EXAMPLE 9.11

Forces $2\mathbf{i} - 3\mathbf{j} - 2\mathbf{k}$, $-\mathbf{i} + 4\mathbf{k}$ and $-\mathbf{i} + 3\mathbf{j} - 2\mathbf{k}$ are acting at the points $(-1, 3, 0), (2, 1, 1)$ and $(4, 0, 1)$ respectively.

a Show that this set of forces form a couple.
b Calculate the magnitude of the resultant moment produced by these forces about the origin.
c Calculate the magnitude of the resultant moment produced by these forces about the point $P(2, 3, 1)$.

Continues on next page

a $2\mathbf{i}-3\mathbf{j}-2\mathbf{k}+-\mathbf{i}+4\mathbf{k}+-\mathbf{i}+3\mathbf{j}-2\mathbf{k}=\mathbf{0}$

For a couple the resultant force must be $\mathbf{0}$ N.

b $\mathbf{M}=\sum \mathbf{M}_i=\sum (r_i \times F_i)$

$$\mathbf{M}=\begin{pmatrix}-1\\3\\0\end{pmatrix}\times\begin{pmatrix}2\\-3\\-2\end{pmatrix}+\begin{pmatrix}2\\1\\1\end{pmatrix}\times\begin{pmatrix}-1\\0\\4\end{pmatrix}+\begin{pmatrix}4\\0\\1\end{pmatrix}\times\begin{pmatrix}-1\\3\\-2\end{pmatrix}$$

$$\mathbf{M}=\begin{pmatrix}-5\\-4\\10\end{pmatrix}$$

$$|\mathbf{M}|=\sqrt{(-5)^2+(-4)^2+10^2}=11.874\,342\,09\ldots$$

$$=12\,\mathrm{N\,m}$$

c   A displacement vector of a point acting along the line of action of the force $2\mathbf{i}-3\mathbf{j}+\mathbf{k}$ from P is $-3\mathbf{i}-\mathbf{k}$.

You need the position vector measured from the point where the moment will be calculated about for each force.

A displacement vector of a point acting along the line of action of the force $\mathbf{i}-4\mathbf{j}$ from P is $-2\mathbf{j}$.

A displacement vector of a point acting along the line of action of the force $2\mathbf{i}+3\mathbf{j}-2\mathbf{k}$ from P is $2\mathbf{i}-3\mathbf{j}$.

$$\mathbf{M}=\sum \mathbf{M}_i=\sum (r_i \times F_i)$$

$$\mathbf{M}=\begin{pmatrix}-3\\0\\-1\end{pmatrix}\times\begin{pmatrix}2\\-3\\-2\end{pmatrix}+\begin{pmatrix}0\\-2\\0\end{pmatrix}\times\begin{pmatrix}-1\\0\\4\end{pmatrix}+\begin{pmatrix}2\\-3\\0\end{pmatrix}\times\begin{pmatrix}-1\\3\\-2\end{pmatrix}$$

$$\mathbf{M}=\begin{pmatrix}-5\\-4\\10\end{pmatrix}$$

$$|\mathbf{M}|=\sqrt{(-5)^2+(-4)^2+10^2}=11.874\,342\,09\ldots$$

You need the magnitude for the moment.

$$=12\,\mathrm{N\,m}\ (2\ \mathrm{s.f.})$$

Round to an appropriate degree of accuracy.

In this exercise, distances are measured in metres and forces are measured in newtons.

1 A force $\mathbf{F}_i$ acts at the point P_i. Find the moment about the origin for each of these situations.

    a   **i** $\mathbf{F}_1 = -\mathbf{i} + 3\mathbf{j}$ and $P_1 = (2, 3)$

         ii $\mathbf{F}_1 = \mathbf{i} + 3\mathbf{j}$ and $P_1 = (-2, 5)$

    b   **i** $\mathbf{F}_1 = -2\mathbf{i} - 3\mathbf{j}, \mathbf{F}_2 = -\mathbf{i} + \mathbf{j}$ and $P_1 = (-1, 0), P_2 = (3, 1)$

         ii $\mathbf{F}_1 = 3\mathbf{j}, \mathbf{F}_2 = 3\mathbf{j} - 2\mathbf{i}$ and $P_1 = (4, 5), P_2 = (-1, -1)$

    c   **i** $\mathbf{F}_1 = \mathbf{i} - 5\mathbf{j}, \mathbf{F}_2 = -2\mathbf{i} + \mathbf{j}, \mathbf{F}_3 = -2\mathbf{i} - \mathbf{j}$ and $P_1 = (1, 1), P_2 = (0, 1), P_3 = (1, 3)$

         ii $\mathbf{F}_1 = 3\mathbf{j}, \mathbf{F}_2 = \mathbf{i} + \mathbf{j}, \mathbf{F}_3 = 6\mathbf{i} + 5\mathbf{j}$ and $P_1 = (-2, -1), P_2 = (2, -3), P_3 = (4, 1)$

2 Use the cross product to calculate the resultant moment for each part in question 1.

3 A force $4\mathbf{i} + 3\mathbf{j}$ acts at the point $(6, 3)$ and a force $-4\mathbf{i} - 3\mathbf{j}$ acts at the point $(3, -1)$. Show that this system of forces forms a couple. Find the moment of the couple.

4 A force $-2\mathbf{i} + \mathbf{j}$ acts at the point $(-2, 1)$ and a force $2\mathbf{i} - \mathbf{j}$ acts at the point $(2, 4)$. Show that this system of forces forms a couple. Find the moment of the couple.

5 Three forces are represented by the vectors $-2\mathbf{i} - 3\mathbf{j}, 3\mathbf{i} + 4\mathbf{j}$ and $-\mathbf{i} - \mathbf{j}$, and act at the points $(2, 0), (0, 3)$ and $(1, 1)$ respectively. Show that this system of forces forms a couple and find the magnitude of the couple.

6 Forces $\mathbf{i} - 3\mathbf{j} + \mathbf{k}, 2\mathbf{i} - 4\mathbf{j} + \mathbf{k}$ and $-2\mathbf{i} - 2\mathbf{k}$ act at the points $(-1, 0, 0), (3, -1, 2)$ and $(4, 0, 1)$ respectively. Calculate the magnitude of the resultant moment produced by these forces about the origin.

7 Forces $3\mathbf{j} + \mathbf{k}, 5\mathbf{i} + 3\mathbf{j}$ and $2\mathbf{i} + \mathbf{j} - 3\mathbf{k}$ act at the points $(1, 1, 1), (-2, 0, 3)$ and $(2, -1, 5)$ respectively. Calculate the magnitude of the resultant moment produced by these forces about the point $P(-3, 4, -2)$.

8 Forces $a\mathbf{i} + b\mathbf{j}$ and $6\mathbf{i} - 4\mathbf{j}$ act at the points $(-2, -2)$ and $(3, -1)$ respectively. This system of forces forms a couple. Find a and b, and the magnitude of the couple.

9 Three forces are represented by the vectors $2\mathbf{i} - 3\mathbf{j}, x\mathbf{i} + y\mathbf{j}$ and $-2\mathbf{i} - \mathbf{j}$, and act at the points $((1, 1), (-1, 3)$ and $(2, -1)$ respectively. This system of forces forms a couple. Find the values of x and y, and the magnitude of the couple.

10 Points A, B, C and D have coordinates $(3, 1), (1, 3), (-2, 1)$ and $(-2, -2)$ respectively relative to the origin O. The forces $3\mathbf{i} + 3\mathbf{j}, 4\mathbf{i} - 5\mathbf{j}, -5\mathbf{i} + 2\mathbf{j}$ and $2\mathbf{i} + 3\mathbf{j}$ act at points A, B, C and D respectively. A couple of moment $\mathbf{M}$ N m anticlockwise and a force $\mathbf{F} = a\mathbf{i} + b\mathbf{j}$ acting through the point $(2, 1)$ are added to the system. The system is now in equilibrium. Find $\mathbf{M}, a$ and b.

11 Given that this system of forces has a resultant force of zero, find the values of a and b. Hence prove that the system of forces is in equilibrium about the origin:

    $\mathbf{F}_1 = a\mathbf{i} - \mathbf{j} + \mathbf{k}$ acting at the point $\mathbf{i} + \mathbf{j}$

    $\mathbf{F}_2 = b\mathbf{i} - 2b\mathbf{j} - 5\mathbf{k}$ acting at the point $3\mathbf{i} - a\mathbf{j} + 5\mathbf{k}$

    $\mathbf{F}_3 = -\mathbf{i} - a\mathbf{j} + 4\mathbf{k}$ acting at the point $-2\mathbf{j} + 4\mathbf{k}$.

> 💡 **Tip**
>
> If a system of forces is in equilibrium then the resultant force and moment is zero.

12 Let **F** be a force. Prove that the moment calculation $\mathbf{m} = \mathbf{r} \times \mathbf{F}$ is independent of the position vector **r** chosen along the line of action of **F**.

13 Prove that the moment of a couple is independent of the reference point chosen for calculating the couple.

Section 4: Problem solving using moments and couples

You need to be able to model situations involving moments and couples.

WORKED EXAMPLE 9.12

A uniform ladder of length 12.5 m rests with one end against a smooth wall and the other on rough horizontal ground 3.5 m from the wall. If the foot of the ladder is on the point of slipping, find the coefficient of friction between the ladder and the ground.

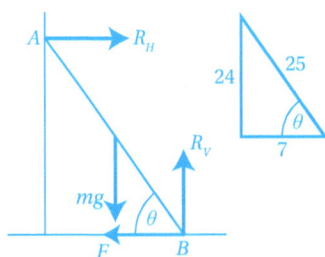

Draw a diagram.

Resolving vertically:
$R_v - mg = 0$

The ladder is in equilibrium.

It is on the point of slipping, so:
$F = \mu R_v = \mu mg$

Friction is at a maximum. You met the coefficient of friction in A Level Mathematics Student Book 2, Chapter 18.

Taking anticlockwise moments about A:

$mg \cos \theta \times 6.25 + F \sin \theta \times 12.5 - R_v \cos \theta \times 12.5 = 0$

There are too many unknowns, so you can use moments to remove the reaction force at A.

$mg \cos \theta \times 6.25 + \mu mg \sin \theta \times 12.5 - mg \cos \theta \times 12.5 = 0$

$\cos \theta + 2\mu \sin \theta - 2 \cos \theta = 0$

$2\mu \sin \theta = \cos \theta$

$2\mu \dfrac{24}{25} = \dfrac{7}{25}$

Simplify and use the $(7, 24, 25)$ Pythagorean triple for $\sin \theta$ and $\cos \theta$.

$\mu = \dfrac{7}{48} = 0.15 \,(2 \text{ s.f.})$

Give your final answer to an appropriate degree of accuracy.

WORKED EXAMPLE 9.13

A model crane is shown in the diagram. The crane is in equilibrium.

a Find the magnitude of the tension T.
b State a modelling assumption about the jib (BC).

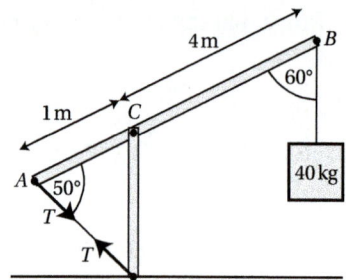

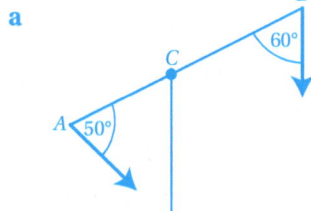

a

Draw a simpler diagram.

Taking anticlockwise moments about C:

$T \sin 50° \times 1 = 40g \sin 60° \times 4$

$T = \dfrac{160 \sin 60°}{\sin 50°}$

$T = 1772.6 \text{ N}$

You don't know anything about the reaction forces at the pivot C, so you can take moments about this point to discount them.

Give your final answer to an appropriate degree of accuracy.

b The jib (BC) can be modelled as light, i.e. weight is not considered.

You don't know the weight of the jib, so you made a modelling assumption that it was negligible.

WORKED EXAMPLE 9.14

$ABCD$ is a rectangle with $AB = 6$ m and $BC = 3$ m. Forces of 4 N, 2 N, 3 N and 5 N act along AB, BC, CD and DA respectively.

a Calculate the magnitude and direction of the single force F that could replace this system of forces.
b The line of action of the single force cuts the line containing AB at the point P. Find the length of AP.

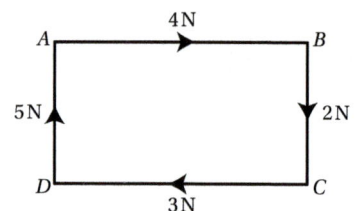

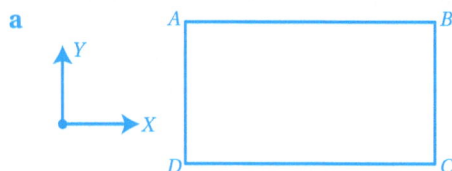

a

Draw a diagram. You can introduce two components for the single force F, X and Y.

Continues on next page

Resolving parallel to AB:

$4 - 3 = X$

$X = 1\,\text{N}$

Find the equivalent horizontal force.

Resolving parallel to DA:

$5 - 2 = Y$

$Y = 3\,\text{N}$

Find the equivalent vertical force.

$F = \sqrt{1^2 + 3^2} = 3\,\text{N}\,(1\,\text{s.f.})$

The question asked to calculate the magnitude of the force F.

Direction $= \arctan \dfrac{3}{1} = 71.566\,05118\ldots$

$= 70°\,(1\,\text{s.f.})$

The question also asked to calculate the direction of the force F.

b

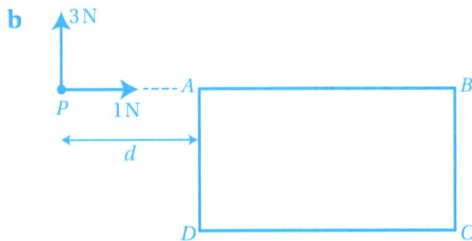

The turning effect of the system of forces should be the same so you can equate the two systems.

Taking clockwise moments about A and equating the two systems:

$2 \times 6 + 3 \times 3 = Y \times d$

$21 = 3d$

$d = \dfrac{21}{3}$

$= 7\,\text{m from } A \text{ along the line}$
containing AB.

WORKED EXAMPLE 9.15

A light rod AB has length 4 m. The rod is on a smooth horizontal table and is acted upon by two horizontal forces of magnitude $\sqrt{6}$ N and $\sqrt{2}$ N. The forces are arranged as in the diagram.

a A force P N is added to the rod AB so that the system of forces forms a couple. Calculate the magnitude and direction of P.

b Calculate the largest possible magnitude of the moment of the couple.

c State the sense of the couple.

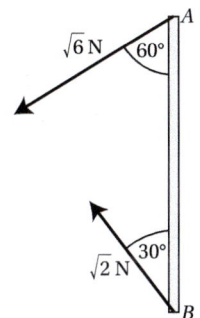

Continues on next page

a

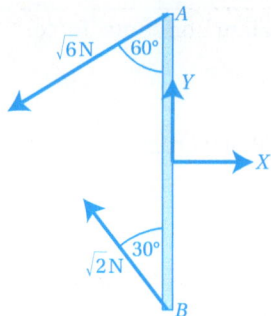

Draw a diagram with the force P marked on in components X and Y.

$\sqrt{2}\cos 30° - \sqrt{6}\cos 60° + Y = 0$

For a couple the resultant force is zero.

$$\sqrt{2} \times \frac{\sqrt{3}}{2} - \sqrt{6} \times \frac{1}{2} + Y = 0$$

$$0 + Y = 0$$

$$Y = 0\,\text{N}$$

Resolving perpendicular to AB, in the direction of X:

$X - \sqrt{2}\sin 30° - \sqrt{6}\sin 60° = 0$

$X = \sqrt{2}\sin 30° + \sqrt{6}\sin 60°$

$X = \sqrt{2} \times \dfrac{1}{2} + \sqrt{6} \times \dfrac{\sqrt{3}}{2}$

$X = 2\sqrt{2}\,\text{N}$

$P = 2\sqrt{2}\,\text{N}$ in the direction of X, perpendicular to AB.

b

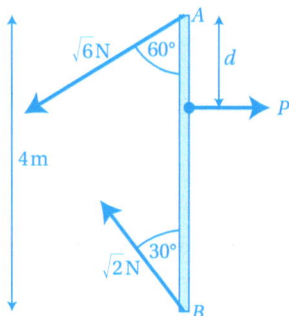

Draw a diagram, labeling a general position for P along the rod AB.

Taking anticlockwise moments about A:

$d \times P - 4 \times \sqrt{2}\sin 30° = d \times 2\sqrt{2} - 2\sqrt{2}$

To maximise the magnitude of the couple, $d = 4$ m.

$4 \times 2\sqrt{2} - 2\sqrt{2} = 6\sqrt{2}\,\text{N m}$

The couple is independent of the point taken to calculate the moment. So you can take moments about any point and work to maximise the magnitude of the moment.

c Anticlockwise.

WORKED EXAMPLE 9.16

A uniform cylinder of mass 5 kg and radius 0.2 m rests in equilibrium with its curved surface in contact with two rough planes, where the coefficient of friction between each plane is μ and each plane is inclined at 20° to the horizontal. The line of intersection of the planes and the axis of the cylinder are horizontal. The maximum couple that can be applied to the cylinder, in the plane perpendicular to its axis, so that the cylinder remains in equilibrium is 5 N m.

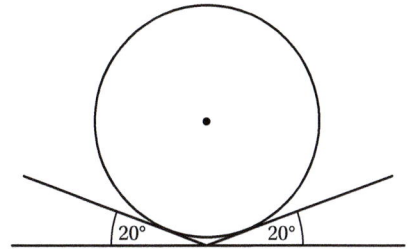

Find μ.

If the cylinder is in equilibrium, then the couple cannot exceed the moment created by the maximum frictional force of the cylinder on the two rough planes.

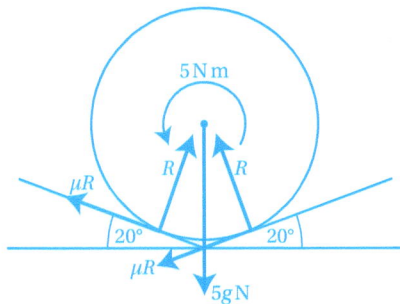

Let R be the reaction force between the cylinder and each plane.

Using symmetry, the reaction force between the cylinder and each inclined rough plane is the same.

Resolving forces perpendicular to the horizontal:

$5g + \mu R \sin 20° = \mu R \sin 20° + R \cos 20° + R \cos 20°$

$5g = 2R \cos 20°$

$R = \dfrac{5g}{2\cos 20°}$

Taking moments about the centre of the cylinder:

$0.2 \times \mu R + 0.2 \times \mu R - 5 = 0$

$\mu = \dfrac{5}{0.2 \times R \times 2}$

$\mu = 0.5 \ (1 \text{ s.f.})$

The direction of the couple will be opposite to the direction of the moment created by the frictional forces.

Give your answer to an appropriate degree of accuracy.

1 *ABCD* is a rectangle.

  i Calculate the magnitude of the single force that can replace the given system of forces.

  ii The line of action of the single force cuts the line containing *AB* at the point *P*. Find *AP*.

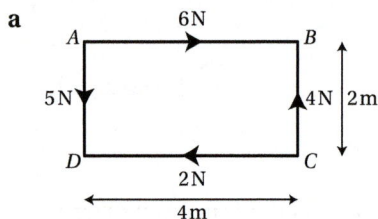

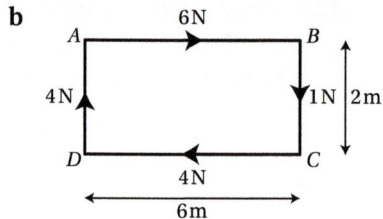

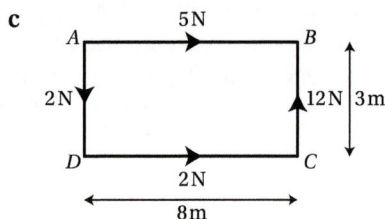

2 A uniform ladder of length *L* m rests with one end against a smooth wall and the other on rough horizontal ground *D* m from the wall. If the foot of the ladder is on the point of slipping, find the coefficient of friction between the ladder and the ground when:

  a i $L = 10$ and $D = 3$ **ii** $L = 20$ and $D = 5$

  b i $L = 15$ and $D = 4$ **ii** $L = 12$ and $D = 4$

  c i $L = 7$ and $D = 1.5$ **ii** $L = 8$ and $D = 2.2$.

3 A uniform ladder of length 10 m and weight 150 N rests against a smooth vertical wall and stands on a rough horizontal surface. A person of weight 750 N stands on the ladder so that their weight acts at a distance of 7 m from the end in contact with the horizontal surface. The foot of the ladder is on the point of slipping with the ladder making an angle of 30° with the vertical. Find the coefficient of friction between the ladder and the horizontal surface.

4 The image shows a simple crane. At what distance can the loading platform carry each load safely? Can all loads be safely carried?

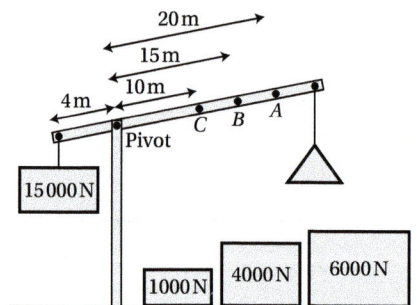

5. *ABCDE* is a framework of seven light rods, freely joined and of the same length. The framework is in equilibrium, supported at *A* and *D*, and has a weight of 750 N hanging from *E*. Using moments, find the forces *R* and *S*.

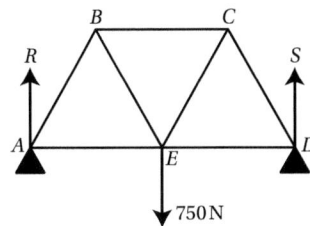

6. A cylindrical roller, of radius 0.75 m and weight 1.5 k N, is on the point of moving up a ledge, of height 0.25 m, by a force applied at the centre of the roller parallel to the horizontal ground. Find the magnitude of this force.

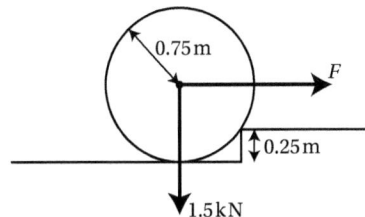

7. A uniform rod *AB* of mass *m* hangs vertically with end *A* freely hinged to a fixed point. The rod is pulled aside by a horizontal force *F*, applied at *B*, until it makes an angle of 60° with the downward vertical. Find *F* in terms of *m* and *g*.

8. The diagram shows a heavy crate with two forces acting. A single force and a couple at *O*, the centre of the create, form an equivalent system.

   a Find the magnitude of the force and of the couple.

   b A third force of 400 N is to be added perpendicular to the side *AD* so that the three forces are equivalent to a single force acting at *O*. Where along *AD* should this force be applied?

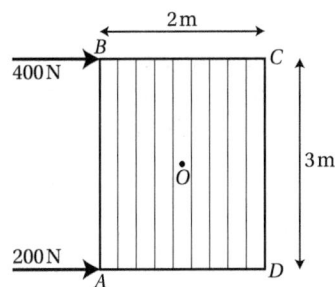

9. A climber of mass 75 kg has their feet resting against a vertical wall and is attached to a rope for support. Their body is inclined at an angle of 60° with the upward vertical at the wall. The rope is attached at the point through which the climber's weight acts and is at right angles to the line of action of their body.

   a Find the tension in the rope.

   b Find the magnitude and direction of the reaction at the wall.

10. A uniform steel girder *AB*, of weight 350 N and length 3 m, is freely hinged at *A* on a vertical wall. The girder is held in a horizontal position by a cable attached to the girder at *B* and to the vertical wall at *C*, vertically above *A* at a distance of 1.5 m. A load of weight 150 N is suspended from the girder at *D*, where *AD* = 2 m. The girder is horizontal and in equilibrium.

    a State two modelling assumptions needed in this situation.

    b Find the tension in the cable.

✐ Checklist of learning and understanding

- The moment of a force F about a point P is:

$$\text{moment} = Fd \sin \theta$$

  where d is any distance between the line of action of the **force** F and the **point** P and θ is the **angle**, as shown.
  The units of moment are **newton metres** (N m).

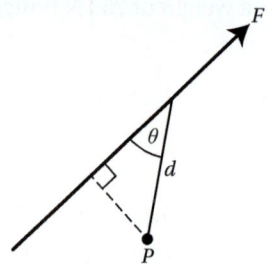

- To find the resultant moment about a point, find the sum of the clockwise and the sum of the anticlockwise moments separately.
  The resultant moment will be the difference between the two sums, in the direction of the larger moment.
- When considering the moments about a point on a rod, you can find the components of the forces acting perpendicularly to the rod, instead of finding the perpendicular distance from the point to the line of action of each force.
  The component acting parallel to the rod will have no effect on the moments, since each parallel component will act through the point about which the moments are being calculated.
- A couple has a turning effect but cannot produce a translation effect (the resultant force is zero).
  The effect of a couple on a rigid body is to cause it to rotate.
  The turning effect of a couple is independent of the point about which the turning takes place.
- The resultant moment $\mathbf{M}$ is the sum of the individual moments $\mathbf{M_i}$ for the forces $\mathbf{F_i}$ about an arbitrary centre O:

$$\mathbf{M} = \sum \mathbf{M_i} = \sum (\mathbf{r_i} \times \mathbf{F_i}),$$

  where $\mathbf{r_i}$ is the position vector measured from O to any point along the line of action of the force vector $\mathbf{F_i}$.

Mixed practice 9

1 A uniform horizontal shelf *CD* of mass of 4 kg is freely hinged to a vertical wall and is supported by a chain *AB*.

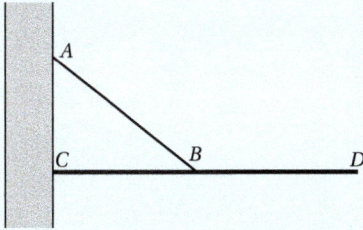

The tension in the chain is 100 N, *CB* = 10 cm and the angle *ABC* = 45°. Find the length of *CD*. Choose from these options.

  A 18 cm   **B** 9 cm   **C** 72 cm   **D** 36 cm

2 A light rod is pivoted about a point *O*.

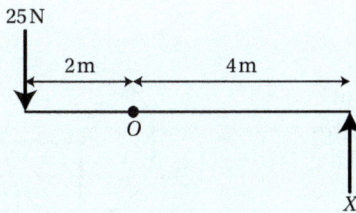

The forces acting form a couple. Find the magnitude of the moment. Choose from these options.

  A 25 N m   **B** 150 N m   **C** 50 N m   **D** 100 N m

3 Forces $3\mathbf{j}+\mathbf{k}$ and $2\mathbf{i}+\mathbf{j}-3\mathbf{k}$ act at the points $(1,0,-3)$ and $(1,-1,2)$ respectively. Calculate the magnitude of the resultant moment produced by these forces about the point $P(-1,2,-1)$. Choose from these options.

  A $2\sqrt{14}$ N m   **B** $2\sqrt{22}$ N m   **C** $6\sqrt{11}$ N m   **D** $2\sqrt{51}$ N m

4 A uniform ladder of length 10 m rests with one end against a smooth wall and the other on rough horizontal ground 2 m from the wall. If the foot of the ladder is on the point of slipping, find the coefficient of friction between the ladder and the ground. Choose from these options

  A 0.306 (3 s.f.)   **B** 0.102 (3 s.f.)   **C** 0.980 (3 s.f.)   **D** 0.612 (3 s.f.)

5 A cylindrical roller, of radius 0.5 m and weight *W*, is on the point of moving up a ledge, of height 0.1 m, by a force 2 k N applied at the centre of the roller parallel to the horizontal ground. Find *W*.

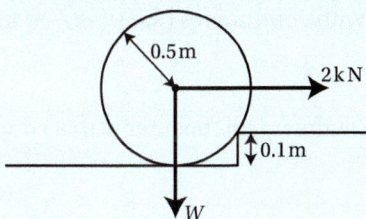

6   Three forces, $-\mathbf{i} + \mathbf{j}$, $4\mathbf{i} - 2\mathbf{k}$ and $-3\mathbf{i} - \mathbf{j} + 2\mathbf{k}$, act at the points whose coordinates are $(0, 2, 1)$, $(3, -1, 0)$ and $(4, 0, -5)$ respectively.

   a Find the resultant of these three forces.

   b Find the moment of these three forces about $(0, 0, 0)$.

   c Explain why these three forces are equivalent to a couple.

   [© AQA 2011]

7   The system of forces:

   $\mathbf{F_1} = a\mathbf{i} + 2\mathbf{j} - 3\mathbf{k}$ acting at the point $(1, -1, 2)$

   $\mathbf{F_2} = \mathbf{i} + b\mathbf{j} + 2\mathbf{k}$ acting at the point $(2, 1, -1)$

   $\mathbf{F_3} = -3\mathbf{i} + \mathbf{j} + c\mathbf{k}$ acting at the point $(2, 0, 1)$

   $\mathbf{F_4} = \mathbf{i} - 2\mathbf{j} + 4\mathbf{k}$ acting at the point $(0, 1, -2)$

   reduces to a couple. Find:

   a a, b and c

   b the magnitude of the couple.

8   A cylindrical roller, of radius r and weight W, is on the point of moving up a ledge, of height h, by a force F applied at the centre of the roller parallel to the horizontal ground. Show that F is given by $W \tan\left(\arccos\left(\dfrac{r-h}{r} \right) \right)$.

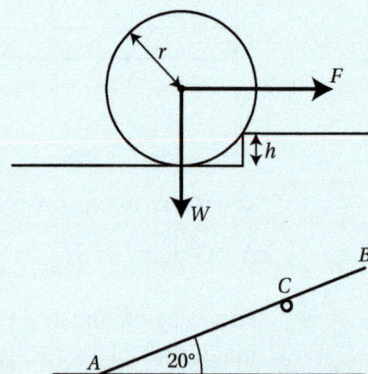

9   A uniform rod AB, of length 4 m and mass 6 kg, rests in equilibrium with one end, A, on smooth horizontal ground. The rod rests on a rough horizontal peg at the point C, where AC is 3 m. The rod is inclined at an angle of $20°$ to the horizontal.

   a Draw a diagram to show the forces acting on the rod.

   b Find the magnitude of the normal reaction force between the rod and the ground.

   c **i** Find the normal reaction acting on the rod at C.

   ii Find the friction force acting on the rod at C.

   d In this position, the rod is on the point of slipping.

   Calculate the coefficient of friction between the rod and the peg.

   [© AQA 2010]

10   Three forces, $\begin{bmatrix} 2 \\ 1 \end{bmatrix}$, $\begin{bmatrix} 5 \\ -4 \end{bmatrix}$ and $\begin{bmatrix} 0 \\ a \end{bmatrix}$ newtons, act at the points with coordinates $(3, 4)$, $(-2, -3)$ and $(2, 0)$ metres respectively.

   This system of three forces is equivalent to a force, $\mathbf{F}$, acting at the origin together with a couple of magnitude 24 N m.

   a Determine the two possible values for a.

   b Write down the force, $\mathbf{F}$, corresponding to each value of a.

   [© AQA 2013]

11 A uniform cylinder of mass 6.5 kg and radius r rests in equilibrium with its curved surface in contact with two rough planes, where the coefficient of friction between each plane is 0.55 and each plane is inclined at 15° to the horizontal. The line of intersection of the planes and the axis of the cylinder are horizontal. The maximum couple that can be applied to the cylinder, in the plane perpendicular to its axis, so that the cylinder remains in equilibrium is 200 N m.

Find r.

12 A light rod has its ends at the points $P(-2, -1, 4)$ and $Q(4, 1, 6)$. A force $\mathbf{F}$ acts at the point M, the midpoint of PQ, where $\mathbf{F} = a\mathbf{i} + \mathbf{j} - 2\mathbf{k}$.

a Show that $\overrightarrow{PM} = 3\mathbf{i} + \mathbf{j} + \mathbf{k}$.

b Find the moment of $\mathbf{F}$ about the point P, giving your answer in terms of a.

c Given that the magnitude of the moment is $5\sqrt{2}$, find the two possible values of a.

[© AQA 2012]

13 The moment of a non-zero force $\mathbf{F}$ about a point A is the same as its moment about another point B. Show that the line of action of the force $\mathbf{F}$ is parallel to AB.

14 A uniform ladder PQ, of length 8 metres and mass 28 kg, rests in equilibrium with its foot, P, on a rough horizontal floor and its top, Q, leaning against a smooth vertical wall. The vertical plane containing the ladder is perpendicular to the wall and the angle between the ladder and the floor is 69°.

A man, of mass 72 kg, is standing at the point C on the ladder so that the distance PC is 6 metres. The man may be modelled as a particle at C.

a Draw a diagram to show the forces acting on the ladder.

b With the man standing at the point C, the ladder is on the point of slipping.

i Show that the magnitude of the reaction between the ladder and the vertical wall is 256 N, correct to three significant figures.

ii Find the coefficient of friction between the ladder and the horizontal floor.

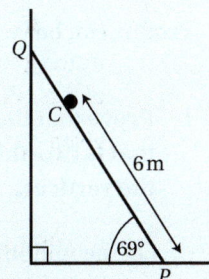

[© AQA 2012]

15 A box of breakfast cereal, of total mass 0.4 kg, rests on a rough horizontal plane. It can be assumed that the centre of the mass of the box with its contents is on a vertical line through the centre of the box. The diagram shows a vertical cross section $ABCD$ through the centre of mass of the box and its contents, where $AB = 0.2$ m and $BC = 0.28$ m. A horizontal force of magnitude P is applied at A, in the direction of AB.

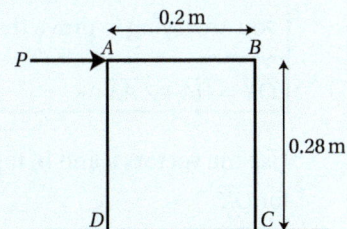

The coefficient of friction between the box and the plane is μ. As P is gradually increased from zero, the box slides before it topples if, and only if, $\mu < k$. Find the value of k.

[© AQA 2013]

In Chapter 8, the formulae for the centres of mass of uniform triangular laminas were stated and used without proof. You will now explore why the centre of mass lies at the intersection of the medians. Then you will find out how you can set up proofs of the formulae, based on this fact and making use of vector arguments.

Justify the statement: the centre of mass of a uniform triangular lamina lies at the intersection of the medians.

You learned that the centre of mass of a uniform lamina lies on any axis of symmetry. A uniform triangular lamina does not have an axis of symmetry unless it is isosceles. In the diagram the lamina has been divided into numerous trapezia parallel to OA. You can approximate these trapezia as uniform rods with centres of mass lying on BM, the median from B to OA. Since the centres of mass of all of these rods lie on BM it follows that the centre of mass of the whole lamina lies on BM. The same argument would apply if you started from either of the other two vertices, so the centre of mass must lie at the intersection of the medians, known as the **centroid**.

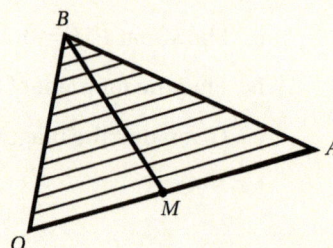

Vectors can be very useful in geometry and you can use them in proofs.

1   **Prove that the intersection of the medians of a triangle lies at a point that is two-thirds of the distance along the medians, measured from the vertices.**

   Let the midpoint of OA be M and the midpoint of OB be N. Consider the medians AN and BM. Let the intersection of these be X.

   You can use vectors to find alternative expressions for the position of X.

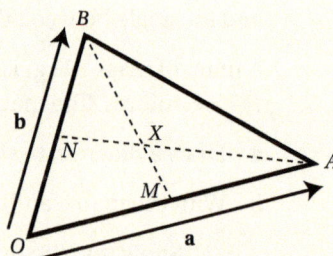

$\overrightarrow{OX} = \overrightarrow{OA} + \overrightarrow{AX}$	$\overrightarrow{OX} = \overrightarrow{OB} + \overrightarrow{BX}$
$\overrightarrow{AX} = \lambda \overrightarrow{AN}$	$\overrightarrow{BX} = \mu \overrightarrow{BM}$
X lies part-way along AN and BM; use λ and μ to indicate this; you are trying to prove that $\lambda = \mu = \dfrac{2}{3}$.	
$\overrightarrow{OX} = \overrightarrow{OA} + \lambda \overrightarrow{AN}$	$\overrightarrow{OX} = \overrightarrow{OB} + \mu \overrightarrow{BM}$

   Use the vectors **a** and **b,** together with the constants λ and μ to find two alternative vector expressions for $\overrightarrow{OX}$.

   You may now equate coefficients of **a** and **b** in the two expressions to get two simultaneous equations. Solve these to find values for λ and μ.

   You should be able to prove that point X is two-thirds of the distance along the medians from the vertices.

2 **Prove that, for a uniform triangular lamina:** $\begin{pmatrix} \bar{x} \\ \bar{y} \end{pmatrix} = \begin{pmatrix} \dfrac{x_1 + x_2 + x_3}{3}, \dfrac{y_1 + y_2 + y_3}{3} \end{pmatrix}.$

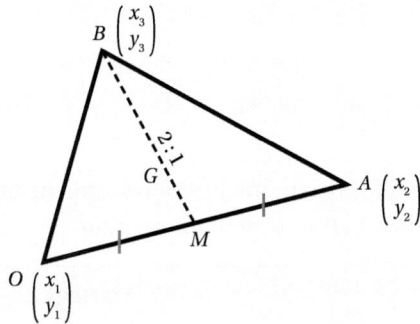

Consider a triangle having vertices with position vectors $O\begin{pmatrix} x_1 \\ y_1 \end{pmatrix}$, $A\begin{pmatrix} x_2 \\ y_2 \end{pmatrix}$ and $B\begin{pmatrix} x_3 \\ y_3 \end{pmatrix}$.

Let the midpoint of OA be M and the centre of mass be G. Remember that the centre of mass of the triangle lies on MB, such that $MG : GB$ is $1 : 2$.

The position vector of the centre of mass, G, is:

$$\begin{pmatrix} \bar{x} \\ \bar{y} \end{pmatrix} = \begin{pmatrix} x_1 \\ y_1 \end{pmatrix} + \overrightarrow{OM} + \overrightarrow{MG}$$

$$= \begin{pmatrix} x_1 \\ y_1 \end{pmatrix} + \overrightarrow{OM} + \frac{1}{3}\overrightarrow{MB}$$

Find vector expressions for $\overrightarrow{OM}$ and $\overrightarrow{MB}$ in terms of $x_1, y_1, \ldots, x_3, y_3$ and substitute them to prove the formula.

Alternative approaches

You know that there are different methods for solving a quadratic equation, such as factorising, completing the square or using the quadratic formula. Choose the method that takes you most quickly to the result(s) you need.

Here the focus is on two Mechanics problems that you can approach in different ways.

Problem 1

An elastic string of unstretched length l has one end fixed at point O. A bob is attached to the other end and dropped from O. Find the maximum speed of the bob in the subsequent motion.

Strategy 1	Strategy 2
You can use conservation of energy to derive an expression for v^2 in terms of the extension, x, of the elastic string. $$mg(l+x) = \frac{\lambda x^2}{2l} + \frac{1}{2}mv^2$$ This will give you an expression for v^2 which is a quadratic in x. To maximise this quadratic in x you will either need to use calculus or complete the square to find the maximising value of x in terms of m, l, λ and g.	When speed is maximised, acceleration is zero, likewise the resultant force. Resultant force: $mg - \frac{\lambda x}{l} = 0$ This takes you straight to $x = \frac{mgl}{\lambda}$. You can substitute your value of x into the energy equation to find v^2: $$mg(l+x) = \frac{\lambda x^2}{2l} + \frac{1}{2}mv^2$$ The common theme in both strategies is application of the principle of conservation of energy: $$mg(l+x) = \frac{\lambda x^2}{2l} + \frac{1}{2}mv^2$$

Problem 2

A small smooth sphere sliding across a smooth surface is acted on by an impulse directed towards the centre of the sphere. The speed of the sphere is increased from u to v, and its direction of motion is diverted through angle α. Values for u, v and α are given. Find the magnitude, I, and direction, β, of the impulse.

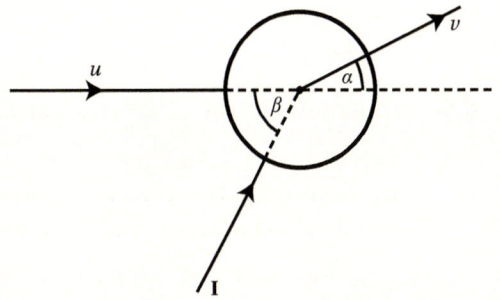

Strategy 1

You can use an impulse-momentum triangle.

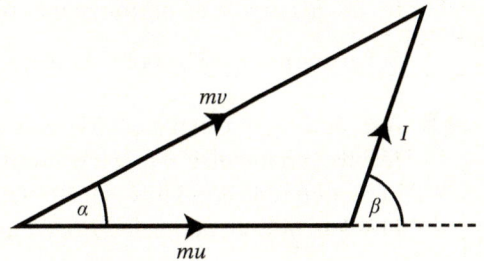

You can use the cosine rule to find the value of I from values given for u, v and α.

$$I^2 = (mu)^2 + (mv)^2 - 2 \times mu \times mv \times \cos \alpha$$

You will have an expression for I in terms of m, unless the value of m is also given.

You can use the sine rule in the vector triangle and hence find β.

$$\frac{\sin \beta}{mv} = \frac{\sin \alpha}{I}$$

Take care with your vector triangle. Make sure that the directions of the arrows on the sides are correct, with mu and mv coming away from the same point and $I = mv - mu$.

Don't forget to use momentum in the triangle rather than velocity to make the triangle dimensionally consistent.

Little algebraic rearrangement is necessary in this solution.

Strategy 2

You can resolve the final speed into components and use conservation of momentum.

Parallel to u: $mu + I \cos \beta = mv \cos \alpha$

Perpendicular to u: $mv \sin \alpha = I \sin \beta$

These are simultaneous equations and you need to eliminate either I or β.

You obtain: $mu + \dfrac{mv \sin \alpha}{\sin \beta} = mv \cos \alpha$

Substitute the values for u, v and α to obtain β and hence I.

Take care to resolve velocities and to apply conservation of momentum correctly.

Simultaneous equations are a standard technique, but you need to take care with your rearrangements.

QUESTIONS

1 In this question, use $g = 9.8 \text{ m s}^{-2}$, giving your final answers to an appropriate degree of accuracy.

An elastic string is fixed at one end at the point O. A bob of mass 200 grams is attached to the other end of the string. The string has natural length 50 cm and its modulus of elasticity is 3.92 newtons. The bob is held next to O and dropped. Find:

a the maximum speed of the bob as it descends

b the maximum extension of the string.

Solve this problem by both of the described methods and compare your answers.

2 A smooth sphere of mass 2.5 kg is sliding across a smooth horizontal floor with a speed 2 m s^{-1} when it receives an impulse acting towards its centre. The sphere slows to a speed of 1.2 m s^{-1} and its direction of motion is diverted through $60°$. Find the magnitude and direction of the impulse. Solve this problem by both of the described methods and compare your answers.

A simple pendulum consists of an inextensible string of length l fixed at one end, with a mass m attached to the other end; you can call the mass the bob. The bob will hang in equilibrium immediately below the fixing point unless it is displaced. If the bob is displaced out of the vertical and then released, it will swing back and forth along the arc of a circle.

Assuming that any resistances to motion are negligible, you can derive an equation of motion of the pendulum bob. You need to consider the transverse acceleration of the pendulum bob, and apply Newton's second law:

$$ml\ddot{\theta} = -mg\sin\theta$$

This equation of motion simplifies to $\ddot{\theta} + \frac{g}{l}\sin\theta = 0$. As for free fall under gravity, the equation of motion of a pendulum bob is independent of mass. Thus the solution of the equation would be the same for a 10 g bob and a 2.5 kg bob.

The equation of motion of the pendulum bob is similar in form to – but not the same as – the equation for simple harmonic motion: $\ddot{\theta} + \omega^2\theta = 0$, where $\omega^2 = \frac{g}{l}$.

> **Tip**
>
> θ is measured away from the vertical, but angular acceleration is always directed towards the vertical, so $\ddot{\theta} \propto -\sin\theta$, rather than $\ddot{\theta} \propto \sin\theta$.

It would be possible to solve $\ddot{\theta} + \frac{g}{l}\sin\theta = 0$ by numerical methods, but the theory of the simple pendulum relies on some of your work on complex numbers and the Maclaurin series in Further Mathematics Student Book 1. You learned that $\sin\theta = \theta - \frac{\theta^3}{3!} + \frac{\theta^5}{5!} - \cdots$ so that, when $\theta \approx 0$, all terms are vanishingly small except the first. Thus if $\theta \approx 0$, then $\sin\theta \approx \theta$.

Now the equation of motion for the pendulum bob can be approximated: $\ddot{\theta} + \frac{g}{l}\theta = 0$ and you can use your knowledge of simple harmonic motion to solve the equation.

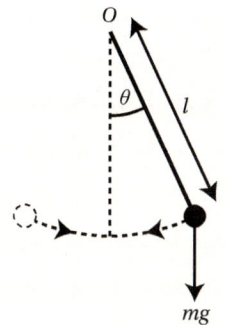

QUESTIONS

1 Use the theory of simple harmonic motion to write down an expression for how θ varies with time, in terms of g and l, given that the pendulum bob is displaced so that the string makes an angle θ_{max} with the vertical and is then released.

2 Work out the period of oscillation for a simple pendulum of length 2.45 metres, as a multiple of π.

3 Sketch a graph of angular displacement against time (θ against t), given that a bob, attached to an inextensible string of length 2.45 metres, is displaced to $\frac{\pi}{24}$ radians from the vertical and then released.

4 Assume that $\theta = \frac{\pi}{24}\cos 2t$. Differentiate to find an expression for $\dot{\theta}$. Also, derive an expression for the transverse velocity v from the angular velocity $\dot{\theta}$.

5 Find the maximum value for the transverse velocity, giving the answer to 4 significant figures.

6 To get an idea of the accuracy of the model you can compare the velocity calculated, using the simple harmonic motion approximation to the velocity calculated from the conservation of mechanical energy.

$$mgl(1 - \cos \theta_{max}) = \text{KE at bottom of swing}$$

$$= \frac{1}{2} m v_{max}^2$$

$$\therefore v_{max} = \sqrt{2gl(1 - \cos \theta_{max})}$$

Taking $\theta_{max} = \frac{\pi}{24}$ and $l = 2.45$ metres, as shown, calculate v_{max} from the energy equation, to four significant figures (4 s.f.). Find the percentage error predicted in v_{max} by the SHM model.

7 Now repeat the steps in questions 2–6 for pendulums with different starting displacements.

    a Use $\frac{\pi}{12}$.   **b** Use $\frac{\pi}{6}$.

CROSS-TOPIC REVIEW EXERCISE 2

A This exercise is for A level students only.

1 A particle P, of mass 0.8 kg, is moving in a straight line with speed 6.5 m s^{-1}. An impulse of magnitude 4 N s deflects P through an angle θ and reduces its speed to 3 m s^{-1}.

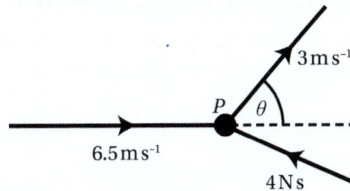

By considering an impulse–momentum triangle:

a show that $\cos\theta = \dfrac{35}{52}$

b find the angle that the impulse makes with the original direction of motion of P.

2 A small ball is moving across a horizontal plane floor when it strikes a smooth vertical wall. The coefficient of restitution between the ball and the wall is e. Just before impact the direction of motion of the ball makes an angle of 60° with the wall. Immediately after impact the direction of motion of the ball makes an angle of 45° with the wall.

a Find the fraction of the kinetic energy of the ball that is lost in the impact.

b Find the value of e.

3 A light rod of length 0.75 metres has one end freely hinged at a fixed point O and a particle P, of mass m kg, is attached to the other end. The rod is set in motion and P makes complete circles about O. The speed of P at the top of the circle is half of its speed at the bottom of the circle. Find the maximum speed of P in terms of g.

4 A region A is defined by the curve $y^2 = 10x$, the line $x = 2.5$ and the x-axis. A uniform solid is formed by rotating A through 2π radians about the x-axis.

a Show that volume of the solid is $\dfrac{125\pi}{4}$.

b Show further that the x-coordinate of the centre of mass of the solid is $1\frac{2}{3}$.

5 Three forces $\begin{pmatrix} -3 \\ 1 \end{pmatrix}$, $\begin{pmatrix} 2 \\ 5 \end{pmatrix}$ and $\begin{pmatrix} 0 \\ a \end{pmatrix}$ newtons, act at the points with coordinates (3, 2), (−2, −1), and (1, 0) metres respectively.

This system is equivalent to a force, **F**, acting at the origin together with a couple of magnitude 3 N m.

a Determine the two possible values for a.

b Write down the force, **F**, corresponding to each value of a.

6 A particle of mass 0.8 kg is moving in a straight line on a smooth horizontal surface. A horizontal force then acts on the particle for 4 seconds. This force acts in the direction of motion of the particle and at time t seconds has magnitude $(5t − 2)$ newtons.

When $t = 4$, the velocity of the particle is 50 m s^{-1}.

a Find the magnitude of the impulse of the force on the particle between $t = 0$ and $t = 4$.

b Hence find the velocity of the particle when $t = 0$.

c Find the value of t when the velocity of the particle is 70 m s^{-1}.

7 A particle P, of mass m kg, is attached to one end of a light inextensible string of length 0.5 metres. The other end of the string is attached to a fixed point O. The particle is hanging in equilibrium at point A, directly below O, when it is given a horizontal speed of $4.5\,\mathrm{m\,s^{-1}}$. When OP has turned through an angle θ and the string is still taut, the tension in the string is T.

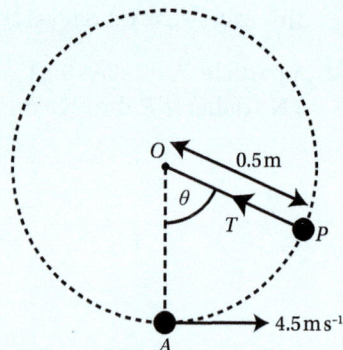

a Find an expression for T in terms of m, g and θ.

In this question, use $g = 9.8\,\mathrm{m\,s^{-2}}$, giving your final answers to an appropriate degree of accuracy.

b Find the height of the particle above A at the instant when the string goes slack.

c Find the maximum height above A reached by P before it starts to fall down again.

8 In this question, use $g = 9.8\,\mathrm{m\,s^{-2}}$, giving your final answers to an appropriate degree of accuracy.

A uniform ladder AB, of length 10 metres and mass 30 kg, rests in equilibrium with its foot, B, on rough horizontal ground and its top, A, leaning against a smooth vertical wall. The angle between the ladder and the ground is 70°.

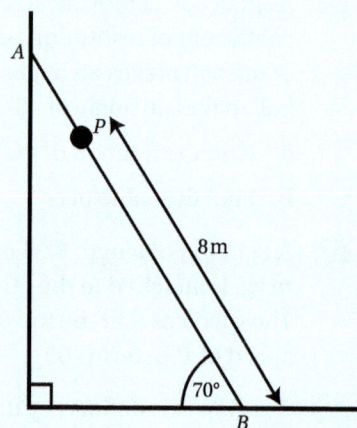

A man, of mass 75 kg, is standing at point P on the ladder so that the distance BP is 8 metres. The man may be modelled as a particle at P.

With the man standing at the point P, the ladder is on the point of slipping.

a Show that the magnitude of the reaction between the ladder and the vertical wall is 270 N, correct to 2 significant figures.

b Find the coefficient of friction between the ladder and the ground.

9 A small smooth ball of mass m, moving on a smooth horizontal surface, hits a smooth vertical wall and rebounds. The coefficient of restitution between the wall and the ball is $\frac{3}{4}$.

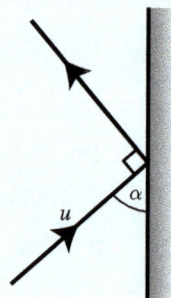

Immediately before the collision, the ball has velocity u and the angle between the ball's direction of motion and the wall is α. The ball's direction of motion immediately after the collision is at right angles to its direction of motion before the collision, as shown in the diagram.

a Show that $\tan\alpha = \dfrac{2}{\sqrt{3}}$

b Find, in terms of u, the speed of the ball immediately after the collision.

c The force exerted on the ball by the wall acts for 0.1 seconds.

Given that $m = 0.2$ kg and $u = 4\,\mathrm{m\,s^{-1}}$, find the average force exerted by the wall on the ball.

[© AQA 2008]

10 A uniform solid consists of a hemisphere of radius r and a cylinder of base radius r and height h, fixed together so that their bases coincide. The solid can rest in equilibrium with any point on the curved surface of the hemisphere in contact with a horizontal plane. Find h in terms of r.

11 A particle is placed at the highest point P on the outer surface of a fixed smooth hemisphere of radius a and centre O. The hemisphere is placed with its plane face on a horizontal surface. The particle is projected horizontally from P with speed u ($u < ag$) and initially moves along the surface of the sphere. The particle leaves the sphere at point Q, where OQ makes an angle θ with the upward vertical through O, as shown.

a Find an expression for $\cos\theta$ in terms of u, g and a.

The particle strikes the horizontal surface with speed $\sqrt{\dfrac{3ag}{2}}$.

b Find the value of θ.

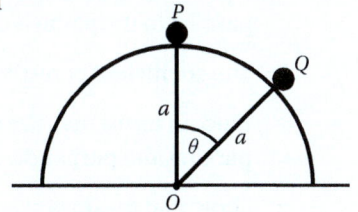

12 The forces $3\mathbf{i} - 2\mathbf{j}$, $4\mathbf{i} - \mathbf{j} + 2\mathbf{k}$, and $3\mathbf{j} - 4\mathbf{k}$ act at the points with coordinates $(-1, 1, 0)$, $(2, 0, 5)$ and $(-6, 2, 1)$ respectively.

a Find the total moment of these forces about the origin.

b This system of forces is equivalent to a single force $\mathbf{F}$.

   i Find $\mathbf{F}$.

   ii Determine a vector equation in the form $\mathbf{r} = \mathbf{a} + \lambda\mathbf{b}$ for the line of action of $\mathbf{F}$.

[© AQA 2015]

13 A child's toy is formed by joining two solid cones so that their circular bases coincide. The cones have the same uniform mass density and the same base radius. The heights of the cones are $1.5h$ and h.

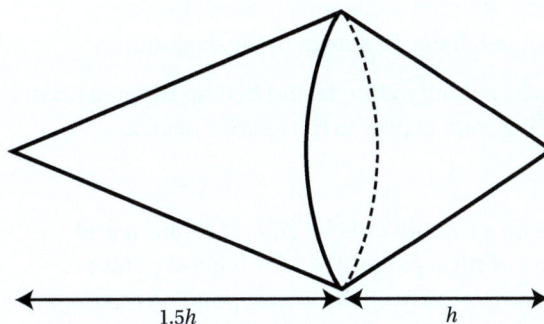

a Find the distance of the centre of mass of the toy from the vertex of the larger cone.

The toy is now placed on horizontal ground with the sloping surface of the smaller cone in contact with the ground. The object rests in equilibrium but is on the point of toppling.

b Find the radius of the base of the cones as an exact multiple of h.

14 A small smooth ball is dropped from a height of h above a point A on a fixed smooth plane inclined at an angle θ to the horizontal. The ball falls vertically and collides with the plane at the point A. The ball rebounds and strikes the plane again at a point B, as shown in the diagram. The points A and B lie on a line of greatest slope of the inclined plane.

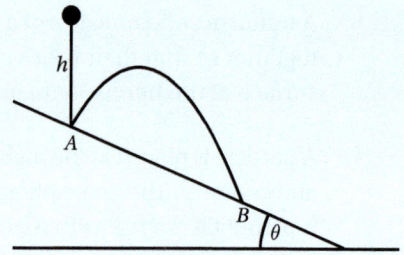

a Explain whether or not the component of the velocity of the ball parallel to the plane is changed by the collision.

b The coefficient of restitution between the ball and the plane is e.

Find, in terms of h, θ, e and g, the components of the velocity of the ball parallel and perpendicular to the plane immediately after the collision at A.

c Show that the distance AB is given by $4he(e+1)\sin\theta$.

[© AQA 2014]

15 **a** A uniform lamina is bounded by the curve $y = 4 - x^2$ and the x-axis, as shown in the diagram.

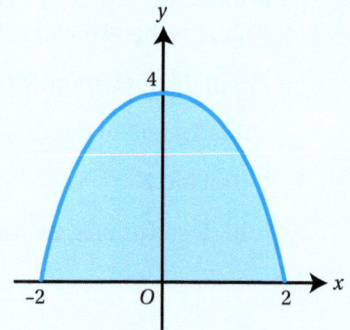

Given that the area of the lamina is $\dfrac{32}{3}$ square units, find the y-coordinate of the centre of mass of the lamina.

b The cross-section of a uniform prism is the same shape as the lamina in part **a**. The prism is placed on a plane inclined at an angle α to the horizontal with the rectangular base of the prism in contact with the inclined plane, as shown in the diagram.

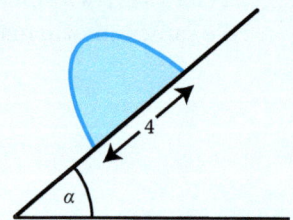

Given that the prism is just about to topple and that no slipping occurs, find the value of α, giving your answer to the nearest degree.

[© AQA 2009]

16 A bead, of mass m, moves on a smooth circular ring, of radius a and centre O, which is fixed in a vertical plane. At P, the highest point on the ring, the speed of the bead is $2u$; at Q, the lowest point on the ring, the speed of the bead is $5u$.

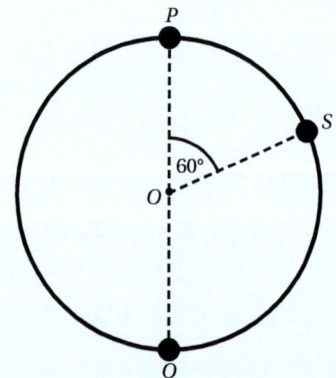

a Show that $u = \sqrt{\dfrac{4ag}{21}}$.

b S is a point on the ring so that angle POS is $60°$, as shown in the diagram.

Find, in terms of m and g, the magnitude of the reaction of the ring on the bead when the bead is at S.

[© AQA 2013]

45 minutes, 40 marks

This paper forms part of a 1 hour and 30 minutes sitting to complete two papers worth 40 marks each.

1 A particle moves in a circular orbit, of radius 0.2 m at a constant angular speed of 6 revolutions per minute. Find the linear speed of the particle. Choose from these options.

A $\frac{\pi}{5}\,\mathrm{m\,s^{-1}}$ B $\frac{\pi}{25}\,\mathrm{m\,s^{-1}}$ C $\frac{72\pi}{25}\,\mathrm{m\,s^{-1}}$ D $\frac{72\pi}{5}\,\mathrm{m\,s^{-1}}$ [1 mark]

2 The string on a guitar is plucked, creating a wave. The velocity, v, of the wave depends upon the mass, m, of the string, its length, l, and the tension, T, in the string so that $v = km^a l^b T^c$, where k is dimensionless. What can you say about the values of a, b and c? Choose from these options.

A $a = b = c$ B $a = b = -c$ C $a = -b = c$ D $-a = b = c$ [1 mark]

3 A particle of mass 400 grams is attached to a light inextensible string of length 80 cm. The string is fixed on a smooth horizontal table and the ball moves in a circular path with a linear speed of 3 m s^{-1}. Calculate the tension in the string.   [2 marks]

4 A car of mass 1000 kg moves along a horizontal road against a constant resistive force of 300 N.

a Find the greatest speed, in m s^{-1}, that the car can move if the engine cannot exert more than 12 kW.   [2 marks]

The car is now attached to a tow rope which pulls a trailer of mass 250 kg. The resistance to motion for the trailer is 200 N and the resistance to the car's motion has not changed. Let T be the tension in the rope. At the instant when the speed is 8 m s^{-1}, the engine is working at 12 kW.

b Find:

  i the tension in the rope   [4 marks]

  ii the acceleration of the car and trailer.   [2 marks]

c State **two** modelling assumptions you have made about the tow rope.   [1 mark]

5 Two spheres, A and B, of masses $2m$ and $3m$ respectively, are attached to opposite ends of a light inextensible string of length l. They are placed next to each other on a horizontal table and sphere A is projected vertically upward with a speed of $\sqrt{6gl}$ m s^{-1}.

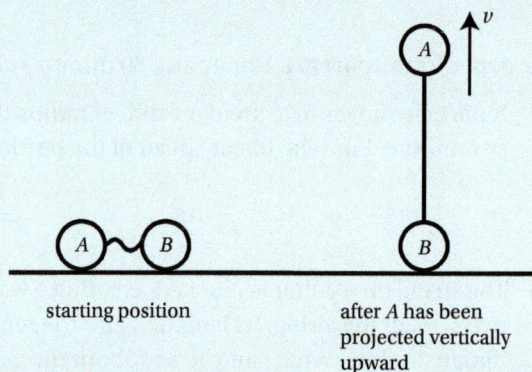

starting position

after A has been projected vertically upward

a Find the speed of sphere A at the instant the string becomes taut. [3 marks]

b Comment on how the modelling assumption 'the two spheres are placed next to each other' will affect your answer to part **a**. [1 mark]

c Show that, at the instant immediately after the string becomes taut, the velocity of B is $0.8\sqrt{gl}$ m s^{-1}. [2 marks]

d Calculate the height that sphere A reaches above the horizontal table when it first comes to an instantaneous rest. [3 marks]

e Calculate, in terms of m, g and l, the loss in kinetic energy due to the tightening of the string. [3 marks]

6 Two smooth spheres, X and Y, with equal radii and masses 0.6 kg and 0.4 kg respectively, are moving on a smooth horizontal surface. The spheres are moving towards each other and before they collide each sphere is moving at a speed of 5 m s^{-1}. After the collision, X moves with a speed of 2.4 m s^{-1} in the opposite direction to its initial motion.

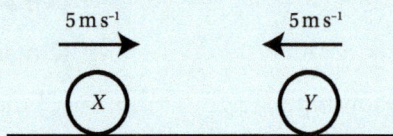

5 m s^{-1} 5 m s^{-1}

X Y

Calculate the coefficient of restitution between the two spheres. [4 marks]

7 A car P of mass 1250 kg starts at A and moves along a horizontal road with a driving force of 2000 N and a variable resistance to motion force that is proportional to the square of the distance from A. At the instant when P is a distance of 20 m from A, the resultant force is 1920 N.

Find the total work done, in kilojoules (kJ), by the car when it has travelled a distance of 50 metres. [5 marks]

8 In this question use $g = 10$ m s^{-2}, giving your final answers to an appropriate degree of accuracy.

A ball of mass 0.4 kg is attached to one end of an elastic spring of natural length 0.6 m and stiffness 40 N m^{-1}. The other end of the spring is suspended from a point on a ceiling and the particle is pulled down and released from rest when the length of the spring is 0.9 m.

Calculate the length of the spring when the particle is at its highest point. State clearly any assumptions you have made. [6 marks]

A LEVEL PRACTICE PAPER

A This paper forms part of a 2 hour sitting to complete two papers worth 50 marks each.

1 A remote-controlled car of mass 35 000 g is brought to rest from a speed of 5 m s^{-1} after a head-on collision with a wall. What is the magnitude of the impulse on the remote controlled car? Choose from these options.

    A 175 kN s   **B** 7 N s   **C** 7 kN s   **D** 175 N s   [1 mark]

2 A 45 cm length of elastic extends 3 cm when a force of 6 N is applied to it. What is the value of the modulus of elasticity? Choose from these options.

    A 90 N   **B** 270 N   **C** 22.5 N   **D** 2.5 N   [1 mark]

3 A smooth bead of mass m kg is threaded onto a smooth circular wire with centre O and radius 1 metre. The circular wire is fixed in a vertical plane. The bead is projected from its lowest point on the wire, with speed $\sqrt{g}$.

  a Calculate the maximum vertical height, in metres, above the point of projection that the bead reaches.   [3 marks]

  b Describe one way in which the model you have used could be refined.   [1 mark]

4 A particle of mass m is attached to one end of a light elastic string of modulus of elasticity mg and natural length l. The other end of the string is attached to a fixed point O on a smooth table so that the particle is moving in a horizontal circle centre O.

  a Find an expression for the force towards the centre of motion, when r is the radius of the circular motion.   [2 marks]

  b Given that the particle is moving at $\dfrac{k}{\pi}$ revolutions per second, find an expression for the radius of the circular motion.   [4 marks]

  c Sketch a graph of r against k, for $l = 1$ metre.   [2 marks]

If the tension in the 1 metre long elastic string reaches mg N, the string will break.

  d Comment on your sketch from part **c** with reference to the values of k that can be chosen for this model.   [2 marks]

5 A solid object is formed by rotating the area under the curve $y = \dfrac{1}{x}$ through 360° around the x-axis between the lines $x = a$ and $x = b$.

  a Show that the distance of the centre of mass from $x = a$ is $\dfrac{a\left(a - b - b\ln\left(\dfrac{a}{b}\right)\right)}{b - a}$.   [5 marks]

A solid object is created, as described, with $a = 1$ and $b = 5$. The solid shape is placed on a very rough plane inclined at an angle of θ to the horizontal, with the largest flat face in contact with the inclined plane. It does not slide.

  b Find the angle θ at the point of toppling, giving your answer correct to three significant figures (3 s.f.).   [2 marks]

6 A uniform ladder, inclined at $60°$ to the vertical, is at rest with one end on a rough horizontal ground and the other end against a smooth vertical wall. The ladder is on the point of slipping. Find the coefficient of friction between the ladder and the ground. [5 marks]

7 A particle P is attached to one end of a string of length l. The other end of the string is attached to a fixed point O. A second particle Q of the same mass as P is attached to one end of another identical string and the other end of the string is attached to the first particle P. The whole system moves with a constant angular speed of ω rad s^{-1} about the downward vertical through O. The upper string OP makes an angle of α with the downward vertical through O and the lower string PQ makes an angle of β with the downward vertical through P.

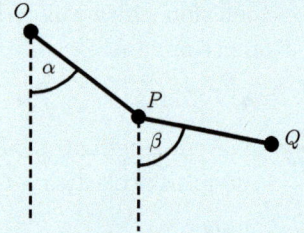

a State two assumptions that you should make about the string in order to model the circular motion of P and Q. [1 mark]

b By considering the forces and the circular motion at Q, show that

$\tan \beta = \dfrac{l\omega^2}{g}(\sin \alpha + \sin \beta).$ [4 marks]

c By considering the forces and the circular motion at P and taking into account part **a**, show that

$\tan \alpha = \dfrac{l\omega^2}{2g}(2\sin \alpha + \sin \beta).$ [4 marks]

8 In this question use $g = 9.8$ m s^{-2}, giving your final answers to an appropriate degree of accuracy.

A particle of mass 25 kg slides down a slope inclined at $30°$ to the horizontal. The particle increases its speed from 3 m s^{-1} to 5 m s^{-1} while sliding 8 m down the slope.

a Calculate the gain in kinetic energy for the particle. [2 marks]

b Calculate the work done against the resistance to motion. [5 marks]

There is a constant frictional force between the particle and the slope, and this force is the only resistance to motion.

c Calculate the coefficient of friction between the particle and the slope. [3 marks]

d For what value of the coefficient of friction will the particle slide down the slope at a constant speed? [3 marks]

Constant acceleration

$$s = ut + \frac{1}{2}at^2 \qquad \mathbf{s} = \mathbf{u}t + \frac{1}{2}\mathbf{a}t^2$$

$$s = vt - \frac{1}{2}at^2 \qquad \mathbf{s} = \mathbf{v}t - \frac{1}{2}\mathbf{a}t^2$$

$$v = u + at \qquad \mathbf{v} = \mathbf{u} + \mathbf{a}t$$

$$s = \frac{1}{2}(u+v)t \qquad \mathbf{s} = \frac{1}{2}(\mathbf{u}+\mathbf{v})t$$

$$v^2 = u^2 + 2as$$

Centres of mass

For uniform bodies

Triangular lamina: $\frac{2}{3}$ along median from vertex

Solid hemisphere, radius r: $\frac{3}{8}r$ from centre

Hemispherical shell, radius r: $\frac{1}{2}r$ from centre

Circular arc, radius r, angle at centre 2α: $\dfrac{r\sin\alpha}{\alpha}$ from centre

Sector of circle, radius r, angle at centre 2α: $\dfrac{2r\sin\alpha}{3\alpha}$ from centre

Solid cone or pyramid of height h: $\frac{1}{4}h$ above the base on the line from centre of base to vertex

Conical shell of height h: $\frac{1}{3}h$ above the base on the line from centre of base to vertex

Answers

All answers are given to 3 significant figures (3 s.f.), where appropriate.

1 Work, energy and power 1

BEFORE YOU START

1 15 km

2 11 270 N

3 20 m s^{-2}

EXERCISE 1A

1 60 J

2 20 kJ (2 s.f.)

3 2.7 m (2 s.f.)

4 6 J

5 125 J

6 a 30 000 J b 18 000 J

7 3500 J (2 s.f.)

8 23 125 J

EXERCISE 1B

1 5.04 kJ

2 96.9 kg

3 37.8 km h^{-1}

4 a 14.0 J b 14.0 J c 1.40 m

5 a 147 kJ (3 s.f.)

   b 97.2 kJ (3 s.f.)

6 6.6 m s^{-1} (2 s.f.)

7 4950 N

8 38.6 kN

9 1.6 N (2 s.f.)

10 7.0 m s^{-1} (2 s.f.)

EXERCISE 1C

1 1200 J (2 s.f.)

2 200 kJ (1 s.f.)

3 5.4 m (2 s.f.)

4 310 grams (2 s.f.)

5 Answers given to 2 s.f.

   a 28 J b 11 J

   c 39 J d 41 m s^{-1}

6 a 1700 J (2 s.f.) b 6400 J (2 s.f.)

   c 15 m s^{-1} (2 s.f.)

   d Model Anita as a particle leaving the surface of the highboard and entering the water at a single instant. No resistance to motion. No account taken of bending of the highboard.

7 Answers given to 2 s.f.

   a 2.6 J b 1.7 J

   c 4.3 J d 12 m s^{-1}

8 2100 J (2 s.f.)

9 a 59 J (2 s.f.) b 12 m s^{-1} (2 s.f.)

10 90 N (2 s.f.)

11 a 600 J b 4000 J (2 s.f.) c 64 m (2 s.f.)

EXERCISE 1D

1 310 kW

2 41 kW (2 s.f.)

3 30 kW (2 s.f.)

4 16.7 kW

5 41.7 kN

6 150 W (2 s.f.)

7 14 MJ (2 s.f.)

8 340 W (2 s.f.)

9 Answers given to 2 s.f.
   a 5900 J b 760 J c 6600 W

10 11 N (2 s.f.)

11 0.24 m s^{-2} (2 s.f.)

12 $u = 16$ m s^{-1} (2 s.f.)

13 Proof.

14 a 5.8 s (2 s.f.) b 8.3 m s^{-2} (2 s.f.)

MIXED PRACTICE 1

1 Answers given to 2 s.f.

   a 31 J b 370 J

   c 400 J (2 s.f.); 18 m s^{-1} (2 s.f.)

2 Answers given to 2 s.f.

   a 12 000 J   **b** 11 000 J

   c 23 000 J; 27 m s^{-1}

3 **a** 16 J   **b** 245 J

   c 260 J (2 s.f.); 32 m s^{-1} (2 s.f.)

4 **a** 1270 J   **b** Proof.   **c** 14.3 m s^{-1}

5 Proof.

6 290 W (2 s.f.)

7 **a** 31 000 J (2 s.f.)   **b** 800 J **c** 540 W (2 s.f.)

8 3.2 m s^{-1} (2 s.f.)

9 26 N (2 s.f.)

10 **a** Proof.   **b** 1.71 m s^{-2}

11 **a** Proof.   **b** 125 kW

12 0.318 m s^{-2}

13 **a** 20 000 N   **b** 1220 m

14 17.1 kJ

15 Proof.

16 96 W

17 **a** 9750 W   **b** 3375 W   **c** 6075 W

2 Dimensional analysis

BEFORE YOU START

1 **a** r^4 **b** r^{12}

   c $\dfrac{1}{16}$ **d** $\sqrt{2}$

2 $x = \sqrt{\dfrac{y(t+1)}{zt^3}}$

3 $x = 4, y = -2$

4 $P = \dfrac{2}{9}$

5 **a** $\dfrac{4}{3}\pi \times 3^3 = 36\pi$ cm^3 **b** $4\pi \times 3^2 = 36\pi$ cm^2

6 m s^{-1}

7 $\theta = \dfrac{5}{4} = 1.25$ rad

8 5 m s^{-1}

9 0.7 m s^{-2}

10 4 m s^{-2}

11 6.3 m s^{-1} (2 s.f.)

EXERCISE 2A

1 **a** $\mathbf{LT^{-2}}$ **b** $\mathbf{LT^{-2}}$ **c** $\mathbf{MLT^{-2}}$

   d $\mathbf{MLT^{-2}}$ **e** $\mathbf{MLT^{-1}}$

   f Dimensionless.

   g $\mathbf{L^3}$ **h** $\mathbf{ML^{-3}}$

   i $\mathbf{ML^2T^{-2}}$ **j** $\mathbf{ML^{-1}T^{-2}}$

2 Dimensionless.

3 Dimensionless.

4 **a** $\mathbf{ML^2T^{-2}}$ **b** Yes, the same.

5 **a** $\mathbf{ML^2T^{-2}}$ **b** The same.

6 Dimensionless.

7 Dimensionless.

8 $\mathbf{MLT^{-3}}$

9 **a** $\mathbf{ML^2T^{-2}}$ **b** $\mathbf{MLT^{-2}}$

10 $\mathbf{M^{-1}L^3T^{-2}}$

11 $\mathbf{ML^2T^{-1}}$

EXERCISE 2B

1 **a** $\mathbf{L}$ **b** $\mathbf{L^2}$ **c** $\mathbf{L^3}$

2 **a** $\mathbf{ML^1T^{-1}}$ **b** $\mathbf{ML^2T^{-2}}$

   c $\mathbf{ML^2}$ **d** $\mathbf{L}$

3 $\mathbf{L}$

4 **a** Consistent.   **b** Not consistent.

   c Consistent.   **d** Consistent.

   e Not consistent.

5 **a** $\mathbf{T^{-2}}$

   b Dimensionally consistent.

6 **a** $m\dfrac{\mathrm{d}^2x}{\mathrm{d}t^2} = -kx$ **b** $\mathbf{MT^{-2}}$

7 **a** $\mathbf{ML^2T^{-1}}$

   b $\mathbf{MLT^{-1}}$; not the same.

   c $\left[\text{angular momentum}\right] = \mathbf{L}\left[\text{linear momentum}\right]$

8 **a** $\mathbf{ML^2T^{-2}}$ **b** $\mathbf{ML^2T^{-2}}$; the same.

9 **a** $E = \dfrac{Fl}{xA}$ **b** $\mathbf{ML^{-1}T^{-2}}$

10 **a** $\dfrac{gx}{2v^2}\sec^2\theta$ **b** Change the x to x^2.

WORK IT OUT 2.1

Solution 2 is correct.

EXERCISE 2C

1 $\mathbf{ML^2T^{-3}}$

2 $\mathbf{L^2T^{-2}}$

3 $\mathbf{T^{-3}}$

4 $\mathbf{MLT^{-3}}$

5 $[\text{Area}] = \mathbf{L}^2$

$\left[\frac{1}{2}ab\sin C\right] = \left[\frac{1}{2}\right][a][b][\sin C] = [a][b]$ as $\frac{1}{2}$ and $\sin C$ are dimensionless.

$[a][b] = \mathbf{L} \times \mathbf{L} = \mathbf{L}^2$

6 a $[x] = \mathbf{L}$

$[a\sin\omega t] = [a][\sin\omega t] = [a] = \mathbf{L}$ as $\sin\omega t$ is dimensionless.

They are dimensionally consistent.

b $\mathbf{T}^{-1}$

7 a $\mathbf{MLT}^{-2}$ **b**   0.45 N

8

$\left[\dfrac{a}{\sin A}\right] = [2R^\alpha]$

$\left[\dfrac{a}{\sin A}\right] = \dfrac{[a]}{[\sin A]} = \mathbf{L}^\alpha = \mathbf{L}^1$

$[2R^\alpha] = [2][R]^\alpha = \mathbf{L}^\alpha$

$\therefore \alpha = 1$

9 a Dimensionless.   **b**   50 dB

10 a $\mathbf{LT}^{-2}$

    b   **i** $[A] = \mathbf{T}^{-1}$ **ii** $[B] = \mathbf{T}^{-2}$

11 a $\mathbf{MLT}^{-2}$ **b** $F = 0.5\rho A(v_1^2 - v_0^2)$

12 a $\mathbf{MLT}^{-2}$ **b** $t = 2\pi\sqrt{\dfrac{ml}{F}}$

13 a $\beta = \gamma = -\dfrac{\alpha}{2}$ **b** $F_r = v\sqrt{\dfrac{1}{gh}}$

14 $\tan\theta = \dfrac{v^2}{rg}$

EXERCISE 2D

Quantity	Dimension	SI unit
Time	T	second (s)
Mass	M	kilogram (kg)
Weight (mg)	$\mathbf{MLT}^{-2}$	newton (N)
Length/ displacement	L	metre (m)
Area	$\mathbf{L}^2$	m^2
Volume	$\mathbf{L}^3$	m^3
Velocity	$\mathbf{LT}^{-1}$	m/s or m s^{-1}
Acceleration	$\mathbf{LT}^{-2}$	m/s^2 or m s^{-2}
Acceleration due to gravity	$\mathbf{LT}^{-2}$	m/s^2 or m s^{-2}
Force (ma)	$\mathbf{MLT}^{-2}$	newton (N)
Kinetic energy $\left(\frac{1}{2}mv^2\right)$	$\mathbf{ML}^2\mathbf{T}^{-2}$	joule (J)
Gravitational potential energy (mgh)	$\mathbf{ML}^2\mathbf{T}^{-2}$	joule (J)

Continued

Quantity	Dimension	SI unit
Work done (force × distance moved)	$\mathbf{ML}^2\mathbf{T}^{-2}$	joule (J)
Moment of a force $(\text{force} \times \text{distance})$	$\mathbf{ML}^2\mathbf{T}^{-2}$	newton metres (N m)
Power $\left(\text{rate of doing work: } \dfrac{dW}{dt}\right)$	$\mathbf{ML}^2\mathbf{T}^{-3}$	watt (W)
Momentum (mv)	$\mathbf{MLT}^{-1}$	kg m s^{-1}
Impulse $(\text{force} \times \text{time})$	$\mathbf{MLT}^{-1}$	newton seconds (N s)
Moment of Inertia $\left(\sum mr^2\right)$	$\mathbf{ML}^2$	kg metre^2
Angular velocity $\left(\omega = \dfrac{d\theta}{dt}\right)$	$\mathbf{T}^{-1}$	radians per second
Density $\left(\dfrac{\text{mass}}{\text{volume}}\right)$	$\mathbf{ML}^{-3}$	kg per m^3
Pressure $\left(\dfrac{\text{force}}{\text{area}}\right)$	$\mathbf{ML}^{-1}\mathbf{T}^{-2}$	pascal (Pa)
Periodic time (time for one complete cycle)	T	seconds (s)
Frequency $\left(\dfrac{1}{\text{periodic time}}\right)$	$\mathbf{T}^{-1}$	hertz (Hz)
Surface tension $\left(\dfrac{\text{force}}{\text{length}}\right)$	$\mathbf{MT}^{-2}$	kg per second^2

MIXED PRACTICE 2

1   C

2   B

3 a   T   **b** $\mathbf{LT}^{-3}$

4 $[\text{Area}] = \mathbf{L}^2$

$\left[\sqrt{s(s-a)(s-b)(s-c)}\right] = \sqrt{[s][s-a][s-b][s-c]}$

$[s] = \mathbf{L}$

$[s-a] = [s] - [a] = \mathbf{L} - \mathbf{L} = \mathbf{L} = [s-b] = [s-c]$

$\sqrt{[s][s-a][s-b][s-c]} = \sqrt{\mathbf{L.L.L.L}} = \sqrt{\mathbf{L}^4} = \mathbf{L}^2$

Therefore it is dimensionally consistent.

5 a $[\text{Tension}] = \mathbf{MLT}^{-2}$

b i Inconsistent; $\dfrac{mv}{r}$ is the inconsistent term.

ii Consistent.

iii Inconsistent; $g\cos\theta$ is the inconsistent term.

6 a $\mathbf{ML^2T^{-2}}$ **b** 52 J

7 a $\mathbf{L}$ **b** $\mathbf{MT}^{-2}$

8 $\alpha = 1, \beta = 2, \gamma = -1, F = \dfrac{mv^2}{r}$

9 a $\mathbf{MLT}^{-2}$

b $\beta = \gamma$ as the two masses must make a similar contribution to the attractive force.

c $F = \dfrac{Gm_1m_2}{r^2}$

10 a $\mathbf{T}^{-2}$ **b** $[A] = \mathbf{T}^{-1}$

c $B = \dfrac{g}{l}$

11 a $\mathbf{MT}^{-2}$ **b** $d = A\sqrt{\dfrac{S}{\rho g}}$ **c** 2.00 (3 s.f.)

12 a $[\text{Tension}] = \mathbf{MLT}^{-2}$

b $\alpha = -1, \beta = \dfrac{1}{2}, \gamma = -\dfrac{1}{2}; f = \dfrac{1}{2l}\sqrt{\dfrac{F}{\mu}}$

13 $\alpha = 0, \beta = 2$ and $\gamma = -1$

14 a $\mathbf{ML^{-1}T^{-2}}$ **b** $\mathbf{ML^{-1}T^{-1}}$

c $v_T = A\dfrac{r^2g(\rho - \rho_1)}{\mu}$

15 $\alpha = 1, \beta = 2, \gamma = 1; F = k\rho v^2 A$

16 $\alpha = \dfrac{1}{2}, \beta = 0$ and $\gamma = \dfrac{1}{2}$

17 a $\mathbf{MT}^{-2}$ **b** $\mathbf{ML}^{-3}$

c $h = \dfrac{AS}{\rho rg}$ **d** 98 mm (2 s.f.)

18 $F = cd^2u^2\rho$

3 Momentum and collisions 1

BEFORE YOU START

1 $x = -\dfrac{1}{2}, y = 2$

2 11 m s^{-1} (2 s.f.)

3 a m s^{-1} **b** m s^{-2} **c** N

4 7.5 m s^{-2}

5 0.8 J

EXERCISE 3A

1 a 2250 kg m s^{-1} **b** 22.5 kg m s^{-1}

c 0.2 kg m s^{-1} **d** 20 000 kg m s^{-1}

e 28 000 kg m s^{-1}

2 900 m s^{-1}

3 1.2 tonnes

4 120 N s

5 720 N s

6

Positive direction		
Initial velocity (m s^{-1})	Final velocity (m s^{-1})	Impulse N s
$\to 4$	$\to 6$	$(+6m) - (+4m)$ $= +2m$
$\to 4$	$\to 2$	$2m - 4m$ $= -2m$
$\to 4$	$6 \leftarrow$	$-6m - 4m$ $= -10m$
$8 \leftarrow$	$3 \leftarrow$	$-3m - -8m$ $= 5m$
$3 \leftarrow$	$\to 8$	$8m - -3m$ $= 11m$

7 5 m s^{-1}

8 240 seconds or, equivalently, 4 minutes.

9 20 m s^{-1}

10 10 m s^{-1}

11 17.5 N s away from the wall.

12 50 N s away from the wall.

13 125 N opposing the direction of motion.

14 150 N

15 $(42\mathbf{i} + 32.4\mathbf{j})$ m s^{-1}

16 $(-400\mathbf{i} - 700\mathbf{j})$ N

17 33 m s^{-1}

18 2.5

WORK IT OUT 3.1

Solution 3 is correct.

EXERCISE 3B

1

m_1	m_2	u_1	u_2	v_1	v_2
3	4	+10	+2	$\dfrac{14}{3}$	+6
2	4	+6	−2	−2	2
2	5	8	+2	+0.5	+5
2	5	+8	−2	−1	+1.6

2 2.25 m s^{-1}

3 1.2 m s^{-1}

4 1.4 m s^{-1}

5 a $\frac{14}{3} \text{ m s}^{-1}$ **b** 2 m s^{-1}

6 0.125 m s^{-1} in the direction that A was travelling before the collision.

7 0.96 kg

8 $\frac{50}{9} \text{ m s}^{-1}$

9 9 m s^{-1}

10 9.6 m s^{-1}; assumptions, for example: balls are spherical, balls are same size, impact is along line of centres, contact is smooth.

11 a $v_1 = \dfrac{5m-9}{m+3}; v_2 = \dfrac{9-5m}{m+3}$

  b $5 \text{ kg and } \frac{3}{7} \text{ kg}$

12 Proof.

EXERCISE 3C

1

	i	ii	iii	iv	v
a	1.2	10	0	32	6
b	5.2m	20m	60m	72m	16m
c	7.28m	0	1800m	288m	32m

2 Both change direction. Speed of P is 1.4 m s^{-1} and of Q is 3.1 m s^{-1}.

3 a 0.2 m s^{-1} towards A. **b** $\frac{1}{20}$

4 a $\frac{3}{4}$

  b 42 N s away from the wall.

  c 84 J

5 a $\frac{mv}{J}$

  b $mv + J$ away from the wall.

  c $\frac{1}{2} m \left(\left(\frac{J}{m} \right)^2 - v^2 \right)$

6 a 20 m s^{-1} **b** 0.625 **c** 46.875 J

7 $3 \text{ m s}^{-1}; \frac{1}{2}$

8 a Velocity of A is 7.12 m s^{-1} and B is 4.08 m s^{-1}, moving in opposite directions to each other.

  b 6.05 N s

9 0.7 m (1 s.f.)

10 a Velocity of A is $0.25u \text{ m s}^{-1}$ and B is $4u \text{ m s}^{-1}$, both in the original direction of motion.

  b $4.375mu^2$

11 Velocity of A is 3.3 m s^{-1} and B is 5.7 m s^{-1}, both in the original direction of motion.

12 $1 : e^2$

13 a Velocity of A is 3.6 m s^{-1} and B is 5.4 m s^{-1}, both in the original direction of motion.

  b 0.6

14 a 4.2 m s^{-1} **b** 0.8 **c** 0.288 N s

15 a $(4.8\mathbf{i}+0.2\mathbf{j}) \text{ m s}^{-1}$ **b** 43.8 J

16 $\frac{\sqrt{10}}{2}(2+\sqrt{5})$

17 $\frac{\sqrt{35}}{7}$

MIXED PRACTICE 3

1 C

2 E

3 1.68 m s^{-1}

4 7.5 kg

5 $(3.9\mathbf{i}+4.1\mathbf{j}) \text{ m s}^{-1}$

6 a 1.5 **b** 2

7 1.5

8 1.25 m s^{-1} or 2.75 m s^{-1}

9 a i Proof. **ii** $\frac{u}{9}$

  b $e > 0.6$

  c Equal radii and velocities parallel to line of centres.

10 a $v_A = \dfrac{5u-3eu}{2}; v_B = \dfrac{5u+eu}{2}$

  b Proof. **c** $2.5mu \text{ N s}$

11 a Proof; $v_B = u$ **b** Proof; $v_B = \dfrac{9u-ux}{3(3+x)}$

  c Proof. **d** $2.5u$

12 a $4mu$ **b** $v_A = \dfrac{8u}{9}; v_B = \dfrac{20u}{9}$

  c Proof. **d** $\dfrac{3s+7r}{10}$

13 $e > \dfrac{1}{9}$

14 $e > \dfrac{10}{17}$

4 Circular motion 1

BEFORE YOU START

1 108 m

2 $\begin{pmatrix} -5 \\ 7 \end{pmatrix}$

3 53.1°

4 $v = 3t + 2$

$s = \dfrac{3t^2}{2} + 2t + 3$

5 $\dfrac{5\pi}{6}$ rad

WORK IT OUT 4.1

Solution 3 is correct.

EXERCISE 4A

1 a i 10.2 m s^{-1} **ii** 0.422 m s^{-1}

  b i 1.75 m **ii** 16 m

  c i 0.167 rad s^{-1} **ii** 22.4 rad s^{-1}

  d i 0.251 m s^{-1} **ii** 3.14 m s^{-1}

2 a i $\omega = 0.419 \text{ rad s}^{-1}$ **ii** $r = 71.6 \text{ m}$

  b i $\omega = 4.19 \text{ rad s}^{-1}$ **ii** $r = 2.39 \text{ m}$

  c i $\omega = 0.105 \text{ rad s}^{-1}$ **ii** $r = 47.7 \text{ m}$

3 a $\omega = 0.107 \text{ rad s}^{-1}$ **b** 58.9 s

4 a $\omega = 0.140 \text{ rad s}^{-1}$

  b $v = 0.0140 \text{ m s}^{-1}$

  c $r = 7.16 \text{ m}$

5 $\omega = 0.25 \text{ rad s}^{-1}$

6 a 57.3 s **b** $\omega = 0.219 \text{ rad s}^{-1}$

7 a That its orbit is circular.

  b i $\omega = 0.002\,38 \text{ rev minute}^{-1}$

       $\omega = 0.000\,249 \text{ rad s}^{-1}$

   ii $v = 31.9 \text{ km s}^{-1}$

EXERCISE 4B

1 a i 0.313 m **ii** 1.29 m

  b i 3.57 m **ii** 1.41 m

  c i 2.26 m s^{-1} **ii** 1.46 m s^{-1}

  d i 3 rad s^{-1} **ii** 12.2 rad s^{-1}

2 a i $a = 4 \text{ m s}^{-2}$ **ii** $F = 8 \text{ N}$

   iii

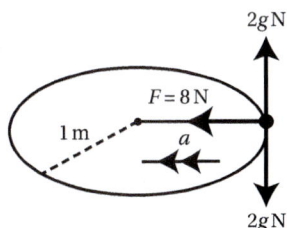

b i $a = 3.78 \text{ m s}^{-2}$ **ii** $F = 11\,000 \text{ N}$

  iii

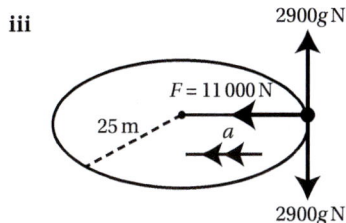

c i $a = 0.0148 \text{ m s}^{-2}$ **ii** $F = 0.002\,96 \text{ N}$

  iii

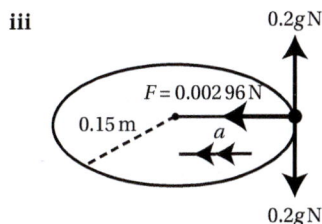

3 $a = 1.38 \text{ m s}^{-2}; F = 4820 \text{ N}$

4 a $T = 60 \text{ N}$ **b** $T = 21.6 \text{ N}$

5 Emily will feel an increase in force by a factor of $\dfrac{4}{3}$.

6 a $v = 26.4 \text{ km h}^{-1}$

  b No it is not a sensible estimate; this is a very low speed to drive around a bend of 55 m radius.

7 $\mu = 0.0209$

8 $v = 1.3 \text{ m s}^{-1} \text{ (2 s.f.)}$

9 a Assume only friction force acting on the car is from the road surface. Assume the car is on the point of slipping away from the centre.

  b i $v = 47.8 \text{ km h}^{-1}$ **ii** $v = 52.0 \text{ km h}^{-1}$

  c For asphalt reduce max safe speed from 47.8 km h^{-1} to 28.2 km h^{-1} when wet.

     For concrete reduce max safe speed from 52.0 km h^{-1} to 37.8 km h^{-1} when wet.

  d Depending on where the road is to be built could influence this decision. For a city with a lower speed limit asphalt would be cheaper and suitable.

10 a, b Proof.

EXERCISE 4C

In this exercise all answers are given to two significant figures, unless stated otherwise.

1 a i 21 N **ii** 42 N

  b i 36 N **ii** 47 N

  c i 2.3 rad s^{-1} **ii** 2.3 rad s^{-1}

  d i $39°$ **ii** $84°$

2 **a** $\theta = 89°$ **b** $\omega = 3.4$ rad s^{-1}

   c $T = 110$ N   **d** $m = 5.2$ kg

3 **a** $T = 13$ N   **b** $\omega = 6.8$ rad s^{-1}

4 **a** $\left(\frac{4}{5}mg + \frac{324}{625}m\omega^2 \right)$ N

   b $\left(\frac{432}{625}m\omega^2 - \frac{3}{5}mg \right)$ N

   c $w > 2.9$ rad s^{-1}

5 **a** 1.9 rad s^{-1} **b** 57 N

   c 17 N, compression.

6 **a** $R = \frac{5}{3}mg$ **b** $v = 4\sqrt{\frac{rg}{15}}$

7 **a** $T_A = 42$ N   **b** $\omega = 3.3$ rad s^{-1}

   c $T_B = 18$ N away from the centre B.

8 $T = 37$ N; $r = 1.2$ m

MIXED PRACTICE 4

In this exercise all answers are given to two significant figures, unless stated otherwise.

1 C

2 A

Ⓐ 3 D

4 **a** $\omega = 1.6$ rad s^{-1}

   b $t = 3.9$ s

   c $F = 2.6$ N

Ⓐ 5 **a**

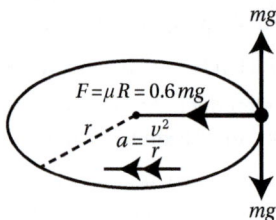

   b $v = 1.33$ m s^{-1} (3 s.f.)

6 **a** 13 m s^{-2} **b** 6.7 N

7 1300 N

8 Proof.

9 13 rad s^{-1}

Ⓐ 10 **a** $T = \frac{25\,mg}{7}$ **b** $v = 2\sqrt{42\,gL}$

   c There was no frictional force acting.

Ⓐ 11 **a** Proof.   **b** 6.3 m s^{-1}

   c $2\pi^2$ m s^{-2} **d** 3.9 N

Ⓐ 12 **a** Centre $(1, 2)$; radius 3 m.

   b 6 m s^{-1} **c** $\begin{pmatrix} -12\cos 2t \\ -12\sin 2t \end{pmatrix}$ m s^{-2}

Ⓐ 13 **a** $v = 20$ km h^{-1} (1 s.f.)

   b **i** $v = 10$ km h^{-1} (1 s.f.)

     ii $v = 30$ km h^{-1} (1 s.f.)

Ⓐ 14 **a** Proof.

   b $T = \frac{mv^2}{l} - mg\sin\theta$

   c Proof.

Ⓐ 15 **a** $R = \frac{mg}{9}$ **b** Yes

   c $T = \frac{80}{69}mg$

Ⓐ 16 **a** Radius 6 m; centre $(-1, 3)$.

   b $v = \begin{pmatrix} -6\pi\sin\pi t \\ 6\pi\cos\pi t \end{pmatrix}$ m s^{-1};

     $a = \begin{pmatrix} -6\pi^2\cos\pi t \\ -6\pi^2\sin\pi t \end{pmatrix}$ m s^{-2}

   c Proof.

Ⓐ 17 $\begin{pmatrix} -2\sin\pi t - 2 \\ -2\cos\pi t + 1 \end{pmatrix}$ m; X is moving in the clockwise direction.

18 17 m s^{-1}

19 **a** 7.00 rad s^{-2} (3 s.f.)   **b** 2.10 m s^{-1} (3 s.f.)

   c 0.898 s (3 s.f.)

20 1.5 m

Ⓐ 21 **a** Proof.   **b** 3.48 m s^{-1}

Ⓐ 22 **a** Proof.   **b** 1.84 m s^{-1}

5 Work, energy and power 2

BEFORE YOU START

1 196 J

2 661 J

3 0.0120 N

4 2

EXERCISE 5A

1 **a** 12.5 J   **b** 5 J

   c 5π J   **d** 625 J

2 $k = 90$

3 $a = 64$

4 9.70 m s^{-1}

5 75.9 m s^{-1}

6 $d = 39.5$ m

7 78.7 m

WORK IT OUT

Solution 2 is correct.

EXERCISE 5B

1. 26.6 N

2. 42.9 N

3. $k = 367\ \text{N m}^{-1}$ (3 s.f.); $\lambda = 220$ N

4. 0.124 m

5. 0.10 m (2 s.f.)

6. $k = 30.6\ \text{N m}^{-1}$; $\lambda = 34$ N (2 s.f.)

7. 33.3 N

8. 0.446 m

9. 3.38 J

10. 32.6 J

11. $\lambda = 523$ N

12. 0.542 m

13. $x = 0.23$ m (2 s.f.)

14. **a** $x = 0.90$ m (2 s.f.)

    b $30.1\ \text{m s}^{-2}$ upwards.

15. $OP = 1.50$ m

16. $OQ = 0.987$ m

17. **a** 5.5 J   **b** $5.91\ \text{m s}^{-1}$

18. Proof.

Ⓐ EXERCISE 5C

1. 117 J

2. 1.96 kJ

3. 73.3 m

4. 23.0 N

5. 55.2°

6. 20.7 J

7. 169 J

8. 30.8 m

9. **a** 450 J (2 s.f.)   **b** 450 J (2 s.f.)

10. **a** 840 J   **b** 570 J (2 s.f.)   **c** $5.2\ \text{m s}^{-1}$ (2 s.f.)

EXERCISE 5D

1. **a** 100 J (2 s.f.)   **b** 15 W (2 s.f.)

2. **a** 2.93 J (2 s.f.)   **b** $2.6\ \text{m s}^{-1}$ (2 s.f.)

3. 6°

4. **a** $1.9\ \text{m s}^{-1}$ (2 s.f.)   **b** 1.2 m (2 s.f.)

5. 16 s (2 s.f.)

6. $1.0\ \text{m s}^{-1}$ (2 s.f.)

7. $\lambda = 30$ N (2 s.f.)

8. **a** Proof.   **b** $3.2\ \text{m s}^{-2}$ (2 s.f.)

9. **a** $0.105\ \text{m s}^{-2}$ **b** $9.6\ \text{m s}^{-1}$ (2 s.f.)

10. **a** Proof.   **b** $22\ \text{m s}^{-1}$ (2 s.f.)

MIXED PRACTICE 5

Ⓐ 1. **a** 97 J (2 s.f.)   **b** $7.8\ \text{m s}^{-1}$ (2 s.f.)

Ⓐ 2. 276 J

Ⓐ 3. **a** 441 J   **b** 8820 J

   c 9261 J; $16.0\ \text{m s}^{-1}$

4. $9.40\ \text{m s}^{-1}$

5. **a** 12.5 J   **b** Proof.

   c $1.0\ \text{m s}^{-1}$ (2 s.f.)

Ⓐ 6. **a** 84.4 J   **b** Proof.   **c** Proof.

7. 41.7 m

Ⓐ 8. **a** Proof.

   b **i** 4.1 m (2 s.f.) **ii** $6.0\ \text{m s}^{-2}$ (2 s.f.)

9. **a** **i,ii** Proof.   **b** 62.5 J   **c** 1.6 m (2 s.f.)

10. **a** Proof.

    b There is no EPE until Carol has fallen 26 metres.

    c 66 m (2 s.f.)

    d **i** 38 m (2 s.f.) **ii** $25\ \text{m s}^{-1}$ (2 s.f.)

11. **a** Proof.

    b **i** 0.2 m   **ii** 44.1 J

    iii 0.017 m above A.

12. **a** 96.8 J   **b** 13.6 N

    c Proof.

    d 2.12 m   **e** 7.12 m

13. **a** Proof.

    b **i** 0.196 m   **ii** Proof.

    iii Proof.

    iv 0.208 m

14. **a** 2400 J   **b** 12.5 m   **c** 7.55 m

A **15** 170 kW (2 s.f.)

16 **a** Proof. **b** 0.30 m s^{-2}

  c 17 m s^{-1} (2 s.f.)

17 8300 kW (2 s.f.)

18 **a** Proof. **b** 0.44 m s^{-2}

  c 59 m s^{-1} (2 s.f.)

19 $\theta = 1.15°$

Focus on ... Proof 1

1 Proof.

2 $\omega_1^2 - \omega_0^2 = 2\alpha(\theta_1 - \theta_0)$

  $(\theta_1 - \theta_0) = \omega_1 t - \dfrac{1}{2}\alpha t^2$

  $(\theta_1 - \theta_0) = \dfrac{1}{2}(\omega_1 + \omega_0)t$

3 50 rad s^{-1}

4 Proof.

Focus on ... Problem solving 1

1 2 m (1 s.f.)

2 0.9π seconds

3 5.3

Focus on ... Modelling 1

1 6.6 m s^{-1}

2 2.05 m

3 Yes. The ball reaches the bell.

4 No. The ball does not reach the bell.

Cross-topic review exercise 1

1 $\alpha = 1, \beta = 2, \gamma = 1; v = \sqrt{\dfrac{2D}{C\rho A}}$

2 $\mathbf{v} = (16\mathbf{i} + 12\mathbf{j})$ m s^{-1}

3 9.87 N

A **4** 60° (1 s.f.)

A **5** 40 kW (1 s.f.)

6 Proof.

A **7** $k = 3.2g$ N m^{-1}

8 0.66 s (2 s.f.)

A **9** 4.1 (2 s.f.)

10 **a** $\mathbf{MLT}^{-2}$ **b** $\mathbf{ML}^{-1}\mathbf{T}^{-2}$

11 2 m s^{-1} away from the wall.

12 0.75

A **13** 1 m^3 (1 s.f.)

6 Momentum and collisions 2

All answers are given to 3 significant figures, where appropriate.

BEFORE YOU START

1 9 kg m s^{-1}

2 $e = \dfrac{v}{u}$

3
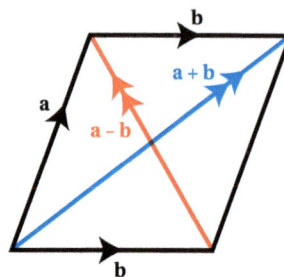

4 Horizontal $F\cos 60°$; vertical $F\sin 60°$.

5 $\sqrt{45} = 3\sqrt{5}$

6 9

EXERCISE 6A

1 **a** 45 N s **b** 30 N s

  c 26 N s **d** 2.5 N s

2 **a** 17.25 m s^{-1} **b** 13.5 m s^{-1}

  c 12.5 m s^{-1} **d** 6.625 m s^{-1}

3

Mass (kg)	Initial velocity (m s^{-1})	Final velocity (m s^{-1})	Constant force (N)	Time (s)
2	0	$8\mathbf{i} + 10\mathbf{j}$	$3.2\mathbf{i} + 4\mathbf{j}$	5
1	$2\mathbf{i} - \mathbf{j}$	$14\mathbf{i} + 15\mathbf{j}$	$3\mathbf{i} + 4\mathbf{j}$	4
2	$-3\mathbf{i} + 5\mathbf{j}$	$-7\mathbf{i} + 11\mathbf{j}$	$-2\mathbf{i} + 3\mathbf{j}$	4
0.5	$2\mathbf{i} + 7\mathbf{j}$	$-10\mathbf{i} + 19\mathbf{j}$	$-\mathbf{i} + \mathbf{j}$	6
4	$4\mathbf{i} + 13\mathbf{j}$	$1.5\mathbf{i} - 8\mathbf{j}$	$-2\mathbf{i} - 4\mathbf{j}$	5

4 $(1.4\mathbf{i}+2.4\mathbf{j})\text{ m s}^{-1}$

5 $(1.1\mathbf{i}+2.1\mathbf{j})\text{ m s}^{-1}$

6 a 36 N s **b** 18.4 m s^{-1}

7 a $(1.5\mathbf{i}+0.5\mathbf{j})\text{ m s}^{-1}$ **b** 37.5 J

8 a i 10 N s **ii** 110 N s

    b 16 m s^{-1}

9 a i 4 N s **ii** 0 N s

    b 4 m s^{-1}

10 4 s

EXERCISE 6B

1 a $a=4; b=-4.2$ **b** 5.8 m s^{-1}

2 a $a=1; b=-4.8$ **b** 25.92 J

Ⓐ 3 a 2.5 m s^{-1} **b** $2.5\sqrt{3}\text{ m s}^{-1}$

    c $-1.25\sqrt{3}\text{ m s}^{-1}$

    d 3.31 m s^{-1} (3 s.f.) at $40.9°$ (3 s.f.) to the wall.

4 4.44 m s^{-1} (2 d.p.) at $13.0°$ (1 d.p.) to the wall.

5 a $u\cos\theta\text{ m s}^{-1}$ **b** $u\cos\theta\text{ m s}^{-1}$

    c $u\sin\theta\text{ m s}^{-1}$ **d** $-eu\sin\theta\text{ m s}^{-1}$

    e $u\sqrt{\cos^2\theta+e^2\sin^2\theta}\text{ m s}^{-1}$ **f** Proof.

6 a 3.30 m s^{-1} (3 s.f.) at $31.0°$ (3 s.f.) to the wall.

    b 3.62 N s (3 s.f.)

7 5 m s^{-1} at $-36.9°$ to the positive $\mathbf{i}$ direction.

8 8.33 J

9 5.04 N s

10 a 4.695 m s^{-1} at $29.3°$ **b** 0.237 J

11 Speed $=eu$ at $(90-\theta)°$ to the side of the table.

MIXED PRACTICE 6

1 B

2 C

Ⓐ 3 a Proof.   **b** 3.248 m s^{-1}

4 a 10 N s **b** 8230

5 2

6 a 9 **b** 7

Ⓐ 7 a 0.813 **b** Proof.

    c $\dfrac{2.4}{u}$

---

    d Smooth cushion means impulse perpendicular to the cushion.

8 a 417 N s **b** 1.95 m s^{-1}

9 a 2 N s **b** 0.75

Ⓐ 7 Circular motion 2

BEFORE YOU START

1 9.4 m (2 s.f.)

2 $v=1.2\text{ m s}^{-1}$

3 1.32 m

4 17 N (2 s.f.)

WORK IT OUT 7.1

Solution 3 is correct.

EXERCISE 7A

In questions 1 and 2 give all answers to 2 s.f.

1 a i 2.8 m s^{-1} **ii** 1.4 m s^{-1}

    b i 0.91 m s^{-2} **ii** 25 m s^{-2}

    c i 28 N **ii** 1.8 N

    d i $54°$ **ii** $70°$

2 a $v=\sqrt{gr(5+2\cos\theta)}\text{ m s}^{-1}$

    b $h=r\text{ m}$

    c $v=\sqrt{3gr}\text{ m s}^{-1}$

    d $v=\sqrt{5gr}\text{ m s}^{-1}$

3 a It will only reach a height of $h=\frac{1}{2}a\text{ m}$ before coming back down again.

    b The bead will not make a full circle. It will reach a height of $h=\frac{1}{3}a\text{ m}$ before coming back down.

    c A full circle will not occur for this bead as it will have velocity $v=0\text{ m s}^{-1}$ at the top of the circle and will come back down the same way it went up.

4 a $v=2.8\text{ m s}^{-1}$ (2 s.f.)

    b $T=15\text{ N}$ (2 s.f.)

5 $v=\sqrt{u^2-0.8g+0.8g\cos\theta}\text{ m s}^{-1}$

6 a The bob swings a full circle.

    b When the string makes an angle of $116°$ with the downward vertical, tension will be lost and the bob will fall freely under gravity.

c When the string makes an angle of 83.6° with the downward vertical, tension will be lost and the bob will fall freely under gravity.

7 $u > \sqrt{6g}$

8 $T_H = \frac{1}{3}mg$

9 a The maximum speed occurs when all GPE has been converted to KE so when P hangs vertically below O.

$v = 2\sqrt{g}$ m s^{-1}

b $T = 1.5g \sin\theta + 0.5g$

c $\theta = 20°$ (1 s.f.)

10 a $v = 1$ m s^{-1} (1 s.f.)　　**b** $R = 0.5$ N

WORK IT OUT 7.2

Solution 2 is correct.

EXERCISE 7B

In Exercise 7B, all answers are given to 2 s.f., unless stated otherwise.

1 a i 2.1 m s^{-1}　　**ii** 5.2 m s^{-1}

b i 20 N　　**ii** 1.3 N

c i $42°$　　**ii** $72°$

d i 3.6 m s^{-1}　　**ii** 5.3 m s^{-1}

2 a $\sqrt{g} = 3$ m s^{-1} (1 s.f.)　　**b** 2 m (1 s.f.)

3 a 4.4 m s^{-1}

b 0.69 s

c 1.5 m

4 a 7.1 m s^{-1}

b 0.37 s

c 2.3 m

5 a 2.9 m s^{-1}

b 1.1 s

c 2.7 m

6 a 2.4 m s^{-1}

b 0.64 s

c 1.5 m

7 $\theta = 48°$

8 2.3 m s^{-1}

9 a $\theta = 60°$

b $T = 1300$ N

c 5.4 m s^{-1} in the direction 30° to the horizontal.

10 a $v = \sqrt{9 - 2g(0.6 - 0.6\cos\theta)}$

b $T = 0.88\cos\theta - 0.14$

c Proof.

11 a 5.4 m s^{-1}　　**b** 10 m s^{-1}

c The bag will be in contact until $\theta = 36°$ on the second chute and then it will lose contact with the chute.

MIXED PRACTICE 7

1 C

2 D

3 D

4 5 m s^{-1} (1 s.f.)

5 22 N (2 s.f.)

6 a $v^2 = 25 - 2.1g + 2.1g\cos\theta$

b $\theta = 98°$ (2 s.f.)

7 26.2 N (3 s.f.)

8 $u > 2\sqrt{ga}$

9 a $\cos\theta = \dfrac{u^2}{3gr} + \dfrac{2}{3}$　　**b** $u > \sqrt{gr}$

10 a When P is vertically below O as a is at its greatest value here.

b $3\sqrt{gr}$

c $5.5mg$

11 a Proof.

b $19.5°$ (3 s.f.)

12 a Proof.

b i $u = 3\sqrt{ag}$　　**ii** $3 : \sqrt{5}$

13 a 1.5 m s^{-1} (2 s.f.)　　**b** 240 N (2 s.f.)

14 a Proof.

b $45°$ (2 s.f.)

15 a 1.4 m s^{-1} (2 s.f.)　　**b** 2.3 kg (2 s.f.)

16 a Proof.

b $3mg$

c No air resistance.

17 a $\dfrac{1}{2}\sqrt{ag}$　　**b** $29 : 5$

8 Centres of mass

BEFORE YOU START

1 $\begin{pmatrix} -4.5 \\ 4.5 \\ 6 \end{pmatrix}$

2 $\frac{9}{2}\ln 3 - 2$

3 9 N m anticlockwise.

4 $\mu 2g$ N

EXERCISE 8A

1 151 cm

2 3

3 72 cm

4 7.5

5 $\bar{x} = 4.30, \bar{y} = 3.70$

6 $\bar{x} = 4.14, \bar{y} = 4.57$

7 $\bar{x} = 4.89, \bar{y} = 5.22$

8 $\begin{pmatrix} -1.25 \\ 2.25 \end{pmatrix}$ cm

9 $x = 5, y = 3$

EXERCISE 8B

1 $(5.5, 4)$

2 $(3.5, 3.5)$

3 $(1.5, 0.866)$

4 a $(3, 2)$ **b** $(2, 4)$

    c $\left(\frac{2}{3}, \frac{5}{3}\right)$ **d** $\left(-\frac{1}{3}, \frac{1}{3}\right)$

    e $\left(-3, -\frac{1}{3}\right)$

5 2.12 cm

6 a $\left(2, \frac{4}{3}\right)$ **b** $\left(3, \frac{4}{3}\right)$

    c $(2.83, 0.645)$ **d** $(4.94, 1.96)$

7 9.74 cm

8 9.44 cm

9 0.79 radians (2 d.p.)

WORK IT OUT 8.1

Solution 4 is correct.

EXERCISE 8C

1 a $\begin{pmatrix} 2\frac{5}{18} \\ 2 \end{pmatrix}$ **b** $\begin{pmatrix} 2\frac{1}{14} \\ 1\frac{4}{7} \end{pmatrix}$

    c $\begin{pmatrix} 2\frac{9}{14} \\ 2\frac{3}{7} \end{pmatrix}$ **d** $\begin{pmatrix} 2\frac{4}{9} \\ 1\frac{17}{18} \end{pmatrix}$

    e $\begin{pmatrix} 2\frac{11}{27} \\ 1\frac{26}{27} \end{pmatrix}$ **f** $\begin{pmatrix} 2\frac{2}{15} \\ 1\frac{13}{15} \end{pmatrix}$

    g $\begin{pmatrix} 3.49 \\ 4.16 \end{pmatrix}$ **h** $\begin{pmatrix} 4.18 \\ 4.57 \end{pmatrix}$

2 0.616 m

3 $\begin{pmatrix} \bar{x} \\ \bar{y} \end{pmatrix} = \begin{pmatrix} 16.25 \\ \frac{65}{6} \end{pmatrix}$ cm

4 $\frac{5a}{24}$ metres from X.

5 5.5

6 $\bar{x} = \frac{45}{7}$ cm

7 The centre of mass is 1.5 cm from AB and 5 cm from AC.

8 $\begin{pmatrix} \bar{x} \\ \bar{y} \end{pmatrix} = \begin{pmatrix} 3.89 \\ 3.42 \end{pmatrix}$

9 19.0 cm

10 The centre of mass is 0.114 metres from AB and 0.611 metres from BC.

11 14.3 cm

12 8.37 cm

13 7.83 cm

14 Proof.

EXERCISE 8D

1 a $f(x) = 5 - \frac{5}{8}x$ **b** $\left(\frac{8}{3}, \frac{5}{3}\right)$

2 $\bar{x} = 0.6; \bar{y} = 0.75$

3 Proof.

4 $\bar{x} = 2\frac{2}{3}; \bar{y} = 2\frac{2}{3}$

5 $\bar{x} = 3; \bar{y} = 0$

6 $\bar{x} = 2.33; \bar{y} = 0$

7 a 9k   **b** 2.25   **c** 2.7k

8 3.6

9 $\bar{x} = \dfrac{4R}{3\pi}; \bar{y} = \dfrac{4R}{3\pi}$

10 0.467

EXERCISE 8E

1 21.8°

2 56.3°

3 45°

4 45°

5 33.7°

6 54.2°

7 a 5.57 cm   **b** 24.0°

8 a $\begin{pmatrix} \bar{x} \\ \bar{y} \end{pmatrix} = \begin{pmatrix} 8.64 \\ 4.09 \end{pmatrix}$ cm

   b 41.7°

9 a $\bar{y} = 20$ cm, $\bar{x} = 33\frac{1}{3}$ cm   **b** 9.46°

10 21.8°

11 38.7°

12 $200\sqrt{3}$

13 a 15.3°   **b** 1.8 N (2 s.f.)

14 $\dfrac{\sqrt{3}mg}{2}$

15 a $F = 2g$ **b** $F = 2.5g$

16 $k = \dfrac{5}{14}$

MIXED PRACTICE 8

1 1.9 m

2 $\bar{x} = 10.6, \bar{y} = 7.71$

3 $\bar{x} = 6.67, \bar{y} = 3.87$

4 a $\bar{x} = 5.13$ cm, $\bar{y} = 2.88$ cm

   b $\alpha = 43.2°$

5 a Symmetry.

   b $\bar{x} = 6.26$ cm

   c $\alpha = 32.6°$

6 a Proof.

   b i

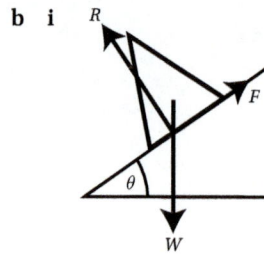

   ii $\theta = 26.6°$

   c Condition for sliding is met before the condition for toppling.

7 21.3 N

8 1.25

9 a i $y = x$ is axis of reflective symmetry.

   ii $\bar{x} = \bar{y} = \dfrac{a}{3}$

   b i Proof.

   ii $k = \dfrac{1}{2}$

10 a $P = \dfrac{mg}{\cos\theta}$

   b Proof.

   c $\mu < \dfrac{\cos\theta}{\cos\theta - \sin\theta}$

   d No, because the inequality in part **c** is independent of mass.

11 a $P = \dfrac{W}{4\cos\theta}$

   b Proof.

   c $\mu < \dfrac{1}{3}$

12 a Proof.

   b i Proof.

   ii $k = 1.5$

13 a $\dfrac{57r}{49}$

   b i Proof.

   ii $P_{\min} = \dfrac{3W}{2\sqrt{2}}$

   iii $\theta = 45°$

14 a i Proof.   **ii** Proof.

   b i 0.8 m   **ii** Proof.   **iii** 1.04 m

   c 18° (to the nearest degree).

15 a–c Proof.   **d** $\left(\dfrac{\sqrt{2}}{2}a, \dfrac{\sqrt{2}}{2}b \right)$

9 Moments and couples

BEFORE YOU START

1 21 N (2 s.f.)

2 6 N m anticlockwise

3 For rectangle $OABC$ with corner O at the origin and A at $(0, 3)$, the centre of mass is at $(3, 1.5)$.

4 $12\mathbf{i} + 19\mathbf{j} + 2\mathbf{k}$

WORK IT OUT 9.1

Solution 3 is correct.

EXERCISE 9A

In Exercise 9A, all answers are given to 2 s.f., unless stated otherwise.

1 a i 5 N m clockwise.

  ii 9 N m clockwise.

 b i 18 N m anticlockwise.

  ii 9 N m anticlockwise.

 c i 0 N m   **ii** 0 N m

2 a i 42 N m clockwise.

  ii 4.2 N m clockwise.

 b i 0.92 N m clockwise.

  ii 28 N m anticlockwise.

3 a i 72 N m clockwise.

  ii 20 N m clockwise.

 b i 69 N m clockwise.

  ii 4.0 N m clockwise.

4 a i 220 N m anticlockwise.

  ii 83 N m clockwise.

 b i 98 N m anticlockwise.

  ii 170 N m clockwise.

5 50 N (1 s.f.)

6 3 N (1 s.f.)

7 1 kg; 8 m (1 s.f.)

8 $\dfrac{mg}{\sqrt{6}}$ N

9 Proof.

EXERCISE 9B

1 a i A couple; 40 N m clockwise.

  ii Not a couple; equilibrium.

 b i A couple; 10 N m anticlockwise.

  ii Not a couple.

 c i A couple; 19 N m clockwise.

  ii A couple; 17 N m anticlockwise.

2 a i Not a couple.

  ii A couple; 18 N m anticlockwise.

 b i Not a couple.

  ii A couple; 12 N m clockwise.

3 a i

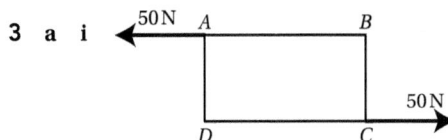

  ii

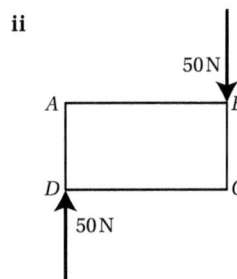

 b i

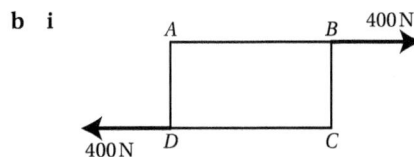

  ii

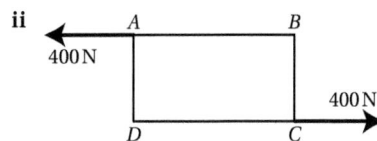

 c i

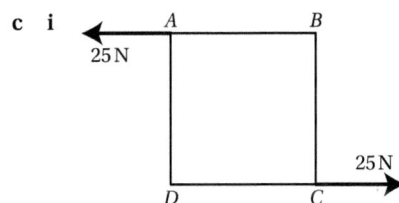

ii

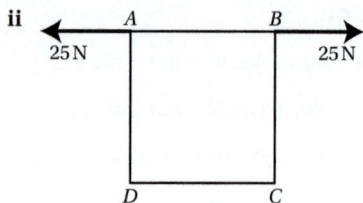

4 6 N m

5 $X = 6$ N, $Y = 1$ N; forces are equivalent to a couple of magnitude 3 N m clockwise.

6 $\dfrac{M}{X}$ N

7 3550 N; 280 N m anticlockwise.

EXERCISE 9C

1 a i 9 N m anticlockwise.

   ii 11 N m clockwise.

  b i 7 N m anticlockwise.

   ii 7 N m anticlockwise.

  c i 1 N m anticlockwise.

   ii 13 N m anticlockwise.

2 a i 9**k** N m   **ii** −11**k** N m

  b i 7**k** N m   **ii** 7**k** N m

  c i 1**k** N m   **ii** 13**k** N m

3 Proof; 7 N m clockwise.

4 Proof; 10 N m clockwise.

5 Proof; 15 N m clockwise.

6 $9\sqrt{2}$ N m or 10 N m (1 s.f.)

7 $\sqrt{5361}$ N m or 70 N m (1 s.f.)

8 $a = -6$, $b = 4$; 26 N m

9 $x = 0$, $y = 4$; 13 N m

10 $a = -4$, $b = -3$, $\mathbf{M} = -14\mathbf{k}$ N m

11 Proof; $a = 3$, $b = -2$.

12–13 Proof.

EXERCISE 9D

1 a i 4 N (1 s.f.)

   ii 12 m (to the left of A)

  b i 4 N (1 s.f.)

   ii 4.7 m (to the left of A)

  c i 12 N (2 s.f.)

   ii 10 m (2 s.f.) (to the right of A)

2 a i 0.157 (3 s.f.)   **ii** 0.129 (3 s.f.)

  b i 0.138 (3 s.f.)   **ii** 0.177 (3 s.f.)

  c i 0.110 (3 s.f.)   **ii** 0.143 (3 s.f.)

3 0.385 (3 s.f.)

4 6000 N at C, 4000 N at B; cannot carry 1000 N without a turning effect.

5 $R = S = 375$ N

6 1700 N (2 s.f.)

7 $F = mg\,\dfrac{\sqrt{3}}{2}$ N

8 a 600 N; 300 N m

  b 1.75 m away from A, along AD.

9 a 640 N (2 s.f.)

  b 370 N (2 s.f.); 60° (2 s.f.) to the vertical wall.

10 a The cable is light and inextensible.

  b 610 N (2 s.f.)

MIXED PRACTICE 9

1 D

2 B

3 C

4 B

5 2.7 kN (2 s.f.)

6 a **0** N   **b** $-4\mathbf{i} + 12\mathbf{j} + 2\mathbf{k}$

  c Proof.

7 a $a = 1$, $b = -1$, $c = -3$

  b $\sqrt{3}$ N m

8 Proof.

9 a

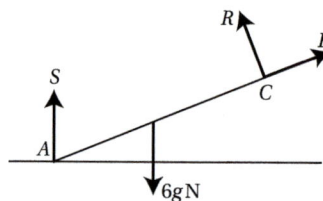

  b 19.6 N (3 s.f.)

  c i 36.8 N (3 s.f.)   **ii** 13.4 N (3 s.f.)

  d 0.364 (3 s.f.)

10 a $a = 3$ or -21 **b** 7**i** or 7**i** − 24**j**

11 1.5 m (2 s.f.)

12 **a** Proof.

   b $-3\mathbf{i}+(a+6)\mathbf{j}+(3-a)\mathbf{k}$

   c $a = -2$ or -1

13 Proof.

14 **a**

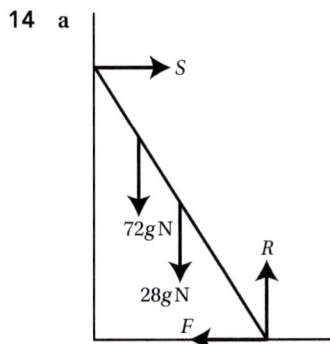

   b **i** Proof. **ii** $0.261\,(3\text{ s.f.})$

15 $k = \dfrac{5}{14}$ or $0.357\,(3\text{ s.f.})$

Focus on ... Proof 2

1 Proof.

2 Proof.

Focus on ... Problem solving 2

1 **a** v is maximised when $x = 0.25$ and $v = 3.5\text{ m s}^{-1}\,(2\text{ s.f.})$.

   b $x = 0.81\text{ m}\,(2\text{ s.f.})$

2 $I = 4.36\text{ N s}$; $\beta = 36.6°$ to the original direction of motion.

Focus on ... Modelling 2

1 $\theta = \theta_{\max}\cos\left(\sqrt{\dfrac{g}{l}}\,t\right)$

2 $T = \pi$

3

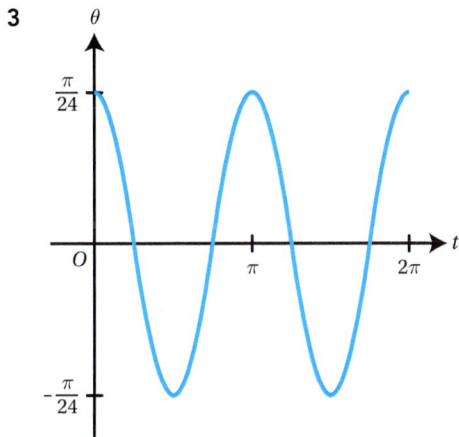

4 $\theta = \dfrac{\pi}{24}\cos 2t \therefore \dot{\theta} = -2\times\dfrac{\pi}{24}\sin 2t$ and

   $v = -2.45\times 2\times\dfrac{\pi}{24}\sin 2t$

5 $\left|v_{\max}\right| 0.6414\text{ m s}^{-1}$

6 $\left|v_{\max}\right| = \sqrt{2gl\left|(1-\cos\theta_{\max})\right|}$ and $\theta_{\max} = \dfrac{\pi}{24}$, $v_{\max} = 0.6410\text{ m s}^{-1}$; the bob is going 0.06% more slowly than the SHM model predicts.

7 **a** $\left|v_{\max}\right| \approx 1.2828\text{ m s}^{-1}$ from SHM model.

   $v_{\max} \approx 1.2792\text{ m s}^{-1}$ from the energy equation; the bob is going 0.3% more slowly than the SHM model predicts.

   b $\left|v_{\max}\right| \approx 2.5656\text{ m s}^{-1}$ from SHM model.

   $v_{\max} \approx 2.5364\text{ m s}^{-1}$ from the energy equation; the bob is going 1.2% more slowly than the SHM model predicts.

Ⓐ Cross-topic review exercise 2

1 **a** Proof.

   b $\alpha = 26.3°$

2 **a** $\dfrac{1}{2}$ **b** $e = \dfrac{\sqrt{3}}{3}$

3 $v = 2\sqrt{g}$

4 **a** Proof.

   b Proof.

5 **a** -4 or 2 **b** $\begin{pmatrix}-1\\2\end{pmatrix}$ or $\begin{pmatrix}-1\\8\end{pmatrix}$

6 **a** 32 N s **b** 10 m s^{-1}

   c 4.8 seconds

7 **a** $T = 3mg\cos\theta + 20.9m$

   b height $= 0.86\text{ m}\,(2\text{ s.f.})$

   c Total height gained $= 1.0\text{ m}\,(2\text{ s.f.})$

8 **a** Proof.   **b** $0.26\,(2\text{ s.f.})$

9 **a** Proof.   **b** $\dfrac{\sqrt{3}u}{2}$ **c** 10.6 N

10 $h = \dfrac{\sqrt{2}r}{2}$

11 **a** $\cos\theta = \dfrac{u^2 + 2ga}{3ga}$

   b $\theta = 60°$

12 **a** $\begin{pmatrix}-6\\-8\\-21\end{pmatrix}$

   b **i** $\begin{pmatrix}7\\0\\-2\end{pmatrix}$ **ii** $\begin{pmatrix}-4\\3\\0\end{pmatrix}+\lambda\begin{pmatrix}7\\0\\-2\end{pmatrix}$

13 a $\bar{x} = \frac{11h}{8}$ **b** $r = \frac{\sqrt{2}h}{4}$

14 a No change because both ball and plane are smooth.

  b $\sqrt{2gh} \sin\theta$ parallel to the plane;
  $\sqrt{2gh}e \cos\theta$ perpendicular to the plane.

  c Proof.

15 a $\bar{y} = 1.6$

  b $\alpha \approx 51°$ (to the nearest degree).

16 a Proof.

  b $R = \frac{53}{42}mg$

Practice papers

AS LEVEL PRACTICE PAPER

1 B

2 D

3 4.5 N

4 a $40\,\text{m s}^{-1}$

  b i 400 N

   ii $0.8\,\text{m s}^{-2}$

  c Light and inextensible.

5 a $2\sqrt{gl}$

  b If the two spheres are not next to each other you cannot assume that A moves a distance of l before the string becomes taut. The answer to part **a** would be larger since the height that A would travel would be smaller.

  c Proof. **d** $\frac{33}{25}l$

  e $\frac{12}{5}mgl$

6 0.85

7 91.7 kJ

8 0.5 m

(A) A LEVEL PRACTICE PAPER

1 D

2 A

3 a 0.5 m

  b Include friction in the model.

4 a $T = \frac{(r-l)mg}{l}$ **b** $r = \frac{lg}{g - l4k^2}$

  c

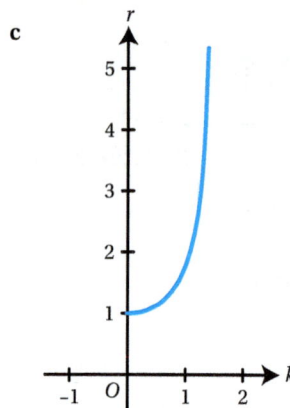

  d There is an asymptote at $k = \frac{1}{2}\sqrt{g}$. For the string not to break, $1 < r < 2$ so $0 < k < \frac{1}{2}\sqrt{\frac{g}{2}}$.

5 a Proof. **b** 44.7°

6 0.87 (2 s.f.)

7 a Light and inextensible.

  b Proof.

  c Proof.

8 a 200 J **b** 780 J

  c 0.46 (2 s.f.) **d** 0.58 (2 s.f.)

Glossary

Acceleration vector: The rate of change of the velocity vector of an object.

Angular speed: The rate at which a particle changes its angle, in radians, in a given time.

Centre of mass: A single point through which the mass of an object can be considered to act.

Centripetal force: The force directed towards the centre of a circle that holds a moving object in a circular path.

Composite body: A body made from a combination of shapes.

Conical pendulum: A particle fixed to the end of a string or rod, suspended from a pivot point, so that the particle moves in a horizontal circle with constant angular speed, with the string or rod tracing out the curved surface of a cone.

Couple: A moment that has a turning effect but no translation effect.

Dimensionless: Numerical constants that do not affect the units of a quantity.

Dimensions: These describe the type of quantity you are measuring, in terms of mass, length and time.

Displacement: The distance moved in a particular direction.

Elastic limit: When an elastic string is stretched beyond its elastic limit it does not return to its original length when the force is removed.

Elastic potential energy: Energy stored in an elastic string when it is stretched, or an elastic spring when it is compressed.

Elastic spring: A spring that can be compressed when a force is applied but will return to its original length when the force is removed.

Elastic string: A string that can be stretched when a force is applied but will return to its original length when the force is removed.

Energy: This is required for work to be done.

Friction: A force that acts to resist motion between surfaces.

Gravitational potential energy: Energy possessed by an object because of its position above the ground.

Impulse: When a force acting on an object changes its momentum, it exerts an impulse on the object.

Kinetic energy: Energy transferred by a moving object.

Lamina: A two-dimensional object that lies in a plane.

Median: A line joining a vertex of a triangle to the midpoint of the opposite side.

Modulus of elasticity: A number that measures the resistance of an object to being deformed elastically when a force is applied to it.

Momentum: The product of mass and velocity of a moving object.

Power: The rate at which energy is transferred when a force does work.

Propulsive forces: Forces that promote movement.

Radial direction: The direction from the centre of a circle along a radius.

Resistive forces: Forces that oppose movement.

Rigid body: A single or composite object, consisting of rods, wires and laminas, that is fixed in shape.

SI: The international system of units based on the kilogram, metre and second.

Scalar: A quantity that has magnitude but not direction.

Stiffness: A measure of the resistance of an object to being deformed.

Tangential direction: The direction along a tangent at a point on a curve.

Tangential speed: The linear speed of an object moving along a circular path.

Tension: A force that is transmitted through a string.

Thrust (in a spring): A force that opposes a compressive force.

Tractive force: The driving force of an engine.

Uniform lamina: A two-dimensional object that has constant mass per unit area.

Vector: A quantity that has both magnitude and direction.

Velocity vector: The rate of change of the position of an object. The magnitude gives the speed and the vector direction gives the direction of the speed.

Work done: A force does work when it moves an object.

Work–energy principle: An essential idea in mechanics that enables you to calculate the work necessary to cause a change in energy.

Index

Acknowledgements

The authors and publishers acknowledge the following sources of copyright material and are grateful for the permissions granted. While every effort has been made, it has not always been possible to identify the sources of all the material used, or to trace all copyright holders. If any omissions are brought to our notice, we will be happy to include the appropriate acknowledgements on reprinting.

Thanks to the following for permission to reproduce images:

Cover image: Peter Medlicott Sola/Getty Images
Back cover: Fabian Oefner www.fabianoefner.com

Eric Raptosh Photography/Getty Images; Hulton Archive/Getty Images; VIPDesignUSA/Getty Images; Hulton Archive/Getty Images; Phil Jason/Getty Images; Steve Lindridge/Getty Images; Marin Tomas/Getty Images; Cylonphoto/Getty Images; Jennifer McCallum / Snapwire/Getty Images; strixcode/Getty images; SBDIGIT/Getty images

AQA material is reproduced by permission of AQA.